From the Pages of
HOLLYWOOD ON LAKE MICHIGAN

"Chicago has this reputation of being a city with muscle. I kind of borrowed that strength from that city's self image. Filmmakers may have internal doubts but you need a certain confidence to say, 'okay, I'm going to direct that picture, give me that $45 million. I will spend it wisely.' "
—Harold Ramis, writer/director/producer

"I owe an awful lot to Chicago. I think of myself as a Chicago actor and I think of my style of acting as a Chicago style."
—John Mahoney, actor

"I think Chicago is the most down to earth place in America. People still take you at face value."
—Tim Kazurinsky, writer/actor

"As a kid, I always lived near and used the El. It represented the arteries and veins of the city to me. Growing up near and having worked in the steel mills—the image of huge girders and the squeal of metal on metal—became a signature of life in Chicago."
—Andrew Davis, writer/director/producer

"Chicago is a logical place for me to be. I can see myself in a kind of broad tradition of the Nelson Algrens, the Studs Terkels—people who try to do socially meaningful work. So I think it's a city that's an appropriate place for a socially conscious filmmaker to be."
—Frederick Marx, producer/editor, *Hoop Dreams*

"For me as a filmmaker, being familiar with my environment is important....That's why I come back to town to write and stay creative. Chicago keeps me grounded."
—George Tillman, Jr., from the Foreword

Other Books By Lake Claremont Press

Chicago Haunts: Ghostlore of the Windy City
by Ursula Bielski

Know More, Spend Less: A Native's Guide To Chicago, 3rd Edition
by Sharon Woodhouse,
with expanded South Side coverage by Mary McNulty

Coming In 1999

Graveyards of Chicago
by Matt Hucke

A Native's Guide To Chicago's South Suburbs
by Christina Bultinck and Christy Johnston-Czarnecki

A Native's Guide To Chicago's Northern Suburbs
by Jason Fargo

A Native's Guide To Chicago's Western Suburbs
by Laura Mazzuca Toops and John Toops

A Native's Guide To Chicago's Northwestern Suburbs
by Martin Bartels

Chicago Resource Guide for the Chronically Ill and Disabled
by Susan McNulty

Great Chicago Fires
by David Cowan

HOLLYWOOD ON LAKE MICHIGAN

100 Years of Chicago and the Movies

by Arnie Bernstein

Lake Claremont Press
4805 North Claremont Avenue
Chicago, Illinois 60625
http://members.aol.com/LakeClarPr

Hollywood on Lake Michigan: 100 Years of Chicago and the Movies
by Arnie Bernstein

Published December, 1998 by:

Lake Claremont Press
4805 N. Claremont Ave.
Chicago, IL 60625
773/784-7517; LakeClarPr@aol.com
http://members.aol.com/LakeClarPr/

ISBN: 0-9642426-2-1: $15 Softcover
Library of Congress Catalog Card Number: 98-85568

Publisher's Cataloging-in-Publication
(Provided by Quality Books, Inc.)

Bernstein, Arnie.
   Hollywood on Lake Michigan : 100 years of Chicago and
the movies / by Arnie Bernstein. — 1st ed.
   p. cm.
   Includes bibliographical references and index.
   Preassigned LCCN: 98-85568
   ISBN: 0-96424262-1

   1. Motion picture industry—Illinois—Chicago—
History. 2. Chicago (Ill.)—Guidebooks.   I. Title.

PN1993.5.U4B47 1998   384'.8'0977311
                               QBI98-1153

**Printed in the United States of America by United Graphics—
an employee-owned company in Mattoon, Illinois.**

To Cheryl

FOREWORD

The first film I saw in Chicago was *Cooley High*, which was made in Chicago by director Michael Schultz. I decided I really wanted to be a director myself after watching that film. Seeing the audience laugh and cry at the same time made me feel like I wanted to be a part of that. To really play with an audience's emotions and make them feel things. Just watching *Cooley High*, I knew I wanted to be involved in the movies. Either in front of or behind the camera, I wanted to be involved somehow.

Chicago is such a big movie town. I remember the first film I saw shooting there was *Child's Play*. It was actually being shot on Wabash. I was in film school at the time, and the inspiration of seeing a professional movie being shot right around the corner from my dormitory kept me going.

After working on countless commercials, music videos and feature films, I decided I wanted to shoot my first major studio feature in Chicago. I wanted to be a part of Chicago film history. Chicago filmmakers such as John McNaughton and Steve Jones, the filmmakers of *Hoop Dreams*, Janusz Kaminski, and the creators of *Go Fish*—these were the guys who inspired me.

That's part of the reason I came back to shoot *Soul Food* in Chicago. Hopefully I can inspire someone else hanging out on the set, observing what's going on. My partner Bob Teitel and I named our company State Street Pictures because Chicago is a part of us, and we continue to like working there.

For me as a filmmaker, being familiar with my environment is important. I don't want to get caught up in this whole Hollywood thing, raking money in and having people ask you to do projects that are not personal. That's why I come back to town to write and stay creative. Chicago keeps me grounded.

—George Tillman, Jr.
Writer/Director, *Soul Food*

CONTENTS

Downtown movie locations, plus interviews with Roger Ebert, Gene Siskel, Joe Mantegna, Tim Kazurinsky, Denise DeClue, Bill Kurtis, Harold Ramis, George Tillman, Jr., Bob Teitel, and Studs Terkel; and articles on the Chicago Film Critics Association, "Early Edition," *Chicago Filmmakers on the Chicago River*, *Mickey One*, and *Native Son*.

North Side and North Suburban movie locations, plus interviews with Jim Sikora, Del Close, John Mahoney, Tom Palazzolo, John McNaughton, Steve Jones, Ron Dean, and Herschell Gordon Lewis; articles on *Go Fish*, The Second City and the Movies, Facets Multimedia, Kartemquin Films, Chicago Cemeteries in the Movies, The Music Box Theater, and *The Package*; and The Pool Halls of *The Color of Money* and The *Home Alone* Tours.

West Side and West Suburban movie locations, plus interviews with Frederick Marx, Peter Gilbert, and Dennis Franz; articles on *Hoop Dreams*, Balaban and Katz Theaters, Robert Altman's *A Wedding*, and The Restoration of Orson Welles' *Othello*; and The *Wayne's World* Tour.

South Side and South Suburban movie locations, plus interviews with Jane Alderman, Andrew Davis, Philip Kaufman, Irma Hall, and Darryl Roberts; articles on *A Raisin In the Sun* and *Call Northside 777*; and The *Backdraft* Tour.

ACKNOWLEDGMENTS

film is often described as a collaborative process, while writing is considered more of a solo effort. Putting together this book has blown that philosophy out of the proverbial water, at least in my own mind. *Hollywood on Lake Michigan* is seeing the light of day thanks to the generosity of many wonderful and extraordinary individuals who believed in the project and went out of their way to help me:

Richard Moskal of the Chicago Film Office and Ron Ver Kulien and Joe Amari of the Illinois Film Office answered numerous questions, opened countless doors, and gave this project immeasurable support. I cannot thank them enough for all of their help.

John Iltis of Iltis Sikich Associates was another early supporter who provided help, encouragement, and those all-important contacts. He's also a genuine mensch.

George Tillman, Jr. showed his generosity of spirit in writing this book's forward.

Special thanks to the city's First Movie Fan, Mayor Richard M. Daley, for providing his thoughts on the film business in Chicago.

The many film actors, producers, directors, writers, and other professionals who took the time to talk with me and were generous with their knowledge and memories: Jane Alderman, Tony Bill, Debra Crable, Andrew Davis, Jerry Blumenthal, Ron Dean, Denise DeClue, Del Close, D.P. Carlson, Michael Dawson, Dennis Franz, Peter Gilbert, Joel Goodman, Irma Hall, Steve James, Steve Jones, Philip Kaufman, Tim Kazurinsky, Bill Kurtis, Herschell Gordon Lewis, Joe Mantegna, John Mahoney, Michael J. Malone, Frederick Marx, Michael S. Ojeda, Tom Palazzolo, Steven B. Poster of ASC, Gordon Quinn, Harold Ramis, Julia Rask, Salli Richardson, Darryl Roberts, Avery Schrieber, Jim Sikora, Studs Terkel, Bob Tietel, Guinevere Turner, and Jim Vincent.

For their perspective on the viewer's end of the movie business: reporters and critics Roger Ebert, Dann Gire, Gene Siskel, and Bill Zwecker; and the exhibitors: Milos Stehlik of Facets Multimedia, Inc., Chris Carlo and Bob Chaney of the Music Box Theatre, Michael J. Kutza and Judy Gaynor of the Chicago Film Festival, and Brenda Webb of Chicago Filmmakers.

The assistants, agents, producers, and publicity people: you all came through for me time and again and were wonderful to work with: Chip Altholz, Stuart Cleland, Joan Dry, Leslie Kaye, Tawny Klipper, Brian Schwartz, Cynthia Snyder, Gardenia Spiegel, Kathy Riordan, Peter Strain—I salute you!

The Chicago location managers and scouts who provided me with stories and suggestions: Robin Agron-Breen, Stephen Andrzejewski, Jacolyn J. Baker, Demetra Diamantopoulos, TG Glazer, and Bob Hudgins.

At Columbia College: Paula Brian and Bob Blinn of the Placement Office and Ric Coken of the Film/Video Department; at St. Augustine College: Carmen I. Dominguez and Pablo E. Rodriguez; and at Prairie State College: Denise Czuprynski, Jeannie Moses, Pamela Caddick, Debbie Griffin, Kathleen Maher, Marietta Turner, the library staff who fetched a lot of books and video tapes for me, and everyone who listened to my crazy babbling about movies while providing relentless encouragement.

George Scheetz of the Champaign Public Library for all his help with the silent era and providing some wonderful illustrations and Marc Chery of the Carter G. Woodson Regional Library in Chicago for his leads and suggestions regarding Chicago's silent African-American filmmakers. Staff members and facilities of: the Chicago Public Library overall—the Carter G. Woodson Regional Library and Harold Washington Library in specific, the Chicago Historical Society, and the Newberry Library.

For introductions and contact information I am indebted to Remy Billups of the Southern Illinois University Alumni Office and my Manhattan comrade, Richard H. Levey of *Direct Magazine*.

Kelly Leonard of Second City and Stephanie Howard of Steppenwolf Theatre, who opened doors and provided information.

Steve Jacoby of the Chicago Police Department, retired Midway Airport airline worker Bill Blaney, and Etel Billig of the Illinois Theatre center for leads, suggestions, and stories.

Special thanks to Martin J. Keenan for his photographs for the Oscar Micheaux section.

For lending me movies, providing an introduction or two, furnishing unlimited moral support, and just because they're good people: Sheila and Gene Bernstein, Nancy and Charles Diddia, Gladys Allen, Ruth Mooney, Jamie and John Peirce, and especially Hannah Lynn and Cameron Michael Peirce.

The late Max and Maria Bernstein, who are with me always.

Special thanks to Jan Grekoff-Pagoria, my former guardian angel at Columbia College, who helped me learn how to spread my own wings; and Steve Levinthal for computer support, creative ideas, and showing me what real friendship is all about.

For advice in matters legal and professional: Alan Jacobson and the

National Writers Union respectively.

The many other friends, relatives, internet correspondents, countless publicity and public relations people from the many public and private institutions chronicled in this book, and other good people who gave help, suggestions, leads, and moral support. There's not enough room here for everyone's name but hopefully you can take some satisfaction in knowing that I truly appreciate your help.

The amazing Bruce Eldon Clorfene for editing my pile of glop into a book.

The invaluable Holly Pluard who helped with research, took marvelous photographs, and had her patience stretched on numerous occasions on behalf of this book. Aren't you glad you took Theatre 103, Holly?

And last, but certainly far from least, the visionary Sharon Woodhouse of Lake Claremont Press, who took a chance on one guy's crazy notions and made them a reality. My deepest and sincere thanks for all your advice, encouragement, and belief in every phase of this project.

And special thanks to the immortals Charlie Chaplin and Groucho Marx for sparking my romance with the movies.

Again, a million and one kudos to each and every one of you. Dear reader, all glory in this book belongs to these wonderful people; all missteps are mine.

—A.B.

INTRODUCTION

Though New York and Los Angeles are commonly thought of as America's film capitals, Chicago has been in the movie business since 1896. When Hollywood was nothing more than a tiny community in southern California, the Windy City was on the cutting edge of the motion picture industry.

Are you looking for a movie made in Chicago sometime over the last 100 years or so? Consider the following:

His New Job. Call Northside 777. Mickey One. The Sting. The Tramp and the Dog. Ferris Bueller's Day Off. The Monkey Hustle. Henry: Portrait of a Serial Killer. My Best Friend's Wedding. Hunting Big Game in Africa. Damien: Omen II. Roger Touhy, Gangster. A Raisin in the Sun. Goldstein. love jones. Groundhog Day. Within Our Gates. My Main Man from Stony Island. Light of Day. Nothing in Common. Bullet on a Wire. North by Northwest. Hoop Dreams. Wayne's World. Breed of Men. The Prime Time. Looking for Mr. Goodbar. Natural Born Killers. Soul Food. Continental Divide. The Fugitive. Red Heat. Gladiators. The Coming of Columbus. The Blues Brothers. The Gore-Gore Girls. Things Change. Flatliners. Backdraft. Hero. Dreamy Dud: Joyriding with Princess Zlim. Hoffa. How U Like Me Now. Home Alone.

These titles are just a smattering of what you'll find if you want to see a film made in Chicago. Some are box office hits. Some are cult favorites. Some are good, some are great, some are unwatchable. And some disintegrated into dust a long ago.

In the past 100-plus years, the Chicago area has generated a spoil of movie-related riches. The very basics of the business—cameras and projectors—were invented here, and two of the world's first film studios were headquartered on the North Side. At the same time, Chicago's South Side was a thriving home to the forerunners of today's independent film community.

The weekly serial, a staple of movie-going in the early days of cinema, was born here. So was an essential element of 1960s drive-in theaters, the gore film, which emerged with a deliciously bloody impact from Chicago's advertising world. We've nurtured writers like David Mamet, directors like Andrew Davis, and producers like Carl Laemmle. Our acting talent ranges from Gloria Swanson to Joe Mantegna. Balaban and Katz built theaters that

A "Movie" Dialogue

"Let's go to the 'Movies' to-night."

"All right; where shall we go—to the Iris Theater?"

"No, let's go to the Ideal; I like the shows there better."

"How about the Apollo? Remember the wonderful serial we saw there last week?"

"Yes, but how do we know it is going to be there again; maybe it is at the Iris to-night."

"Come on now, children; quit your quarreling," said the father of the family as he entered the living room. "Look in the advertisements under 'Motion Picture Theaters' in The Daily News and you will find just what is appearing at each of these theaters to-night and then you can make up your minds where to go."

Pretty good advice.
Are *you* following it?

Chicagoans have had a wealth of moviegoing choices from the very beginning. *Chicago Daily News* ads from September 13, 1915 (*left*) and September 18, 1915 (*right*).

turned moviegoing into an event. Siskel and Ebert used their thumbs to tell us what was worth seeing.

This book is about the Chicago area and the movies. That's a short way of saying it's about a lot of things. The locations, the anecdotes, the films themselves, and most importantly—the people, from conniving Colonel Selig and his Polyscope to the inspirational trio who lived and breathed *Hoop Dreams* (1994)—they're all a part of the Windy City's century-long love affair with the movies. I've also included some television production, a growing factor in Chicago's filmmaking circles.

"Films and filmmaking have become as much a part of Chicago's cultural fabric as our architecture, music, and theater," says Mayor Richard M. Daley. "Not only do movies capture the beauty and texture of our neighborhoods, lakefront, and skyline, they showcase the combined talents of a thriving and nationally-acclaimed filmmaking community."

Though *Hollywood on Lake Michigan* lists many addresses and neighborhoods where films have been shot, there's no way I could include everything. This volume is part history and part guidebook. Had I included an entire century's worth of movie locations, *Hollywood on Lake Michigan* would easily have turned into an encyclopedia. What I've done is boil a massive list down to some of its more interesting essences, many instantly recognizable, others that might best be categorized as "trivia." By the way, don't look for such films as *Some Like It Hot* (1959) or *The Man with the Golden Arm* (1955) in these pages. Though Chicago is an important part of these and other Hollywood studio movies, this book sticks with the films made in the city and suburbs.

For obvious reasons, private residences are not included among the movie locations. While it may be fun to take a look at the house where Tom Cruise ran his bordello in *Risky Business* (1983), one can understand why the homeowner wouldn't want tourists showing up at the doorstep. Consequently, you won't find out where Macaulay Culkin was left *Home Alone* (1990) either.

The few private homes to be found in these pages are due to their historical significance and all are part of the public record. I have also included apartment buildings where significant; it's understood that the reader will respect the privacy of all residents.

Other movie-related sites, like Planet Hollywood, Facets Multimedia, Doc Films at the University of Chicago, and the Music Box Theatre all have a place here. I've also pointed out a few suburban locations as part of the larger Chicago moviemaking arena.

Naturally, profiles of Chicago-made films and filmmakers are included. Some are familiar names, others more obscure. That's part of the beauty of our diverse filmmaking community. From big stars to feisty independent filmmakers, Chicago has it all. We know the powerhouses: John Hughes, Oprah Winfrey, and Andrew Davis. But our independent movement, marked by filmmakers who raise their own money and make movies their way, has grown into a thriving part of Chicago's movie industry.

Consider this: in 1980, 12 film and television productions were shot in Chicago and Illinois, generating $16 million in revenue and 9,707 jobs. Those figures include part-time jobs for crew members, actors, extras, caterers, security, and other necessary positions, with money going toward salaries, food, hotel, merchandise, equipment rental, and other goods and services. Compare the 1980 numbers with 1997: 41 productions, $104 million in revenue and 18,239 people hired.

"The success of filmmaking is due in large part to the cooperation we received from the community and neighborhoods," says Rich Moskal, director of the Chicago Film Office.

Notes Mayor Daley, "Chicago actors, writers, directors, production technicians, and artists contribute to what has become a respected and prosperous local industry."

"It is that genuine, undeniable quality of being a great American city that captures the imagination of filmmakers and compels them to tell their stories here," Daley adds. "Chicago is not only a great place to tell a story, it is a great place to hear a story told. Thanks to the power and far-reaching influence of the movies, Chicago is now being appreciated by film-going audiences from around the world."

Though I've done my best to be objective, I am, like all cinephiles, rife with personal preferences and prejudices. I hope you'll find this book to be thorough, albeit a biased thorough. If I've left out a personal favorite of yours, please forgive me. On the other hand, if *Hollywood on Lake Michigan* sends you breathlessly hunting for a movie you might never have heard of before, you'll make me a very happy guy.

—Arnie Bernstein

CHICAGO MOVIE TIMELINE

➡ **1893**

The Edison Kinetoscope was supposed to be exhibited at the Columbian Exposition, but never made it on time.

➡ **1895**

After years of working in various aspects of show business, "Colonel" William Nicholas Selig returns to his native Chicago with plans to develop a film projection system and opens office an at 43 Peck Court (now East Eighth Street).

In Waukegan, George K. Spoor fronts money to Edwin Hill Amet to develop a film projection system.

Selig meets Andrew Schustek. The two begin to develop what eventually becomes the Selig Standard Camera Selig Polyscope.

Selig opens a second office at 3945 N. Western Avenue. He eventually founds film studio, first called Mutoscope & Film Company, then W.N. Selig Company, and finally, The Selig Polyscope Company.

➡ **1896**

Selig shoots *The Tramp and the Dog*, the first narrative film made in Chicago. After presenting his projection system, the Magniscope, Amet sells his interest in the machine to Spoor. Spoor opens the National Film Renting Company at 62 N. Clark Street, which distributes films and projectors to nationwide theaters.

➡ **1901**

Walt Disney is born in Chicago on December 5.

➡ **ABOUT 1906**

William G. Anderson (formerly Max Aronson), a.k.a. "Bronco Billy," leaves Thomas Edison's New Jersey film studios and joins the Selig Polyscope Company.

➡ **1907**

Selig Studios now include both indoor and outdoor facilities, encompassing the area surrounded by Western Avenue, Irving Park Road, Claremont Avenue, and Byron Street. Around this period, Selig also opens downtown offices at 45 E. Randolph Street. Anderson leaves Selig and goes into business with Spoor, forming Peerless Film Manufacturing Company.

In August, Peerless is renamed Essanay Film Manufacturing Company after Spoor and Anderson's initials, "S and A."

Spoor and Anderson open an office at 501 N. Wells Street. The first Essanay film, *An Awful Skate or the Hobo on Rollers*, starring Ben Turpin, is filmed outside the Wells Street headquarters.

Essanay employees Donald J. Bell and Albert S. Howell form their own motion picture equipment company, Bell & Howell.

The Green Mill, a jazz bar which becomes important to Chicago films as a setting for on- and off-screen action, opens under the name "Pop Morse's Roadhouse" at Lawrence and Broadway.

➡ **1908**

Essanay builds a studio at 1333 W. Argyle Street, which is ultimately expanded to 1345 W. Argyle.

Essanay Western Company is opened in Niles Canyon, about 20 miles south of Oakland, California.

Essanay, Selig Polyscope, and seven other production companies form the Motion Pictures Patent Company.

Barney Balaban opens his first movie theater.

➡ **1909**

Selig shoots *Hunting Big Game in Africa* in anticipation of Theodore Roosevelt's safari success.

➡ **1910**

Selig films first movie version of *The Wizard of Oz*, based on books by Selig writer, L. Frank Baum.

➡ **1911**

Selig shoots *The Coming of Columbus* at the Jackson Park Yacht Basin; the film becomes first movie ever screened at the Vatican.

John Freuler opens the American Film Manufacturing Company at 6227 N. Broadway with offices at 207 S. State Street and studios located at Devon and Western Avenues. Freuler eventually moves to California and merges with Mutual Films.

An inside look at the arduous process of early-20th century film editing and perforation at Chicago's American Film Company. (*Chicago Historical Society photo ICHi-26006.*)

➡ **1913**

Selig, in conjunction with the *Chicago Tribune*, creates movie serial, *The Adventures of Kathlyn*, starring Kathlyn Williams.

William Foster opens Foster Photoplay Company, the first African-American owned and operated film production company in the United States at the Grand Theater at 3110 S. State Street (then 3312 S. Wabash Street) and produces a two-reel comedy, *The Railroad Porter* (a.k.a *The Pullman Porter*).

➡ **1914**

Economic recession forces Selig to temporarily shut down his Chicago studio, while Selig's California facility grows in stature.

The Peter P. Jones Film Company opens at 3704 S. Prairie Avenue, later moving to 3849 S. State Street. It produces a two-reel comedy, *Sambo and Dinah*, and the documentary, *For the Honor of the 8th Ill. U.S.A.*

A teen-aged Gloria Swanson is hired as an extra at Essanay.

Charlie Chaplin is signed by Essanay for $1,250 per week, a then-record figure for any film actor.

➡ **1915**

Chaplin makes *His New Job* at Argyle Street studios, co-starring Ben Turpin and with Gloria Swanson in a bit part. Dissatisfied with Chicago facilities, Chaplin moves to Essanay's California studio.

Supreme Court rules that the Motion Pictures Patent Company violates the Sherman Anti-Trust Act and orders the confederation to disband.

Historical Feature Film Company opens offices at 105 W. Monroe Street.

Balaban enters business partnership with Sam Katz. The Balaban and Katz name eventually becomes synonymous with grand movie theater palaces.

➡ **1916**

Unique Film Company (3519 S. State Street) produces its only picture,

Shadowed by the Devil.

Peter P. Jones closes his Chicago office and relocates to New York.

The Dumb Girl of Portici, starring dancer Anna Pavlova, is filmed in Chicago. An uncredited extra in the film, William Henry Pratt, later changes his name to Boris Karloff.

➡ **1917**

Essanay closes its Chicago studio.

William Foster leaves the film production business.

Birth of a Race Photoplay Company opens at 123 W. Madison Street, then moves to 29 S. LaSalle Avenue.

Ebony Film Corporation opens offices at 608 S. Dearborn Street (725 Transportation Building), with studio facilities at 2332 N. California Avenue.

➡ **1918**

Selig shoots *Pioneer Days*, his last Chicago film. He closes his Chicago studio, but maintains an office at 3945 N. Western through 1919.

Intending to produce a screen version of his novel *The Homesteader*, Oscar Micheaux opens The Micheaux Film and Book Company at 538 S. Dearborn, Suites 807-808.

Democracy Photoplay Corporation is briefly in operation.

Birth of a Race debuts at the Blackstone Theater.

➡ **1919**

Ebony Film Corporation folds.

Micheaux's *The Homesteader* debuts.

The Royal Gardens Motion Picture Company opens at 459 E. 31st Street.

Delight Film Corporation is briefly in operation.

Cowboy star William S. Hart films *Breed of Men* in Chicago.

➡ **1920s**

So-called "Film Row," located from 800 S. Wabash to Wabash and 15th Street, becomes a hotbed for area film distribution and movie theater supplies. The strip maintains this status into the 1950s.

➡ **1920**

In the wake of Chicago's 1919 race riots, Micheaux's depiction of mob lynching in *Within Our Gates* becomes a center of controversy.

Royal Gardens Motion Picture Company releases *In the Depth of Our Hearts*, but folds soon afterwards.

Pyramid Picture Corporation is briefly in operation.

Micheaux begins transferring production to New York, while maintaining business offices in Chicago.

➡ **1921**

Balaban and Katz open their flagship palace, the Chicago Theater, on North State Street.

➡ **1922**

Fife Productions Company is briefly in operation.

➡ **1925**

D.W. Griffith shoots *That Royale Girl*, starring W.C. Fields, in Chicago.

Balaban and Katz open the Uptown Theater.

➡ **1926**

Micheaux closes his Chicago office.

➡ **1929**

Universal shoots scenes for *King of the Rodeo* in Chicago.

➡ **1930**

20th-Century Fox films *Three Girls Lost* in Chicago.

➡ **1930s**

With the rise of sound features and the Hollywood studio system, Chicago ceases to be a center for feature film production. Only the occasional feature comes to town for background shooting.

➡ **1934**

John Dillinger is killed by FBI agents outside Lincoln Avenue's Biograph Theater on July 22nd.

➡ **1936**

Balaban sells two-thirds of the Balaban and Katz movie theater chain to Paramount Studios. Balaban will eventually end up running Paramount.

➡ **1942**

All-American News, located at 2901 S. Prairie Avenue, produces newsreels for African-American audiences.

➡ **1947**

James Stewart, director Henry Hathaway, and 70 cast and crew members spend ten weeks in Chicago shooting the 20th-Century Fox drama *Call Northside 777*, which is based on an unsolved local murder case.

➡ **1948**

In the case of *U.S. vs. Paramount*, the Supreme Court rules that film studios have an unfair stranglehold on movie distribution. The ruling has a major effect on Balaban and Katz theaters.

➡ **1951**

Author Richard Wright plays protagonist Bigger Thomas in the first screen version of his Chicago-set novel *Native Son*. Though most of *Native Son* is shot in Argentina, some location work is done in Chicago.

➡ **1955**

The Compass Players, which evolve into The Second City theater company, stages its first revue in Hyde Park. The impact of Compass and succeeding Second City colleagues will have an indelible impact on American films.

➡ **1959**

Alfred Hitchcock, Cary Grant, James Mason, and Eva Marie Saint shoot scenes for cross-country thriller *North by Northwest* at the Drake Hotel, along Michigan Avenue, and at Midway Airport.

➡ **1960**

Herschell Gordon Lewis directs his first film, *The Prime Time*.

Tom Palazzolo begins studies at Chicago's Art Institute, then goes on to become one of the city's leading documentary filmmakers.

➡ **1961**

Exteriors for *A Raisin in the Sun* are filmed in Chicago.

➡ **1964**

Philip Kaufman directs his first film *Goldstein*, which wins the Prix de la Nouvelle Critique, the Cannes Film Festival prize for new filmmakers.

Mickey One, directed by Arthur Penn and starring Warren Beatty, shoots in Chicago.

➡ **1965**

Michael Kutza founds the Chicago International Film Festival.

➡ **1966**

Roger Ebert is hired as a reporter for the *Chicago Sun-Times* and becomes a film critic six months later.

Kartemquin Films is formed.

Aardvark Cinematheque, a not-for-profit group, screens avant-garde films at various Old Town locations.

➡ **1967**

Kaufman directs his second feature, *Fearless Frank* (also known as *Frank's Great Adventure*), starring Jon Voight in his film debut.

➡ **1968**

Richard Dreyfuss stars in the Chicago-made teen exploitation film, *The Young Runaways*.

The Democratic National Convention is held in Chicago, during which police clash in riots with Vietnam War protesters. Haskell Wexler and camera crew shoot the feature film *Medium Cool* within the turmoil.

➡ **1969**

The Second City attempts to create a Chicago-based film studio with their science fiction comedy, *The Monitors*.

Gene Siskel is hired as a reporter for *Chicago Tribune* and becomes a film critic seven months later.

➡ **1971**

The Community Film Workshop of Chicago, funded in part by the American Film Institute and the Chicago Office of Economic Opportunity, opens with the mission to provide inexpensive, hands-on film training.

➡ **1972**

Herschell Gordon Lewis makes his last feature, *The Gore Gore Girls*.

Television's "The Bob Newhart show" debuts; opening credits establish its Chicago setting.

➡ **1973**

The Sting, Oscar winner for Best Picture, shoots scenes in Chicago.

➡ **1974**

Gary Sinise, Jeff Perry, and Terry Kinney form Steppenwolf Theatre Company in a Highland Park church basement. In the next two decades, the Steppenwolf ensemble will produce some of America's leading film actors.

Credit sequence for the television series "Good Times" is shot at Cabrini-Green public housing complex.

➡ **1975**

The television program "Opening Soon at a Theater Near You," a WTTW Channel 11-produced program featuring Siskel and Ebert reviewing current movies, debuts. The title is later changed to "Sneak Previews."

Ebert wins a Pulitzer Prize for his film criticism.

➡ **1976**

In an effort to attract more Hollywood productions to the state, Gov. James Thompson establishes the Illinois Film Office. The city establishes the Chicago Film Office soon afterwards.

Two major Hollywood films, *Silver Streak* and *Looking for Mr. Goodbar,* shoot in Chicago.

➡ **1977**

Andrew Davis shoots his first feature, *Stony Island* (a.k.a. *My Main Man from Stony Island*), which is also the film debut for Organic Theatre actor Dennis Franz.

➡ **1978**

Towing, an independent feature made entirely with Chicago talent behind the camera, features Franz and Joe Mantegna in his feature film debut.

➡ **1979**

My Bodyguard shoots in Chicago, making extensive use of Chicago talent, including Tim Kazurinsky and Denise DeClue as uncredited screenwriters and local actors Adam Baldwin, Joan Cusack, and Jennifer Beals who make their film debuts.

Wheaton native John Belushi, along with pal Dan Aykroyd and Chicago-born director John Landis, tears up the town filming *The Blues Brothers*.

➡ **1980**

Women in the Director's Chair, a collective for female filmmakers, is formed.

Opening sequence for hit television program "Hill Street Blues" is filmed at the Maxwell Street police precinct and other city locations.

Chicago native Michael Mann makes his directorial debut in his home town, shooting *Thief* with James Caan and Second City actor James Belushi.

➡ **1981**

Siskel and Ebert move to WGN Channel 9, with their show re-titled "At the Movies."

Director Michael Mann in D.P Carlson's *Chicago Filmmakers on the Chicago River.* (*Photo by Jessica Feith.*)

The Fine Arts Theater opens in the Fine Arts Building on Michigan Avenue, utilizing space formerly occupied by Studebaker Theater.

➡ **1983**

Chris Carlo and Bob Chaney reopen the shuttered Music Box Theatre on North Southport Avenue. Ultimately, the Music Box becomes one of the nation's best venues for film exhibition.

John Hughes begins his 1980s reign as the North Shore's unofficial director-in-residence when he films the first "brat pack" movie *Sixteen Candles* starring Molly Ringwald and Anthony Michael Hall. John Cusack also has small on-screen role.

➡ **1984**

Oprah Winfrey is hired to host WLS-TV Channel 7 morning show "A.M. Chicago." Within a year, the program is renamed "The Oprah Winfrey Show," and Winfrey begins building her broadcast/media empire.

Hughes shoots his study of teen angst, *The Breakfast Club.*

The television shows "Punky Brewster" and "Webster" become the next television series to use Chicago as their settings in the opening credits.

➡ **1985**

Short-lived television cop/action series "Lady Blue" is shot on location in Chicago.

Major Hollywood films shot in Chicago and suburbs include *About Last Night...*, *Ferris Bueller's Day Off*, *Manhunter*, *Raw Deal*, *Running Scared*, and *Wildcats*.

➡ **1986**

Siskel and Ebert sign long-term contract with Buena Vista television. Their program is re-titled "Siskel and Ebert."

Research and fundraising begin for the documentary *Hoop Dreams.* Shooting begins 15 months later.

Amid hoopla and hyperbole, Geraldo Rivera opens Al Capone's "vault" on national television, revealing the notorious gangster's secret cache of empty bottles.

Major Hollywood films shot in Chicago and suburbs include *The Big Town*, *The Color of Money*, *Light of Day*, *She's Having a Baby*, and *The Untouchables.*

Michael Mann produces the locally-shot television series "Crime Story,"' featuring former Chicago cop Dennis Farina.

John McNaughton and Steve Jones shoot *Henry: Portrait of a Serial Killer.*

➡ **1987**

Broadcast newsman Bill Kurtis forms Kurtis Productions, which becomes an important player in the growing cable market. Kurtis Productions will eventually become a powerhouse for television documentaries.

Major Hollywood films shot in Chicago and suburbs include *Above the Law; Adventures in Babysitting; Betrayed; Midnight Run; Planes, Trains and Automobiles; Poltergeist III; Red Heat;* and *Things Change.*

➡ **1988**

The Chicago Film Critics Association is formed.

Major Hollywood films shot in Chicago and suburbs include *Child's Play, Major League, Men Don't Leave, Next of Kin,* and *When Harry Met Sally.*

➡ **1989**

Major Hollywood films shot in Chicago and suburbs include *Flatliners, Music Box, The Package, Opportunity Knocks,* and *Uncle Buck.*

Television series "Anything But Love," starring Jamie Leigh Curtis and Richard Lewis, shoots its opening credits in Chicago.

Darryl Roberts shoots his first independent feature *The Perfect Model* (a.k.a.: *Sweet Perfection*).

➡ **1990**

John Hughes writes and produces and Chris Columbus directs the slapstick kid comedy *Home Alone,* starring Macaulay Culkin, Joe Pesci, and Daniel Stern. *Home Alone* ultimately becomes the biggest grossing comedy in film history, while term "home alone" enters the lexicon of television news reporters across the country. *Home Alone* inspires two sequels, also filmed in Chicago and its suburbs.

With New York film production facing union difficulties, Ron Howard moves his fire fighting epic, *Backdraft*, to Chicago.

Major Hollywood films shot in Chicago and suburbs include *Child's Play II*, *Curly Sue*, *Only the Lonely*, and *V.I. Warshawski*.

➡ **1991**

Major Hollywood productions hit new records in Chicago, with numerous films shooting in city and suburbs. Films include *The Babe*, *Candyman*, *Dutch*, *Folks!*, *Gladiators*, *Hero*, *Mad Dog and Glory*, *Mo' Money*, *Prelude to a Kiss*, *The Public Eye*, *Straight Talk*, and *Wayne's World*

Darryl Roberts shoots his second independent feature, *How U Like Me Now*?

➡ **1992**

Major Hollywood films shot in Chicago and suburbs include *Dennis the Menace*, *Groundhog Day*, *Hoffa*, *Home Alone II: Lost in New York*, *Rookie of the Year*, and *Sleepless in Seattle*.

Local comic Emo Phillips stars in off-beat independent feature *Meet the Parents*.

Syndicated television series of "The Untouchables" begins shooting exclusively in Chicago and suburbs.

➡ **1993**

Major Hollywood films shot in Chicago and suburbs include *Baby's Day Out*, *Blankman*, *Blink*, *The Fugitive*, *The Hudsucker Proxy*, *I Love Trouble*, *Major League II*, *My Life*, *Natural Born Killers*, *Rudy*, *Wayne's World II*, and *With Honors*.

Oprah Winfrey produces and stars in the television film "There Are No Children Here," based on Alex Kotlowitz's reportage of life in Chicago housing projects.

➡ **1994**

Hoop Dreams and *Go Fish* debut at Sundance Film Festival to great audience and critical acclaim; both films become independent box office hits.

Snubbed by the Academy at Oscar nomination time, *Hoop Dreams* goes on to become the highest grossing documentary in film history.

NBC and CBS television networks film scenes for their respective hospital dramas, "ER" and "Chicago Hope," at various city locations.

Amid glitz and glamour, national restaurant chain Planet Hollywood, co-owned by Bruce Willis, Demi Moore, Sylvester Stallone, and Arnold Schwarzenegger, opens a Chicago branch.

Major Hollywood films to shoot in Chicago and suburbs include *Losing Isaiah*, *Miracle on 34th Street*, *Richie Rich*, *Stuart Saves His Family*, and *While You Were Sleeping*.

➡ 1995

Normal Life and *A Family Thing* among the independent films made in Chicago and suburbs.

Major Hollywood productions to shoot in Chicago and suburbs include *Primal Fear* and *The Relic*.

Second City veteran Bonnie Hunt films credits for her Chicago-set sitcom, "The Bonnie Hunt Show," around town.

➡ 1996

The CBS television network fantasy drama "Early Edition" begins shooting exclusively in Chicago.

Director Theodore Witcher and directing/producing team George Tillman, Jr. and Robert Teitel—all graduates of Columbia College—return to Chicago to shoot *love jones* and *Soul Food* respectively.

Northwestern University graduate David Schwimmer directs *Dogwater* in Chicago. The film is eventually turned into the television movie "Since You've Been Gone."

Major Hollywood films shot in Chicago and suburbs include *The Chamber*,

Home Alone 3, Hoodlum, The Jackal, and *My Best Friend's Wedding.*

➡ **1997**

Films shot in Chicago and suburbs include *The Negotiator* and *Payback.*

➡ **1998**

Films shot in Chicago include *American Reel, Light It Up, Message in a Bottle,* and *A Stir of Echoes.*

"Early Edition" begins its third season, with the majority of production based in Chicago

Jeremy Piven, son of Chicago acting talents/teachers Joyce and Byrne Piven, stars in and produces "Cupid," a weekly ABC network television series, which he brings to Chicago for production.

THE
SILENT
ERA

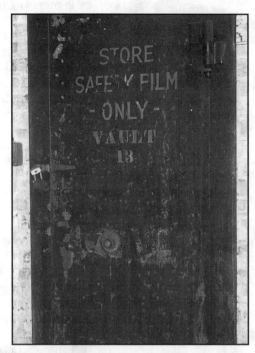

A remaining Essanay film vault (*left*) still stands in its original location, now the basement of St. Augustine College on Argyle Street. (*Photo by Holly Pluard.*) The now-demolished McVickers Theater at 25 W. Madison (*below*) was a vaudeville house before eventually becoming part of the Balaban and Katz movie theatre chain with the evolution of popular entertainment. (Chicago Historical Society photo, DN-483, taken in 1902.)

THE SILENT ERA

➡ SILENT MOVIES - "THE BEGINNING"

The neighborhood at Western Avenue and Irving Park Road, bordered by Byron Street and Claremont Avenue, is as typical as any stretch of Chicago. A gas station on the corner of Western and Irving. A block of apartments along Claremont. It's a quiet, residential area, with only the sounds of traffic flying through the air.

There is one oddity to the neighborhood: a building at the northeast corner of Byron and Claremont with an anonymous letter "S" emblazoned in concrete above a doorway. Imprinted in a diamond shape, that "S" is the only hint that this neighborhood was once a thriving hub for moviemaking.

The building is the last remnant of one of Chicago's major silent film factories. At its peak, this lot was teeming with movie people, equipment, and a menagerie of exotic animals. The cacophony of those lions, monkeys, wolves, and actors have long been replaced by the more innocuous sound of traffic. The distinguishing "S" was the trademark emblem of the Selig Polyscope Company, where "Colonel" William Selig presided over his personal moviemaking workshop.

A few miles south and east of Col. Selig's former film studio is St. Augustine College, a bilingual facility for Chicago's Hispanic community. Located at 1333-1345 W. Argyle Street, St. Augustine is another link to Chicago's great silent movie past. The entrance at 1345 W. Argyle features an Indian head logo set in

Though now condos, the former Selig Polyscope Co. building at Claremont and Byron still bears the trademark "S."
(*Photo by Holly Pluard.*)

colored terra cotta. This doorway marks the former entrance to Essanay Film Manufacturing, Chicago's most important silent film studio.

Today, students walk through the same buildings once used by Charlie Chaplin, Gloria Swanson, Wallace Beery, Ben Turpin, and Essanay's

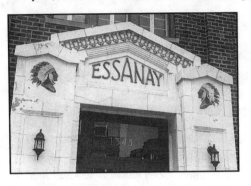

leading heartthrob Francis X. Bushman. One of popular cinema's first matinee idols, Bushman spent his off hours tooling around Chicago in a lavender sedan. Fans were known to follow him in packs whenever he went shopping in the Loop. Eventually, one store was forced to ask Bushman to no longer frequent their place of business—they couldn't keep up with the herd that always followed the good-looking actor!

The entrance to Essanay Film Manufacturing (1345 W. Argyle), the most significant silent film studio in Chicago, now home to St. Augustine College. (*Photo by Holly Pluard.*)

In the first two decades of the 20th century, the impact of motion pictures was felt at every level of society. "The time is not far in the distant future when the moving picture apparatus will be in the equipment of every schoolhouse," wrote one *Chicago Daily News* columnist in 1911. "The attempt to teach without it will be absurd." Replace the words "moving picture apparatus" with "computer technology" and you have a better understanding how revolutionary motion pictures were to everyday culture. In a much-criticized move, social reformer Jane Addams exhibited films at her Hull House location on 800 S. Halsted Street. Charging five cents admission, the same as local theaters, Addams's in-house motion picture venue became a neighborhood staple. An audience was an audience in Addams's mind. She realized the power of motion pictures as an important tool for both entertainment and enlightenment.

As Chicago once more enjoys status as a world-class center for film production, it's important to consider the city's history with the motion picture. Though the technologies have undergone radical change in 100 years, the basic techniques of telling a story on screen remain virtually unchanged.

➡ THE CHICAGO SILENT ERA

Chicagoans were first to be introduced to moving pictures at the Columbian Exposition of 1893 with a special pavilion devoted to Kinetoscopes, a viewing machine created by Thomas Edison's labs in Orange, New Jersey. Developed under Edison's supervision by his assistant William Kennedy Laurie Dickson, the Kinetoscope was the forerunner to the modern motion picture. Basically, the Kinetoscope was a large box that contained several spools and a 50-foot loop of exposed moving picture film. By looking into the eyepiece at the top, viewers could watch such entertainments as Edison worker Fred Ott sneezing, dancers performing, and other simple motion attractions.

However, due to production delays, the Kinetoscopes never arrived in time and the fair closed before the machines could be installed. Though many Chicagoans claim to have viewed Kinetoscope films at the Columbian Exposition, these early moving picture devices would have to wait a bit longer before arriving in Chicago.[1]

Despite this inauspicious beginning, the movies eventually took their hold on Chicago in a big way. By the first decade of the new century, Chicago was a thriving center for moving picture production, while nickelodeon theaters opened throughout the city. As advancing technology brought moving pictures out of the Kinetoscope and projected onto screens, nickelodeons became the new standard for film exhibitors. Charging five cents for admission (hence the name "nickelodeon"), these theaters operated out of storefronts and other handy locations. Musical accompaniment was usually provided by a piano player improvising popular tunes to fit the on-screen action.

With the proliferation of movies and exhibition spaces came the need for many moving picture-related jobs. Chicagoans eager to get in on the many aspects of the film industry began advertising in the *Daily News, Tribune,* and other newspapers, offering a wide variety of film-related services. "Moving picture music especially arranged is taught by Chas. Quinn, 59 E. Van Buren, Room 206"[2] and "Experienced lady pianist desires position in first class picture theater. Drexel 6051"[3] were typical classified ads, focusing on the unique musical needs of nickelodeons.

Other advertisements attracted would-be movie stars with such enticing copy as: "Motion picture instruction. Gilbert Shorter has new department under direction of competent director who has been connected with several feature productions. Exceptional opportunity for competent students. Day and evening classes. 50 Auditorium Building."[4]

While fans flocked to the nickelodeons, studios and entrepreneurs worked throughout the city to provide moving picture entertainments. The movies became an important aspect of Chicago's artistic and business world.

→ **SELIG POLYSCOPE COMPANY (1896 - 1919)**
- **43 Peck Court (Now East 8th Street)**
- **3945 N. Western Avenue**
  (southeast corner of Western Avenue and Irving Park Road)
- **45 E. Randolph Street**

A product of the Chicago streets, William Nicholas Selig brought a good sense for show business, along with his personal style of savvy and bluster, to the fledgling movie industry. Born in Chicago on March 14, 1864, Selig experienced ill health as a young man that forced him to relocate to a more hospitable climate. First moving to Colorado and then to California, Selig's well-being improved and he became manager of a West Coast health spa ironically named "Chicago Park."

Eventually Selig found his calling in the world of vaudeville and sideshows. He took up magic and achieved some success as a parlor performer. Eager to expand in the world of show business, Selig adopted the sobriquet "Colonel" and put together a traveling minstrel show. One member of the troupe was a young performer named Bert Williams, who would later achieve great success as a comedian in the Ziegfield Follies.

While traveling through Texas in 1895, Selig saw his first Kinetoscope parlor. With his show business sensibilities, the Colonel perceived the enormous financial potential of further developing moving picture technology. Driven to carve out his own piece of this fledgling business, Selig returned to his hometown and rented office space at 43 Peck Court (now East Eight Street), in the heart of what was then Chicago's brothel-filled "tenderloin" district. Selig had no interest in opening his own string of Kinetoscope parlors. Understanding that the real money was to be in filling theaters, Selig turned his attention to developing technology that would project film strips onto a wall or screen.

To keep his cash flow going, Selig operated a photography studio out of his Peck Court office. His major source of income was providing carbon prints for Chicago portrait studios and working on landscape photography for the railway industry. In the meantime, Selig began looking at the attempts of other early film projection pioneers. He was particularly interested in the efforts of Major Woodville Latham, a retired Confederate soldier, and Louis Lumière of France. In 1895, after seeing an exhibit of Latham and Lumière's machines at Chicago's Schiller Theater at 103 E. Randolph Street, Selig knew what he was up against.

Major Latham had developed a successful motion picture projection system while working on expanding the Edison Kinetoscope. Latham's so-called "Latham Loop," a basic set-up in threading motion picture film through a projector, has essentially remained the same since its invention in 1895. Lumière, who had seen an exhibition of the Kinetoscope in Paris, coupled moving picture technology with his own ideas. His invention, dubbed the Cinématographe, was capable of both recording movement and projecting the exposed film onto a screen.

Through his talent as a conniver, Selig got his hands on both Latham and Lumière movie samples and began experimenting in his Peck Street office with projection machines. His trial runs were successful ventures. Often Selig's offices would be teeming with friends interested in seeing the Colonel's moving picture exhibitions. Yet Selig still was frustrated by his inability to create his own technology.

In desperation, he turned to the Union Model Works—a local Chicago machine shop located at 193 N. Clark Street—hoping to find a mechanic who could help develop his ideas. Selig met Andrew Schustek, the leading machinist and model maker for the shop.

Serendipity ensued.

It seemed that Schustek had been deeply involved in creating machine parts for a mysterious, foreign-born customer. This gentleman had been coming to the shop week by week, asking Schustek to reproduce specific items for some sort of mechanical device. Though the enigmatic stranger never revealed what he was developing, Schustek had taken an interest in the project and carefully sketched out plans for each piece.

Finally Schustek learned that his customer was French and had been involved with the Lumière demonstration at the Schiller Theater. Essentially, the tight-lipped client was having Schustek reproduce a Lumière Cinématographe piece by piece. Who this customer was and why he had Schustek create the device is a great unknown. The Frenchman paid Schustek $210 cash for his work (350 hours of labor at the sum of 60 cents an hour) and never left a name. What he did leave was a perfect set of plans, created by Schustek, for building a motion picture recording and projection machine.

When Selig met Schustek to explain his own interest in motion pictures, the Colonel looked on Schustek's workspace and was amazed to see a blueprint for the Lumière Cinématographe. A deal was quickly hatched and Schustek left Union Model Works for employment with Selig.

Needing a larger place to work, Selig opened a second office at 3945 N. Western Avenue, located on the far reaches of Chicago. Settling into the southeast corner of the intersection at Western Avenue and Irving Park Road, Selig and Schustek devised a plan to recreate the Lumière Cinématographe, make slight changes and give the contraption a new name to avoid any claims of patent infringement. Essentially, they created a front with Schustek building cameras and projectors for a sole customer, who of course was Selig. The Lumière Cinématographe, as developed by the two men, became the Selig Standard Camera for recording film and the Selig Polyscope, which was the projection system.

Christening his business "Mutoscope & Film Company," then "W.N. Selig Company," and finally "The Selig Polyscope Company," Selig opened up one of the world's first film studios at his Western and Irving Park space. Using this North Side setting as a headquarters, Selig made his first narrative, *The Tramp and the Dog*, in 1896. Shot in a wooded area in what is today the Rogers Park neighborhood, this simple film involves a hobo going door to door, looking for a meal. At one house he is met by an acrimonious bulldog who chases the tramp over a fence. Since such movie conventions as stunt men and trained animals were years away, Selig's comedy took an unexpected turn when the dog sank his teeth into the actor's pants while the camera continued rolling. It was said that the look on the hobo's face was genuine fear—the original method actor. This misfortune aside, the 150-foot film was a popular attraction when shown in Chicago vaudeville houses. Selig was on his way.

Selig's ventures into the fledgling film industry continued with smaller (and safer) productions—essentially 50-foot reels documenting the city on-film. Audiences, slowly warming up to this new medium, watched the films as filler in between acts at Chicago vaudeville houses. Selig Polyscope produced such titles as *Chicago Police Parade, Gans-McGovern Fight, Chicago Fire Run, View of State Street*, and *Chicago Fireboats on Parade*. Realizing that audiences wanted to see other locales besides their neighborhoods, Selig sent camera crews out to Colorado and the southwestern states.

Meanwhile, on the East Coast, Thomas Edison was attempting to broaden the base of motion picture audiences by creating "story films." His first success was the 1903 film, *The Great Train Robbery*, directed by Edwin S. Porter. *The Great Train Robbery* was a landmark picture on many fronts. It was one of the first American films to effectively tell a story by editing together different shots from various locations. As an adventure of the Old West, it introduced many motifs, such as bandits, train robberies, and wild shoot-outs, which became stock elements of Westerns well into the sound era. *The Great Train Robbery* featured a young actor by the name of William G. Anderson (formerly Max Aronson). Anderson, a fledgling stage actor and magazine model, was trying to work his way into the growing motion picture business. He took on the screen name "Bronco Billy" for his alleged horse riding-skills, though Anderson's saddle experience was largely the product of his imagination. Early in the filming of *The Great Train*

Robbery, Anderson was thrown from his horse and ended up missing a good deal of production time. Consequently, most of his scenes were completed sans bronco.

Nevertheless, Anderson was hooked on the movie business. Brushing up his horsemanship, Anderson moved west to Chicago. To compete with the success of *The Great Train Robbery*, the Colonel hired Anderson to produce, direct, and star in Selig Polyscope Westerns. Circus horse riders were hired to play cowboys and Native Americans were brought in from Michigan as Selig's Indians. Teepees were erected on the studio lot, doubling as both housing for the Native American actors and sets for the Selig Westerns.

These films proved to be a financial success, though not without certain production problems inherent to shooting movies near a major metropolis. Scenes occasionally had to be scrapped when the exposed footage revealed western landscapes with laundry flapping in the breeze. Other problems involved curious neighborhood children who could be seen hiding in the shrubbery to watch cowboy shoot-outs.

Selig, realizing that authentic western locations would attract even more viewers, ordered Anderson and a cameraman to California. In autumn, Anderson became the first filmmaker to set up shop in the Golden State, working on the outskirts of Los Angeles. He filmed numerous location Westerns for Selig, beginning with *The Girl from Montana* (filmed in both California and Montana), *His First Ride,* and *The Bandit King*. The results were more realistic-looking pictures that raked in money for the Colonel.

By 1907, Selig was developing into a genuine movie mogul. The Western Avenue studio grew to include both indoor and outdoor facilities. Now bounded by Western Avenue, Irving Park Road, Claremont Avenue, and Byron Street, the Selig Polyscope studio billed itself as "the biggest motion picture plant in the country...(with) the largest skylight of any west of the Hudson River." By the end of the year, Anderson left Selig to form his own company with Spoor (see below), though the defection barely made a dent in the Selig operation. Expanding the market beyond Westerns, Selig Polyscope also produced romances, comedies, jungle stories, pirate adventures, and historical pictures.

In the fall of 1908, Selig had some high-level meetings with former president Theodore Roosevelt who was planning a hunting trip in Africa. Selig pitched the idea of documenting Roosevelt's exploits with a camera crew and even proposed taking Roosevelt's son Kermit to Chicago to teach him how to use a Polyscope camera. Roosevelt was sold on the idea and Selig made trips back and forth from Chicago to Washington to finalize plans. By Christmas, it was obvious that things were changing. Roosevelt was more hesitant, though he insisted that the Selig deal was still good. By the spring of 1909, however, it was obvious that Selig was off the project. Roosevelt, who made arrangements for his trip through the Smithsonian Institution, left for Africa in May, taking along an English camera crew hired by the museum.

Not to be outdone, Selig developed an alternative plan. He revamped one section of his studio to resemble an African location. A local actor well-known for his Teddy Roosevelt impersonations was hired to play the former president. Selig next went up to Milwaukee, where a failing zoo was in the process of selling off its menagerie. An aging, yet still feisty lion was acquired for $400 and brought back to the Selig lot. Local African-Americans were hired as members of Roosevelt's hunting party and outfitted in "native" costumes. With all the players set up, Selig's African hunting party was ready for production.

According to accounts, Selig's Roosevelt was a lousy shot, so a marksman was hired to shoot the lion from off-screen while the on-screen actor fired blanks. "Roosevelt," his hunting party, and the lion were contained in a cage on the set. Unfortunately the hired gunman missed the beast on his first shot. The lion became angry at being smacked with a blank cartridge from "Roosevelt's" prop gun. A second shot by the marksman hit the beast in the jaw, further enraging the animal. As the cameras continued rolling, the hunting party escaped through an emergency door while the faux Roosevelt scrambled to the top of the cage. Hanging onto the top with a very real and very angry lion roaring beneath him, the actor sweated it out while Selig's director Tom Persons stopped the camera and reset the scene for a close-up. With "Roosevelt" quaking above, the lion was finally killed by the marksman. One costume change and camera set-up later, "Roosevelt" posed as the Great White Hunter, standing triumphantly above the lion's corpse.

After completing production, Selig bided his time. Finally, word came from overseas that the real Roosevelt had felled his first lion. As newspaper headlines throughout the nation trumpeted this news, Selig rushed his film, dubbed *Hunting Big Game in Africa*, to the theaters. Though Roosevelt was never mentioned by name in either the film or the advertisements, audiences assumed the movie was authentic. *Hunting Big Game in Africa* was extremely popular, making Selig Polyscope an enormous amount of money in the process. Once he learned of the situation, Roosevelt was outraged. But there was nothing the former president could do to stop Selig.

With the success of *Hunting Big Game in Africa*, Selig developed a livestock company of animal performers. He specialized in exotic creatures which could be used for jungle films, as well as adventures set in the frozen North. In 1911, one writer visiting the Selig lot cataloged the menagerie as "12 lions, 9 lion cubs, 1 elephant, 10 leopards, 7 leopard cubs, 5 pumas, 1 monkey, 3 bears, 2 deer, 10 Eskimo dogs, 8 grey wolves, not to mention mules, geese, dogs, horses, etc."[5]

The Colonel also built up a stock troupe of human actors, drawing on the large pool of talent living in the area. Centrally located, Chicago was a logical home for many vaudeville performers of the day. He also maintained a strong stable of off-screen talent, including writer L. Frank Baum. Baum got started in Chicago as a reporter for the *Chicago Evening Post*, then switched to penning children's stories. He hit the jackpot with his 1900 book *The Wizard of Oz*. In 1908, Baum turned to theatrical entertainment, creating a combination stage and film show called *Fairylogue and Radio-Plays*. Eventually Baum ended up at Selig, who released the film portion of *Fairylogue* in 1910. Selig also made the first film version of Baum's best known work that same year. But rather than remain with Selig, Baum decided to strike out on his own. By the end of the year, he had moved to California and later opened his own film studio devoted to producing *Oz* films, the Oz Film Manufacturing Company. Featured as the Tin Man at Baum's studio was a rotund comic actor named Oliver Hardy.

As the Western Avenue studio thrived, Selig opened up a suite of offices at 45 E. Randolph Street. Selig even maintained a special room at his Randolph Street office specifically for local censors to screen films. The Chicago Film Board was formed in 1907 to regulate the content of the

A zebra at the Selig Movie "Zoo"—one amongst a growing number of animals the Colonel kept on hand for use in films, 1914.
(*Chicago Historical Society photo DN 62, 843.*)

growing movie industry. Fearing the possible moral corruption of audiences who flocked to the movies, the City Council gave the Board power to ban any seemingly objectionable film. Rather than fight this governing body, Selig played the game by their rules and consequently experienced no trouble at all.

Conforming to stereotypes of the day, Selig used ethnic actors to give his films a sense of "realism," or at least realism as viewed through archetypes that motion picture producers relied on. In addition to hiring Native Americans, Selig often used local African-Americans to play "natives" in his jungle adventures. A 1909 exploit in the "Arctic" used Japanese acrobats as authentic-looking "Eskimos." Sent to a wintry location in Michigan that doubled for the North Pole, the troupe tracked down and shot a domesticated polar bear for Selig's cameras.

Selig made rather imaginative use of Chicago and the surrounding area. The Indiana Dunes served as the Sahara Desert for one Selig adventure. The Des Plaines River near the Chicago Canal doubled for a Boer War location. And in one of his most ambitious and internationally successful films, Selig turned the yacht basin at Jackson Park into the landing site of Christopher Columbus.

The Colonel had come into possession of three ships, replicas of the Nina, the Pinta, and the Santa Maria, left over from the Columbian Exposition of 1893. Originally brought to Chicago by the Spanish government, the vessels were now in pretty sorry shape. Nevertheless, Selig made the ships seaworthy (or Lake Michigan-worthy as the case was) and hired crews to sail them into the Jackson Park Yacht Basin. Shooting, however, was delayed by bad weather. Complicating matters, Columbus (played by Selig actor Charles Clary) and his crewmates, unused to choppy water, got seasick. Once they recovered, the production ran into further problems when the Santa Maria became stranded on a sandbar. Finally, as the recreation of this historic landing was about to unfold for the cameras, the filmmakers encountered a problem never imagined by the real Columbus. Scores of curiosity seekers circled the three ships in small boats of their own, eager to get a glimpse of the moviemaking process.

Despite the difficulties, Selig's *The Coming of Columbus* was completed and went on to phenomenal success. Audiences around the world flocked to see this cinematic re-enactment. In a special showing for Pope Pius X, *The Coming of Columbus* earned a historical footnote of its own as the first movie to be screened at the Vatican. The Pope was highly impressed with Selig's film and awarded the Colonel an honorary medallion for his efforts.

Another Selig innovation was buying stories for movie adaptation. Convinced by 1905 that filmmakers would eventually run out of ideas, Selig began looking for a source of fresh material. He made an initial contact with Moses Koenigsberg, editor of the William Randolph Hearst-owned *Chicago American*, then began working with a New York publishing representative to obtain new stories.

Though Edison had pioneered the movie serial with *What Happened to Mary?* in 1912, Selig took the form a step further. In 1913, the Chicago newspaper world was in the midst of a circulation war. Seven papers were competing for daily readership. It was nothing for a newspaper to publish 17 editions in a single day in a desperate effort to stymie the competition. On a typical day, the *Chicago Evening American* would bombard readers with a new headline every 45 minutes. Selig, sensing opportunity, went to the *Chicago Tribune* with a proposal.

The result was *The Adventures of Kathlyn*, a 13-chapter serial for both film audiences and newspaper readers. Each week, the plucky Kathlyn, played by Selig actor Kathlyn Williams, went through a series of torrid events, leading up to a high-pitched cliffhanging ending. The thin storyline revolved around an American woman who inherited a royal title in India. Debuting on December 29, 1913, *The Adventures of Kathlyn* was popular in both mediums. Viewers headed to the theaters week after week for another breathless installment, while simultaneously following Kathlyn's exploits in the *Tribune*. If figures are to be believed, *Tribune* circulation went up ten percent as a direct result of *The Adventures of Kathlyn*.

Williams, who was known as "The Selig Girl," appeared in Selig's best known work, the first screen version of *The Spoilers* in 1914. This tale of the Alaskan gold rush was based on a novel by popular author Rex Beach. Realizing the money to be made in the picture industry, Beach demanded a whopping sum of $2,500 for the rights to his story. Selig hammered out a compromise with the author, arranging a royalty payment while the Colonel maintained story rights. This marked the first time an author was given royalties on a movie project. Shot at the Western Avenue studio, *The Spoilers* featured Williams along with Selig's top leading man, William Farnum. If the title sounds familiar, it's

Ad for Selig/Tribune serial
The Adventures of Kathlyn
in the *Chicago Tribune*,
January 6, 1914.

because *The Spoilers* was remade on several occasions. A 1930 version featured Gary Cooper, and the best known remake, released in 1942, starred John Wayne, Randolph Scott, and Marlene Dietrich.

Realizing that Chicago's winter climate was not conducive to year-round filming, Selig began branching out to warmer climates. He opened one film studio in Jacksonville, Florida and another on the outskirts of Los Angeles at the corner of Eighth and Olive Streets. Though his California studio was growing, he still maintained Chicago as his base of operations.

An unexpected recession in 1914 temporarily shut down Selig's Chicago operation. Though he was soon back in business, Selig's eyes remained on California. His studio out west was growing in size and stature, with such notables as Tom Mix and Roscoe "Fatty" Arbuckle launching their film careers with Selig Polyscope. The outfit was even beginning to dabble in animation, creating short cartoons dubbed "Seligettes." Sticking to his sense for showmanship, Selig launched a well-planned publicity stunt in the summer of 1915. The Colonel chartered a train—dubbed the Selig Movie Special—as part of a two-week excursion to the Panama Pacific Exposition in San Francisco. This was followed by a trip to the Selig California headquarters. At the cost of $128 per person, the tour attracted a wide variety of movie fans, news writers, and studio personnel, with Selig cameras on hand to faithfully record the tour.

Chicago Tribune ads urge readers to theaters to see *The Adventures of Kathlyn.* December 30, 1913 (*top*) and January 4, 1914 (*bottom*).

Certainly the film industry had grown in California, with studios such as Biograph and Keystone doing a thriving business in the Los Angeles suburb of Hollywood. Realizing the future of the movie business was California, Selig had all but shut down his Chicago operations by 1918. The studio made only a few more films in the Windy City, including *The Crises*. This Civil War drama, based on a novel by Winston Churchill (a cousin of the future British prime minister), featured Tyrone Power, Sr. (father of the better known Tyrone Power, Jr.) in the lead. However, *The Crises* did poorly at the box office. *Pioneer Days*, a recreation of the famed Fort Dearborn massacre, was shot on location in Wilmette and signaled the end of Selig's Chicago production.

Though Selig maintained an office at 3945 N. Western through 1919, the move to California was permanent. However, Selig's days as the original movie mogul were coming to an end. Though he continued to dabble with independent production as late as 1922 and maintained a stable of exotic creatures for animal adventure films, Selig had grown bored with the production end of the business. Now 50 years old, Selig turned to younger producers and sold them the rights to stories he had bought years before. The gamble he had made years before had paid off handsomely. Retired and rich, Selig lived in happy obscurity until his death in 1948.

➡ ESSANAY FILM MANUFACTURING COMPANY
- **501 N. Wells Street (1907)**
- **1333-45 W. Argyle Street (1908 - 1917)**

Driving down West Argyle Street, you'll pass St. Augustine College. Occupying five acres in Uptown between 1333 and 1345 W. Argyle, St. Augustine's mission is to make higher learning accessible to non-traditional students, with its emphasis on education to America's Hispanic community. The campus buildings, however, have a unique history. A distinctive Indian head logo, on top of an arched door at one entrance, is part of the reason these buildings have earned landmark status from the Chicago City Council. The college's Charlie Chaplin Auditorium also recalls the early days of these buildings. Though an important educational resource today, this Argyle Street location was originally built as the headquarters for the Essanay Film Manufacturing Company.

In its prime, Essanay was the center of Chicago's silent film industry. The studio's star roster boasted such luminaries as Ben Turpin, Gloria Swanson, screen heartthrob Francis X. Bushman, Wallace Beery, and Essanay's biggest talent, Charlie Chaplin.

Essanay was founded by George K. Spoor and the former Selig director

An early photo of the exterior of Essanay Film Studio (1345 West Argyle)—
Chicago's most significant silent film studio.
(*Chicago Historical Society photo ICHi-17852.*)

Essanay Film Studio co-founder George Spoor (in derby) and others with
early photographic equipment, c. 1920-30.
(*Chicago Historical Society photo ICHi-25486.*)

Gilbert M. "Broncho Billy" Anderson. Spoor's entrance into the moving picture business was something of a fluke. In 1895, he owned and operated a newspaper stand at the Chicago & Northwestern station at Kinzie Avenue and Wells Street. Occasionally, in order to make ends meet, Spoor worked in the box office of the Waukegan Opera House in downtown Waukegan.

Meanwhile, Edwin Hill Amet, a Waukegan employee of the Chicago Scale Works, was tinkering with a device for motion picture projection. His previous invention had been a penny scale that could print out a card telling a person's weight. Amet had bigger hopes with his motion picture projector, but craved the advice of an expert.

Figuring someone at the Waukegan Opera House would have inside knowledge on trends of the entertainment industry, Amet approached box office manager Spoor with his experiments. Not letting on that his show business connections were limited to the ticket booth, Spoor agreed to look at Amet's invention. Impressed, though broke, Spoor asked what it would take to complete the projector. Amet estimated his final cost to be $65. Though he barely had the capital, Spoor "advanced" Amet $25, almost all the money Spoor had at the moment.

Dubbed the "Magniscope," Amet completed his projector the following year. Yet, when all was said and done, Amet didn't think the moving picture fad would last. He sold his interest in the invention to Spoor, who quickly established the National Film Renting Company at 62 N. Clark Street. This business distributed films and projectors to the burgeoning moving picture theater circuit nationwide. Before long, Spoor dumped the newspaper stand and began raking in profits from this new entertainment form.

For the most part, Spoor distributed simple films that documented the everyday life of late 19th and early 20th century America. Subjects like rushing streetcars, crowded city streets, or athletic events were popular with audiences craving to see something—anything—moving on the screen. Within ten years of his original $25 investment, Spoor had built up a considerable corporation. Among his many employees were Donald J. Bell, who was in charge of film projector installation, and Albert S. Howell, who headed up the maintenance department. In 1907, the duo left Spoor's outfit to form their own motion picture equipment company, Bell & Howell.

Itching to develop as a film entrepreneur apart from Col. Selig, "Broncho Billy" Anderson paid a visit to Spoor's offices in April 1907. The two agreed that between Spoor's distribution talents and Anderson's filmmaking abilities, a production partnership could result in mutual benefits. Together they formed the Peerless Film Manufacturing Company.

By August, the company had undergone a significant name change. Adopting their initials of "S" and "A," the company was re-christened the Essanay Film Manufacturing Company and settled into office headquarters

One of Essanay's silent screen legends, Ben Turpin, the cross-eyed walrus-mustachioed funnyman, began his career in vaudeville before starring in films with Charlie Chaplin and Laurel and Hardy. (*From the collection of Arnie Bernstein.*)

These 1913 postcards of Essanay Players Billy Mason, Lily Branscombe, and Joseph Allen are representative of early movie promotional shots. (*From the collection of Arnie Bernstein.*)

at 501 N. Wells Street.

The first Essanay release, *An Awful Skate, or the Hobo on Rollers,* was shot on the sidewalk outside the company's Wells Street home. Directed by Anderson, this 1907 comedy starred a cross-eyed funnyman named Ben Turpin. Essentially the film was a mini-documentary as Turpin veered up and down the sidewalk, desperately trying not to smash into innocent pedestrians. Turpin, a vaudeville veteran, made $15 a week doing double duty as Essanay's house comedian and janitor. With his permanently-crossed eyes and walrus mustache, Turpin's offbeat looks were made for comedy. He went on to great success as the ultimate second banana of silent slapstick comedies, working with everyone from Chaplin to Laurel and Hardy. As a joke, his eyes were insured for $1 million by the prestigious Lloyds of London should they ever come uncrossed.

During Essanay's early years, slapstick was the stock in trade. "Home of Comedy Hits," was the studio motto, though Anderson was still churning out Westerns. Like Selig Polyscope, Essanay made effective use of Chicago's prairie-strewn Rogers Park in such films as *The Life of Jesse James* (1908). Occasionally, Anderson would take a camera crew and his actors down to Starved Rock to film in the rugged landscape. As Selig had learned, audiences were growing more sophisticated about the movies, and authentic backgrounds became a necessity.

Once again, Anderson made regular trips to Colorado to film against a bona fide cowboy background. And again, following Selig's lead, these trips became so routine that the studio opened a California branch. The Essanay Western Company was headquartered in Niles Canyon about 20 miles south of Oakland.

Chicago remained Essanay's nerve center, however. With profits reaching record numbers and the public demanding more films, Spoor and Anderson decided to build a larger, more elaborate studio. They acquired property at 1333 W. Argyle Street on Chicago's North Side. Ultimately the studio stretched to 1345 W. Argyle as the complex grew. At its peak, the Essanay film factory housed three studios for shooting, a carpentry shop, prop and wardrobe storage, an area for film processing, a publicity department, and, of course, dressing rooms for the stars. The studio also possessed one of the most sophisticated movie lighting systems of the time, making effective use of both natural conditions as well as a complicated circuitry of artificial lights. An Essanay employee named Alan Dwan, who later became a respected Hollywood director, created a mercury-vapor arc light system, a ground-breaking development in film production.

Essanay, which coined the popular term "photoplay" to describe moving picture entertainments, developed a considerable stable of actors and film talent, led by handsome Francis X. Bushman. Bushman's pictures primarily were historical and dramatic romances, with such turgid titles as *His Friend's Wife*, *The Mail Order Bride*, *White Roses*, *The House of Pride*, and *When Soul Meets Soul*. Another of Essanay's major players was Beverly Bayne. A 16-year-old Hyde Park High School student when she first joined the studio, Bayne was often paired with Bushman as a love interest. Eventually the duo left Essanay for Metro Studios in California. They even married, though the nuptials were kept a secret for some time less the Bushman/Bayne marital status affect their respective careers as matinee lovers.

Essanay screen idol Francis X. Bushman is prominently featured in this *Chicago Daily News* ad. September, 17, 1915.

Understanding the meaning of "clout" in Chicago years before the term came into use, Spoor and Anderson learned how to use public officials and public facilities to their advantage. Anderson did get arrested at one point for setting off a false fire alarm so Essanay cameras could film Turpin on the run from the horse-drawn fire wagons. By 1912, however, there was official cooperation between the studio and a Chicago fire brigade for the Essanay photoplay *Nepatia, the Greek Singer*. City Hall also got in on the act. Mayor "Big Bill" Thompson became very interested in helping out when Essanay offered to film the annual Prosperity Day Parade. It didn't hurt that the event was a pet project of Thompson. And Essanay's stock went up with City Hall, undoubtedly, when the studio hired the mayor's wife to write movie scenarios.

State government got in on the action as well. More than 500 members of the Illinois National Guard were featured as extras in Essanay's epic adventure *In the Palace of the King*. They also got permission to film the drama *Power* at Starved Rock State Park. Casting Illinois Gov. Edward Fitzgerald Dunne in a supporting part inevitably helped to ease the permitting process.

In addition to Turpin, the Essanay comedy wing boasted the talents of Wallace Beery. Beginning his show business career in 1902 as an assistant to the elephant trainer of Ringling Brothers Circus, Beery turned to comic performance for Broadway and vaudeville shows. At Essanay, Beery's burly appearance was put to incongruous use by outfitting him in a blonde wig and long dress. In this drag get-up, Beery starred in a series of comic misadventures as "Sweedie, the Swedish Maid." With titles like *Sweedie the Swatter*, *Sweedie and Her Dog,* and *Sweedie Goes to College*, the series was quite popular with audiences.

Essanay also housed a considerable writing staff. Ring Lardner, Sr., George Ade, and Hobart Chatfield-Taylor penned photoplays for the studio. The scenario department was run by Louella Parsons. Parsons hailed from Freeport, Illinois and came to Chicago to become a writer. Eventually she relocated to Los Angeles, acted in a few pictures, then went to work for the Hearst newspaper chain where Parsons carved out her stake in the American cultural landscape as a nationally-recognized gossip columnist.

Another future writer, Katherine Anne Porter, worked as an extra in many Essanay productions. Porter later moved to Mexico where she worked as a teacher and journalist. She later became an accomplished short story writer and novelist. Her best known work, *The Ship of Fools*, was filmed in 1965 by director Stanley Kramer.

Porter often worked with another Essanay extra, a Chicago teenager named Gloria Swanson. Swanson's aunt was a friend of Spoor's and in June 1914 she brought young Gloria to the Argyle Street complex. While touring the facilities, Swanson was noticed by the Essanay casting director. In a matter of days, she was cast in her first picture, playing the part of a guest at a wedding. For this less than remarkable cinematic debut, Swanson was paid a grand total of $3.25. An undeserved chewing out by a temperamental director nearly caused Swanson to quit the business altogether after her third film.

Essanay had other plans. Swanson was offered a place in the studio's stock of extra players at a guaranteed salary of $13.25 per week, whether she worked one day or four. Saturday work increased her weekly salary to nearly $20.

Swanson wasn't just noticed by the casting people at Essanay. Beery was smitten with the beautiful young woman and often drove her home in his open-top Stutz Bearcat. Whispers of a liaison between the beefy comedian and another young woman ultimately forced Essanay to permanently exile Beery to their California branch. Two years later, when Swanson herself was a rising star in California, Beery became the first of her six husbands.

By far, the biggest name to work at the Essanay Chicago studio was

Charlie Chaplin. In 1914, Chaplin was the most popular film star in the world. His work with Mack Sennett and the gang of crazies at Keystone Comedies had made Chaplin an international audience favorite. Consequently, when his contract was up with Keystone, the British comic found himself in an enviable position for negotiation.

By fall, the contract talks between Keystone and Chaplin had disintegrated. Anderson, out West working on his Bronco Billy films, met with Chaplin to talk over future possibilities at Essanay. After some discussion, Anderson wired Spoor back in Chicago. He proposed they offer America's beloved film star the then-unheard salary of $1,000 per week. However, by the time Anderson heard back from Spoor, Chaplin's asking price had gone up to $1,250 per week. Anderson agreed and even promised Chaplin a signing bonus of $10,000. The deal settled, Anderson and Chaplin boarded a train heading east.

Upon arrival, Chaplin was disappointed to learn that his new boss, Spoor, was out of town. He toasted New Year's of 1915 with Anderson and his family, and all appeared bright for the new Essanay sensation. Yet Chaplin's brief Chicago period ultimately proved to be an unhappy experience for the comic.

It turned out Spoor had deliberately missed Chaplin's Chicago arrival. Chaplin later discovered the real story: while Anderson first suggested hiring Keystone's sensation, Spoor had never heard of the world's most popular comedian. This was an oddly out-of-touch response for someone so deeply involved in the film industry. At the recommendation of Essanay director Jess Robbins, however, Spoor agreed to hire Chaplin. Still, the $1,250-per-week fee seemed excessive to Spoor, particularly when other studio comics were only making $75 per week. Consequently, when Chaplin was due to arrive, the penny-pinching Spoor wasn't around.

Chaplin also had difficulty getting his promised bonus out of Essanay. He was bounced from office to office in a fruitless search for the cash. Though the money eventually was paid, the brusque treatment gave Chaplin a strong indication of things to come.

The snub by Spoor and the withheld bonus were just part of Chaplin's dissatisfaction. He felt Essanay was too regimented as a business and ultimately not hospitable to creativity. Chaplin was horrified to learn Essanay routinely screened original negatives during the editing phase of filmmaking, rather than go through the added expense of making a positive workprint. Bushman, sensing trouble, tried to smooth things over by telling Chaplin that the upfront operations were just the "antithesis" of how Essanay really worked. "But it wasn't," Chaplin wrote in his autobiography. "I didn't like the studio and I didn't like the word 'antithesis.' "

Still, Chaplin settled into Chicago, taking the penthouse suite at the

Brewster Building on 2800 N. Pine Grove. His next stop was the shops on State Street to buy new baggy pants and over-sized shoes, his trademark costume. Despite the turmoil at Essanay's business office, Chaplin was ready to work.

He got back on the creative track and shot his first comedy for the studio, an appropriately-titled film called *His New Job*. Perhaps the picture was an indication of Chaplin's unhappiness with Spoor: the story revolves around a troublemaking handyman (Chaplin) who causes havoc behind the scenes at a film studio. Released in February of 1915, *His New Job* was notable for introducing Chaplin to Turpin. The two comics had good chemistry both on-screen and off and ended up making several films together. Also appearing in *His New Job* was Gloria Swanson. Chaplin had deliberately picked Swanson for the film, hoping the pretty bit player would add some comic sparkle to the film. Swanson, however, was unimpressed with Chaplin's slapstick. "All morning (during shooting) I felt like a cow trying to dance with a toy poodle," she later wrote in her autobiography, *Swanson on Swanson*. As a result, the disappointed Chaplin stuck Swanson in a smaller role, playing a secretary at a job placement office. Many years later after she had achieved considerable success on her own, Swanson told Chaplin she had been deliberately obstinate during the making of *His New Job*. She had her sights set on a dramatic career and didn't want to be typecast as a lowly comic actress.

After *His New Job* was completed, Chaplin wanted to be as far from Spoor as he could. He demanded to work exclusively at Essanay's California studio. When the contract ended in 1916, Chaplin left Essanay for the Mutual Film Corporation, another studio with some Chicago connection.

Chaplin's defection was the beginning of the end for Essanay. A few years earlier, in 1908, Essanay, along with Selig Polyscope and seven other production companies banded together to form the Motion Pictures Patent Company. This business alliance was designed to combat Thomas Edison's claim that other motion picture professionals were infringing on his patents. However, in the process of creating their coalition, the Motion Pictures Patent Company put a stranglehold on other movie companies. They threatened to cancel contracts with George Eastman for raw stock if he dared to sell film to any other motion picture business. Additionally, in order to control all aspects of distribution, the Motion Pictures Patent Company formed the General Film Company, effectively giving the nine studios sole ability to distribute and control product. In 1915, the Supreme Court ruled that this confederation violated the Sherman Anti-Trust Act. The Motion Pictures Patent Company and the General Film Company were both ordered to disband, opening up immense opportunities to new film companies and distributors.

Promotional pennants for some of Essanay's biggest stars: June Keith, Francis X. Bushman, Edna Mayo, G.M. Anderson, Charlie Chaplin, and Richard C. Travers. (*Courtesy of George Scheetz.*)

The movie business learned nothing from this court case. In 1948, with major Hollywood studios controlling film distribution throughout the country, the Supreme Court again broke up a monopoly on how motion pictures were distributed. (For more information, see the Balaban and Katz entry on page 263.)

This legal decision, and the loss of Chaplin, Bushman, Beery, and other Essanay stars to new film companies, ultimately contributed to the studio's tailspin end. Without a stock company of stars, Essanay pictures no longer raked in box office dollars. Other non-movie related factors which effected Essanay's bottom line included a national coal shortage, a raging flu epidemic, and the ongoing war in Europe. Faced by mounting financial troubles, Spoor finally closed Essanay in 1917.

Having retained a good part of his personal fortune, Spoor sunk $4 million into a 3-D film process known as "natural vision." However, the advent of sound films coupled with the Great Depression caused natural vision to flop. Broke but not broken, Spoor left the film business altogether and later recouped his losses by wise investment in Texas oilfields.

Anderson's fate was less fortunate. He tried his hand at producing Broadway shows, but with little success. He headed back to California, hoping to revive his movie cowboy career, but due to copyright laws, Anderson was forced to relinquish his "Bronco Billy" screen name. Though he left the acting trade, Anderson returned to directing when Metro Studios hired him to work on some of their comedies. There Anderson helmed a few comedy shorts starring an up-and-coming comic named Stan Laurel. Laurel eventually left Metro for Keystone, where he entered into a career partnership with Oliver Hardy.

After his contract with Metro ended, Anderson was unable to find work in the film industry. Doomed to Hollywood oblivion, Anderson spent many years floating through a series of menial jobs. However, the first screen cowboy star was not entirely forgotten. In 1957 Anderson was plucked from obscurity by the Academy of Motion Picture Arts and Sciences and awarded an honorary Oscar "for...contributions to the development of motion pictures as an entertainment."

And what of the buildings Spoor and Anderson left in Chicago? After closing Essanay's Chicago doors, Spoor sold the studio facilities to his former employees, Bell and Howell. In 1973, the Bell and Howell corporation donated part of Essanay to WTTW, the Chicago public television station. The buildings later became home to Essanay Stage and Lighting Company, one of Chicago's top rental houses for industrial film and commercial production.

The Argyle Street properties were next passed to St. Augustine College. Though the buildings have undergone significant remodeling, remnants of

Essanay Film Manufacturing's glory days still remain. Recognizing Essanay's importance to the city, on March 26, 1996 the Commission on Chicago Landmarks gave monument status to the Argyle Street building. The students and teachers at St. Augustine still walk past the old Essanay entrance way. The studio where Chaplin shot *His New Job* has been re-christened "The Charlie Chaplin Auditorium." Just above the auditorium, the original catwalk, where Essanay hands scurried about during filming, remains unchanged from its original design. The staircase, located outside the 1345 building, is another studio vestige. And deep within the basement of the 1333 building, there are two vaults, still labeled with warnings on handling fragile silent-era nitrate film.

➡ THE SOUTH SIDE: THE SILENT ERA'S HOME TO AFRICAN-AMERICAN FILMMAKERS

While Selig and Essanay were producing films on the North Side, the South Side also proved to be a fertile ground for moving picture entrepreneurs. As the silent era blossomed, movies reflected the culture of the time—a society that was segregated and racist. African-Americans working in movies were usually relegated to playing jungle natives, such as Selig's films which often hired Pullman porters to play "authentic" Africans. Many on-screen African-Americans were comic buffoons, never full-blown characters. Other roles available typically were the subservient positions of porters, maids, and domestic help, a trend that continued well into the Hollywood sound era. Quite often in silent films, African-American supporting characters were played by Caucasian actors decked out in blackface.

Consequently, entrepreneurial African-Americans, eager to see an accurate screen reflection of their people, began producing their own films. These pictures were often referred to in African-American communities as "Race pictures." Though usually hampered by low-budgets and crude technical aspects, Race moviemakers took on tough issues facing the African-American community, including racial prejudice, poverty, and intra-racial strife. Light skin tone versus darker skin tone was a recurrent theme in many Race pictures.

Certainly African-American audiences were eager to see Race pictures. The films themselves received enthusiastic support from the *Chicago Defender*. Founded in 1905 by Robert S. Abbott, the *Defender* was a weekly newspaper that focused on the concerns of Chicago's African-American community. Pullman porters often carried the paper with them on their train routes, thus giving the young paper a quick national circulation. Today the

Defender publishes six days a week, bringing an African-American perspective to local and national events of the day.

In the April 9, 1910 edition of the *Chicago Defender*, Sylvester Russell, the newspaper's "Foremost Drama Critic," wrote, "The moving picture craze has developed a wonderful stampede among the Negro...theater goers."[6] Indeed, African-American-operated studios popped up around the country, with regional filmmakers headquartered in such disparate sites as Los Angeles, Philadelphia, and Lincoln, Nebraska. As with the white studios, Chicago proved an ideal spot for enterprising African-Americans. Many popular jazz acts and vaudeville performers either lived in or passed through the city, creating a diverse and accessible talent pool. Though the South Side film industry never approached the financial success of Selig Polyscope or Essanay, its impact was felt during the silent era.

➡ FOSTER PHOTOPLAY COMPANY (1913)
- **Grand Theater, 3110 S. State Street**
- **3312 S. Wabash Street**

Like Col. Selig, William Foster's entertainment background served as his entry to the fledgling motion picture industry. Getting his start in New York City, Foster first entered show business as a publicity agent for the Cole and Johnson Company, a popular minstrel show of the late 19th and early 20th centuries. Intrigued by the possibilities vaudeville had to offer, by 1904 Foster was in Chicago, booking acts and serving as business representative for Robert Motts and the Pekin Theater. The Pekin, which was also known as the Pekin Inn and the Pekin Cafe, was located at 2700 S. State Street. This landmark playhouse/nightclub on Chicago's South Side housed an orchestra and stock acting company which catered to African-American audiences. During this period Foster also wrote articles for the *Chicago Defender* using the pseudonym "Juli Jones, Jr." The thrust of his work dealt with African-American show business, though he also dabbled in sportswriting.

By 1913, Foster was ready to branch out on his own. As an answer to the stereotypes of white filmmakers, Foster opened the first African-American owned and operated film production company in the United States, the Foster Photoplay Company. "Nothing has done so much to awaken race consciousness of the colored man in the United States as the motion picture," Foster wrote for the African-American newspaper, the *Indianapolis Freeman*. "It has made him hungry to see himself as he has come to be."

Foster headquartered his outfit at the Grand Theater, located at State and 31st Street (which advertised itself in the *Defender* as "built for the colored people"), before moving to 3312 S. Wabash.

Foster's first picture was a two-reel comedy, *The Railroad Porter* (a.k.a. *The Pullman Porter*). This slapstick comedy featured Lottie Grady and Howard Kelly, two actors Foster had worked with at the Pekin Theater. The innocuous plot followed the adventures of a Pullman porter and ended in a slapstick chase along the lines of Mack Sennett's Keystone Comedies. Foster wrote and directed *The Railroad Porter* and released it with a companion newsreel which featured a Y.M.C.A. parade of African-Americans. Foster's work was very successful in local theaters, as well as in New York and other eastern cities.

Heady with this initial success, Foster continued producing two-reel comedies and went in search of a national distributor. For a time, he even considered relocating to Jacksonville, Florida, where a number of white studios had set up operations.

By 1917, Foster's dream had withered. Shut out by racism from film distribution channels and unable to book his comedies into white-owned theaters, Foster closed his production house. He re-joined the *Defender* as circulation manager, only to leave a few years later to open a coffee distribution firm. Foster continued to show his films to South Side audiences, however. He even sent some of his movies overseas "to the boys in the trenches," the *Defender* told its readers, so African-Americans fighting in World War I could have a small taste of homelife.

Foster made a brief comeback in the movies at the close of the silent era. Relocating to Los Angeles, he was hired as an assistant to the director of Pathe Studios. Foster directed a few musical short subjects featuring African-American performers, then tried to re-establish himself as a producer. Though he incorporated the business and opened up a Los Angeles office in 1928, the second Foster Photoplay Company folded before making a single film.

➡ THE UNIQUE FILM COMPANY (1916)
3519 S. State Street

Formed by businessman Miles M. Webb, the Unique Film Company only produced one picture. *Shadowed by the Devil*, released in 1916, was based on a story by Webb's wife. The drama focused on three major characters, one a spoiled little rich girl and another a poor but hardworking young man. The third character was the devil-possessed son of an entrepreneur, hopelessly trying to free himself from Satan's grip. Beyond this meager description, not much is known about the film or how it was received. In any event, Unique folded after producing this single film.

➡ PETER P. JONES FILM COMPANY (1916)
- **3704 S. Prairie Avenue**
- **3849 S. State Street**

Peter P. Jones came to filmmaking through portrait photography. Originally from Kalamazoo, Michigan, Jone's studio portraits were considered some of the best in the country. He first came to Chicago in 1908. Jone's reputation quickly grew and eventually he opened up a studio at 3519 S. State Street. Many prestigious figures of the early 20th century sat before Jones lens, including social activists W.E.B. DuBois and Booker T. Washington, artist Henry Tanner, and entertainer Bert Williams.

A community activist, Jones made an important contribution to Chicago political history when, in 1912, he became the first African-American to run for the City Council. Aiming for the office of alderman of the 2nd ward, Jones's political ambitions were thwarted when his petitions for a spot on the ballot were officially denied.

Jones turned to moviemaking in 1914. The Peter P. Jones Film Company opened up at 3704 S. Prairie Avenue, then later moved to 3849 S. State Street. His first effort was *Sambo and Dinah*, a forgettable two-reel comedy that relied on stereotyped characters to carry the humor. Jones's second film, however, put him on the map. *For the Honor of the 8th Ill. U.S.A.*, released in September 1914, was a documentary highlighting the exploits of the 8th Illinois regiment, an all-African-American military unit based in Chicago.

Jones continued making newsreels, then in 1916 produced a five-reel comedy, *The Slacker*. The story revolved around a would-be draft dodger who desperately wants to avoid the Great War in Europe. After a dream in which he encounters a battlefield veteran, the protagonist changes his mind and achieves glory on the battlefields of France.

Following *The Slacker*, Jones relocated to New York. He returned to still photography and became the first African-American hired by a major movie studio upon taking a job with Selznick Film Laboratories, a facility run by movie pioneer Lewis J. Selznick. In 1922, Jones tried his hand again at film production in an abortive attempt to make a film with aviator Bessie Coleman. Coleman, the first African-American woman to earn a pilot's license, was a well-known stunt flier and test pilot. The following year Jones produced a two-reel airplane comedy, *How High is Up?*, his last known effort at moviemaking.

➡ BIRTH OF A RACE PHOTOPLAY COMPANY (1917)
- **123 W. Madison Street**
- **29 S. LaSalle Avenue**

In 1915, the *Chicago Daily News* carried advertisements for D.W. Griffith's Civil War epic, *The Birth of a Nation*, noting that seats were being sold four weeks in advance and patrons asked to name two dates for seats if possible. The full-page ad, which at one point trumpeted that the film had been shown "185 Times in Chicago Today and Not an Empty Seat Yet," also listed many of *The Birth of a Nation's* highlights. Viewers were in store for a host of excitements, previously unimaginable in moving pictures. The "gigantic spectacle" promised 3,000 horses, 18,000 people, and 5,000 scenes put together for film audiences at the staggering cost of $500,000. The advertisement also heralded the film's many historical re-enactments, including Sherman's march to the sea, the assassination of Abraham Lincoln, and the "rise of the Ku Klux Klan."

Others were less impressed with Griffith's depiction of the KKK. While *The Birth of a Nation* was a landmark achievement in American movies in its pioneering use of editing, epic story-telling, and rousing climax, it also was an appalling historical rewrite of what developed in the post-Civil War South. The film generated controversy throughout the United States, realistically, the first time in the nation's history that racism in popular culture garnered open public debate. Though President Woodrow Wilson called the film "history written in lightning," other notable figures including Chicago novelist Upton Sinclair (*The Jungle*) and philanthropist George Foster Peabody condemned the production.

In Chicago, Mayor William "Big Bill" Thompson managed to delay the opening of the film for some time. Eventually *The Birth of a Nation* was the subject of debate in the Illinois legislature, leading to a bill prohibiting racially inflammatory material from stage and screen. This bill passed by an overwhelming majority of 111 to 2.[7]

Griffith, the son of a Confederate Army colonel, was shocked and dismayed over the outrage his film generated. Ultimately he was forced to cut and re-cut the picture, opening different versions around the country, often depending on what local attitudes would and would not tolerate on screen. The controversy ultimately broke Griffith. He attempted to answer his critics with *Intolerance*, an epic production examining fanaticism through the ages. The film, while today acknowledged as a masterpiece, was an expensive flop. Though Griffith continued working into the early sound era, he became an alcoholic, unable to shake the personal defeat he experienced with *The Birth of a Nation*.

At the time of *The Birth of a Nation*'s release, the *Chicago Defender* published a letter to the editor against the film written by Booker T. Washington. The letter, which was later printed in African-American newspapers throughout the country, read in part: "No matter how many other artistic and historic features the play may have, its ultimate result will be to intensify race prejudice and thereby do great, lasting harm to both races."[8] Washington also considered what impact his own autobiography, *Up From Slavery* might have if it were turned into a photoplay. In November 1915 Washington died, leaving it for others to take up that challenge.

Emmett J. Scott, who had been Washington's confidential secretary since 1897, continued to pursue the project. Before Washington's death, the two had explored producing a film called *Lincoln's Dream*, a project which ultimately fell apart due to financial difficulties. This fruitless attempt was an ominous prelude to what ultimately happened.

By July 1916, Scott had regrouped. He incorporated The Birth of a Race Photoplay Corporation in Delaware, though production was headquartered in Chicago. Such varied national figures as former President William Howard Taft, Washington's widow, Illinois Gov. Frank Lowden, and noted Sears Roebuck executive and philanthropist Julius Rosenwald all endorsed the idea behind the proposed film.[9] A brochure, inviting investors to buy stock in this new film corporation, stated that *The Birth of a Race* would show "the true story of the Negro, his life in Africa, his transportation to America, his enslavement, his freedom, his achievements, together with his past, present and future relations with his white neighbor and to the world in which both live and labor."[10]

The war in Europe slowed down fundraising, as Scott, concerned over issues facing African-American draftees, became a special adviser to the U.S. Secretary of War, Newton Diehl Baker. Stock for the film continued to be sold, however, and promises made on potential returns. The African-American community of Chicago's South Side bought a considerable amount of shares. Sales were then concentrated in the Jewish community, with additional scenes promised that would bring a public indictment on anti-Semitism in society.

Initially, the film was to be made in conjunction with the Selig Polyscope Corporation. After spending $140,000 on production, Selig dropped the project. It seemed that the stock sales had been grossly mismanaged, though this was carefully shielded from shareholders via a periodic newsletter trumpeting the continuing production. Dismayed at what was happening to the original concept, Rosenwald withdrew his support from the troubled production. Others who had previously endorsed the project also distanced themselves. Then, in the spring of 1918, Chicago stockbroker Giles P. Corey was arrested for fraudulently promoting the actual value and return on stock.

Down, but not out, the production was picked up by Daniel Frohman of the New York-based Frohman Amusement Company. Things seemed to be picking up; after all, Frohman was a reputed show business producer and theatrical impresario. In conjunction with his brother Charles, Frohman controlled many theaters throughout the United States.

As the film changed hands, so did the nature of the story. It was now turning into a Biblical epic, with recreations of Old and New Testament stories. Frohman moved the production to Tampa, Florida to shoot Biblical footage. The original concept of promoting racial tolerance and harmony fell to the wayside as anti-German propaganda was added to exploit wartime sentiments. Scott's name was also dropped as the film's scenarist.

The film was finally completed at Chicago's Rothacker Film Manufacturing Company, a non-entertainment industrial film studio located at 1339 W. Diversey Parkway. In November of 1918, an innocuous advertisement appeared in the back pages of *Variety* to announce the grand opening of *The Birth of a Race* at the Blackstone Theater at 60 E. Balbo Avenue. (Then one of the world's most fashionable venues, today the theater is owned by DePaul University and has been re-christened the Merle Reskin Theater.) To ensure an audience, investors were asked to pay a hefty sum of $10 each for opening night tickets.

The film finally opened in December of 1918. What resulted after the many years of effort and controversy was a complete shambles. The Biblical story and the war story lines in *The Birth of a Race* seemed like two different movies haphazardly stitched together. Promised scenes of racial harmony and enrichment were gone, replaced by a sequence in which a young white boy bullied an African-American child.

Surprisingly, the film earned mixed reviews. Some pronounced the film "clean, sincere" and "worth seeing," if perhaps a bit on the long side.[11] On the other hand, the show business publication *Moving Picture World* declared "the names of three men are given as the authors of the scenario. It would be a deed of charity not to reveal their identity nor the names of the members of the cast. All have well-earned reputations and are probably anxious to live down their connection with the entire affair."[12]

➡ **HISTORICAL FEATURE FILM COMPANY (1915)**
 105 W. Monroe Street

➡ **EBONY FILM CORPORATION (1917)**
 • **608 S. Dearborn Street (725 Transportation Building)**
 • **2332 N. California Avenue**

The Historical Feature Film Company was a white-owned company which produced two-reel comedies. Aimed at both African-American and white audiences, the slapstick shorts relied heavily on Negro stereotypes of the era. Such titles as *A Natural Born Shooter, Money Talks in Darktown,* and *Black and White* were released in 1915.

Two years later, Ebony Film Corporation was founded by a group of white film investors. Run by Luther J. Pollard, an African-American who served as Ebony's figurehead, the studio offices were located downtown on South Dearborn, with production facilities on North California Avenue. Ebony also had an outdoor studio located just outside Oshkosh, Wisconsin. The company of 40 players included Sam Robinson, a cousin of Bill "Bojangles" Robinson who was one of Hollywood's premier tap dancers in the 1930s. Another member of the Ebony stock company was Sam T. Jacks, who would become involved with The Royal Gardens Motion Picture Company in 1919.

As titular head of Ebony, Pollard espoused racial pride in the studio product. "We specialize in comedy, the same as the producers of Charles Chaplin...or any other producers of comedy," he wrote to a Los Angeles-based African-American filmmaker. "You will find (our films) to be clean and without those situations which are usually attributed to the American negro. We proved to the public that colored players can put over good comedy without any of that crap shooting, chicken stealing, razor display, watermelon eating stuff that the colored people generally have been a little disgusted at seeing..."[13]

Ebony comedies, such as *Ghosts, The Porters, The Busted Romance* (all 1917), *The Bully,* and *A Black Sherlock Holmes* (both 1918), tended to be

Chicago Defender movie ads, c. 1917-1918, promoting theaters as well as the photoplays of Ebony Film Corporation.

overacted, ham-fisted comedy, however. The films were well-received in white theaters, where the stereotypes played as appealing low-brow humor. African-American audiences saw the Ebony films in a totally different light.

The *Chicago Defender* printed numerous editorials and letters to the editor, complaining about the nature of Ebony's films. "It was with abject humiliation that myself and many of my friends sat through the scenes of degradation shown on screen," wrote one angry viewer. "...if (the films) were meant for comedy, the meaning certainly miscarried."[14]

Part of the problem was that before Pollard and company actually produced films of their own, they released the Historical Feature Film Company movies under the Ebony name. The earlier films, which were more blatant in their racist stereotypes, resulted in a boycott of Ebony pictures. Led by the *Defender*, theaters catering to African-American audiences gradually stopped booking the Ebony product. This inevitably resulted in financial difficulties for the company and Ebony ultimately folded in 1919.

An article in the May 12, 1917 edition of the *Chicago Defender* reports on a theatre which refused to show one of Ebony Film's movies.

➡ **THE MICHEAUX FILM AND BOOK COMPANY (1918)**
   538 S. Dearborn, Suites 807 - 808

Ambitious and hard-driven, Oscar Micheaux is something of a spiritual predecessor to the American independent film movement of the 1990s. The child of former slaves, Micheaux was born in 1883. Raised in the small town of Metropolis, Illinois, at the very southern tip of the state, Micheaux moved to Chicago in 1900. After working a series of odd jobs, he relocated to Wheaton, where he became a farm laborer. Though this low-paying job largely involved pitching hay, Micheaux lived simply and was able to open a bank account. After a couple of years, he took a job as a Pullman porter.

Though the paycheck amounted to a lowly sum of $40 a week, Micheaux again was able to save while traveling throughout the country.

In 1904, Micheaux put in to buy a plot of government land being sold by lottery in South Dakota. Though unsuccessful in this attempt, Micheaux became a landowner two years later when he was sold a portion of land near Gregory, South Dakota. Although he had no experience in agriculture, Micheaux developed into a proficient farmer.

In frequent business trips to Chicago, Micheaux exhorted other African-Americans to move West, though he had little luck in this campaign. However, Micheaux was still a much-respected figure among African-Americans living in Chicago, and a visit by him often merited a few lines in the *Defender*.

Micheaux had been corresponding over the years with Orlean McCracken, a minister's daughter from Metropolis In 1910, the two were married at a Chicago church. Orlean's father cared little for Micheaux, though, and did not trust his

Farm laborer and Pullman porter turned independent filmmaker and author: Oscar Micheaux. (*Photo from the South Dakota State Archives. Courtesy of Martin J. Keenan.*)

headstrong son-in-law. Micheaux's marriage deteriorated when Orlean could not adapt to the sparse conditions of prairie life. In 1911, she gave birth to a stillborn child. Pressure from his in-laws, coupled with growing crop difficulties, led to Orlean leaving Micheaux for the more hospitable environs of Chicago.

A bad drought ultimately led to the end of Micheaux's life as a farmer. Ever the entrepreneur, Micheaux decided to turn his unique life experiences into fiction. In 1913, Micheaux's thinly-veiled autobiographical novel, *The*

Conquest, was published by Woodruff Press, a company based in Lincoln, Nebraska. Micheaux began traveling around the country, selling his book from town to town. This barnstorming sales technique was a pattern Micheaux would later carry over from his literary career to his life as a filmmaker.

The Conquest proved to be a successful venture for the freshman author and Micheaux wrote his second book, *The Forged Note,* in 1915. His third book, *The Homesteader,* published in 1917, was another roman à clef, detailing Micheaux's life as a homesteader and his failed marriage. It was this novel which led to the next phase of Micheaux's life.

The Homesteader was read by George P. Johnson, an executive with Lincoln Motion Picture Company, an African-American film business with offices in Omaha, Nebraska and Los Angeles, California. After a series of meetings between Micheaux, Johnson, and Johnson's brother Noble, negotiations to bring *The Homesteader* before the cameras broke down. The Johnson's saw Micheaux's story as a short, three-reel movie, whereas Micheaux felt the epic nature of his plot demanded much more significant screen time. (Noble Johnson later became an actor in numerous Hollywood films, including roles as "Queequeg" in the 1930 adaptation of *Moby Dick* and as a tribal chieftain in *King Kong* (1933). He continued playing small supporting and uncredited parts well into the 1940s.)

To this end, Micheaux went into the moviemaking business himself.   In 1918, he opened the Micheaux Film and Book Company with the express purpose of making a movie out of *The Homesteader.* Offices were opened in Sioux City, Iowa and at 538 S. Dearborn in Chicago. Turning to old friends, Micheaux raised funds for the production by selling stock to the white business people and farmers of Gregory.

The Homesteader opened at Chicago's 8th Regiment Armory on Thursday, February 20, 1919. The wordy advertisement for the film read "Passed by the Censor Board despite the protests of three Chicago ministers who claimed that it was based upon the supposed hypocritical actions of a prominent colored preacher of this city!" Undoubtedly, this was a veiled reference by Micheaux aimed at his former father-in-law. Clocking in at almost three hours, an unheard of running time during the silent era, the *Defender* immediately dubbed Micheaux's photoplay "...the greatest of all Race productions..."

Booking his film at numerous South Side movie venues and then at theaters throughout the Midwest, Micheaux managed to turn a healthy profit. The success invigorated Micheaux as he plunged onward as a filmmaker.

One of the reasons Micheaux was able to earn back the investment on *The Homesteader* was his bargain-basement approach to filmmaking. While he was a natural storyteller, Micheaux's cinematic sensibility was crude at best. His films suffered from bad lighting, choppy editing, and a host of other technical blunders. Another criticism Micheaux faced early in his career was his casting of light-skinned African-Americans in heroic roles and darker members of the race as villains. Micheaux even used light-skinned African-Americans to play white characters.

Still, Micheaux forged ahead. Using his time-tested method of promotion and fundraising, he traveled extensively throughout the south to book his films and obtain money for new productions. At its height in Chicago, the Micheaux Film and Book Company turned out three films a year.

In 1920, Micheaux stirred up considerable controversy. The previous year, racial tensions in Chicago exploded into riots after a young African-American, Eugene Williams, was stoned and drowned by a group of whites after Williams accidentally drifted on the lake to a "Whites Only" beach along 29th Street. From July 27 through 31, Chicago was a city under siege by its own citizens. African-Americans battled white mobs in the streets. Ultimately, it took the National Guard and a timely rainstorm to quell the violence. When the violence was finally over, 23 African-Americans and 15 whites were dead, while 537 people were reported injured. Hundreds more had lost their homes in numerous arsons. For a gripping recreation of this horrific moment in Chicago's history, check out the PBS drama *The Killing Floor* (1984).

Tackling these still raw emotional feelings head-on, Micheaux released *Within Our Gates*, a drama notable for a scene in which a white mob lynches an African-American. Initially, the Chicago Board of Movie Censors vetoed any plans to show *Within Our Gates*, fearing the film would incite a second riot. The Board, however, agreed to a second viewing of the film and this time invited area officials and representatives of Chicago's African-American community.

The results were mixed. Alderman Louis Anderson and Edward Wright, the Corporation Counsel for Chicago, believed that the film should be shown despite the unsettling lynch scene. Others, including a coalition of African-American and white clergy, believed that *Within Our Gates* would only cause more problems. On the morning *Within Our Gates* was scheduled to open, the interracial Methodist and Episcopal Minister's Alliance appealed to Chicago's Mayor "Big Bill" Thompson and Chief of Police John J. Garrity. Both officials, however, refused to censor Micheaux's work.

Like any other "controversial" movie throughout film history, *Within Our Gates* was suddenly the film to see. "8,000 feet of sensational realism," cried advertisements. "Cost more than any 10 racial films ever made."

On Monday, January 12, 1920, *Within Our Gates* opened to a packed house at the Vendrome Theater at 3145 S. State Street. *The Defender* called the film "the biggest protests against Race prejudice, (and) lynching...ever written or filmed..."

Emboldened by his success, Micheaux returned to a lynching theme the following year with *The Gunsaulus Mystery*. This drama was loosely based on the case of Leo Frank, a Jewish man murdered in 1915 by an angry mob in Marietta, Georgia. The *Gunsaulus Mystery* was shot in New York, where Micheaux had relocated. Though the Chicago office remained open as a distribution wing for Micheaux Book and Film Company, by the early 1920s, all production had shifted to New York City.

In 1926, Micheaux finally closed what remained of the Chicago office, though he continued making films well into the sound era. Micheaux developed an ensemble of African-American actors to correspond with popular Hollywood figures. Thus, Lorenzo Tucker was billed as "The Black Valentino," Ethel Moses as "The Black Harlow," and Bee Freman as "The Sepia Mae West." His 1924 film *Body and Soul* marked the film debut of the noted African-American actor/singer/activist Paul Robeson, and his 1939 film, *Lying Lips,* featured Robert Earl Jones, the father of noted actor James Earl Jones.

However, the increasing sophistication of Hollywood productions paired with Micheaux's lack of technical panache made it harder for Micheaux to find venues for his work. Illness and financial difficulties forced Micheaux to leave the film business in 1948, so he turned to what he knew how to do best—hit the road and sell his books.

Micheaux died in 1951 and was buried in Great Bend, Kansas. His parents had moved to this quiet Kansas town in the center of the state in the early 1900s, and other family members resided in the area. His grave was marked with a simple metal plate.

This trailblazing director was seemingly relegated to a position of footnote in American film history. However, in the mid-1980s Micheaux was rediscovered by a new generation of moviemakers and film buffs. With the growth of independent cinema and the rise of such African-American directors as Spike Lee, Chicago-born Robert Townsend, and Julie Dash (all disciples of the late filmmaker), Micheaux was finally recognized as a cinematic pioneer. His surviving films, including *Within Our Gates*, were featured in retrospectives across the United States. In 1986, the Directors Guild of America gave Micheaux a posthumous honor with a Golden Jubilee Special Directorial Award, recognizing his efforts to bring African-American stories to the screen. On February 13, 1987, Micheaux was given the ultimate in Hollywood honors: his own star on the Walk of Fame along Hollywood Boulevard.

On October 8th of the following year, a small group that included some of Micheaux's relatives, Townsend, and James Shabazz of the Black Filmmakers Hall of Fame —gathered at Micheaux's grave site. Together they unveiled a tombstone paid for with money raised by the director's fans and advocates.

The South Dakota gravemarker of American film pioneer Oscar Micheaux. (*Courtesy of Martin J. Keenan.*)

"Oscar Micheaux, Jan. 2, 1884 - Mar. 25, 1951," read the inscription. "Pioneer Black Film Maker & Author. A Man Ahead of His Time."

For more information on this groundbreaking director, check out the Web site http://www.greatbend.net/gbcc/history/micheaux/index.html

➡ THE ROYAL GARDENS MOTION PICTURE COMPANY (1919)
459 E. 31st Street

The Royal Gardens, run by Virgil L. Williams, was a popular nightclub and restaurant with Chicago's African-American community. Clarence Muse, who went on to play supporting parts in numerous Hollywood features, including Jim to Jackie Coogan's *Huckleberry Finn* (1931) and Snoe in *The Black Stallion* (1979), was often hired by Williams to stage floorshows at the club. Another regular was jazz legend King Oliver. Between 1918 and 1921, the King Oliver Band, featuring trumpeter Louis Armstrong, was a steady attraction for the Royal Gardens.

In 1919, Williams attempted to pick up where William Foster had left off. Working with Sam T. Jacks, who had acted in several pictures for the Ebony Film Company, Williams entered the movie business by establishing a new branch of his entertainment ventures, The Royal Gardens Motion Picture Company. His intent was to create a center where African-Americans could learn the craft of filmmaking.[15]

Royal Gardens only produced one picture of note, *In the Depth of Our Hearts*, in 1920, with shooting taking place around the city and in rural Wisconsin. Williams took particular pride in the technical qualities of his film, which he felt were better than most "Race" pictures showing in South

Side theaters. Though forgotten today, *In the Depth of Our Hearts* was praised by the *Defender* in 1920 for both its dramatic qualities as well as some "wonderful amount of action of the thrilling sort—hand to hand fights between red blooded men which will make you sit up and take notice..."

By 1920, Williams' dream succumbed to financial difficulties and the filmmaking operation folded.

➡ **DEMOCRACY PHOTOPLAY CORPORATION (C. 1918)**
➡ **DELIGHT FILM CORPORATION (C. 1919)**
➡ **PYRAMID PICTURE CORPORATION (C. 1920)**
➡ **FIFE PRODUCTIONS COMPANY (C. 1922)**

Little is known about either the Democracy Photoplay Corporation or the Delight Film Corporation. Like Ebony Pictures, both companies were white-owned and operated. Democracy produced at least one known film, titled *Democracy or a Fight for Right*. Advertised as a "Smashing Virile Story of Our Race Heroes," the film was not well received.[16]

Delight was another matter entirely. Rumored to be producing a version of Shakespeare's *Othello*, using an entirely African-American cast, the company proved to be something of a fly-by-night operation. Spied on by an agent from Lincoln Motion Picture Company, an African-American photoplay operation located in Los Angeles, the Delight operation does not emerge from history with glowing credentials. According to the Lincoln agent, "the whole place looks like a swindling joint." The attitudes of the studio's white owners came through clearly in advertising campaigns that read "colored people are funny."[17] In any event, the Delight Film Corporation, like so many of its peers, folded without making much of an impact.

There were at least two other Chicago-based African-American production companies operating during the silent era. Other than their names, there is little information on the Pyramid Picture Corporation (c. 1920) and Fife Productions Company (c. 1922).

➡ **OTHER SILENT PRODUCTIONS**

Though records are scant, there were a handful of other films shot in Chicago in the silent era, the most notable being *That Royale Girl*, a 1925 feature directed by D. W. Griffith and featuring W. C. Fields in a rare dramatic role. At this point in his career, Griffith was all but washed up. In the wake of *The Birth of a Nation* controversy and the financial misfortunes of *Intolerance*, Griffith had fallen from his august position as cinematic pioneer to studio hack.

That Royale Girl was produced by Famous Players-Lasky/Paramount, which allowed Griffith to do some location work in Chicago. Most notable were scenes shot at the famed Saint-Gaudens statue of Abraham Lincoln, just east of what is now the Chicago Historical Society in Lincoln Park.

Ultimately, *That Royale Girl* did little to impress either critics or moviegoers. By 1925, Griffith's brand of drama and overwrought emotion was passé. The film died a quick death at the box office and was instantly forgotten. Since its release, however, *That Royale Girl* has disappeared, unless perhaps an errant print is hidden in someone's attic or mislabeled and buried inside a studio vault. In 1980, *That Royale Girl* was put on the American Film Institute's list of the "ten most wanted" lost films, which were determined on their historical and/or artistic merits. As of this writing, the film remains lost in movie history.

Other notable silent films shot in Chicago include a 1914 adaptation of *The Jungle*, which was the first dramatization of Upton Sinclair's muckraking novel about the city's meatpacking industry. Cowboy star William S. Hart came to Chicago in 1919 to film his Western, *Breed of Men*. A 1916 feature, *The Dumb Girl of Portici*, has some significance as well. Produced by Universal Pictures, this tale of a poor Italian girl in love with a Spanish nobleman in the midst of political upheaval is the only known film of the renowned Russian ballet star Anna Pavlova. The film also features an uncredited extra by

William Hart, cowboy silent film star, appeared in 1919's *Breed of Men*. (*From the collection of Arnie Bernstein.*)

the name of William Henry Pratt. Fifteen years later, Pratt, using the stage name Boris Karloff, would gain international acclaim as the Creature in Universal Picture's 1931 horror classic *Frankenstein*.

The departure of Selig Polyscope and Essanay to the West and Oscar Micheaux to the East put an effective conclusion to Chicago's golden age of silent film. And in 1927, with the release of the musical *The Jazz Singer*, the entire movie industry was forever transformed by the revolutionary breakthrough of sound technology.

In the 1930s, as Los Angeles blossomed into the world capital for moviemakers, Chicago developed into a center for training films and commercial work. Occasionally Hollywood productions, looking for gritty urban locations (such as *Call Northside 777* in 1946), came to the Windy City. Yet for the most part between 1930 and the early 1960s, a Chicago-based film was usually shot on a Hollywood soundstage.

It would be another 35 years following *The Jazz Singer*'s debut before feature filmmaking would slowly begin its return to Chicago and eventually flourish along Lake Michigan's southern shore.

[1] Ramsaye, Terry, *A Million and One Nights: A History of the Motion Picture Through 1925* (New York: Touchstone, 1986), 85.

[2] *Chicago Daily News* classified ads, September 2, 1911.

[3] *Ibid.*, September 1, 1911.

[4] *Ibid.*, April 30, 1915.

[5] Lahue, Kalton C., editor, *Motion Picture Pioneer: The Selig Polyscope Company* (Cranbury, New Jersey: A.S. Barnes and Company, 1973.).

[6] *Chicago Defender*, April 23, 1912.

[7] Schickel, Richard, *D.W. Griffith: An American Life* (New York: Simon and Schuster, 1984), 296.

[8] *Ibid.*, 298.

[9] Leab, Daniel J., *From Sambo to Superspade: The Black Experience in Motion Pictures*. (Boston: Houghton Mifflin Company, 1975), 60.

[10] *Ibid.*, 61.

[11] Cripps, Thomas, *Slow Fade to Black: The Negro in American Film, 1900-1942* (London: Oxford University Press, 1977), 75.

[12] Sampson, Henry T., *Blacks in Black and White: A Source Book on Black Films*. (Metuchen, New Jersey: Scarecrow Press, Inc., 1995), 209.

[13] *Ibid.*, 202.

[14] *Ibid.*, 205.

[15] Kenney, William. "Chicago's 'Black-and-Tans,'" *Chicago History Magazine* (Fall 1997): 22.

[16] Cripps, 84.

[17] *Ibid.*

Much of the material in this silent era section was drawn from the historical record, including the following resources:

Chaplin, Charles. *My Autobiography*. New York: Pocket Book, 1966.

Cripps, Thomas. *Slow Fade to Black: The Negro in American Film, 1900-1942.* London: Oxford University Press, 1977.

Lahue, Kalton C., editor. *Motion Picture Pioneer: The Selig Polyscope Company*. Cranbury, New Jersey: A.S. Barnes and Company, 1973.

Leab, Daniel J. *From Sambo to Superspade: The Black Experience in Motion Pictures*. Boston: Houghton Mifflin Company, 1975.

Ramsaye, Terry. *A Million and One Nights: A History of the Motion Picture Through 1925*. New York: Touchstone, 1986.

Robinson, David. *Chaplin: His Life and Art*. New York: McGraw-Hill, 1985.

Sampson, Henry T. *Blacks in Black and White: A Source Book on Black Films*. Metuchen, New Jersey: Scarecrow Press, Inc., 1995.

Schickel, Richard. *D.W. Griffith: An American Life*. New York: Simon and Schuster, 1984.

Sheetz, George H. *The Chicago Film Industry: Beginnings to 1918*. Unpublished Senior Thesis. University of Illinois at Champaign-Urbana, Department of English, Spring 1974.

Swanson, Gloria. *Swanson on Swanson*. New York: Random House, 1980.

INDEX OF ARTICLES

River North and
North Michigan Avenue

➡ RUSH STREET & DIVISION STREET AREA

New York may have had its Studio 54, but Chicago had its Rush Street. Anybody who was hip and happening in the 1970s inevitably found themselves gravitating towards the allure of the bars along Rush and Division: Faces, BBC, and many more. That dizzying nightlife center was dismally captured in *Looking For Mr. Goodbar* (1977), an adaptation of Judith Rossner's novel. The story revolved around a naive Catholic woman (Diane Keaton), whose double life as teacher of the deaf/party girl comes to a violent end when she picks up the wrong guy on a fateful New Year's Eve.

The film is definitely a product of its time. Hairstyles and clothing on some characters must truly be seen to be believed. Ultimately, *Looking for Mr. Goodbar*, at its best, is a morass of turgid movie clichés. Gay men are flaming queens (keep in mind, this is eight years after 1969's groundbreaking *Midnight Cowboy*), women suffer from the Madonna/whore complex, and straight men are psychopaths ready to boil over.

Yet, within this mass of stereotypes, director Richard Brooks managed to provide a fairly intriguing documentary look at Chicago's nightlife in the mid-1970s.

➡ MOTHER'S
26 W. Division Street

A mecca among singles' bars, Mother's played a prominent role in the yuppie romance, *About Last Night...* (1986). Have a drink here and you can pretend to see where Demi Moore and Rob Lowe loved and fought—in reality only the exterior of Mother's was used in the film. The bar's decor was faithfully recreated on a Hollywood soundstage!

Mother's sister bar, Shenannigans (16 W. Division St.), is another popular Division Street watering hole. It had a small part in *Nothing in Common* (1986), a Tom Hanks comedy/drama about the difficulties faced by a man who's parents are divorcing. *Nothing in Common* turned Shenannigans (normally a singles' nightspot) into the favorite neighborhood watering hole of Hanks's curmudgeon father, played by Jackie Gleason.

➡ THE DRAKE HOTEL
140 E. Walton Place

One of Chicago's most elegant hotels, the Drake opened its doors on New Year's Eve 1920. The hotel was conceived by John Burroughs Drake, a well-known hotelier of the era, as a place for his sons John and Tracy to manage. Quickly gaining a reputation as a place to see and be seen, the Drake attracted guests from around the globe. The hotel's Gold Coast Room hosted lavish floor shows, which were directed by Marshall, who maintained a strong interest in day-to-day operations. In the 1930s, the Gold Coast Room was home to big band radio broadcasts heard nationwide over WGN radio.

In its many decades of operation, the Drake has been an overnight home to an eclectic collection of Hollywood celebrities, world leaders, and other noted individuals. Movie-wise, the Drake Hotel always rates high on the posh meter. In *Mission Impossible* (1996), a simple mention of "a room at the Drake" is all it takes for secret agent Jon Voight to impress his colleagues in the international spy game—no mean shakes in a cinematic profession known for impeccably high standards.

New York food critic Julia Roberts stayed at the Drake while plotting

Julia Roberts, a New York food critic in *My Best Friend's Wedding*, stayed at the elegant Drake Hotel (140 E. Walton) off of Michigan Avenue. (*Photo couresty of the Drake Hotel.*)

the downfall of her rival Cameron Diaz in *My Best Friend's Wedding* (1997). In the dark social satire *Risky Business* (1983), Tom Cruise and Curtis Armstrong drank pricey hot chocolates in the Drake's Palm Court while waiting to confront high-priced call girl Rebecca DeMornay. Unfortunately for the three of them, Guido the killer pimp (Joe Pantoliano) is also there, flashing his nasty smile and a nastier gun. Scenes from the bland basketball drama *Heaven is a Playground* (1991) were also shot here, as well as footage for *The Blues Brothers* (1980) and the made-for-television movie "Man Against the Mob" (1988).

The Drake played a climactic role in *Hero* (1992). It was here where Andy Garcia, a homeless man turned accidental hero, decides to jump off a ledge rather than face the truth and his reporter/love interest Geena Davis. As a teeming mob watches from below, Garcia is ultimately bullied back inside by Dustin Hoffman, an off-kilter crank with real hero credentials.

Preparation for this night-time scene took more than six weeks. Part of this involved construction of a realistic-looking ledge outside a hotel window, plotting out camera and lighting set-ups, and corralling more than 300 extras. Yet, despite all these preparations, the film crew faced an extra-large snafu when it was time for cameras to roll.

On the same night this scene was to be shot, Chicago's second biggest star, Oprah Winfrey, was hosting a tribute at the Drake to Chicago's mega-star, Michael Jordan. The production crew was forced to stop all work as a seemingly non-stop parade of limousines dropped off a coterie of high-powered luminaries. The delay threw *Hero*'s director, Stephen Frears, into an over-the-top temper tantrum. Screaming for someone to get rid of the limos, Frears was greeted with a notable cool on the part of Chicago's Finest. Crew members were told by police: "Tell that guy to settle down or we're gonna lock him up!" Finally, with Oprah, Air Jordan, and their intimates safely ensconced deep within the Drake, an army of 300-plus extras was moved in, Garcia crawled out on a ledge, and shooting commenced—only to stop once more when it was time for tribute dinner guests to return back to their squadron of limos.

For reservation and restaurant or catering information, call the Drake Hotel at 312-787-2200.

➡ **FOUR SEASONS HOTEL**
120 E. Delaware Place (at 900 N. Michigan Avenue)

Located in the heart of Michigan Avenue's shopping district, the Four Seasons Hotel has shown up in a handful of films. The opening reception in *The Fugitive* (1993) takes place at the Four Seasons, and in fact, Harrison

Ford, the film's star, stayed here while the production was in Chicago. *Chain Reaction* (1996) and *Miracle on 34th Street* (1994) also shot scenes here.

To make reservations at the Four Seasons, call 312-280-8800. You can check out the hotel's Web site at http://www.fshr.com/locations/Chicago/index.html.

➡ **THE JOHN HANCOCK BUILDING**
875 N. Michigan Avenue

Towering over North Michigan since 1969, the John Hancock Building is one of Chicago's signature skyscrapers, ranking it as the thrid tallest, just behind the Sears Tower and the Amoco Oil Building. Its 100 stories hold offices, condominiums, and a variety of shops. Counting the antennas atop the building, the Hancock checks in at 1,127 feet tall. The 94th floor viewing deck offers a spectacular view of Lake Michigan and many points beyond, while the building's signature restaurant, the 95th, is one of the city's most chi-chi eateries.

Movie-wise, the Hancock is another of those characteristic "Chicago" buildings filmmakers love to use in opening shots. A few (very few) directors have also ventured through the doors to take advantage of the Hancock's interior.

The Hancock Building was turned into a haunted house of sorts for *Poltergeist III* (1988), as poor Heather O'Rourke was followed by spooks for a third outing while Aunt Nancy Allen and Uncle Tom Skerritt did a lot of helpless screaming. On a more dramatic note, Tom Cruise and Rebecca DeMornay had a poignant final scene over drinks at the 95th in *Risky Business* (1988).

It took *The Blues Brothers* (1980) to exploit the Hancock's status as one of the world's tallest buildings. As part of the climactic chase sequence, Jake and Elwood Blues (John Belushi and Dan Aykroyd) lead neo-Nazi Henry Gibson and one of his henchmen on a wild ride through expressway construction. A quick turn saves the Blues Brothers but sends Gibson's vehicle hurtling off an unfinished ramp. Soaring into the air, we see the car hit its peak, then rapidly descend with the John Hancock Building in the background to provide scale.

To accomplish this shot, the automobile was hoisted some 1,200 feet into the air via helicopter and then dropped into a vacant lot along the Chicago River. Incidentally, the chase leading up to this bizarre sight was a fine example of geography by editing. Though portions of the scene were shot along Chicago expressways, director John Landis used an unfinished

Milwaukee expressway as the launching pad for Gibson's car. Look carefully in the background and you'll see a distinctively non-Chicago skyline in some shots.

Sadly, the John Hancock Building gained fame as the final crash pad for one of Chicago's favorite funny guys. In December 1997, the body of Chris Farley was found in the comedian's Hancock condo. Official cause of death was later determined to be a combination of drugs, alcohol, and Farley's weight.

For information on the John Hancock Observation Deck call 312-751-3681. To make reservations at the 95th, call 312-787-9596.

➡ WATER TOWER PLACE
835 N. Michigan Avenue

Boul Mich's shining shopping mall is anchored by Marshall Fields and boasts many terrific shops, dining areas, and two sets of movie theaters. Movies shot here include *Poltergeist III* (1988) and *Mo' Money* (1992). The remake of *Miracle on 34th Street* (1994), a tale of a young lady who learns a few things about Christmas and Kris Kringle, made obvious use of Water Tower Place for its wonderful shopping atmosphere. However, the most memorable movie moment for Water Tower Place was in the minor comedy *Class* (1983). Prep student Andrew McCarthy enters Water Tower's trademark glass elevators a naive innocent but exits a little wiser after he's seduced in the vertical see-through people-mover by Jacqueline Bisset, the mother of a school chum. Certainly one of the most preposterous movie scenes ever shot in Chicago, but oddly memorable nonetheless!

SISKEL & EBERT
TWO THUMBS WAY UP

There's a block of Erie Street, between Fairbanks Court and McClurg Court, that's been officially renamed by the Chicago City Council as "Siskel and Ebert Way." Honorary street names often indicate some pull with the city, but the clout Gene Siskel and Roger Ebert wield has repercussions with movie-goers throughout the country. Their long-running television show, "Siskel & Ebert," is seen on more than 200 stations throughout the country and is the highest-rated syndicated half-hour on television today.

Yet Siskel and Ebert are not a two-headed movie critic named "Siskbert," as they've sometimes been called. Though the show has been on since 1975, both had developed as film critics and journalists by the time they hit the airwaves, and both remain quite distinctive personalities.

Ebert is from downstate Champaign and graduated from the University of Illinois, where he was editor of the *Daily Illini*. He also attended the University of Chicago and studied at the University of Cape Town, South Africa on a Rotary Fellowship. In 1966, he was hired as a reporter by the *Chicago Sun-Times*. Six months later, he was given the job of film critic. "When I started at the *Sun-Times*," says Ebert, "we were just emerging from the era of pseudonyms for critics. The *Tribune*, for example, had 'May Tinee'—a play on the word 'matinee'—as their film critic, and anybody could be May Tinee. But there was a new film generation starting up in the late 1960s (with) films like *Blow Up, The Graduate, Bonnie and Clyde, Easy Rider,* and the European films earlier in that decade. I think as a result of the space that the *Sun-Times* gave me and the commitment they made to film criticism, the other Chicago papers at that time had to respond. So really, if I have made a historical contribution to Chicago, it is kind of through bringing in a different kind of film criticism.

"I love to write. My reviews are a dialog with the reader and in a way, I've been doing this for so long and I've written so many reviews that when I'm actually writing a movie review it's like I'm having a conversation with some idealized reader. I try to write in a way that will be of interest to people who don't care about the movie. My bargain with you is, if you will read this review, I will try not to bore you even though you have no intention of going to see this film and, indeed, maybe you have no interest in the film.

Ebert quickly built a reputation as an intelligent and thoroughly knowledgeable critic. "I consider it more of a vocation than a job," he says. Ebert's devotion to the craft and his genuine love for writing about the movies earned him a 1975 Pulitzer Prize for criticism. He is the only film critic to be honored with this prestigious award, though Ebert maintains "that will not last. A lot of people deserve the Pulitzer who haven't won it and they should."

In 1969, Ebert began teaching film classes through the University of Chicago Fine Arts Program, which he continues to do some 30-plus years later. "I teach primarily to educate myself," says Ebert. "I take a subject I need to know more about, like the Japanese cinema or the documentary or the French New Wave, the German New Wave and teach a class in it. That way I have to do a little research and a little reading on my own and have to see a film and deal with it over a period of a couple of hours. This has been extremely useful to me in my cinematic education."

One of Ebert's most intriguing explorations as an academician is his shot-by-shot examination of a single film. "We go through a film a shot at a time over of a period of about eight to ten hours, stop action, in the dark, everybody talking, everybody in the room contributing, talking about visual strategy, about structure, about message, about acting, about color, about sound, about anything," says Ebert "Going through a lot of films in that sort of highly detailed way is an extremely useful exercise in preparing you to see a new film in a screening or a film festival."

Aside from his regular *Sun-Times* reviews, which are syndicated nationally, Ebert is heavily involved with the movie community and blasts around the world via the Internet. "I've been on line since the early 80s on CompuServe. In 1990, I was given a section of the 'Show Biz' forum where I could hang out. That was an extremely interesting experience because on a daily—or several times a week—basis, I was getting feedback. The Internet also gave me a chance to eavesdrop on other message threads written by some extremely perceptive people. There are a lot of film critics and people who work on movies, such as cinematographers, sound editors, film editors, screenwriters, even directors, who have hung out there over the years, and it's like an instant feedback, instant correction, agreement, dissent.

"When you write an article in the paper, people may be reading it but they don't necessarily write you a letter to tell you what they thought. If they do, it might come a week or two later. With the Internet, your review goes up Friday morning and by Friday afternoon you'll have three or four people telling you what they think."

Another aspect to Ebert's career is his own brief stint as a screenwriter for director Russ Meyer. Meyer, a pioneering exploitation director, built his reputation on fast-paced, cartoonish films featuring large-breasted women. Though his work is not for all tastes, Meyer enjoys a much-deserved cult reputation. His editing style has won a good deal of critical praise, drawing seemingly unlikely comparisons between Meyer and the great Soviet director/film theorist Sergei Eisenstein.

"I enjoyed Meyer's films when I was an undergraduate at the University of Illinois, Ebert notes. I went to see *The Immoral Mr. Teas* (1959), which I think played for more than a year at a theater in Champaign-Urbana. *The Immoral Mr. Teas* was the first American nudie and I had read about it in a famous review by the critic Leslie Fiedler.

Fiedler called *The Immoral Mr. Teas* the best American comedy of 1959.

"When *The Wall Street Journal* did a front page article about Russ, I wrote a letter to the editor saying that I thought he was a very interesting American filmmaker who deserved attention. Russ wrote to me to thank me for that letter and we met the next time he came to Chicago.

"When he was hired by 20th Century-Fox to do *Beyond the Valley of the Dolls* (1970), he asked me to write the screenplay. It was really one of the peak experiences of a lifetime and a very valuable experience for a film critic. I actually moved into offices on the lot of 20th Century Fox and attended the birth of a motion picture from the yellow pad stage to opening night."

The film, which has nothing to do with the trashy camp classic *Valley of the Dolls* (1967), tells the story of an all-girl rock band and their transsexual manager. It's laced with liberal doses of sex, drugs, and often bizarre humor. "We made up that movie out of thin air," Ebert recalls. "I was involved to some degree in the shooting and visited the set and so forth and in the casting and in the revisions and in the backstage struggles and in the front office with its input and in the promotion. "The first go-around grossed $44 million in 1970 dollars."

Additionally, Ebert is a prolific book author on a wide variety of subjects. Naturally, his forte has been film: *Roger Ebert's Video Companion, Ebert's Little Movie Glossary: A Compendium of Movie Cliches, Stereotypes, Obligatory Scenes, Hackneyed Formulas, Shopworn Conventions, and Outdated Archetypes, Roger Ebert's Book of Film, Questions for the Movie Answer Man, Two Weeks in the Midday Sun: A Cannes Notebook, A Kiss Is Still a Kiss,* and *Roger Ebert's Movie Yearbook.* Additionally, he's written a pulp novel, *Behind the Phantom's Mask: A Serial.* Ebert has co-written one other book: *The Future of the Movies: Interviews With Martin Scorsese, Steven Spielberg, and George Lucas* with his television partner, Gene Siskel.

A graduate of Yale, Siskel started as a *Chicago Tribune* reporter in 1969. Within seven months, he became the paper's film critic. He held court as the *Tribune's* leading movie writer for 19 years, then was named syndicated film columnist. In this capacity, Siskel continues to write reviews, critical "think-pieces," and interviews. He also provides a weekly column for "TV Guide" and critiques movies locally for the Chicago CBS affiliate and nationally on "CBS This Morning." "The reason why I do these various pieces," Siskel says, "is the irresistible opportunity to reach a huge audience with one's opinion. I feel I'll steer people towards good pictures and steer them away from junk."

Like Ebert, Siskel takes his role as a critic very seriously. "I know that I'd rather see things I haven't seen before," he says emphatically. "As a critic, that's one bias I do have. Also, remember I'm a reporter so I have an interest in documentary material. I like finding out what's really going on. I like observing raw data and finding out what's real.

"I love documentaries. I tend to prefer documentaries to fiction films because they are more interesting. They have less 'phoniness' about them, by definition. They exist in a real place and time, unlike most films that live in 'movie world,' whatever that is. They're interchangeable and just a bunch of things happening to set up action sequences. There's no real life there."

Another important aspect for Siskel is passion on the part of the filmmaker. "Do you think anybody seriously wanted to see a movie about a couple of robots 20 years ago?" he says, using *Star Wars* (1977) as an example. "That wasn't on my radar screen. But somebody loved those robots and somebody was passionate enough to create a whole world in which they were a logical part, and that's what connected."

In 1975, the careers of Ebert and Siskel were forever changed. Both writers were approached by Chicago's public television station, WTTW Channel 11, to do a movie criticism program. "It was a sheer fluke that someone in Chicago had the idea for a weekly review of the arts in Chicago on the public television station," says Siskel. "They started with movies because that was the most popular. Because of film clips, movie reviewing lends itself to television very well."

The show was called "Opening Soon at a Theater Near You." Its format was brilliant in its simplicity. Siskel and Ebert, holding court on a television set resembling a movie theater, showed film clips, then gave their respective opinions. More often than not, the discussion would lead to a heated debate over a respective film's merits. "It turned out that these two guys had, I guess, chemistry!" says Siskel in retrospect. "We also looked different in the classic comic forms; but it's the chemistry that made everything work."

Within two years, the wordy title was changed to "Sneak Previews." The show syndicated to Public Broadcasting System stations throughout the country and though originally slated as a monthly venture, it quickly became a weekly series. In 1981, the two left "Sneak Previews" for commercial television. Their new show was titled "At the Movies," and was based at WGN. In 1986, the two switched once more, signing a long-term contract with Buena Vista Television. The program was titled "Siskel & Ebert." Siskel's top billing was chosen by a time-tested method: the flip of a coin.

In 1989, Ebert introduced a new idea that has been forever linked with the duo. Films either critic liked were given a "thumbs up," while non-recommended movies were given a "thumbs down." Simple and to the point, the Siskel and Ebert thumb rating is today an indelible part of our pop culture. Countless movie advertisements use this shorthand (or thumb) validation to attract viewers. "The 'thumbs up' and 'thumbs down' gave an extra little life to our opinions," says Siskel.

Over the years, Siskel and Ebert built a solid reputation for fair-minded reviews, as well as their on-camera rapport. "The fact is we we're competitors," says Siskel. "We don't fake our relationship. It's been described as the most honest relationship on television because we don't pretend to like each other." Indeed, Siskel and Ebert can often be wildly at odds with each other, which makes for heated debate and occasional on-camera sniping.

Both are affirmed Chicagoans. "I do think Chicago is a beautiful city, and I'm happy to live here," says Ebert. "There are neighborhoods in Chicago that nobody has seen, and directors who grew up here, like Andrew Davis, have been extremely successful at finding Chicago locations that are new even to some Chicagoans."

Unlike downstate native Ebert, Siskel was born and bred in the city. "I will often ask actors who are from Chicago 'is there anything "Chicago" about you?' " he says. "I think what comes across in most of the responses—and I think that it applies to Roger and me—is that we Chicagoans are pretty straightforward and direct. We're not unsophisticated. I hope our comments are appropriately sophisticated at times, but we're straight talkers. You're not going to catch us performing or striking a pose. In my opinion, I think we're upfront, and I think that's the nature of this city."

"It is strange if you think about it," he notes, "that the national movie review program comes from Chicago as opposed to New York, the media capital of the United States, and indeed the world, or Los Angeles, the movie capital of the United States or the world."

To read Ebert's on-line database of reviews and essays, check out http://www.suntimes.com/ebert/ebert.html. Siskel's current reviews can be found on-line at http://www.chicago.tribune.com/leisure/movies. For more information on the two critics and their respective opinions regarding movies past and present, head to http://www.siskel-ebert.com. A good starting point for *Beyond the Valley of the Dolls* (1970) on the Web is at http://web.wwa.com/~jjf/.

➡ **NBC TOWER**
455 N. Cityfront Plaza/454 N. Columbus Drive

Home to WMAQ-TV, Chicago's NBC affiliate, the NBC Tower is an art deco style building created by the architectural firm of Skidmore, Owings, and Merrill. At the top of this 38-story limestone structure is a shiny spire, decorated with the NBC peacock logo. Opened in 1989, the NBC Tower looks almost like something out of the Manhattan skyline, moved west and plunked down along Chicago's lakefront.

In the movies, the NBC Tower was the headquarters for television news reporter Geena Davis in *Hero* (1992). One scene, shot outside the Tower, required literally hundreds of extras which ultimately whipped an overwhelmed NBC security force into a lather.

If you're interested in picking up some swell mementos of hit NBC shows like "ER" or "Frazier," then check out the Tower gift shop. They have tee-shirts, coffee mugs, and other assorted tchotchkes from all your television favorites.

The WMAQ-TV Web site can be found at http://www.nbc5chi.com/.

Chicago Film Critics Association

Say the words "Chicago film critics" to an out-of-towner and inevitably the response will be "Siskel and Ebert." On the surface, that seems like a fair assessment. Through their respective writings, various television gigs, and their overwhelmingly successful syndicated television show, Gene Siskel and Roger Ebert have more or less put a very public face on film criticism emanating from our town.

But to assume Chicago film criticism begins and ends with Siskel and Ebert short-changes a wealth of talent throughout the city's many media outlets. Indeed during the silent era one of the Windy City's most influential literary lions—Carl Sandburg—was a film critic for the *Chicago Daily News*. Today, in addition to Siskel, the *Tribune* features the intelligent film writing of Michael Wilmington, as well as the work of freelancers and staff writers like John Petrakis and Achy Obejas. *The Reader,* one of Chicago's two major free weekly papers, has nationally-respected critic Jonathan Rosenbaum ruling their critical roost. Over at the *Reader*'s competition, *New City*, Ray Pride handles much of the movie reviewing chores. Turn on the radio every Saturday morning around 9:30 a.m. and you'll hear the entertaining banter of Roy Leonard and Nick Digilio as they discuss new movies on WGN AM 720. WGN also features the irrepressible "Marilyn at the Movies" on the Kathy and Judy Show. And that's just a start. There's also a substantial number of freelance reviewers in town, as well as film critics for such suburban newspapers as the *Daily Herald* and *Daily Southtown*.

In 1981, film critics from several city and suburban newspapers attempted to unite under an umbrella called the Chicago Film Critics Circle. It was formed by two schools of thought: 1) as critics they should celebrate the art of film, and 2) as Chicago film critics they should somehow divert all the movie-reviewing glory from Siskel and Ebert. Needless to say, the group didn't last long.

Despite its limited existence, the Chicago Film Critics Circle did get a few like-minded people thinking about the state of movie criticism in Chicago. In 1988, Sue Kiner, a communications consultant who reviewed films with partner Sharon Lemaire on WGCI radio, reworked the idea of uniting area movie critics. The result was the Chicago Film Critics Association (CFCA). A board, including Leonard, Wilmington, Petrakis, *Daily Herald* critic Dann Gire, then-WMAQ entertainment reporter/critic Norman Mark, and publicists John Iltis and Sherman Wolf, were picked to oversee this new group.

In its ten-plus years of existence, the CFCA has grown considerably. Given the wide range of film reviewers throughout the city and suburbs, core membership varies, though more than 40 local writers vote in the CFCA's annual Chicago Film Critics Awards.

Like the CFCA's counterparts in New York and Los Angeles, the Chicago Film Critics Awards recognizes the best of the previous year's movies. Honors are given to best picture, foreign language film, director, screenplay, cinematography, original score, actor, actress, supporting actor and actress, and most promising actor and actress. The ceremony—a sort of Chicago version of the Oscars—is held in late February. Winners have been known to fly in to accept their awards, bringing such prestigious names as Robert Duvall, Spike Lee, Tom Hanks, Nicholas Cage, and Oliver Stone to town.

Additionally, the CFCA gives two honorary awards at the annual ceremony. The Commitment to Chicago Award is handed to well-known personalities who maintain strong ties and creative commitments to the city. Past winners include John Hughes, Gary Sinise, and John Mahoney. The Big Shoulders Award goes to a local organization which has made significant contributions to the Chicago film community.

Recipients of this award include the Chicago Film Coalition and Kartemquin Films.

Though the awards ceremonies are fun and bring in illustrious names to the city for a glamour-filled night, the CFCA does a lot more than hand out prizes. In a unique educational endeavor, the CFCA sponsors a program called "Send a Needy Kid to a Movie." Working with various organizations, including the Chicago Board of Education and the not-for-profit "Grant-A-Wish" foundation, the CFCA sends city school classes on a field trip to the movies. Afterwards, students hold an in-class discussion and write a critique of what they've seen. Since 1992, more than 4,000 Chicago schoolchildren have participated in this wonderful project. "Send a Needy Kid to a Movie" has also received generous support from several film personalities, including Kevin Costner, Dustin Hoffman, Steve Martin, and Robin Williams.

The CFCA has a non-voting wing, "Friends of the Critics," which is open to the public. Annual membership provides several perks including screening passes, invitations to roundtable discussions, and other movie-related events.

For membership information contact the Chicago Film Critics Association at (773) 509-8155 or check out their homepage at http://www.ChicagoFilm.org/cfca/About_Us.html.

➡ **BILLY GOAT TAVERN**
430 N. Michigan Avenue

"Cheezbooga! Cheezbooga! Cheeps! No Coke, Pepsi!" The cry was made famous by John Belushi on "Saturday Night Live" in the mid-1970s in a series of sketches revolving around a grimy, little diner. Of course, Belushi didn't create this catch phrase out of thin air—he picked it up hanging out at the famed Billy Goat Tavern, located beneath Michigan Avenue, just off Hubbard Street. With its handy location near the Sun-Times building and the Tribune Tower, Billy Goat's has long been a favorite of Chicago journalists, most notably the late, great Mike Royko.

Ironically, Royko was a friend of Belushi's family from way back. Years later, Chicago's curmudgeon laureate became the model for Belushi's "Ernie Souchak" character in the film *Continental Divide* (1981). Comparing real life to reel life in one of his columns, Royko opined:

As to the plot of the movie itself, I had mixed reactions. Some of it was realistic and some of it was ridiculous...(w)hen the beautiful birdwatcher (Blair Brown) turns up in Chicago...(Belushi) takes her to eat in the restaurant on the ninety-fifth floor of the John Hancock. That's unrealistic. At that joint's prices, she'd have to eat cheeseburgers in Billy Goat's.[1]

The Goat opened around 1934. The original tavern was located on the West Side, near the old Chicago Stadium, before eventually moving to its present location. Of course, everyone in Chicago knows the story about the original owner, Sam Sianis, who attempted to bring his billy goat to the 1945 World Series in Wrigley Field. Kicked out by Cubs' ownership, Sianis put a hex on the team as his vengeance, claiming they would never be in another World Series. 'Nuff said.

Once you enter the Billy Goat, it's hard not to think you've stepped into a 1940s movie. The tavern is dimly lit, and the bar is littered with photos of famous and infamous elbow benders who've called the Goat their home away from home. Yes, you'll hear the order-taker loudly shouting that joyful "Cheezbooga! Cheezbooga!" refrain but you're in for a big surprise if you ask for Pepsi. To the shock of many, the Billy Goat Tavern serves 'Coke, no Pepsi!'

Surprisingly, other than the SNL connection, the Billy Goat Tavern hasn't been used much by Hollywood. The short-lived television shows "Jack and Mike" and "Missing Persons" both shot scenes here, but other than those brief flings with the camera, the Billy Goat Tavern is still waiting for its big movie break.

Billy Goat Tavern can be reached at 312-222-1525. Two sister taverns are located in the Loop: Billy Goat II at 309 W. Washington 312-899-1873 and Billy Goat's Tavern and Grill at 316 S. Wells Street 312-554-1442. The cheeseburgers are just as good, but neither of these locations have the same goofy energy that permeates the Michigan Avenue Goat.

[1] Royko, Mike, *Like I Was Sayin'* (New York: Jove Books, 1985), 162-3.

➡ **THE WRIGLEY BUILDING**
400 and 410 N. Michigan Avenue

If ever a location defined Chicago in the movies, it's the Wrigley Building. Situated on Michigan Avenue along the north bank of the Chicago River, the distinctive terra cotta exterior and two-story, four-faced clock tower is wonderfully photogenic. Illuminated at night by powerful lamps installed along the south bank of the river, the Wrigley Building's regal presence has been a filmmaker favorite for decades.

Over the years, it has become a cinematic keynote to establish that "we're in Chicago." The structure served this purpose in such varied movies as *Native Son* (the original 1950 version, with Richard Wright playing his fictional creation Bigger Thomas) to the science fiction thriller *The Relic* (1996). The building is also a regular on television's "Early Edition."

Having the Wrigley Building appear in a window is always a sign you're dealing with high-powered characters. This is best exemplified by Tommy Lee Jones's investigation room with a clock tower view in *The Fugitive* (1993) and Vanessa L. Williams's legal office in *Soul Food* (1997).

The Wrigley Plaza at the base of the building is one of the city's best locations for people-watching. This scenic walkway is also the starting point of one of the many action sequences in the slam-bang thriller *Mercury Rising* (1998).

In *Call Northside 777* (1948), the Wrigley Building itself was vital to the plot. It was here where reporter James Stewart meets Kasia Orzazewski, a proud Polish woman who cleans offices at night in an effort to free her son from prison. It's hard to forget the haunting scene where the two first meet, with Stewart's heels echoing through the darkened hallway as Orzazewski quietly scrubs the floor.

Gore flick disciples must come to the Wrigley Building if they want to tread the former stomping grounds of their lord and master, Herschell Gordon Lewis. In the late 1960s and early 1970s, Lewis's ad agency and filmmaking headquarters occupied a suite of offices here. (For more information, see Lewis's profile on p. 237.)

With the release of *Safety Last* (1923), Harold Lloyd's thrill comedy about a "human fly" who scales a towering structure, the Wrigley Building hosted a rather bizarre publicity stunt. The high point of *Safety Last*, literally and figuratively, is the famous sequence where Lloyd dangles from the hands of a tower clock, numerous stories above

An aerial view of the Wrigley Building (400 and 410 N. Michigan), which served as Vanessa L. Williams's law office in *Soul Food* and is regularly featured on CBS's "Early Edition." (*Photo by Holly Pluard.*)

terrified onlookers. To promote the feature, Lloyd was scheduled to break a bottle of champagne on the Wrigley Building clock tower. Though wary of the idea, Lloyd didn't have much choice in the matter. With 10,000 fans gathered in the Wrigley Plaza, the reluctant comedy star was brought to the top of the building. There he was greeted by a steeplejack dressed in Lloyd's signature coat and glasses.

According to plan, the double was to be lowered to the clockface while sitting on a boatswain's seat attached to a rope. This being the Windy City, the gales whipping around the clock tower, 425 feet above Michigan Avenue, weren't exactly the most favorable for such a flimsy device. The faux Lloyd, an expert on safety in high places, took one look at his working

---

 # HOT DOGS

Which of these three is endemically correct?

a) In *While You Were Sleeping*, Sandra Bullock has lunch with her boss near the Wrigley Building Plaza, pouring her heart out while munching on a pushcart hotdog.

b) In an episode of NBC's "ER," George Clooney orders a hotdog with everything from a pushcart vendor working Michigan Avenue.

c) In Mel Brooks' *The Producers*, down and out Broadway impresario Zero Mostel invites neurotic accountant Gene Wilder to dine "al fresco" in Central Park on lunch of pushcart hotdogs.

If you guessed "c," you're clearly a native Chicagoan. While eating hotdogs sold out of pushcarts might be a way of life for New Yorkers, you'll have a hard time finding such vendors in Chicago. We've got churros and hot pretzel salesman near the Shedd Aquarium, and we've got the occasional Italian ice vendors working the neighborhoods, but buying hotdogs from pushcarts is simply not part of the Chicago dining repertoire.

For what it's worth, the original script for *While You Were Sleeping* actually was set in New York; the movie hotdog vendor was simply a carryover that out-of-town producers clearly took for granted when they relocated to Chicago.

Whatever you do, don't pass the ketchup.

conditions and announced "Gentlemen, I need the money but I don't want to commit suicide." With the double out of the picture, promoters wondered if Lloyd himself could be lowered to the clockface. Fortunately, Lloyd's insurance, and good common sense, prevented him from taking any chances.

Yet all was not lost, at least from a movie publicist's perspective. Returning to the street, the bespectacled comic took a megaphone and jumped onto the roof of a nearby taxi cab. "I told them exactly what had happened," Lloyd later recalled. "I told them I didn't want to commit suicide and had no intention. Of course, it became a big joke. We got tremendous play in the Chicago papers, more than if we had gone through with the stunt."[1]

[1] Dardis, Tom, *Harold Lloyd: The Man on the Clock* (New York: Viking Penguin, 1984), 125-8.

> **SUN-TIMES BUILDING**
> **401 N. Wabash Avenue (at the Chicago River)**

Sitting on the banks of the Chicago River, the *Sun-Times* Building is headquarters for one of Chicago's two competing daily newspapers. Built in 1957 by Naess and Murphy, the building once housed both the *Sun-Times* and its sister paper, the *Chicago Daily News*, which folded in 1978 after 102 years in the business.

Of Chicago's two daily newspapers, the *Sun-Times* is decidedly more film friendly. Numerous Hollywood productions have incorporated the *Chicago Sun-Times* in one form or another including *While You Were Sleeping* (1995), *I Love Trouble* (1994), and *Straight Talk* (1992). *I Love Trouble* featured Julia Roberts as a *Sun-Times* writer who falls for Nick Nolte, a competitor at the *Tribune*. *Straight Talk*, another *Sun-Times*-based movie, featured an ever more preposterous romance. James Woods, looking painfully uncomfortable, played a hard-bitten *Sun-Times* columnist trying to learn the real story behind sweet-natured radio talk show host Dolly Parton.

Another film took its inspiration from one of the paper's best known writers. *Continental Divide* (1981) featured John Belushi as a Mike Royko-esque columnist who digs up political dirt for the *Sun-Times*. The film's story revolved around another unlikely romance, this one involving Belushi and Blair Brown, a reclusive ornithologist the Belushi character is sent to interview. Brown lives at the top of a Colorado mountain, which means the Chicago-bred scribe has to make some considerable personal compromises get his story.

After the film opened, Royko was besieged by colleagues and fans, all

Exterior of the Sun-Times building (401 N. Wabash), home to film critic Roger Ebert, has also employed many on screen columnists—Julia Roberts, in *I Love Trouble*; James Woods, in *Straight Talk*; and John Belushi, in *Continental Divide*. (*Courtesy of the Chicago Sun-Times.*)

wanting to know how much of *Continental Divide* was real and how much was fiction. Hoping to answer these questions, Royko wrote a tongue-in-cheek column, saying, among other things, "On the way up the mountain, the columnist loses his supply of liquor and cigarettes and is heartbroken. That's stunningly realistic. In fact, I wept during that part of the film."[1]

When Belushi died of a drug overdose the following year, Royko printed a tribute column to the boy he saw grow up into a movie star. "I learned a long time ago that life isn't always fair," wrote Royko. "But it shouldn't cheat that much."[2]

In addition to the building, the *Sun-Times* newspaper often shows up in feature films when a note of Chicago realism is necessary. The paper made for a great punch line in *Ferris Bueller's Day Off* (1986), with its headline story about the movie's title character.

Of course, the *Sun-Times* is the home paper to several of Chicago's leading entertainment writers, including film critic Roger Ebert, legendary columnist Irv Kupcinet, and genial celebrity-watcher Bill Zwecker.

[1] Royko, Mike, *Like I Was Sayin'* (New York: Jove Books, 1985), 163.
[2] Royko, Mike, *Like I Was Sayin'* (New York: Jove Books, 1985), 203.

"EARLY EDITION"

D
o you buy the early edition of the *Sunday Sun-Times* on Saturday? There's a certain vicarious thrill in doing that, a little joke on yourself that you've got tomorrow's headlines a day in advance. Now take that

joke, throw it into a premise for a television series, and you have another kind of "Early Edition."

"Early Edition," which began in the fall of 1996, is that wonderful rarity: a network television show that slipped the surly bonds of Los Angeles to bring its entire production to Chicago.

Two other current network programs, "ER" and "Chicago Hope," both utilize Chicago settings. Yet location shooting for these programs amounts to a few weekends a year. "Early Edition" has made that important next step: staying in Chicago for the studio work. In economic terms, that makes a world of difference. During its second season, "Early Edition" spent between $18 to $20 million in Chicago, averaging $800,000 to $900,000 per episode.

When the show was originally pitched to Hollywood powers that be, "Early Edition's" creators and producers were insistent that whatever city the show took place in be the actual location for production. Considering that the "Early Edition" concept required that setting be as much a character of the show as the actors, Chicago was the natural choice.

The result has been a love affair between the city and production. "I think that we're all very lucky, because there just aren't that many location TV shows," says Julia Rask, a co-producer on the show. "It's a real treat to be able to shoot a show that's on location six out of eight days."

"Early Edition" is headquartered at a West Side studio, where offices and a few standard sets, such as star Kyle Chandler's apartment, are located. But the heart of the show lies elsewhere. "We're out in the streets so much," says Rask. "We want to shoot historic sites and neighborhoods. You learn so much about a city doing this kind of shooting."

To no surprise, one of the most cooperative partners with "Early Edition" has been the *Chicago Sun-Times*. "They've certainly gotten a lot of recognition nationally because of the show," says Rask. Scenes for the show have been shot in the newsroom and other parts of the Sun-Times building. "We couldn't dress a set of what the *Sun-Times* newsroom looks like," Rask notes.

"Early Edition" even did some shooting at Soldier Field during a Bears football game. On November 2, 1997, series stars Kyle Chandler and Fisher Stevens (who grew up in Lake Forest and Highland Park respectively) suited up before the Bears/Redskins game. The scenario, in which they rescue the Bears' star quarterback, was played out before thousands of screaming fans, eager to get in on the fictional action.

Part of that week's story involved the Bears making the playoffs—a highly fictional detail considering the episode was shot in the midst of a terrible losing streak by the real-life team. "We were a little embarrassed by all the press we got that day," admits Rask. "The TV Bears were playing better than the real Bears."

"Early Edition" turns out 23 episodes a season. Between preparation work and shooting a year's worth of scripts, the show is in Chicago about 10 months out of the year. It takes eight days to film an episode, with six of those days usually devoted to location-shooting.

"Early Edition" has been a real champion of the city. Besides the Sun-Times Building, the show has also utilized such well-known sites as the Cultural Center, City Hall, the Field Museum, the Blackstone Hotel, the Drake Hotel, Marina Towers, Holy Name Cathedral, Graceland Cemetery, O'Hare Airport, and Michigan Avenue. "Producers love the El—El platforms, streets with Els in the background, El stops. A lot of times they'll pick a location based on the El," notes Robin Agron, one of the two "Early Edition" location managers.

The show also solicits location ideas from location manager, Robin Agron and her colleagues, then develops a story around these suggestions. Ultimately, this brings about a variety to the series that you won't find on other television programs shot here or anywhere else. "Early Edition" cameras show up at obscure pawn shops, neighborhood hangouts, and little side streets. They've ventured out to Blue Island and Oak Park, and shot in Chicago's most neglected film location, the gorgeous Beverly area.

Another important aspect, at least as far as Chicagoans are concerned, is the work "Early Edition" provides for local actors. One of the series regulars, Shanesia Davis-Williams, is a graduate of the Goodman School of Drama. As a Chicago-based actor, she has had parts in such locally-made productions as *Backdraft* (1991) and the television series "Missing Persons." Other Chicago actors, including Ron Dean, show up from time to time in supporting roles. Even Tim Kazurinsky took time out from his screenwriting day job to make a guest appearance as a slightly cracked inventor.

➡ THE CHICAGO RIVER AND ITS BRIDGES

One of the city's most enduring symbols is the Chicago River. The North Branch runs from Lake Michigan for 35 miles out to Lake County, while the South Branch is four miles long to its end at the Chicago Sanitary and Ship Canal. Between 1882 and 1900, as motion picture technology was being developed inland, another major feat of engineering was taking place along the mouth of the Chicago River. After a cholera and typhoid epidemic,

The Chicago River bridges from Michigan Avenue to the Lake have provided a picturesque background for a wealth of cinematic action in films such as *Chain Reaction* and *Mercury Rising*. (*Photo by Holly Pluard.*)

caused in part because of pollution in Lake Michigan, it was decided to reverse the river flow away from the lake. It took some $40 million and the efforts of more than 8,500 workers, but eventually this overwhelming task was completed.

Filmmakers have been drawn to the river since cameras started turning in Chicago. And why not? As a location it provides a wealth of opportunity. Do you want romance? Check out Julia Roberts and Dermot Mulroney's slow dance on a Wendella tour boat in *My Best Friend's Wedding* (1997). Male bonding? Check out the scene in *About Last Night...* (1986) as James Belushi and Rob Lowe stumble stone drunk along the riverside arguing about women. Danger? *V.I. Warshawski* (1991) staged a speedboat chase down the Chicago River. And that Windy City tradition, dyeing the Chicago River green for St. Patrick's Day, is faithfully documented in *The Fugitive* (1993).

The many bridges spanning the river offer filmmakers a different viewpoint and a certain ambiance that's hard to resist. Each one provides a unique perspective.

In a breathless chase sequence in *Chain Reaction* (1996), Keanu Reeves scrambles up a raised Michigan Avenue Bridge to escape his pursuers. It's certainly a hair-raising stunt and not one that was easily accomplished. Shooting required five nights in which the bridge had to be raised and lowered numerous times. To make those five nights productive, six months of preparation work went into the scene. Bridge engineering, stunt choreography, lighting the set, and actor and crew safety were among the many variables which had to be taken into account before cameras could roll. (The Michigan Avenue Bridge was also the site of a chase sequence in the 1998 Bruce Willis action feature *Mercury Rising*.)

Another great stunt took place off the Wells Street Bridge. In *Code of Silence* (1985), cop Chuck Norris struggles with a bad guy atop a moving CTA El train. As the train crosses Wells Street, both criminal and hero take a dive from the moving train into the river below.

The Wells Street Bridge also played a crucial role in *The Fugitive*. Harrison Ford, as the fleeing Dr. Richard Kimble, uses a phone booth to call

Julia Roberts and Dermot Mulroney sailed on a Wendella tour boat on the Chicago River in *My Best Friend's Wedding.* (*Photo by Holly Pluard.*)

the office of Tommy Lee Jones, the U.S. Marshal who has been trying to find him. Analyzing a tape of the call, Jones and company detect the sound of a train, as well as bridge warning bells in the background. It doesn't take them long to realize exactly where Ford placed his call from.

In one of the more ridiculous uses of river bridges, Dolly Parton and James Woods have a "cute meet" in *Straight Talk* (1992) along the Wabash Avenue bridge beneath the Chicago Sun-Times building. The scene opens with Parton, a naive Southern belle, accidentally dropping some money off the bridge. She scrambles over the side (in heels no less!) to retrieve her dough and is spotted by newspaper writer Woods from his office window. Thinking she's about to kill herself, Woods gets to the bridge in record time and pulls Parton to safety. There's a million stories in the big city; unfortunately for audiences, *Straight Talk* is one of them that gets told.

On a more cerebral note, one of the moments in *The Untouchables* (1987) takes place along the Michigan Avenue Bridge. Kevin Costner, playing no-nonsense cop Elliott Ness, walks alone along the bridge, dejected over his inability to stop gangster Al Capone (Robert DeNiro). In the dark of night, Costner is confronted by a street-wise beat officer played by Sean Connery. "You want to get Capone?" sneers Connery. "Here's how you get him: he pulls a knife, you pull a gun. He sends one of yours to the hospital, you send one of his to the morgue. It's the Chicago way and that's how you get Capone."

Other films to use Chicago River bridges include *Prelude to a Kiss* (Kinzie Street), *The*

Aerial view of the Michigan Avenue Bridge, as seen in *Chain Reaction* and *Mercury Rising.* (*Photo by Holly Pluard.*)

Package (Kinzie Street), *Blues Brothers 2000* (Roosevelt and Courtland), *Hope Floats* (Roosevelt and Kinzie), *Hoodlum* (Courtland), *The Negotiator* (Clark), and *Soul Food* (Roosevelt).

For a scenic trip along the Chicago River, take a Wendella boat ride, which launches from the northwest corner of the Michigan Avenue Bridge at the Wrigley Building. Phone 312-337-1446 for more information or visit their Web site at http://www.wendellaboats.com.

Chicago Filmmakers on the Chicago River

 Chicago filmmaker D.P. Carlson conjured up an idea for a documentary on the creative process that offers a great deal of complexity within its simple setup. Chicago Filmmakers on the Chicago River places Chicago-bred directors on boats, sends these personalities on a journey down one of our town's most enduring symbols, and lets them talk about their work.

"Basically, Chicago Filmmakers on the Chicago River kind of came out of a conversation my buddies and I were having one night," says Carlson. "We were talking about how the Chicago River has never been used as a character in a film. You see it as a backdrop, you see it as an establishing shot, you'll see a scene on the river, but you never see it as a recurring character. We threw around some narrative ideas to do a fiction-type film and joked that it might be fun to get in- a boat one day and float around with a camera, take a few beers and monkey around.

"Then it occurred to me that it might be kind of cool to touch base with different filmmakers I knew and ask them about the river. The idea was to just throw them on different boats and do a documentary about film directors from Chicago. The river would be used as a kind of metaphor for the creative process because it was the big transportation route in Chicago history with early settlers coming up the river and carving out different waterways.

"So I started asking certain people who I knew to be in it, mostly independent filmmakers. Then I decided maybe I should get a Hollywood-type guy, and I went after Andy Davis. I thought I'd do a short film, maybe a half-hour movie about this creative process and have it build up to Davis, our most successful, most true-to-form kind of

Chicago filmmaker in that he brings films back here all the time."

Once Davis agreed to do the film, Carlson decided to ask other former Chicagoans, now working in Hollywood, to participate. "I was trying to stay specific to people who were from the Midwest and from Chicago. I got Haskell Wexler to climb on board and Harold Ramis and all of the sudden my idea of having one character represent the Hollywood side of things turned into a handful of guys and the project got bigger."

The film doesn't discriminate when it comes to talent. In addition to Davis, Hollywood stalwart John Landis went along for the ride; so did local independents Jim Sikora and Heather McAdams. Other filmmakers who've gone down the river for Carlson's camera are Stuart Gordon and Michael Mann (representing the established "Hollywood" crowd) and all levels of independent filmmakers, including John McNaughton, Steve Jones, Jerry Blumenthal, Gordon Quinn, Tom Palazzolo, Ayanna U'Dongo, Louis Antonelli, Katy Maguire, Ross Marks, Loretta Smith, Mike Dawson, and Zeinbau Davis.

One of the most important elements of the film was choosing what kind of boat to represent each interviewee. With the assistance of Friends of the Chicago River, Carlson was able to secure boats that best reflected each filmmaker's distinctive personality and style. "If you were an independent filmmaker I stuck you in a canoe or a paddle boat where you sort of have to provide your own power to get around," said Carlson. "If you're more established, like a Michael Mann, I put you in a cigarette boat and you're sort of sitting back; or if you're Andy Davis, I put you on a fireboat which is kind of a blue-collar ethnic type of thing. Stuart Gordon [who directed 1985's over-the-top horror film *Re-Animator*] was on a freakish houseboat that had beaver skulls on it.

"I was talking to Haskell Wexler in 1996 prior to him coming out here for a *Medium Cool* (1969) retrospective when the Democratic Convention was held in

D.P. Carlson on the
Chicago River.
(*Photo by Jessica Feith.*)

Chicago," says Carlson. "He hadn't locked in for an interview yet and he said, 'Tell me about your project.' I said, 'It's about independent filmmakers up to feature film directors and what types of movies they've done in Chicago.'

"He interrupted me and said, 'Don't you mean feature film directors up to independent filmmakers?'

"That was very interesting. It actually changed my perspective on the film. I had to sort of step back and go, 'you know what? There's something about the creative process in terms of an independent filmmaker having a lot more creative control over a project as opposed to the larger Hollywood features where you have to compromise a lot more in your typical art versus commerce kind of conflict.' "

➡️ **MARINA CITY**
300 N. State Street

Built in 1964, the Marina City Towers were considered the ultimate in efficient architecture despite their resemblance to corn cobs sprouting along the Chicago River. Designed by Betrand Goldberg Associates, each tower is 62 stories tall. The first 18 floors of each building are for parking; the remaining floors hold offices, shops, and a bank, as well as apartments. Depending on where the apartment is situated, the view from the semicircular balconies of a Marina City residence can be spectacular. A former ground-level movie theater has been transformed into one of Chicago's tragically hippest night spots, the House of Blues, co-owned by ex-Second Citizens James Belushi and Dan Aykroyd. The bosses are known to stop in from time to time, and the club is a great space for people-watching.

With their unusual design, the Marina City Towers are one of many visual clichés moviemakers use to signify a Chicago location. The Marina City parking lot served as a home away from home for the Jeep of yuppie prince Tom Hanks in *Nothing in Common* (1986). But the ultimate use of these lots belongs to Steve McQueen's 1980 action-thriller, *The Hunter*.

In the film's most compelling sequence, McQueen (playing a character based on real-life bounty hunter Ralph "Papa" Thorson) drives a tow truck pell-mell through the serpentine Marina City lots in fevered pursuit of a dangerous bond jumper. The social miscreant leads the chase

The 62-story Marina City was a pivotal location in *The Hunter* with Steve McQueen. The villain taking a wrong turn, crashes through the parking lot fence, and plunges into the Chicago River below. (*Photo by Holly Pluard.*)

in a green 1980 Grand Prix Pontiac but takes a wrong turn at the 15th floor—hurling the car through the protective cable fence of the garage and plunging it into the Chicago River.

Setting up a stunt like this took considerable planning on the part of the filmmakers in cooperation with Chicago police. Paramount Pictures, making sure nothing would be missed, set up six cameras, including one stowed in a helicopter above the Dearborn Street Bridge to film the plunge. A stunt man started the engine, then quickly left the driving to a well-placed dummy as the Pontiac went charging over the edge at 40 miles per hour. Some 1,500 spectators had gathered at street level to watch this bizarre commuter nightmare.

Three cars had been prepared in case anything went wrong, but happily the first take was right on the money. The car hit the water, floated for a moment, then sank to the mucky river bottom.

By sinking, the auto ultimately changed the course of the film. In the original script, the driver survives and is taken into custody. Thus McQueen's on-screen professional decision, to bring the man back to California dead or alive, was conveniently made.

For a more surreal look at the Towers, check out *Mickey One* (1965). Warren Beatty and Alexandra Stewart join a crowd gathered at the base of Marina City, where an eccentric artist has set up a Rube-Goldberg contraption. After setting his creation in motion, the artist lights up his opus in a fiery blaze of creative glory. The Chicago Fire Department rushes to the scene and douses the burning artwork with chemical foam. In the dream-like sequence, Marina City glows like two eerie candles while gobs of white foam float through the air towards the camera.

➡ **MERCHANDISE MART**
350 N. Wells Street (at the Chicago River)

Designed by Graham, Anderson, Probst, and White and opened in 1930, the Merchandise Mart has about 4 million square feet of floor space, which technically makes it one of Chicago's largest buildings. What it lacks in height, it makes up for in volume. Until the construction of the Pentagon, this was the world's largest building by floor area.

The Merchandise Mart is situated on the Chicago river, and is home to one of the city's busiest El stops as well. More than 5,000 manufacturers and designers use the mart to house furniture and other interior decorating wares. Once owned by the Marshall Field family, the Merchandise Mart was purchased by Joseph P. Kennedy in 1945. Since then, many Kennedy family members, including in-law and presidential-wannabe Sergeant Shriver, have been ensconced in powerful positions at the Mart. In 1998, the Mart was sold to Vornado Realty Trust.

Its imposing size worked well for the Cohen frères Joel and Ethan in their dizzy satire *The Hudsucker Proxy* (1994). The building, which spans two city blocks, served as the exterior of Hudsucker Industries, the mammoth company run by Paul Newman's character. The Mart exterior has also shown up in countless other films in background and establishing shots to let everyone know we're in downtown Chicago.

Additionally, the Mart El stop was used by Andrew Davis in *The Package* (1989) during one of the film's many exciting chase sequences.

➡ **PLANET HOLLYWOOD**
633 N. Wells Street

Sure, it's aimed at the tourist market and may be the ultimate in kitschy theme restaurants, but taken in the right spirit, dining at Planet Hollywood is a good ol' time. Where else in town can you eat Cap'n Crunch-coated chicken beneath the gaze of the creature from *Predator* (1987), while ogling cardboard (and occasionally live) movie stars?

As everyone within earshot of an "Entertainment Tonight" broadcast knows, Planet Hollywood is the co-creation of restaurateur Robert Early; film producer Keith Barish—the brains behind such divergent fare as *Sophie's Choice* (1982), *9 1/2 Weeks* (1986), and *The Fugitive* (1993); and three of the movie world's biggest guns: Arnold Schwarzenegger, Sylvester Stallone, and Bruce Willis. The original restaurant, located in New York, premiered in 1991.

Chicago's division opened in 1994 with a star-studded event worthy of

Interior of Planet Hollywood (633 N. Wells Street), which features glass encased movie memorabilia, props, costumes, and pictures, with a heavy emphasis on films shot in Chicago. (*Photo courtesy of Planet Hollywood.*)

a Hollywood premiere. The three heavyweights showed up, along with several big-name pals and Willis's missus, Demi Moore. Keeping with Hollywood tradition, handprints and signatures were eternalized in cement and mounted along the outside of the restaurant. Those prints have been joined by many others, including a few Chicago luminaries: James Belushi, Dan Aykroyd, Roger Ebert, and Gene Siskel.

Before entering Planet Hollywood, prepare your eyes for sensory overload. The place is teeming with movie memorabilia, historic props and costumes, pictures, video screens, music, and, of course, live, warm bodies. The food isn't bad either.

Eating, of course, is just part of Planet Hollywood's appeal. Another obvious reason film fans swarm here is for the movie and TV memorabilia. There are costumes in glass cases, props hanging off the ceiling, and old lobby cards, posters, and autographed pictures mounted on the wall. So what exactly can the movie fan leer at?

There's certainly an emphasis on made-in-Chicago movies. John Belushi and Dan Aykroyd's original *Blues Brothers* (1980) costumes receive shrine-like status. There's also a "Chuckie" doll from *Child's Play*

(1988), Sean Connery and Kevin Costner's costumes and guns from *The Untouchables* (1987), Matthew Broderick's sweater from *Ferris Bueller's Day Off* (1986), and one of Schwarzenegger's pistols from *Red Heat* (1988). For the kids, an entire exhibit is devoted to *Home Alone* (1990). Devotees of classic cinema just might swoon to be in the presence of Al Pacino's handgun from *The Godfather* (1972). One of Faye Dunaway's costumes from *Bonnie & Clyde* (1967) and a Darth Vader helmet from *Star Wars* (1977) are also on display.

No reservations are needed to dine at Planet Hollywood. Call 312-266-7827, for more information

➡ **INDEPENDENT FEATURE PROJECT/MIDWEST**
676 N. LaSalle Street, Suite 400,
Chicago, IL 60610

One of the best resources for Chicago-based moviemakers is the Independent Feature Project/Midwest. A not-for-profit organization, the IFP brings together directors, writers, camera people, editors, and other movie technicians for education, socializing, and—most important—advice and assistance in taking your independent film from concept to screen.

The IFP/Midwest is part of the national IFP network, which includes chapters in New York, Los Angeles, Minneapolis, Miami, and other cities. The group is devoted to helping independent filmmakers through seminars, special programming, and screening opportunities.

Every spring the IFP/Midwest hosts Chicago's Independent Filmmakers Conference. Packed with seminars, workshops, and a wide range of speakers, the conference is an invaluable experience. Sessions focus on budgeting issues, casting and other creative decisions, film festivals, and the many legal considerations faced by independent moviemakers. Best of all, local talents made good, along with national figures, provide afternoon workshops that give the inside scrapes and scrabbles faced on the road to independent success.

For membership information, contact the Independent Feature Project/ Midwest at 312-587-1818.

The Loop

➡ **THE EL**

> "As a kid I always lived near and used the El.
> It represented the arteries and veins of the city to me."

—Andrew Davis

Snaking through the city, and stretching out into the northern and western suburbs, the Chicago Transit Authority's elevated train and subway system is commonly referred to as the El. Since the 1890s, commuters have been depending on the city's train system, which came under the CTA's authority in 1945. And filmmakers love the El. It's the motherlode of Chicago locations, having been used in countless film and television productions.

Hollywood has shown us all aspects of the El. Consider that staple of action films, the chase sequence. In Andrew Davis' *Code of Silence* (1985), Chuck Norris duked it out with a bad guy along the top of a moving train, before both took a dive into the Chicago River off the Wells Street bridge. A few years later, Davis used the El for a tense game of cat and mouse in *The Fugitive* (1993). Billy Crystal and Gregory Hines went on an unlikely but wildly entertaining chase in *Running Scared* (1986), driving their battered automobile down the El tracks in pursuit of criminals. And would-be superhero Damon Wayans created a special vehicle to ride the rails at maximum velocity in the goofy comedy *Blankman* (1994).

How about romance? In *While You Were Sleeping* (1995), Sandra Bullock played a fetching Sedgwick Avenue station CTA clerk. She fantasizes over one of the El-riding station regulars, handsome Peter Gallagher. Ultimately this obsession leads Bullock into a contrived, though entertaining movie love story. The comedy begins when Gallagher falls off the platform into the path of an on-coming train. Bullock leaps from her post, saves Gallagher's life, and quickly finds herself intertwined with Gallagher's family—and his equally handsome brother, Bill Pullman. (The Sedgwick El stop was also utilized in 1994's *Blink.*)

Yet the romantic entanglements of *While You Were Sleeping* are a mere pittance compared to the ultimate film for train lovers: *Risky Business* (1983). In a deeply sensual sequence, high school student and future business leader Joel Goodson (Tom Cruise) makes love to his girlfriend-for-a-night, Lana (Rebecca DeMornay), while aboard a CTA train. This encounter takes the duo around the city, above ground and below, in a passionate tour of Chicago's many El stops. Director Paul Brickman punctuated this erotic sequence with a wicked joke, sending a jolt of electricity sparking off the third rail in the love train's wake.

The television program "ER" makes extensive use of the El, particularly the Chicago-Wells station. Located just north of the Loop, the curving tracks of this El stop provide a marvelous view of the downtown skyline. Couple that with station signs reading "Chicago," and a director couldn't ask for a nicer shot to establish location. The television series "Chicago Hope" has also used this stop, as did the movies *Blankman* and *Blink*.

As some of the El stops are still in their original, if less than pristine state, they provide a wonderful opportunity for period filmmakers. The Oscar-winning *The Sting* (1973) is a good example of this, using the old station at 43rd and Calumet for a scene where Robert Redford has to go on the lam. Incidentally, this sequence also points out one of *The Sting's* historical errors. Station signs indicate the stop is for "A" and "B" trains, a service that wasn't instituted by the CTA until after World War II, well past the early 1930s era of *The Sting*. (The "A" and "B" stop system was subsequently dropped in 1995.)

The eclectic face of the El system is another boon to filmmakers. Though much of the system runs through the inner city, portions of the El tracks run along both the Kennedy and Dan Ryan Expressways. This helped producers of the far-fetched action thriller *Mercury Rising* (1998) when it came to creating one action sequence.

The film's slender plot has disgraced FBI agent Bruce Willis protecting a ten-year-old autistic boy from the nefarious clutches of shadowy government agents. In one scene, Willis is forced to pull over on the Kennedy Expressway, alongside the El tracks near the Addison Street stop. Jumping over the retaining wall between the expressway and the train tracks, Willis takes a moment to assess his situation. Meanwhile, the boy wanders onto the tracks into the path of an oncoming CTA train. Quickly Willis runs to the child

One of Chicago's most popular film locations are the elevated train tracks, seen here winding towards The Loop from the Chicago Avenue "El" stop.
(Photo by Holly Pluard.)

as another train heading the opposite direction comes screaming down the line. Willis has to leap with the boy into a tiny ditch between the two high-speed trains, pulling off this gymnastic maneuver in the nick of time—which he does quite handily, this being an action movie after all!

When the Chicago portion of the production came to an end, the *Mercury Rising* team bought a train car from the CTA. The rest of the sequence, which involved a gun fight aboard the train and a bad guy getting thrown onto the tracks, was shot on a Hollywood soundstage.

Other films which have used the El include *Backdraft* (1991), *Flatliners* (1990), *Go Fish* (1994), *Medium Cool* (1968), *Michael* (1996), *Mickey One* (1965), *Native Son* (1986), *Red Heat* (1988), and *The Hunter* (1980).

➡ **MARSHALL FIELD'S**
   111 N. State Street

Marshall Field's is a Chicago shopping institution that pre-dates the Chicago Fire of 1871. The store has undergone countless changes since its founder Marshall Field first came to Chicago in 1856. After going into partnership with Potter Palmer and accountant Levi Z. Leiter, Field opened his first State Street store in 1868. Like much of the downtown retail area, the six-story building was destroyed in the Great Chicago Fire. Field rebuilt on the same site two years later, only to see that building burn to the ground as well in 1877.

But Field refused to quit. Once more, he erected a department store on the corner of State and Washington and the result was a manor house for consumers. Designed by Daniel Burnham, the store went up in 1892, with additional facilities added in 1904 and 1907. The interior is marked by wide courts, grilled railings, and wonderful skylights. Outside you'll find beautifully ornate clocks at State and Washington and State and Randolph. These timepieces are State Street landmarks and the phrase "meet me under the clock" has become a motto for many Marshall Field's tag-team shoppers. Every Christmas the Field's windows are gaily decorated with holiday scenes. Visiting this display, gazing at the enormous Christmas tree inside the store, and a visit to the Field's Santa is an annual tradition for countless Chicago-area families.

Hollywood has captured the beauty of this Chicago tradition in many films. Judge Reinhold (inhabited with the personality of his pre-teen son, Fred Savage) worked here in *Vice Versa* (1988). *Curly Sue* (1991) and *Straight Talk* (1992) also shot scenes here. *Looking for Mr. Goodbar* (1977) staged a misfired fantasy sequence with the Field's Christmas windows, having Diane Keaton imagining herself a star figure skater while gazing at

Marshall Field's famous Walnut Room, where Julia Roberts dined in *My Best Friend's Wedding*. (*Photo courtesy of Marshall Fields*.)

the holiday display.

Looking for some good dining in between cash registers? Check out the Walnut Room and see where Julia Roberts had a bite to eat in *My Best Friend's Wedding* (1997).

Then there's *Baby's Day Out* (1994). A slapstick comedy in the tradition of *Home Alone* (1990) and the Three Stooges, the film revolves around a group of bumbling kidnappers who can't keep track of the baby they've snatched. The baby has a wild day on the town, the trio (led by Joe Mantegna) gets knocked around, and everyone lives happily, if improbably, ever after.

The basic joke of the movie hinges on the premise that absolutely no one would possibly notice a happy baby crawling around Chicago by himself. In the fantasy world of Hollywood that might be all right, but within the realistic environs of the Loop, a lone baby would definitely be noticed. One scene in *Baby's Day Out* (1994) called for the youngster to crawl out of Field's and accidentally end up in a taxi cab while Mantegna and company watch in comic horror. The scene was shot on a Saturday afternoon, a busy time for the store. Enormous crowds had gathered to watch a 27-inch-tall man outfitted with a latex baby head and hands crawl his way from the store to the street. As with many movie locations, the Chicago Police Department had set up barricades around Field's to prevent onlookers from interfering with the 180-person movie crew. Of course the inevitable happened.

The "baby" crawled out of Field's. With a large crowd, including many of Chicago's Finest, watching, one hapless couple, unaware the scene was fictional, broke through the police line to rescue the roving tot. From beneath his latex baby head, the little man screamed, "Put me down!" The couple, terrified of this bizarre child whose lips didn't move though he screamed like a rabid trucker, totally freaked out. Whether this well-meaning pair chose to play Good Samaritans ever again is unknown, but the incident has become a legend among Chicago film crews.

Joe Mantegna

He's played a romantic interest opposite Mia Farrow in Woody Allen's *Alice* (1990), appeared as Al Pacino's nemesis in *The Godfather: Part III* (1990), and shared a touching moment watching "Itchy and Scratchy" cartoons with Bart Simpson. However, Joe Mantegna's career is indelibly linked to his hometown and his friend from the 1970s Chicago theater scene, David Mamet.

"The first professional thing I did in Chicago was the play *Hair*." In fact my wife and I were both in the same show; that's where we kind of hooked up. We did that at the Shubert Theatre and then we moved to the Blackstone and after that I did Godspell at the Studebaker. So I was kind of on the musical comedy track early on. It was actually when I did that, while I was in *Hair* that I met Andre de Shields who was in the same company. He became a good friend of my wife and me.

"When *Hair* closed, Andre was asked to go back to the Organic Theater, which he did. I was doing *Godspell* at the time when they were doing *Warp* at the Organic. Andre, being a friend of ours, said, you've got to come and see this play we're doing. There were a couple of plays he did there actually. There was the play *Poe*, based on Edgar Allen Poe; then they did *Warp* which was this huge success which they ultimately took to Broadway.

"After *Warp* closed, [the company] came back from New York. Some of them decided to stay in New York, some of them decided to move on, some of them decided to continue. Coincidentally, *Godspell* was closing. Stuart Gordon, who I had met informally through Andre coming to see their plays and stuff, he had seen me do *Godspell*. He was looking to reform the Organic and asked me and Richard Atwood and Meshach Taylor, who was a friend of mine from *Hair*, if we wanted to read for his company. I remember Richard Atwood had already made plans to move out to California, but Meshach and I both decided, yeah, we'll give this a shot and we did and that was the beginning. We did *The*

Wonderful Ice Cream Suit. That was the first show we did. I wound up staying for about five years. I think Meshach was the same.

"I'm trying to remember the first time I met David Mamet. I think basically he and I just bumped into each other on the stairs of the Goodman Theater, as I recall. I think he kind of said to me at the time 'hey man, I know you, I've seen you.' He had seen me in Organic Theater stuff. He introduced himself and said he was a playwright and hoped we could somehow hook up and I was like 'yeah, great.' And I remember that he offered me [a part in] the original production of *Sexual Perversity in Chicago*, which the Organic was doing, but I couldn't do it...I was an understudy in the show 'Lenny,' which was big time. It was a New York show coming to town. It was paying well. Even as an understudy I was making more than I would have doing *Sexual Perversity*! Ultimately, Mamet and I hooked up later. I think the first full-length play I did for him was *A Life in the Theater* with Mike Nussbaum and then it was on from there."

While working at the Organic, Mantegna, like many Chicago actors, also worked in industrial films and occasional commercials. Then, in 1976, he was asked to do his first character role in front of the camera, playing the developmentally disabled nephew of fellow Organic member Jack Wallace.

"We basically did it for nothing; it was a student film. But we liked the script very much, we did it, it was a 20-minute short film, but it turned out really well. It was a very uplifting little film. But for me it was a way to get my feet wet, because I really had no film experience prior to that really."

This student short led to Mantegna's first feature film, *Towing* (1978). Based on the escapades of the notorious Lincoln Towing Company, immortalized in song by folksinger Steve Goodman as "The Lincoln Park Pirates," *Towing* was a goofy little satire that didn't get much play outside of Chicago. Still, it gave Mantegna an opportunity to further develop his craft.

"It was with some known people. Sue Lyon from *Lolita* (1962) fame and Jennifer Ashley, she was from some kind of movie like *Pom-Pom Girls* (1976). At that time it was like some kind of big deal.

"My first day of shooting, here I was, I hadn't really done much filming at all, all of the sudden they say: 'okay, in this scene you're going to be driving this tow truck, pulling a car behind it.' And I did. I never had driven a tow truck before, let alone hauling a car behind it. From the world of the theater you had weeks to rehearse things like this. In subsequent films I've done in different conditions, it's not so far-fetched.

Sometimes you get thrown into stuff. You just do it. You just jump in and do it."

Throughout this period, Mantegna developed an accomplished acting resume. He appeared in several Mamet plays and ultimately won both a Joseph Jefferson Award and Tony Award for his searing performance of the amoral salesman Richard Roma in Mamet's *Glengarry Glen Ross*. With his fellow members of the Organic Company, Mantegna created an improvisational play based on what they observed watching the Cubs play at Wrigley Field. *Bleacher Bums*, a play in nine innings, looked at baseball from the fan's prospective. The piece was a huge success and was performed in both New York and Los Angeles, where Mantegna served as the show's director. A television version, done for the Public Broadcasting System at Channel 11, ended up winning an Emmy Award.

In 1977, Mantegna headed to California, where he landed a recurring role in the spoof sitcom "Soap." He continued doing small television and film roles, as well as theater, then got a huge break when he was cast as the conniving lead in *House of Games* (1987), the directorial debut of his old pal Mamet. The next year, Mantegna came back to Chicago to appear in Mamet's mobster fairy tale, *Things Change* (1988). Mantegna was cast as a low-level mobster assigned to baby-sit an innocent Italian shoeshine man, played by Don Ameche.

"*Things Change* was a great experience in a lot of ways. It's always fun working with Dave. Doing all the three or four movies I've done with him, it always seems like it's one long movie because you get back together. A lot of the faces are the same and we just kind of all click. It's like a reunion in a way.

"We wrapped the movie on my 40th birthday in Chicago, and Dave's birthday is actually only two weeks later than mine, so we combined the wrap party and made it a double birthday party for the two of us. At the party, somebody in the Mayor's office who we kind of knew, was able to get this done. They read this proclamation. At the time it was Mayor Washington, [and] he made it 'Joe Mantegna Day' in Chicago. It was November 13, 1987."

After *Things Change*, Mantegna played a series of gangster and cop roles, including Joey Zaza in Francis Ford Coppola's *The Godfather: Part III*, (1990) a Jewish detective torn by his faith in Mamet's *Homicide* (1991), and actor George Raft in Barry Levinson's crime saga *Bugsy* (1991). In 1994, Mantegna returned to Chicago to play the lead kidnapper in the John Hughes-scripted slapstick comedy *Baby's Day Out* (1994).

"That was like a dream come true, to be able to come into Chicago and spend that much time there. We were there almost four months, and that was great to be able to do that. I really loved the fact that Hughes opened a studio in Chicago. The other two guys in the movie, Brian Haley and Joe Pantoliano, they'd always get a kick out of it because we'd be shooting on a location either downtown or wherever else and guys would ride by on a bike or walking by, something like that, 'Hey Joe, it's me, Angelo, from high school!' Everyday there might be somebody, either a relative or a friend out of my past that would come up on the set and Brian and Joe were like, 'hey do you know everybody in this town?'

In 1997, Mantegna took on the role of executive producer, as well as actor, when he became involved with *Jerry and Tom* (1997), a movie based on the three-actor comic hitman play *Tom and Jerry*, by Rick Cleveland. *Tom and Jerry* debuted at Chicago's American Blues Theater (now the American Theater Company) in their 1995-1996 season. A dark comedy of a professional killer and his apprentice, the script's black humor appealed to Mantegna almost immediately.

Joe Mantegna is well-known for his local theater work and association with playwright David Mamet, as well as his film work in *House of Games* (1987), *The Godfather: Part III* (1990), *Homicide* (1991), *Bugsy* (1991), *Baby's Day Out* (1994), and others. (*Photo courtesy Peter Strain & Associates, Inc.*)

"I had some, not really problems, but in the sense of things that I thought needed to be done at least for me to be interested in it. Some of it was conceptual. I was afraid if they don't go along with this, I'll probably have to move on but if they go along with it maybe we got something, and as it turned out they agreed with this basic one concept idea I had. The main thing was, in the play, all the victims were played by one actor. I said, 'you know, in the play that works but in a movie, I don't think that's gonna work, and second of all, this would give you a great opportunity to hire some terrific actors to do these different victims, almost like cameo parts, whereas if you do it with one person, it's going to be like 'The Robin Williams Show.' The movie is much stronger than that. The script that you've written is not about that. Maybe as a play, maybe that was a black comedy gimmick. But now, it's not about 'oh let's see how this actor is going to play this part as a victim.'

"So they agreed with that, and he [Cleveland] re-wrote the whole thing based on different actors playing it, and it worked out really well. I got involved as the producer of it, [because] it was like, 'if I'm going to do this, you know, I'm going to help try to get it made. I'll make the phone calls I need to make to try to get other actors involved.' I suggested we do a reading of it over at this theater that I'm connected with. We wound up doing about three different readings of it and those were of immense value. It was a small audience, just to get feedback and stuff. We wound up doing that and we wound up putting the cast together. Ted Danson, William H. Macy, Charles Durning were some of the victims. I was able to help bring in friends of mine that there normally would not have been a role for had it been done the other way.

"We took it to the 1998 Sundance Film Fest and Miramax bought it. *Jerry and Tom* certainly lived up to all of our expectations. One reviewer at *Variety*, when they reviewed the films at Sundance, said it was the best film work Ted Danson had done on the big screen in his life. It was just basically two days he worked on it to do that one little part. That's what it was like, they were little gems, these little roles that Macy played, that Durning played, that Danson played, that Peter Reigert played, that made it worthwhile for them to do it without a lot of commitment. The writing was just so good. Rick did a great job. In fact, Miramax bought, apparently, his next script based on that.

"We just shot a few days in Chicago. There's a bar in it they call Zacek's which is basically an homage to Dennis Zacek of Victory Gardens. Mike Nussbaum's in one of the scenes they shot in Chicago—he's obviously a very dear, close friend of mine. So there's a definite Chicago connection.

"Chicago is accommodating. It's indigenous to the kind of people that are in Chicago in the first place. Its what makes Chicagoans and people from the midwest different from the east coast and the west coast, period. I mean, I love New York and obviously I like California; I live here. But the midwest, there is a different temperament in a way. It's the center of the country and it's a different kind of thing there."

Ironically, one of Mantegna's most recent roles took him directly back to his roots at the Organic Theater. "We made the movie of *The Wonderful Ice Cream Suit* (1997) which was the play we did at the Organic in 1973. It was based on the Ray Bradbury story. So 25 years later the movie's going to come out for Disney, and Stuart Gordon directed it just as he did the play, and I play the same character I played in the original. It's not the original cast because of the nature of the play; mostly it's a Hispanic cast with Edward James Olmos and Esai Morales, wonderful Hispanic actors like that. But Stuart was able to use some of the old guys from the play in little cameo bits. Dennis Franz was going to do something, but he had to work that day on "NYPD Blue" but he would have done it just for kicks."

A quarter of a century after doing the play in Chicago, Mantegna was thrilled to be recreating *The Wonderful Ice Cream Suit* with Gordon. "It was fantastic, it was just wonderful. It was like déjà vu all over again because it was fun to play the role 25 years later. Ray Bradbury was there everyday almost because he wrote the screenplay, which was something. In a way, [he] helped us get the project done.... Bradbury had loved our original production of it, I think he saw it five or six times. But the thing went through various incarnations in Hollywood. Steven Spielberg had the rights for awhile, Harry Belafonte had the rights for awhile, everybody wanted to do something with the thing but never wound up doing anything with it, and I don't think anybody was totally interested in Bradbury being that involved. They wanted to basically buy the rights to it, as they would often do to writers and say 'thanks a lot, we'll call you when its done.'

"But in this case, we were like the Tortoise and the Hare. We just persisted and after 25 years it came around again and Stuart was in the position now to go to Bradbury and say, 'look, I've got Disney interested to make this movie and you can write the screenplay and we'll do it,' and that's what we did. Ninety-nine percent of the words that are coming out of our mouths Bradbury wrote down, which was great, and he still gave us some freedom to ad lib a bit in it and stuff, which we had always done with the play anyway. So that was great, that was a wonderful, wonderful experience, and I'll be real anxious when that comes out, especially for the people who hopefully enjoyed seeing the play version 25 years ago. I think they'll be pleased because it's pretty much inspired by what we did then."

Mantegna, who studied at the Goodman School of Drama, now hosts an annual scholarship fundraiser for DePaul University Theater School. "They gave me an honorary doctorate, so basically now they own me because they were nice enough to do that. I went to the Goodman School for two years, but then left before I really completed my studies to go do *Hair*. So then, like, over 20 years later when DePaul came to me and said, 'we'd like you to give a commencement speech this year and give you a doctorate,' it was like 'wow!' So I did. That was in 1988 and then they told me about this idea they had to instigate this kind of yearly event and if I would be interested in hosting it, which I did, and now this will be the 10th year of it. So every year I bring in these film celebrities and we give them achievement awards and we have this really nice evening. The money that the people pay to come see us at this black-tie event goes to the scholarship fund. It's kind of like my Jerry Lewis telethon I do every year. And for me it's nice because it's a way for me and my family to come into Chicago and it's usually the week of Mother's Day, so that works out. It gives me a chance to come home at least that one time a year because a lot of times that may be the only time I get back."

➡ CHICAGO THEATER
162 N. State Street

On October 26, 1921, Barney Balaban and Sam Katz opened the doors to the flagship of their movie theater empire, the Chicago Theater. Though it may not have quite lived up to its nickname "The Wonder Theatre of the World," the Chicago Theater set the standard for other film palaces.

Designed by Cornelius and George Rapp, who created many of Balaban and Katz theaters, the Chicago Theater featured a five-story lobby. The grand staircase, modeled after that of the Paris Opera, took guests to balcony seats of the seven-story auditorium. Crystal chandeliers hung from the ceiling. The orchestra pit was outfitted for up to 50 musicians, as well as a mighty Wurlitzer pipe organ. The marquee was just as grand, featuring a sculpted mini-replica of France's Arc de Triomphe.

The opening night show was *A Sign on the Door*, starring Norma Talmadge, one of the era's most popular stars. Talmadge's brother-in-law,

Buster Keaton (then married to Natalie Talmadge), provided live entertainment, while the Chicago Plan Commission chair, Charles M. Wacker, served as the evening's host.

Over the next four decades, the Chicago Theater was the place to see great films and live entertainment. John Philip Sousa, Duke Ellington, Benny Goodman, Jack Benny, Will Rogers, Al Jolson, Sophie Tucker, Eddie Cantor, Frank Sinatra, Milton Berle, Bob Hope, the team of Dean Martin and Jerry Lewis, Sid Caesar, Sally Rand, and many other headline entertainers all trod the Chicago Theater boards.

The influence of television and the decline of the city's downtown theater district, however, provided a double whammy to the Chicago Theater. By the 1970s, this once shining palace had deteriorated into a third-rate movie house. Eventually its owners, the Plitt Theater chain, decided it would be more cost effective in the long run to simply close up shop. On September 19, 1985, the once-bright lights of the Chicago Theater marquee were dimmed, seemingly for the last time.

The fate of this building became a cause célèbre. A committee of concerned businesses and citizens, calling themselves the Chicago Theater Restoration Associates, was formed. With some help from city

Aerial view of State Street featuring the Chicago Theater. (*Photo by Holly Pluard.*)

officials, the Chicago Theater was purchased from Plitt and some $25 million put forth towards its reconstruction.

In less than a year, the miracle was complete. With hard work on the part of Daniel P. Coffey and Associates and A.T. Heinsbergen and Company, the Chicago Theater was restored to its former grandeur. In a move that was symbolic of the theater's rich history, Frank Sinatra was booked as the new theater's opening act. The Chairman of the Board sang to a sold-out crowd on September 10, 1986.

Though the theater had its ups and downs after the much-ballyhooed opening, the Chicago Theater hit the jackpot when it booked the Andrew Lloyd Webber-Tim Rice musical *Joseph and the Amazing Technicolor*

Dreamcoat. Featuring former teen heartthrob Donny Osmond in a sparkling performance, this Biblically-based musical comedy played to record crowds. The Chicago Theater was truly reborn as an exciting new venue for live downtown performance.

What's more, the restoration inevitably attracted film production. Charles Grodin and Robert DeNiro shared some aggravation here in the cross-country caper *Midnight Run* (1988). DeNiro later returned to film some scenes for *The Untouchables* (1987). For the *Blues Brothers 2000* (1998), some stuff was shot in front of the theater as well.

➡ LEO BURNETT BUILDING
35 W. Wacker Drive

At the corner of Wacker and Dearborn stands the mighty Leo Burnett Building, a towering homage to the power of advertising. The agency itself was founded by Burnett, a former police reporter, in 1935. Beginning with just eight employees, Burnett's ad agency grew into a corporate giant. Today Leo Burnett Advertising has offices around the world and more than 7,500 employees. The business has always been headquartered in the Windy City and the Leo Burnett Building, designed by Kevin Roche, gives the company a magnificent home.

The talent at Burnett is second to none—several ex-Burnett creatives have gone on to work in Hollywood. Among the alumni are Tim Kazurinsky and the team of Jeffrey Price and Peter S. Seaman, who wrote the screenplay for *Who Framed Roger Rabbit?* (1988) and *Doc Hollywood* (1991).

The Leo Burnett Building is a rather versatile movie location. Kevin Bacon worked in its offices in *She's Having a Baby* (1988) and Kelly Lynch kept her law practice here in *Curly Sue* (1991). It has also showed up in *Midnight Run* (1988) and *Betrayed* (1988) and impersonated a ritzy Manhattan location (like almost everything else in the so-called Second City!) for *Home Alone II: Lost in New York* (1992).

Tim Kazurinsky & Denise DeClue

SCREENWRITING FROM CHICAGO

Screenwriters aren't supposed to live the good life. They're embittered failures, clutching at fragments of hope, like William Holden in *Sunset Boulevard* (1950) or maddened geniuses, like John Turturro in the title role of *Barton Fink* (1991), wrestling in an unholy war between inner muses and bloated studio bosses. One thing for certain, screenwriters aren't supposed to be comfortable Midwesterners.

So how did the team of Tim Kazurinsky and Denise DeClue end up working in Chicago instead of striking out to Hollywood like so many others? With an uncredited scripting job on the charming *My Bodyguard* (1980) and the box office success of *About Last Night...* (1986), the answer was a simple one. "*About Last Night...* did extremely well and sort of put Denise and I on the map as screenwriters," says Kazurinsky. "And we didn't have to move to California. That was the great thing! I had just done four years on "Saturday Night Live," my head was reeling from all that *mishegoss*, being a TV celebrity, those monsters of fame: drugs, all that craziness, but Chicago keeps me sane and honest. I got married and started a family. Where do I want to be: in Hollyweird or Manhattan? I thought, no I wanted to be here. Luckily, when *About Last Night...* (1986) hit, it was like 'oh good, I get to stay in Chicago!' " Adds DeClue, "I remember somebody once quoted our agent as saying, 'Denise and Tim don't give a shit about the business. They just want to take the money and lead a normal life in Chicago.' In a way, it was kind of true."

Kazurinsky was born in Australia, then came to the United States at age 16. After living in Johnstown, Pennsylvania, he moved to Chicago and attended Wright Junior College. Following studies at the University of Pittsburgh and the University of Illinois, Kazurinsky returned to Johnston where he became a newspaper reporter. "But I didn't want to be a starving writer," he said, "so I switched to advertising." For a while he worked in St. Louis doing ad work for a department store, then came back to Chicago and got a job with Leo Burnett. "I was a lousy presenter of commercials," said Kazurinsky. "So I took classes at Second City." The idea, in Kazurinsky's mind anyway, was to improve his presentation skills through improvisational comedy techniques. Instead, he found himself getting more involved in Second City and eventually joined the mainstage company. One night John Belushi caught the show and was impressed by Kazurinsky's style. He became the younger comedian's mentor and eventually got Kazurinsky hired as a writer-performer at Belushi's former place of employment, "Saturday Night Live."

DeClue got her creative start as a journalist. "I started a couple of lefty, alternative newspapers," she recalled, "the *Chicago Daily Planet* and the *Chicago Express*. I went to work for *Follett's* as an editor for awhile. Quit there, had a baby, then I went to work for the *Chicago Reader*." DeClue also freelanced for the major papers, including the *Chicago Daily News*. One assignment ultimately led to a career turnabout.

"I always wanted to do something like Second City, so I went to do an article about them. The thing was, for the *Daily News* "Panorama" section you got $68 if it was an 'inside' story, but if it was on the cover you got $150. I went for a cover story. My assignment was the Chicago Comedy Festival. The story was about the people who had started Second City and a lot of people were coming in for this festival. The festival hadn't started yet so I had to pump a story about something that hadn't happened into a front page story. So I thought, 'where do comedians come from?' It turned out they had workshops at Second City, so I said 'okay, well, now they must come out of these workshops. 'So I went and did a workshop with Del Close, who was running it that day. I really had a great time and finally I remember Del saying, 'you know, there are paying customers here, Denise. You can't take personal journalism this far. Get off the stage!'

"So then I signed up for some workshops, and I met Tim there. I was attracted to the political aspects of Second City and just the basic attitude of the place. I kept saying, 'I want to quit doing journalism and start doing more narrative prose or plays, more fiction and maybe this would help.' So I was doing that and Tim was trying to improve his advertising and sales pitches. I think we were both hams and we stayed. He was the smartest guy I worked with in any of the workshops. When we did exercises on stage we could tease each other and give each other handicaps in improvising. We just became really good friends.

"By that time, I guess I had gotten involved with Second City to the extent that I had told Bernie Sahlins why don't you pay me what the *Reader* was paying me and I'd help him develop ideas for TV and movies. I was sort of on staff as a writer, although I didn't write things for the mainstage."

The big break came when Tony Bill brought *My Bodyguard* (1980) to Chicago. Needing help with the script, Bill turned to Second City and asked if anyone there could punch up the dialog. "Bernie Sahlins took the job and asked: can anybody write?" said DeClue. She and Kazurinsky took the assignment and gave the screenplay a complete overhaul. Essentially, the duo wrote the script as the film was being made.

"Well, eight to ten weeks later, we'd pretty much rewritten every word of the movie," said Kazurinsky. "That was our first exposure to screenwriting." The film featured several Chicago area high schoolers in the cast, including Joan Cusack of Evanston Township High School and Jenevive (later Jennifer) Beals of Francis Parker. Cast in the title role was New Trier East student Adam Baldwin.

Following completion of the film, Kazurinsky went to Canada where he'd been hired to work on a John Candy television project called "Big City Comedy." DeClue remained in Chicago and when *My Bodyguard* opened in the spring of 1980, both fledgling writers got the wonderful shock of a lifetime. "I went to the screening," DeClue said. "The audience cheered the good guys and booed the bad guy. People stood up and clapped when it was over."

Exhilarated with this unexpected success, DeClue quickly got Kazurinsky on the phone. "Denise called me up (in Canada) and said, 'Tim, this movie came out. I gotta tell you, people applauded at the end of this movie.' I said 'were they all extras on the movie?' She said, 'no they were regular people. I've seen it two places. All the extras can't go to the same movie theater!'

"A couple of weeks later I managed to get back to Chicago and went and saw it. It was a huge hit. I remember I couldn't get into the Water Tower Theater and I had to tell them that I actually wrote the movie and that I was in a scene; I was an actor in it. I got the one seat in the front row. And I sat there watching the movie and it was amazing! The people laughed where we hoped they would laugh and they got choked up where we hoped they'd get choked up. I remember sitting there with a crick in my neck, staring up there at the screen, thinking 'I can do this. I got another career.' "

Due to contractual obligations and the general goofiness of the Hollywood system, Kazurinsky and DeClue didn't get screen credit for their work on *My Bodyguard*. What they lost in on-screen kudos however, was made up for in plum assignments. In 1980, the movie rights had been acquired to David Mamet's one-act play *Sexual Perversity in Chicago*, a dark look at the world of dating.

Again, the producers were looking for local talent to write the screenplay, and Kazurinsky and DeClue ultimately became involved in the foreboding task of turning Mamet's acidic stagework into a commercial film. "It became this magnificent obsession of ours that went on for years and years," said Kazurinsky. "Eventually we did 13 drafts, which is not unusual anymore. When you're young and the first thing you do is *My Bodyguard* and you're writing that morning and the lines are going in that night, we thought: this is how they make movies. We didn't know yet there were things like rewrites. We wrote the first draft in 1980 and it was shot in 1986. At one point Jonathan Demme was going to direct it. It had many, many metamorphoses."

In between getting the assignment and completing the final draft, Kazurinsky was hired for "Saturday Night Live." All the while, he and DeClue continued working on the script. Kazurinsky's run as a "Not Ready for Prime Time Player" lasted from 1981 through 1984, and when it was over, he returned to Chicago.

Of course, rewriting David Mamet is in and of itself a considerable task. "It was pretty scary because he's such a hallowed figure," said DeClue. When we set out to do this, I'd seen two productions of *Sexual Perversity in Chicago*. The first one was real intense and sort of like a one-act sketch and it was bitter. Basically Danny and Debbie (the Rob Lowe and Demi Moore characters) were the fools and Bernie and Joan (the James Belushi and Elizabeth Perkins characters) were the hip people, even though they might have had some problems.

"There were hints of homosexuality in Bernie and Joan. It was like a nice, kind of bitter little comedy on the 1970s singles scene, like love isn't possible, it's all over, it'll never happen. But when I saw the play the second time with Jimmy Belushi as Bernie, Bernie liked himself a lot. It changed the whole production in my mind. Instead of being a bitter little comedy, it was maybe an acerbic but really much funnier commentary. But still, Danny and Debbie were the schmucks and Bernie and Joan were the cool guys because they could see that love was impossible.

"When the whole thing came up that would we write this, it wasn't any problem for us to say, 'well it's Hollywood, it's going to have a happy ending.' Both Tim and I had been veterans of the singles scene and knew that loves springs eternal and didn't have any problem saying that Debbie and Danny were the logical protagonists and they would have some logical hope in the end. So that meant then dealing with Mamet's characterization. I think what he did was like commedia dell'arte. You pull these stock characters out every generation. By the time we did *About Last Night...*, it was like 15 years later, so (Mamet's characters were) reinvented again in terms of the early 1980s. So it was scary in the terms of rewriting.

"I've rewritten a lot of people. I did a play based on Nelson Algren's *City on the Make* and *Neon Wilderness* that was well received here and that was really scary. Yet what I always told myself was you don't do the original creator any justice by holding on to what they wrote in one form when your job is to translate it into another form. You have to bring all your skills to bear and respect the ideas but don't assume that the play is a movie and don't assume you can just leave it like it is. You try to take the best and make it work within the context of a film." Kazurinsky concurs. "It's impossible [to rewrite Mamet]. You just go, okay, this is a different beast.

"Mamet had already taken a swipe at the screenplay, which was basically his play with entrances and exits. That was not the movie they wanted. *Sexual Perversity in Chicago* is a tough, one-act play. It's a very dark look at the hopelessness of the singles scene, and it had a lot of stuff going on about the veiled homosexuality of [the characters] Bernie and Joan. The studio was like 'no, we don't want that.' I think our vision of humanity and the singles scenes was a little gentler and kinder. We wanted to throw people a bone."

DeClue and Kazurinsky never discussed the rewrite with Mamet. "I'm sure he would have some choice things to say about it!" Kazurinsky says today with a laugh. "Actually, *About Last Night...* may have ended up making more money for Mamet than anything else he ever did filmwise. He had a huge piece of it. It did better than *House of Games* (1987). But Mamet is a great writer and it is intimidating to go delving; plus, when we started, he hadn't won the Pulitzer or the Obie yet. He was just a playwright. I thought he was a great writer but he hadn't won all these enormous awards yet. We had to throw out great chunks of it. There were lines in there . . . [that wouldn't] play in Des Moines! We were probably trying to be more commercial at that point. We were trying to make a light movie. It's certainly a much more commercial film. It's not *Sexual Perversity in Chicago*! We were always depressed that they changed the title, because we loved it, but the film is really not Mamet's play.

With the screenplay completed, Rob Lowe and Demi Moore were hired to play the leads, with James Belushi and Elizabeth Perkins in support rolls. When cameras started to roll, another former Chicagoan, Edward Zwick, served as the film's director.

Unlike *My Bodyguard*, Kazurinsky didn't have the chance to be involved with *About Last Night's....* shooting in Chicago. "You wait seven years for your movie to be made and it happens when you sign a contract to do a *Police Academy* film!" he woefully recalled. "I was up in Toronto, running around in a cop uniform in *Police Academy III* (1986). There I was, being that no-neck geek cop that I played and *About Last Night ...*was shooting down here and it was killing me because I couldn't be in Chicago. I was only on set two days for the whole shooting of *About Last Night...* and I wanted to be there everyday."

Following the success of *About Last Night...*, Kazurinsky and DeClue penned another comically poignant adolescent film, *For Keeps* (1988). Starring Molly Ringwald, the film was a sensitively-told tale of how teenagers learn to cope with an unexpected pregnancy. In 1997, their off-beat Western, *The Cherokee Kid*, became an HBO telefilm with comedian Sinbad in the title role. In addition to writing the script, Kazurinsky and DeClue also served as producers on the project. A popular writing duo, Kazurinsky and DeClue have now collaborated on more than 30 television and film scripts.

Though their careers are inevitably linked, Kazurinsky and DeClue have also done considerable work apart from each other. In addition to the *Police Academy* films, Kazurinsky has played supporting roles in everything from television programs like "Married...With Children" to the dramatic "Early Edition." On screen, he's appeared in *Somewhere in Time* (1980), with his mentor John Belushi in *Neighbors* (1981) and *Continental Divide* (1981), *Hot to Trot* (1988), and Bobcat Goldthwait's cult comedy *Shakes the Clown* (1992). He had bit cameo parts in *My Bodyguard*, *About Last Night...* (a very funny scene as Demi Moore's nightmare date), and *The Cherokee Kid*. Additionally, Kazurinsky played a villainous role in a 1998 series of promotional ads for the Chicago White Sox.

Though locals still know Kazurinsky from his Second City work and "Saturday Night Live" days, he doesn't feel he gets any special "celebrity" treatment in Chicago. "Even here there's a sensibility about it like nowhere else. Like, in New York you'd be in the vegetable section at the grocery and someone would yell 'Hey! Saturday Night Live! Look, it's the guy from "Saturday Night Live!" ' But here, people sometimes pass you on the street and go 'I liked your work at Second City.' I get a lot of that—'I liked your work' or 'thanks for the laughs.' People drive by your car with a thumbs up and a smile. It's just great, just sort of on the fly. They don't intrude. If you're in a restaurant, they don't come and sit down next to you. You're allowed your space.

"There are pluses and minuses to working out of Chicago. All the guys I know out in L.A. say, 'you know, yeah, you may lose work because you're not here, you're not available, you can't be there, you can't run to location. But Chicago is where your home and family are. You don't have to go to this cool party, this director's son's bar mitzvah, this shindig, this opening night, that opening night, and anybody with the price of lunch can't steal two or three hours of your life. With you, if they're really serious, they have to pop for a plane ticket.'

"Yeah, we lose work, we lose jobs, it is a case of out of sight, out of mind, but it's a trade-off, a quality of life versus quantity of living."

DeClue has been active locally as a producer, working briefly on the television program "Missing Persons," which was based in Chicago. With her husband Robert Schneiger, she put together a television documentary "Uptown Sounds." The program, which looked at Chicago teens staging a play in their drug-infested neighborhood, won three Midwestern Emmy awards. She has also written several solo screenplays and works for the theater.

"The real fun thing about Chicago is being able to live here and have a life and have a job or freelance in the kind of way that you're sort of connected and sort of unconnected," she says. "For me, [the advantage of Chicago is] the fact that you really get to know a lot of people who are really not in one business—they're not in the film business. As a writer your take on life is from real life, not a life that centers around the movie business. If you're a writer it's better to just live your life. I wasn't really interested in becoming a screenwriter. When people ask me 'how did you become a screenwriter?' I say 'just don't want to, until maybe you wind up being one!' "

Tim Kazurinsky, comic actor, prolific screenwriter, and former cast member of "Saturday Night Live" and Second City. (*Photo courtesy of Tim Kazurinsky.*)

➡ OLD STATE OF ILLINOIS BUILDING
160 N. LaSalle Street

Built in 1924 by the Burnham Brothers (sons of city planner Daniel Burnham), this building was originally named after its architects. In 1946 the Burnham Building was bought by the state government as its Chicago headquarters and subsequently was known as the State of Illinois Building. When the Thompson Center was opened in the mid-1980s, Illinois government offices moved out.

Though eclipsed by the gaudy glass and steel of the new state headquarters, the old State of Illinois Building still had one brief, shining moment—it became Coles Department Store in the remake of *Miracle on 34th Street* (1994). Ironically, the new Thompson Center was its competitor.

➡ R.R. DONNELLEY BUILDING
77 W. Wacker Drive

Before the new headquarters of R.R. Donnelly was completed, it made for an intriguing film set. It's here where white supremacist Tom Berenger and undercover FBI agent Debra Winger faced off in *Betrayed* (1988). The scene had Berenger and Winger sneaking onto the construction site with the purpose of shooting a human target on the street below. Winger prevents the assassination, only to learn there's a lot more to the situation then it would appear.

Ten years later, the Donnelly building became the focal point of *The Negotiator* (1998). Samuel L. Jackson, playing a top police negotiator, enters the tower (which, for purposes of the film, became a government building) to prove his innocence when he's accused of masterminding a labyrinth money laundering scheme. Taking hostages within an office suite, Jackson ultimately squares off in a battle of wits with his peer negotiator, Kevin Spacey. While the two play cat and mouse games, Wacker Drive is choked with police cars, barricades, and countless extras, police snipers are poised on surrounding buildings and helicopters buzz around like oversized mosquitoes. Just another night in Chicago, albeit through the world of action movie set pieces!

➡ DOWNTOWN RANDOLPH STREET
Randolph Street between Michigan Avenue and Wells Street

If you take a walk down Randolph Street between Michigan Avenue and Wells Street, you'll find yourself in a bustling throng. Between the business people, bike messengers, and tourists, downtown Randolph is a great place for people watching.

If you're looking for movie locations along Randolph, you'll find plenty. The Cultural Center, Marshall Fields, and the Thompson Center are among the most prominent landmarks (see individual entries). Yet the Randolph Street we know today is very different from what this thoroughfare was just a few years ago.

During the 1940s, Randolph Street was the heart of Chicago's big ticket theater district. Huge neon marquees flashed movies, plays, and special celebrity appearances for theaters like the Apollo, the Garrick, the Oriental, the Palace, the United Artists, and the Woods. The Showman's League, a organization for people in the entertainment business, maintained their headquarters at the corner of Randolph and Wells.

On a hot Saturday night, Randolph Street was the place to be. Slowly, however, the luster of this thriving district began to fade. By the 1970s, blockbuster movies no longer played exclusively at downtown theaters. Randolph's once-proud movie palaces were reduced to playing karate movies, exploitation action flicks, and the more-than-occasional pornographic film. By the mid 1980s, most of the theaters were demolished, though the Oriental and the Palace (renamed the Bismark Palace), merely shut their doors.

Though today this downtown street is largely comprised of business and government buildings, it is making a cultural comeback of sorts. The Oriental has undergone extensive renovation. Under its buffed-up rebirth, this former movie house now caters to big-ticket musicals and other theatrical productions.

If you're nostalgic or just plain curious about old Randolph Street, there are a few films that will give you a glimpse of the theater district's decaying glory. In *Mickey One* (1965), Warren Beatty cruises the street in search of a booking agent. Michael Mann's *Thief* (1981) features an interesting shot of James Caan driving past the glowing Randolph Street marquees. The neon signs are seen as reflections off the hood of star James Caan's car, creating a feverish dream-like ambiance.

Matt Dillon played a small town gambler who comes to Chicago during the 1950s-era drama, *Big Town* (1987). When the production came to town, Randolph Street was on its last legs as a theater district. What showed up on screen was a nice period look, giving the right ambiance to Dillon's world of low-life excitement.

MICKEY ONE (1965)

"I'm the king of silent movies hiding out 'til the talkies blow over."
—Warren Beatty to a perplexed Alexandra Stewart
in *Mickey One*

Mickey One (1965) may be the ultimate in cult pictures: movie zealots know all about it, but precious few acolytes have actually seen this film. It's nearly impossible to find *Mickey One* on video or at a film society screening. Directed by Arthur Penn [*The Miracle Worker* (1962), *Bonnie and Clyde* (1967)] and starring Warren Beatty, *Mickey One* was part crime picture, part art house film. The influence of the French New Wave directors of the late 1950s/early 1960s was clearly evident in this grim black and white movie, as was the work of Italian director Federico Fellini. Throw in 1940s B-movie plotting and characters, along with the nightmare alienation comedy of writer Franz Kafka, and a mournful soundtrack featuring Stan Getz improvisations and you have *Mickey One*.

The plot follows a nightclub comic (Beatty) who's on the run from Detroit mobsters. He hops a freight train to Chicago, lives in the street for a while, and eventually tries to re-establish himself on the nightclub circuit. He can't escape his past though and gets caught up in a world of crime, show biz sleaze, and personal demons.

Penn shot all over the West Side, downtown, and the Rush Street area. His portrait of the city was foreboding, replete with darkened alleys and side streets, eerily-lit nightclubs, and the twisted-metal prairies of auto scrap yards. He made particularly good use of the West Madison Street area. The soup kitchens and storefront missions, greasy spoons, and tenement apartments gave Beatty's nightmare world an everyday reality.

Scenes along Randolph Street in the Loop give a brief glimpse to how the downtown area looked in the early 1960s. Beatty is seen entering the Woods Building (54 E. Randolph) as he pounds the pavement looking for an agent. Next door is the long-gone movie house, the Woods Theater, featuring Otto Preminger's *The Cardinal* (1963) as the main attraction. Other scenes, shot along Rush Street's nightclub district give today's viewers an idea of what Chicago looked like when Lenny Bruce, Woody Allen, and Mort Sahl roamed the comedy circuit.

Penn also made effective use of the Chicago River and the newly-built Marina City Towers (see Marina City entry).

Though the film had its admirers, *Mickey One* was probably too esoteric for its own good. It certainly had its moments, for example, the harsh shots of Beatty being tortured by a stark spotlight piercing through a darkened nightclub. Yet Penn's free-form narrative and dense symbolism ultimately worked against him. "I may have overshot my mark," the director said a few years later. "I was really operating on the symbolic and metaphorical level without engagement between audience and screen....it would have been so easy to tell a really simple narrative, but a binding one," Penn told author Joseph Gelmis in the book *The Film Director as Superstar*.

Still, the film, if you can find it, is well worth a look. For all its strengths and weaknesses, *Mickey One* gives a unique glimpse of Chicago as distilled from early 1960s art film sensibilities.

Source: Gelmis, Joseph. *The Film Director as Superstar*. New York: Doubleday and Company, 1970, 221-2.

➡ **THE CHICAGO FILM OFFICE**
One N. LaSalle Street, Suite 2165, Chicago, IL 60602

➡ **THE ILLINOIS FILM OFFICE**
100 W. Randolph Street, Suite 3-400, Chicago, IL 60601

You're a producer looking for a commuter train running alongside an expressway. You're a director who needs to have neighborhood streets blocked off to local traffic so you can shoot a love scene. Either way, you're looking for professional crew people who have experience working on multi-million-dollar movies. These are the kinds of demands that ratchet up movie budgets if things don't go exactly as planned. That's where the Chicago and Illinois Film Offices come in.

Established in 1976 as Hollywood was gradually rediscovering the beauty of Chicago, the Illinois Film Office (IFO) was set up by Gov. Jim Thompson as a way of creating new revenue streams for Illinois. The Chicago Film Office (CFO) opened shortly thereafter. In the 20-plus years of their existence, these two offices have grown into invaluable liaisons between local concerns and Hollywood necessities.

The IFO is ground zero for any producer thinking about bringing a production to Illinois. "Our job is to make the process go as smooth as possible for both the filmmaker and the community where they're filming," says Ron Ver Kuilen, who serves as managing director. "We have extensive location files on homes, restaurants, bars, and so on. We look at scripts and see what might work. When filmmakers come to town, Joe Amari, our senior location scout, takes them around to give them a feel for the city or other Illinois areas and sell the state to the filmmaker."

Once a producer decides on Chicago, pre-production begins. This includes help with research, finding out what resources are available, and hiring professionals to work behind the scenes. "We're known by many people in Hollywood," says Ver Kuilen. "They're comfortable with our crews, Chicago talent is world-renowned, and we've got first-class facilities. A producer can get on a plane in Los Angeles and find everything here that he possibly could use in making a film." Ver Kuilen points out that between the considerable pool of actors in Chicago, the production personnel, the technical facilities, and the ease of getting around town, the Windy City has become a very attractive location to Hollywood.

Ver Kuilen cites three main reasons Hollywood loves Chicago: the attractiveness of the city, affordability of production, and the availability of locations. Some of the most popular areas to shoot are Michigan Avenue, Wrigley Field, the Milwaukee-North-Damen area, the turnaround basin along the river, Wacker Drive, Grant Park, the near North Side around Clark and Fullerton, and Southport Avenue. Having an elevated train and subway system snaking around town is another aspect of the city producers find very sexy. "The Chicago Avenue El stop is very popular. Producers also like the stations at Wabash and Randolph and Wabash and Madison because of their older look. The North and Clybourn subway is used a lot for the same reason," Ver Kuilen says.

"Movies can do a huge service to us by capturing the look of the city, the character of the city, and putting them up on screens big and small throughout the world," says Richard Moskal, director of the CFO. "Chicago has a great big-city look, but it also has colorful, diverse neighborhoods that lend a lot to telling a variety of different stories. The fact that we're on the lake and have the river cutting through, the historic architecture, the older metropolis-looking stuff—there's a lot of texture and diversity to what Chicago has to offer visually. It's a city that people can identify with—it's very middle American and very cosmopolitan at the same time."

A division of the Mayor's Office of Special Events, the major part of the CFO's job is to coordinate filmmaking needs with city concerns. "The office is the focal point of concerns regarding city services so a production company doesn't have to get involved in bureaucracy. It's the city's way of saying we can accommodate the movie business in a quick and efficient fashion," says Moskal. The CFO also works closely with communities where films are being shot.

"We work closely with the Illinois Film Office. They're dealing with economic development and marketing. They encourage film producers to do work here and do a lot of the initial leg work, hooking them up with resources. The Chicago Film Office gets down to streets. We're an advocate for the industry in terms of getting the films made, but we're also watching out for the city and the communities so that neighborhoods don't necessarily get taken advantage of by what can be very huge demands and challenges," says Moskal.

The two offices also sponsor the biennial Illinois/Chicago Screenwriting Competition. "The idea was to recognize that Chicago has a sizable writing community and as much as a big portion of our efforts are focused on production, all of it begins with a script," says Moskal. To be eligible, the screenplay must be set in Illinois with at least 75 percent of the locations identifiably within the state. The contest is open to any Illinois resident age 18 and up.

Scripts are looked over by a jury of local and national film industry professionals. Out of the numerous submissions (the most recent competition garnered more than 200 scripts) the first-tier judges select 50 semi-finalists. Writers in this group have the option of placing their work on a list for studios and production companies looking for new scripts. The 50 are then boiled down to ten finalists, who are given an opportunity to rewrite their respective scripts. From these ten, three winners are chosen. Each member of the fortunate trio is awarded a cash prize and a trophy. Best of all, their screenplays are submitted to a group of Hollywood studio executives and producers who have an arrangement with the IC Competition.

The Illinois Film Office can be reached at 312-814-3600. The Chicago Film Office can be reached at 312-744-6415. Visit their Web page at http://www.ci.chi.il.us/WorksMart/SpecialEvents/Film Office.

➡ **JAMES R. THOMPSON CENTER/**
STATE OF ILLINOIS BUILDING
100 W. Randolph Street

To some it's a beautiful, post-modern palace. To others, it's a glass and steel nightmare representing the worst modern architecture can belch up. Take it or leave it, inevitably you'll have some kind of business here at the James R. Thompson Center (also known as the State of Illinois Building).

The building, opened in 1985, was designed by architect Helmut Jahn,

Nighttime aerial view of the James R. Thompson Center (100 W. Randolph), also known as the State of Illinois Building. Its eye-catching modern architecture is admired by some, loathed by others. (*Photo courtesy of Illinois Department of Central Management Services.*)

well-known for his forays into glass and steel construction. Jahn was personally chosen by then-Illinois Gov. James Thompson to design the edifice, inspiring one local wag to dub the completed building "Thompsonland." Indeed, with its expansive atrium, towering escalators, glass elevators, and always-buzzing food court, the James R. Thompson Center does have the look and feel of a Disney-inspired attraction. While the design may be attractive to some, it also has a rather significant drawback: the building suffers from perennial heating and air conditioning trouble.

In *Music Box* (1989), Costa-Gavras's story about the trial of a long-hidden Nazi war criminal, federal prosecutors had offices in the Thompson Center. The building's mall-like environment was neatly exploited in *Miracle on 34th Street* (1994), turning the Thompson Center into a Christmas-festooned department store. *Switching Channels* (1988), a sort of broadcast remake of the famed Chicago newspaper play *The Front Page*, by Charles MacArthur and Ben Hecht, also had some fun with the building, making good use of its futuristic ambiance.

The playhouse qualities of Jahn's architecture were pushed to the limits in the Billy Crystal-Gregory Hines cop buddy picture, *Running Scared*

(1986). In the film's climactic sequence, Crystal and Hines leap around the building's atrium liked crazed monkeys, using ropes to swing through open spaces and shooting out the glass elevators. It's a fast and furious mishmash of action, suspense, and Crystal's wisecracks in an unbelievable, yet totally entertaining, package. Just beware of the painful freeze-frame ending that caps the film!

➡ **CITY HALL/COUNTY BUILDING**
   121 N. LaSalle Street/118 N. Clark Street

"Hut! Hut!" That's not the cry of pigeons but the regimented yell of tethered swat team members scrambling down the City Hall columns in *The Blues Brothers* (1980). That film's frenzied climax ended here, with scores of cops and National Guardsmen pouring through the hallways to the County Assessor's office, where Joliet Jake (John Belushi) and Elwood (Dan Aykroyd) complete their mission from God and pay off an orphanage tax bill to mild-mannered clerk Steven Spielberg. Of course, that's the film's biggest joke, since in real life the orphanage would be a tax-exempt organization!

The Cook County Building was built between 1906 and 1907, and City Hall came shortly thereafter, with groundbreaking in 1909 and a grand opening in 1911. Those Corinthian columns *The Blues Brothers'* swat team hopped down are the tallest on any city building, towering at 75 feet apiece.

Aside from Jake and Elwood, City Hall/County Building has been visited by characters in *Miracle on 34th Street* (1994) and *A Family Thing* (1996), among others. The old coal tunnels deep beneath the structure doubled as underground passageways beneath the Field Museum in *The Relic* (1997), when City Hall tunnels proved to be an easier place to film.

Apparently there's something about the City Hall/County Building that attracts movie men on the run. In addition to Jake and Elwood's County Building encounters, poor Dr. Richard Kimble (Harrison Ford) is nearly captured here by U.S. Marshal Sam Gerard (Tommy Lee Jones) in *The Fugitive* (1993). Of course, in real life, Harrison Ford wouldn't be looking up prisoners in the County Building, as he does in *The Fugitive*. On the other hand, the bullet-proof-glass doors that nearly stop Ford dead in his tracks don't exist here, either.

Love, however, does spring eternal in the building's basement. Though often referred to as a "City Hall wedding," marriages are actually a function of Cook County government. So head downstairs, where you and your intended can be married by a Cook County judge, and while you're there, take a few puffs on a good cigar in honor of Groucho Marx. On February 4,

1920, Groucho (a.k.a. Julius Henry Marx) and his first wife, Ruth Johnson, took their vows in a Cook County judge's chambers.[1] This being a Marx Brother marriage, appropriate chaos ensued. A potted plant appeared to blissfully walk around on its own throughout the room during the ceremony, courtesy of a carefully hidden Harpo. And when the justice of the peace solemnly intoned, "We are gathered here to join this couple in holy matrimony," Groucho, in his superlative fashion replied, "It may be holy to you, Judge, but we have other ideas."[2]

Information on the scheduling of City Hall tours for school groups is available from the Inquiry and Information Office at 312-744-6671.

[1] Marx, Groucho, with Hector Arce, *The Groucho Phile: An Illustrated Life* (New York: Bobbs-Merrill, 1976): 34.

[2] Marx, Arthur, *Son of Groucho* (New York: David McKay Company, Inc., 1972): 22.

➡ **RICHARD J. DALEY CIVIC CENTER AND PLAZA**
50 W. Washington Street

One of the best places in the city for people watching, the Richard J. Daley Civic Center and Plaza is a quintessential Chicago site that can't be duplicated. The towering 31-story building, which houses many courts and offices, was opened in 1965 and overlooks Daley Plaza, home to one of the city's most universally recognized symbols, the rust-red Picasso statue.

Movie-wise, the Daley Plaza's scenic beauty is a natural location for filmmakers looking to add a distinctive splash of local color. It's been seen on screen in one form or another in films like *Blink* (1993), *Baby's Day Out* (1994), *Backdraft* (1991), *Ferris Bueller's Day Off* (1986), *The Fugitive* (1993), *Adventures in Babysitting* (1987), and *Mercury Rising* (1998). Still, none of these films can compete with the ultimate Daley Center location shoot in *The Blues Brothers* (1980).

The scene had everything: National Guardsmen by the truckload, cops on foot and horseback, fire trucks, tanks, anti-aircraft guns, and helicopters all crammed on the Plaza in hot pursuit of Blues Brothers, Jake (John Belushi) and Elwood (Dan Aykroyd). Shot over Labor Day weekend in 1979, the scene used more than 500 extras and cost $3.5 million to film. Breakable plate glass was installed in the building, allowing Belushi and Aykroyd (or, more properly, a stunt driver) to blast the Bluesmobile through a window on the Washington Street side of the building, down corridors past a bank of elevators, and then make a quick exit via another obliterated window on the Randolph Street side.

Certainly one of Chicago's most complicated shoots, the *Blues Brothers* mayhem, surprisingly, does not rank as the strangest scene ever filmed in the Daley Center Plaza. That honor goes to *The Naked Ape* (1972), a loose adaptation of Desmond Morris's anthropological study of man, as envisioned by the motion picture geniuses of Chicago's own *Playboy Magazine*. The magazine's short-lived film production wing used the fountain pool at the Plaza's west end on March 15, 1972 as an unlikely respite for two lost Neanderthals (the hapless Ira Rogers and Susan Knox, looking more like refugees from *The Planet of the Apes* (1967) than *homo sapien* predecessors).

And just how did these prehistoric figures end up in the Daley Plaza? According to the film's convoluted logic, Neanderthals, running through a combined animation/live-action sequence, are confronted by the history of architecture, ranging from simple huts to the glass and steel canyons of neoteric cities. In the comically pretentious words of director Donald Driver:

> Neanderthal is being encompassed and encroached upon. He runs into a lake—it's his only out; he's completely surrounded by modern architecture—and the splashing of animated water is soon overtaken by the splashing of real water. The camera pulls back rapidly, and there he is in the middle of the pool of the Civic Center. We pull back from 40 stories to look at him from the top of the Brunswick Building, and there he is: Neanderthal man standing in the middle of an urbanized civilization to which he has never been able to genetically adjust.[1]

Interestingly enough, this cinematic auteur disappeared from the filmmaking scene shortly after *The Naked Ape's* release.

[1] Siskel, Gene, "Culture Shock at the Civic Center Plaza," *Chicago Tribune*, March 16, 1972.

➡ CALDER'S "FLAMINGO" AT THE FEDERAL PLAZA
Dearborn and Adams Streets

The Federal Plaza is surrounded by the Dirksen, Kluczynski, and Metcalfe Federal Buildings, with the United States Post Office-Loop Station off to one side. While these glass and steel towers present an imposing visual picture, what really captures the eye is the abstract sculpture that anchors the Plaza, Alexander Calder's 53-foot tall "Flamingo."

It was in the shadows of the "Flamingo" where Adam Baldwin and Chris Makepeace had a celebratory ride on Baldwin's motorbike in *My Bodyguard* (1980). The joy felt by these two awkward teens is a wonderfully exuberant moment to behold. Baldwin and Makepeace practically radiate energy from the screen.

On a less poetic note, Debra Winger's FBI office headquarters in *Betrayed* (1988) were located in the Dirksen Building.

➡ **THE PUBLIC EYE NEWSPAPER OFFICE**
135 S. LaSalle Street

Once owned by Marshall Field, the 135 S. LaSalle Street Building has been on the corner of LaSalle and Adams Streets since 1934. Its period look was perfect for offices of the *New York Daily News* in the 1940s era drama *The Public Eye* (1992). Joe Pesci starred as a tabloid photographer based on the famed Wee Gee. *The Public Eye* was partially filmed in Chicago, which producers felt had a more realistic New York look and feel than the Big Apple itself.

➡ **THE ROOKERY**
209 S. LaSalle Street

Without a doubt, this is one of downtown's most beautiful buildings. Designed in 1885 by Daniel Burnham and John Wellborn Root, with interior work done by Frank Lloyd Wright, in 1907, and others through the years, the Rookery is glimmering with historical beauty. The building is 11 stories tall, with a dark red facade and elegant window designs framed by stone columns. A stoned arch serves as the main entrance on LaSalle Street. If you look along the granite columns on either side of this entrance, you'll notice a pair of birds carved into the stone. These are rooks, a European relation to the American crow, from where the building gets its name.

The arched entrance on LaSalle Street stood in for Chicago Police headquarters in the big screen version of *The Untouchables* (1987). Scenes from *Folks!* (1992), a laughless Tom Selleck comedy, were shot here, as were a few moments of *Kissing a Fool* (1998), starring David Schwimmer.

Perhaps Hollywood's most careful use of the building was in *Home Alone II: Lost in New York* (1992). The Rookery's exterior served as the entrance for Duncan's Toy Chest, a faux New York emporium. The film was shot during the final stages of the Rookery restoration, with a scene calling for a large, three-dimensional sign to be attached to the building. Not wanting to deface the intensive work that had gone into refurbishing the building, a special sign was created that would stay up yet not be anchored to the Rookery's stone exteriors.

Duncan's Toy Chest is another case of one on-screen place/two real life sets. When actors passed through the Rookery doors, they found themselves, through the magic of editing, transported to the Uptown Theatre on North Broadway near Lawrence Avenue. The beautiful lobby of this former Balaban and Katz palace was the toy store's interior.

➡ CHICAGO BOARD OF TRADE/LASALLE STREET CANYON
141 W. Jackson Boulevard

At the corner of Jackson Boulevard and LaSalle Street stands the mighty Chicago Board of Trade. Designed by the architectural firm of Holabird and Root, the building was opened in 1930 as the center for commodities trading in the Midwest. A classic example of the art deco style, a 36-story tower juts out from the Board of Trade's nine-story base. The building is finished in limestone and capped by a pyramid-shaped roof. Looking out on LaSalle Street from the rooftop is a 31-foot tall statue of Ceres, the Roman goddess of grain and harvest. Along the building's northern face are carvings of a Native American and a Mesopotamian, representing the corn and wheat which were the original stocks in trade here. Between the two reliefs are a clock and an eagle carved into the limestone. South LaSalle Street is nicknamed "The Canyon" and for good reason. With tall buildings lining either side of the street and the looming Chicago Board of Trade serving as an anchor, this corridor is the very essence of an urban

The Chicago Board of Trade (141 W. Jackson) at the end of the LaSalle Street "Canyon." The Canyon has been featured in many films, including *The Untouchables, Mad Dog and Glory, Hoodlum,* and *U.S. Marshals.* (*Photo by Holly Pluard.*)

canyon. It's a visually striking conglomeration of Chicago architecture, stretching between Adams Street and Jackson Boulevard. Crawling with traders, bankers, and business people during the day, the LaSalle Street Canyon has become a playground for filmmakers in recent years.

South LaSalle has been seen in *The Untouchables, Mad Dog and Glory, Folks!,* and *Limit Up,* a lame comedy set among Board of Trade employees. In these films, South LaSalle Street is clearly identified as a Chicago location. Yet the two most interesting uses of the Canyon transformed these environs from the Windy City to the Big Apple.

Hoodlum (1997) featured Laurence Fishburne as Ellsworth "Bumpy" Johnson, a real-life figure from the New York gang wars of the 1920s and 1930s. He'd previously played the character as a supporting part in Francis Ford Coppola's drama *The Cotton Club* (1984), but in *Hoodlum,* directed by Bill Duke, this Harlem-based gangster was at the center of action.

One of *Hoodlum's* biggest set pieces was a shootout between Johnson and thugs sent by his Manhattan rival Dutch Schultz (Tim Roth) outside the New York City Opera House. Director Duke chose the LaSalle Street Canyon for this sequence, exploiting the block's period look. The Board of Trade became the Opera House, old fashioned streetlights and WPA banners were affixed to light poles, and for one brief, bloody moment, LaSalle was transported back in time and location.

Though problems inevitably hit film sets, the *Hoodlum* production crew faced a rather unique concern when it came to filming this sequence. The LaSalle Street shootout, which included gunfire and explosions, was scheduled for production the same week as the 1996 Democratic National Convention, which was being held a few miles west at the United Center. In anticipation of the event, Secret Service agents had scoped out the city from top to bottom to make sure nothing could possibly endanger President Clinton or any of the other top government and political figures visiting the city during Convention Week. When word came that *Hoodlum* was planning to film a violent, albeit fictional, confrontation, the Secret Service quickly nixed the idea. Negotiations between the production and offcials ensued and included Secret Service interviews with many of the movie team's principal behind-the-scenes people. Finally, a compromise was reached, fake bullets and blood were allowed to fly through the air, and the Democrats renominated Bill Clinton without a hitch.

U.S. Marshals (1998), a sequel to the made-in-Chicago thriller *The Fugitive* (1993), took place in a variety of locations, including downstate Illinois, Chicago, and New York. One key sequence involved a briefcase being handed off between two shadowy contacts in the midst of a crowded Manhattan lunch crowd. Through creative set decoration and quick editing, the LaSalle Street Canyon was transformed into its Lower Manhattan colleague, Wall Street. Chicago street signs were camouflaged, New York newspaper boxes were placed on the sidewalk, and a horde of extras was utilized to recreate the madness of Wall Street at lunchtime. The result was a realistic-looking New York location, filmed entirely in Chicago.

For more information about the Chicago Board of Trade, check out their Web site at http://www.cbot.com/.

➡ SEARS TOWER
233 S. Wacker Drive

Depending on which source you want to believe, the Sears Tower ranks as the tallest building in the world. Bounded by Wacker Drive, Franklin and Adams Streets, and Jackson Boulevard, the Tower was completed in 1973. Designed by the firm of Skidmore, Owings, and Merrill, the building has 110 stories, is 1,468 feet tall, and covers three acres of space from bottom to top. It was originally built as headquarters for Sears, Roebuck and Company; however, 20 years later Sears relocated its corporate offices to Hoffman Estates, Illinois.

As one of the Windy City's iconic buildings, the Sears Tower has been used in countless films to establish that "we're in Chicago." It's another case of Hollywood taking a local landmark and turning it into a very tall visual cliché, as in *The Package* (1989) and *Michael* (1996).

Thankfully, the Chicago-based John Hughes understood Sears Tower's appeal to Chicagoans and highlighted the spectacular view from its Skydeck in *Ferris Bueller's Day Off* (1986). It's here where Ferris (Matthew Broderick), his girlfriend Sloane (Mia Sara), and their neurotic pal Cameron (Alan Ruck) lean against the windows and soak up all Chicago has to offer.

For ticket information on the Sears Skydeck, call 312-875-9696.

Depending on who's measuring, the Sears Tower (233 S. Wacker Drive) may be the tallest building in the world. Its Skydeck was featured in *Ferris Bueller's Day Off*. (*Photo courtesy of the Sears Tower.*)

➡ **UNION STATION**
210 S. Canal Street

Bordered by Jackson Boulevard, Adams, Canal, and Clinton Streets, Union Station was built between 1913 and 1925, with a design by Graham, Anderson, Probst, and White. The name came from the "union" of four major rail companies that converged on this important hub. Though rail use has declined with the rise of air traffic, Union Station is still a busy hive of activity. Commuter services and Amtrak passenger trains serve the thousands of passengers who pass through Union Station on a daily basis.

The centerpiece of this building is a gorgeous waiting room, designed by Graham, Burnham, and Company in 1917. The waiting room's wooden benches are surrounded by fluted columns and overhead is an immense skylight. On either side of the waiting room you'll see two bird statues. One is a rooster, representing morning travel; the other is an owl, symbolizing the nighttime voyager.

Union Station's visual appeal was made for the movies. *Chain Reaction, Code of Silence, I Love Trouble, Prelude to a Kiss, Red Heat, The Package, Midnight Run, Vice Versa, love jones,* and *My Best Friend's Wedding* all staged scenes here. *The Sting,* set in 1930s era Chicago, made effective use of the station's period look. The television shows "ER" and "Early Edition" have also shot scenes here.

Yet one Union Station film stands above them all. With *The Untouchables* (1987), director Brian DePalma, actors Kevin Costner and Andy Garcia, and one teetering baby carriage staged what can either be called a brilliant homage or a glossy rip-off, depending on your view of film history.

The scene had Costner, as Elliott Ness, and Garcia, as a member of the fabled cop squad, facing off with some of Al Capone's henchmen on a Union Station staircase. Enter a mother innocently pushing her baby carriage. Amidst all the hullabaloo, the baby carriage breaks free from Mommy and begins a slow-motion roll down the stairs.

Sharp-eyed film buffs, who've often accused DePalma of ripping off Alfred Hitchcock movies, immediately recognized the source of this scene. In 1925, Russian director Sergei Eisenstein filmed *The Battleship Potemkin*, a fictionalized account of a 1905 sailors' revolt. The most dramatic sequence involved a mob of Czarist soldiers attacking the people of Odessa on a public staircase. Amidst all the fireworks, a dying mother releases a baby carriage, sending her infant plummeting down the steps.

Unlike Potemkin's unlucky infant, *The Untouchables'* baby is rescued by Costner and company. A bit unrealistic? Well, of course, but this is still a fun set piece, combining flashy editing and camera work for a nicely choreographed sequence.

Union Station is where the title train of *Silver Streak* (1976) supposedly crashed in the slam-bang finish of a Los Angeles to Chicago run. In reality, the station's interior was recreated at an airplane hanger at Lockheed Aircraft in Los Angeles and a train was sent barreling through the phony set.

BILL KURTIS

"When Kurtis Productions started about ten years ago, little would I know that suddenly we would evolve with cable into the golden age of documentaries."

Though many Chicagoans still remember him as news anchor at WBBM-TV Channel 2 (along with on-air partner Walter Jacobson), Bill Kurtis has been a trailblazer in the field of television documentaries. Originally from Kansas, where he obtained a bachelor's degree in journalism as well as a juris doctor, Kurtis began his career as a television news reporter in Wichita. Moving to Chicago and WBBM in the late 1960s, Kurtis developed a solid reputation as he covered everything from the tumultuous street riots of 1968 to the legal proceedings of the Charles Manson and Chicago Conspiracy trials. In 1973, he was teamed with Walter Jacobson for WBBM's nightly newscast, a partnership that lasted nine years. All the while, Kurtis made it a point to do his own reporting and not to get locked in behind an anchor's desk. This aggressive style brought him to Vietnam two weeks before Saigon fell, the war-torn streets of Northern Ireland, and other world hot spots—all while based at WBBM.

While anchoring the evening news, Kurtis also began an investigative reporting unit, which led to his first efforts in television documentary. His groundbreaking exposé on the defoliant Agent Orange and its long-term health effects on America's Vietnam veterans brought this issue to the attention of a nation.

It was inevitable that a journalist of Kurtis' talent would be sought after by national news organizations. In 1982, Kurtis went to New York and a slot on "The CBS Morning News," where he worked with news star Diane Sawyer. He also hosted several documentaries for the network's "CBS Reports" series. But fed up with internal politics at the network's highest levels, Kurtis returned to Chicago just three years later. His new contract at WBBM provided not only a return as local news anchor, but also a chance for Kurtis to develop a series of hour-long documentaries.

Eventually Kurtis formed his own company, headquartered in Chicago and devoted to producing non-fiction television. "Kurtis Productions came about from a desire to 'save the hour documentary form' and pursue my own dream, which was to really get into long form television. That's what really motivated me to start my own company," Kurtis recalls. His timing for this venture was impeccable. In the mid-1980s, cable television was still a largely uncharted territory, eager for fresh approaches to programming. Today, Kurtis is a solid fixture at the Arts & Entertainment network, producing and hosting three nationally-acclaimed series.

Kurtis Productions' work for A&E has garnered numerous industry and journalism awards and, most important, provided a consistently intelligent alternative for television viewers. With his authoritative, senatorial voice, Kurtis serves as a guide to viewers, letting facts speak for themselves as each program unfolds. His "Investigative Reports" is a news-driven documentary series, examining problems and issues of the day. It was on "Investigative Reports" that Kurtis exposed the world to the shocking "home videos" of imprisoned mass murderer Richard Speck. This broadcast, in which Speck blatantly uses drugs, engages in sexual banter with a fellow prisoner, and brags about the party life behind bars,

Bill Kurtis on location in the Sinai Peninsula for the premier episode of "The New Explorers." (*Photo by Bill Arnold. Courtesy of Kurtis Productions, Ltd.*)

led to a major shakeup in the Illinois prison system. "American Justice," which looks at well-know crimes and trials throughout the 20th century, is a pet project of Kurtis. "I wanted to do [this series] because I'm a lawyer," said Kurtis. "I covered some pretty high profile trials back in the early 1970s, but I was never able to find a specialist spot and really take advantage of my legal education. 'American Justice' enables me to do that."

Finally, there is "The New Explorers." Originally a series for public television, the program has since moved over to A&E (though rebroadcasts on PBS will continue to the year 2000). Unlike Kurtis Productions' news and history-related series, "The New Explorers" "is just kind of following my curiosity," says Kurtis. Examining the world of science through documentary storytelling, Kurtis and his filmmaking crews have provided viewers with a fantastic array of narratives. The program has looked at a dolphin living in the waters off the Sinai Peninsula, delved into the research center of the National Cancer Institute, probed the interior of Bolivia's lush rain forests, and explored many other fascinating paths.

"The New Explorers" has been honored with the prestigious George Foster Peabody Award, won numerous film festival prizes, and earned several Emmy Awards. Most meaningful, however, is the impact the show has on education. Kurtis created the program as a teaching tool, using a documentarian's techniques to blow the dusty image off scientific research. "The New Explorers" has been a part of the Chicago public school curriculum since 1991 and has been picked up by other educational systems across the country.

Despite all his recognition throughout the country, Kurtis deliberately maintains his headquarters in Chicago. "Why Chicago? One reason is that it's a central location. The other reason is that for me Chicago has always provided a window to the world. That sounds like a Channel 11 slogan, but I mean it like this: with all our nationalities here we usually have someone directly connected to any hot spot in the world. You can usually see trends here and get to places easier from Chicago, I think, than from New York or L.A."

Another benefit for Kurtis is Chicago's solid work ethic. "You don't have the competition that you have in L.A. In New York, everybody's maneuvering for the next job. In Chicago, it's easier to just work at your craft. We don't have to worry about politics like in New York. We don't have to worry about the b.s. like in LA. We're here to work."

Kurtis Productions uses in-house talent to create programming and does not accept unsolicited work or résumés.

The Lakefront, Michigan Avenue, and Grant Park

➡ **NAVY PIER**
600 E. Grand Avenue

As an on-screen location, Navy Pier once ranked as Chicago's foremost seedy waterfront. Shoot-outs, drug deals, car chases, and murders have all been a part of this landmark site's movie history. With it's mid-1990s makeover, Navy Pier's cinematic representations have evolved from nightmare alley to dream date location. And with its enormous Cineplex Odeon IMAX Theater, this is also one of the best places in town to watch movies as they were meant to be seen.

The pier was designed by Charles Sumner Frost in 1914. After two years of construction, Municipal Pier (as it was originally known) opened as a recreational spot for Chicagoans. Complete with shopping, restaurants, and its dazzling Grand Ballroom, the city extended streetcar lines for the convenience of Pier visitors. During World War I, Municipal Pier was temporary home to numerous military recruits and Red Cross units. By the war's end, the Pier's status as a tourist spot was reinstated. A theater was opened, restaurants thrived, and the Pier even had its own streetcar line. Throughout the 1920s, it was a thriving center for Chicago culture and entertainment.

Renamed Navy Pier in 1927 as a tribute to Navy personnel who had served in the war, the pier also was used as a dock for freight and passenger boats. Though the stock market crash took its toll on attendance, Navy Pier remained open throughout the 1930s. By the end of the decade, however, fewer boats used this lakefront dock.

After the start of World War II, Navy Pier closed as a tourist site. It was leased to the United States Navy for training, which lasted through 1947. Two aircraft carriers were docked alongside the pier, and at one time a young Navy pilot named George Bush trained here.

Following the war, Navy Pier was used as a branch of the University of Illinois until Circle Campus was built in 1965. Some docking still went on, as well as occasional conventions and city festivals. For the most part, however, the Pier was underused until its rehabilitation in the mid-1990s.

The empty pier, while a ghost of its former self, was a filmmakers' paradise. The empty Grand Ballroom could serve as just about anything, from warehouse to soundstage, and the lengthy pier run was ideal for a variety of situations. Couple that with the wonderful skyline view and access to the lake, and Hollywood just couldn't resist.

The cops and robbers films *Thief* (1981) and *Running Scared* (1986), *Raw Deal* (1986), *Cooley High* (1975), and even the off-beat romantic comedy *Touch and Go* (1986) all staged some of their chase sequences here. The low-budget comedy *Monkey Hustle* (1977) also used Navy Pier for a few nefarious dealings.

Director Brian DePalma brought a Cadillac, a load of guns, and several twisted government agents to Navy Pier for *The Fury* (1978). The idea was to have good guys and bad guys blast away at each other, with the $11,000 Caddie taking a climactic plunge into Lake Michigan. The scene, while full of action, wasn't a complicated shoot until an unforeseen glitch appeared in the form of two news crews, eager to capture this wild chase for their own viewers.

What resulted was a war of camera crews. When asked to leave, a team of German news people graciously picked up their equipment and split. However, a local television outlet stayed, determined to grab some action footage for broadcast. Splitting from the pier for a boat dubbed "The Pizza King," the cameramen and reporter set up off-shore, waiting for DePalma to shout "Action!" Instead, the producer, Frank Yablans, ordered his people to flash high-powered movie lights at The Pizza King in order to ruin any television camera footage. Eventually the police marine unit was called in, sending The Pizza King and its passengers packing. Finally, after a delay of 45 minutes (which cost *The Fury* production some $2,250), the movie cameras rolled and the Cadillac was sent into the drink.

In *The Color of Money* (1986), director Martin Scorsese used Navy Pier for a different sort of shoot-out. The Grand Ballroom was transformed into an Atlantic City casino, where pool legend Eddie Felson (Paul Newman) faces his former protégé, table hustler Tom Cruise.

Meanwhile, Navy Pier was on the verge of rebirth. With the success of ChicagoFest in the late 1970s, the site was once more looked at as a viable cultural center. After some years of negotiation, the Illinois State Legislature authorized creation of the Metropolitan Pier and Exposition Authority. Under this consortium's leadership, Navy Pier underwent a $150 million redevelopment. When all was said and done, the Pier was brighter than ever. Now boasting an auditorium, a Ferris wheel, and a walkway of shops and restaurants, Navy Pier became one of Chicago's hot spots. The days of seedy waterfront filming were gone.

Hollywood's car chases and shoot-outs were replaced by film crews looking for Chicago "color." *Straight Talk* (1992), *I Love Trouble* (1994), and *Losing Isaiah* (1994) all shot scenes at the Pier. The television people came, too, as "ER" and "Chicago Hope" took breaks from their California hospital sets for location work at Navy Pier.

An opportunity to trod the boards where Julia Roberts or James Caan once walked is a good reason for some movie fans to come to Navy Pier. Another reason is to watch movies at the Cineplex Odeon Navy Pier IMAX Theater. One of two such theaters in Chicago (the other is at the Museum of Science and Industry, see p. 295), the IMAX screen and sound system are pure heaven. The gigantic screen is 87 feet wide and 62 feet high, roughly ten times of those puny sheets hanging up at your local mall theater. Images are projected at 48 frames a second, twice the speed of regular movies. The result is a picture of amazing clarity and size. Throw in the Omnimax's unmatched sound system and you have the ultimate in movie projection systems. The IMAX Theater is a division of Canada's IMAX Corporation, which won a Scientific and Technical Achievement Oscar for their breakthrough gizmos.

For more information about Navy Pier activities, call 312-595-7437 or visit their Web page at http://www.navypier.com. For tickets to the Cineplex Odeon Navy Pier IMAX Theater call 312-595-0090.

➤ LOWER WACKER DRIVE

Wacker Drive runs along the south bank of the Chicago River and provides a unique two-level street which comes in handy for drivers trying to negotiate downtown traffic. Though David Letterman once told a Chicago audience that "Wacker" was really his college nickname, this drive was named after Charles H. Wacker, a one-time president of the Chicago Planning Commission. The CPC was instrumental in developing Wacker Drive in the 1920s.

Be careful when you're on Lower Wacker. If we are to believe Hollywood, this underground drive is a haven for car chases. *Thief* (1981), *Primal Fear* (1996), and *Red Heat* (1988) are just some of the films that have exploited Lower Wacker's twists and turns for some action-packed excitement.

In fact, the *Red Heat* chase sequence ultimately led to a change in regulations for filmmakers using Lower Wacker. Before shooting a chase sequence involving a CTA bus, production team members hosed down Lower Wacker so it would have a wet look on screen. Wetting down a street is a popular practice for movies. Apparently the soaked pavement makes for a better street look, at least in the eyes of Hollywood. It's a case of artistic license and movie logic—city streets around the world never stay dry at night.

Unfortunately for the *Red Heat* crew, no one calculated how much oil and grit had accumulated over the years on Lower Wacker. When water hit the pavement, this dry gunk turned to slime, making for extremely dangerous driving conditions. During the first rehearsal of the film's chase sequence, the bus lost control on the slippery asphalt and went careening into a support column. To make matters worse, two minutes later a drunk driver picked the wrong time to head down Lower Wacker. The combination of a boozed-up motorist and street ooze were uncontrollable. The car smashed through a barricade and onto the film set. Though ultimately the chase sequence was filmed a few nights later, new rules were established forbidding filmmakers from ever again wetting down Lower Wacker.

Another terrifying Lower Wacker scene was in *Henry: Portrait of a Serial Killer* (1986). Tag-team killers Henry (Michael Rooker) and Otis (Tom Towles) pull over pretending to have car trouble. When a Good Samaritan stops to help, Otis pulls out a gun and murders the ill-fated benefactor.

→ **OUTER DRIVE EAST**
400 E. Randolph Street

This 40-story high-rise, built in 1963, is well-known for its ground-floor swimming pool, which is covered by a geodesic dome. Movies filmed at this unique poolside location include *Mickey One* (1965), *Medium Cool* (1968), and *Nothing in Common* (1986).

→ **THE STONE CONTAINER BUILDING**
150 N. Michigan Avenue

With its giant, mirrored diamond top sloping across the Chicago skyline, the Stone Container Building certainly isn't for all architectural tastes. Designed by A. Epstein and Sons, this unusually-designed building has been a part of Michigan Avenue's diverse scenery since the early 1980s.

Movie fans will instantly recognize the Stone Container Building for its climactic role in the slapstick comedy *Adventures in Babysitting* (1987). It was here that Elizabeth Shue's wild night came to its over-the-top, if just a tad unrealistic conclusion. Stick around after the closing credits—the film ends with a punchline atop this structure's sloping roof.

➡ CHICAGO CULTURAL CENTER
78 E. Washington Street

The interior boasts the world's largest Tiffany dome, elegant mosaics, marble staircases, and a fine collection of Civil War artifacts. The exterior resembles a palace, with tall columns, graceful arches, and sun-filled windows. Opened as the Chicago Public Library in 1897, the Chicago Cultural Center has been a favorite site of Hollywood filmmakers. This visually rich location has doubled as an opera house, a government building, a courthouse, and much more.

For more than 70 years, the building served as Chicago's central library. By the mid-1970s, however, the building had become too small for such a purpose. The holdings were moved to a book warehouse on North Michigan Avenue, and in 1991 the Harold Washington Library at State Street and Congress Parkway became their permanent home. As for the original library building, it was revamped as a performance and art space and dubbed the Chicago Cultural Center. Dance troupes, theater companies, lecturers, exhibiting artists, and many others provided a renewed energy to the stately architectural monument.

The moviemakers followed.

Code of Silence (1985) used the Cultural Center as an art gallery, where tough cop Chuck Norris follows a young woman to protect her from bloodthirsty mobsters. The building's Romanesque facade served as various New York City period buildings in *The Public Eye* (1992), *The Babe* (1992), the remake of *Miracle on 34th Street* (1994), and *Hoodlum* (1997). It's also been seen on the television programs "Early Edition" and "ER" and the British television film "March in the Windy City," where it housed a political rally for a nefarious office seeker. However, its period look, was best captured in Brian DePalma's gangster drama *The Untouchables* (1987),

The Tiffany dome in Preston Bradley Hall of the Chicago Cultural Center. (*Photo by Degnan/ Moloitis. Courtesy of the Chicago Department of Cultural Affairs.*)

where the Cultural Center doubled as an opera house.

If you want to retrace the steps of straight-jawed Elliot Ness (Kevin Costner) tracking down Capone henchman Frank Nitti (Billy Drago), head to the north staircase. Of course you won't be able to get to the roof, where Nitti took his fatal (and totally fictional) plunge, but head out to Randolph Street and you'll see where he went splat.

Once you're outside, take a look at the steps and dramatic entrance. Now imagine the space as seen through whirling camera angles, mixed film stocks, and a decidedly edgy point of view. That's what Oliver Stone did when he shot the frenzied courthouse scene of *Natural Born Killers* (1994) at the Cultural Center's north entrance, filling Randolph Street with a mob of star-struck fans, tabloid reporters, cops, and one smug, sunglass-festooned killer. As Woody Harrelson's psychopathic killer Mickey Knox declares to the camera, "You ain't seen nothing yet!"

For more information, call 1-312-FINE ART or visit their Web site at http://www.ci.chi.il.us/Tourism/See/CulturalCenter/.

➡ THE ART INSTITUTE OF CHICAGO
Michigan Avenue & Adams Street

In *Ferris Bueller's Day Off* (1986), Matthew Broderick leads girlfriend Mia Sara and hypochondriac pal Alan Ruck on a glorious tour of the Art Institute. Director John Hughes juxtaposes his cast with museum artwork, creating what amounts to a visual poem that sticks out amidst the rest of the film's controlled chaos. Best moments? A quiet kiss shared between Broderick and Sara, framed by the stained glass windows of Marc Chagall, and a stare-off between Ruck and Georges Seurat's *A Sunday on la Grande Jatte*, with Ruck becoming at one with the pointillist masterpiece. (This painting, the most popular attraction at the Art Institute, also inspired the Stephen Sondheim musical, *Sunday in the Park with George*.)

Founded in 1879 as the Academy of the Fine Arts, the museum's name was formally changed to the Art Institute of Chicago in 1882. Surprisingly, only one other feature film has taken advantage of the magnificent settings within the museum—the little-seen, independent film *Watch It* (1993).

For more information, call 312-443-3600.

➡ THE SCHOOL OF THE ART INSTITUTE'S FILM CENTER
Columbus Drive at Jackson Boulevard

Behind the Art Institute of Chicago is its famous school and the Film

Center. Established in 1972 as part of the School of the Art Institute, the Film Center is devoted to bringing audiences films from around the world and from all stages of cinematic history. Through screenings, lectures, discussions, and publications, the Film Center provides Chicagoans with an indispensable movie resource. If you're looking for the latest film from Iran or perhaps a Mary Pickford retrospective, the Film Center has what you're looking for. Internationally acclaimed figures sometimes attend screenings and answer audience questions in post-film discussions.

Festivals at the Film Center include an annual look at Iranian cinema, the Black Harvest International Film and Video Festival, and the Silver Images Festival, which examines how cinema views older adults and aging. (For more information on these festivals, see Appendix A on p. 323.) And lest you think this is a place for motion picture elitists, it should also be noted that for many years the Film Center was the only place in town to see the action-packed pictures of Hong Kong superstar Jackie Chan.

The School of the Art Institute has a distinguished list of alumni, including Ivan Albright, Georgia O'Keefe, Grant Wood, and Leon Golub. Also among the graduates are Tom Kalin, director of the 1992 drama *Swoon*, which was loosely based on the Leopold-Loeb murder case, and animator Tex Avery, head lunatic of the "Termite Terrace" cartoon division at Warner Brothers in the 1930s and 1940s (he later moved to Metro-Goldwyn-Mayer). Avery's enduring slapstick legacies include Bugs Bunny, Tom and Jerry, and television commercials for the insecticide "Raid."

For more information on the Film Center of the School of the Art Institute, call 312-443-3733.

➡ CHICAGO SYMPHONY CENTER/ORCHESTRA HALL
220 S. Michigan Avenue

If you want to catch one of the great orchestras of the world, head to South Michigan Avenue and the Chicago Symphony Center (formerly the Orchestra Hall Building). This magnificent concert hall, designed by D.H. Burnham and Company, first opened its doors in 1905. Home to the Chicago Symphony Orchestra, considered one of the finest classical ensembles in the world, the CSC also has a surprisingly rich movie history.

Next time you're attending an Orchestra Hall concert, close your eyes and imagine it's the early twentieth century. Suddenly the building isn't just a concert hall—it's an extraordinary movie palace. During the silent era, Orchestra Hall offered continuous cinematic and musical entertainment. For the price of a ticket, ranging from 10 to 25 cents, you could see a full-length feature, a travelogue, and a comedy short. The bill would be accompanied by Chicago Symphony musicians and even included pipe organ recitals between films. "A program of this magnitude has never been offered to Chicago," boasted a newspaper advertisement for the 1913 film *The Woman.* "A delightful bill of moving pictures and a really high class concert."[1]

On screen, the Symphony Center is one of the city's most neglected sites. Some films shot along Michigan Avenue provide a glimpse of the building and its entranceway, which is carved with the names of Bach, Mozart, Beethoven, and other composers. The only picture in recent memory to go through the doors and shoot inside is *Home Alone II: Lost in New York* (1992). Even then, Orchestra Hall didn't get to play itself—it doubled for New York's Carnegie Hall!

Then again, maybe Orchestra Hall's biggest impact on movie history is as flashpoint of inspiration for one Chicagoan, Harold Ramis.

Consider Ramis's extensive career, like co-scripting *Animal House* (1978), directing *Groundhog Day* (1993), and acting in pictures like *As Good As It Gets* (1997), while he fondly reminisces:

> When I was in high school I sang in the mixed chorus. I got chosen for an all-city chorus that sang with the Chicago Symphony Orchestra in Orchestra Hall. It was great. It gave me an experience of being on a big stage in a big setting and also through chorus I got to be an extra in the Lyric Opera. So I got to be on stage with some of the greatest singers in the world. Those kinds of experiences built my confidence, and Chicago has this reputation of being a city with muscle. I kind of borrowed that strength from that city's self-image. Filmmakers may have internal doubts but you need a certain confidence to say, 'okay, I'm going to direct that picture, give me that $45 million. I will spend it wisely.'

For more information on Chicago Symphony Center and the Chicago Symphony Orchestra, call the main switchboard at 312- 294-3333. For backstage tours, call 312-294-3100. You can also find out more by visiting their Web site at http://www.chicagosymphony.org.

[1] *Chicago Daily News*, September 3, 1913.

HAROLD RAMIS'S DREAM PROJECT
AN EPIC BIOGRAPHY OF EMMA GOLDMAN

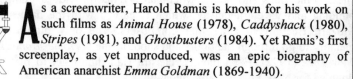

As a screenwriter, Harold Ramis is known for his work on such films as *Animal House* (1978), *Caddyshack* (1980), *Stripes* (1981), and *Ghostbusters* (1984). Yet Ramis's first screenplay, as yet unproduced, was an epic biography of American anarchist *Emma Goldman* (1869-1940).

Goldman was a powerful advocate for free speech, birth control, women's rights, the labor movement, and the anti-war movement surrounding World War I. Her activism took her around the country, blazing a trail for social justice. Goldman, a Russian-Jewish immigrant, was inspired to political action following the 1886 Haymarket Riot in Chicago.

Along with Alexander Berkman, Goldman's comrade in politics and life, she plotted the assassination of Henry Clay Finch, who made national headlines by using armed guards to suppress strikers at his Homestead, Pennsylvania factory. The plot failed and Berkman was sent to prison.

Goldman later became involved with Benjamin Reitman, the legendary "hobo doctor" of Chicago. A strong voice against conscription, she eventually was deported to Russia by J. Edgar Hoover. Disillusioned by the increased political repression that followed the Bolshevik Revolution, Goldman ultimately abandoned the Soviet Union for England.

Following her death in 1940, Goldman's body was brought back to the United States. She was buried outside of Chicago, in Forest Park's historic Waldheim Cemetery. In accordance with her wishes, Goldman was laid to rest near the monument of her political inspirations, the Haymarket Martyrs. Her former love, Ben Reitman, is also buried nearby.

And just how did one of America's premier comedy directors become interested doing a film on Emma Goldman? "I was working at Second City in 1969," said Ramis, "and I was always mouthing off about the Weather Underground and Days of Rage and the Chicago Seven. For a successful urban hippie, I had kind of a radical posture. Bernie Sahlins, Second City's producer, handed me an article, I think from the *Sunday New York Times*, and said 'you didn't invent this.' The article was about

Emma Goldman at 18 and her lover Alex Berkman at 19 attempting to assassinate Henry Fricke. I'm like, 'Wow!' They were living communally, she protested the First World War, counseled draft resisters. So I read Berkman's prison memoir, her autobiography, *Living My Life*, and I was amazed.

"I wrote a screenplay [about Goldman], I guess it was 1970 or '71. I wrote it in Europe and I sent it to Costa-Gravas [director of *Z* (1969) and *State of Siege* (1973)]. I was in London at the time and I tried taking it around to British production companies.

"It was no sale, of course. In fact, I sent it to one major studio and got a letter back saying 'these people may be your heroes but they're certainly not ours.'

"I'd love to [do the picture]. I've talked to Bette Midler about playing Emma Goldman and she was very interested. In fact, we went to Disney together. Talk about irony, pitching *Emma Goldman* to Disney! But I've always thought Helena Bonham-Carter could do it, there's so many actresses who could do it. Holly Hunter would be good. Emma was a small woman and a strong woman. Everyone knows the role."

For more information about this remarkable woman, check out The Emma Goldman Project at http://sunsite.berkeley.edu/Goldman/. Goldman's grave is located at Waldheim Cemetery, Forest Park, Illinois.

➡ **FINE ARTS BUILDING**
  410 S. Michigan Avenue

➡ **FINE ARTS THEATER**
  418 S. Michigan Avenue

Whether you're looking for historical inspiration or the latest in overseas cinema, the Fine Arts has what you're looking for. The building, designed by S.S. Beman, went up in 1884 on land owned by the Studebaker family. Originally used as a carriage factory, the building gradually changed focus with the beginning of the 20th century. Artistic-oriented clients rented rehearsal and studio space throughout the newly-renamed "Fine Arts Building." Supposedly L. Frank Baum wrote some of his *Wizard of Oz* books in an office he rented here; at the time he was also on the payroll as a scenarist for Selig Polyscope, which filmed the earliest screen versions of Baum's *Oz* stories. Another important tenant was the Little Theater, a dramatic group which was harbinger to Chicago's modern off-Loop theater community.

The Fine Arts later housed a theater named after the building's original owners. For many years, the Studebaker Theater was a venue for live performances, before switching over to movies. The theater fell into disuse in the 1960s and for a time served as an outlet for pornographic films. Happily, in 1981, this changed when the auditoriums were overhauled and the theater was re-christened the Fine Arts.

Though the management has changed hands over the years, the Fine Arts' reputation has grown among local movie mavens. Now housing four theaters, this is one of the only places in town that routinely books new foreign films, American independent features, and documentaries.

To find out what's playing at the Fine Arts, call 312-939-3700.

➡ THE AUDITORIUM THEATRE
50 E. Congress Parkway

➡ ROOSEVELT UNIVERSITY
430 S. Michigan Avenue

Officially opened by President Benjamin Harrison on December 9, 1889, the Auditorium Building is a historical work of Chicago architecture designed by the team of Dankmar Adler and Louis Sullivan. At the time of its construction, the Auditorium was Chicago's tallest building and was one of the first multi-purpose constructions to be wired for electrical lighting. Theater-goers also had the option of staying a while—the top floors housed hotel rooms and a restaurant.

Following the stock market crash of 1929, the Auditorium fell into disuse and disrepair, finally closing its doors in 1941. During World War II, soldiers in transit were housed at the Auditorium and the stage, designed for perfect acoustics by Adler, was turned into a GI bowling alley! Once the war ended, the building was acquired by the newly-founded Roosevelt University. Though much of Adler and Sullivan's work was maintained throughout the entire building, the actual theater remained shut. Restoration of the Auditorium proved too costly for the fledgling educational facility.

In 1960, however, a consortium was formed to bring the Auditorium Theater back to its former glory. Three million dollars and seven years later, the theater doors were reopened as a performance venue. Going to the Auditorium today is like stepping, ever briefly, back in time. Sullivan's refurbished sweeping staircases and gorgeous mosaics are still awe-inspiring, recalling a grand era when this theater was Chicago's cultural mecca.

With its consummate nineteenth-century design, the Auditorium has

The exterior of the Auditorium
Building c. 1890 (*above*) and the lobby
of the Auditorium Hotel c. 1890 (*left*).
(*Photos by J.W. Taylor.*) The balcony
of the Auditorium Theatre (*below*)
during the building's 1960s restoration.
The balcony slopes at a steep 41 degrees.
(*Photos courtesy of Bart Swindall at the
Auditorium Theatre.*)

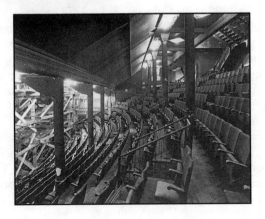

done a fine job for filmmakers who need a period look. *Gaily, Gaily* (1969), Norman Jewison's cliché-ridden adaptation of the memoirs of Chicago journalist Ben Hecht, shot a few scenes in the upper balconies. "...If nothing else in the film had moved me," wrote *New York Times* film critic Vincent Canby, "I still would cherish Jewison's careful recollection of old Chicago scenes and his use of the interior of the Auditorium Theater, one of this country's most beautiful."[1]

The Joan Jett and Michael J. Fox rock musical *Light of Day* (1987) shot some footage here, as did the Joe Mantegna comedy *Baby's Day Out* (1994) and the syndicated television remake of "The Untouchables" (1993-94). Around the corner on Michigan Avenue, be sure to stop in Roosevelt University. The school's magnificent lobby and lush Sullivan staircase doubled for the Lexington Hotel, home to gangster king Al Capone, in the big-screen version of *The Untouchables* (1987).

If you'd like to take a tour of the Auditorium Building, call either Roosevelt University at 312-341-3555 or the Auditorium Theatre at 312-431-2354.

[1] Canby, Vincent, "Movie Based on Hecht Book Begins Its Run," *The New York Times* (December 17, 1969).

➡ **COLUMBIA COLLEGE**
　　600 S. Michigan Avenue (Main Building)
　　1415 S. Wabash Avenue (Film and Video Department)
　　72 E. 11th Street (Getz Theater)
　　4730 N. Sheridan Road (Dance Center)
　　623 S. Wabash Avenue (Brunswick Building)
　　624 S. Michigan Avenue (Torco Building)

Founded in 1890 as the Columbia School of Oratory, Columbia College has been around Chicago even longer than the movies. Originally begun as a school for women's speech studies, today Columbia offers a multi-faceted arts curriculum including undergraduate and graduate programs in fiction writing, dance, theater, graphic design, advertising, public relations, photography, and journalism. What's more, with more than 1,700 students enrolled in its Department of Film and Video, Columbia College ranks as the world's largest film school.

The film schools at New York University, UCLA, and USC are more high profile, but Columbia College alumni have developed a solid reputation in Hollywood. Janusz Kaminski, who won an Oscar for his cinematography on Steven Spielberg's *Schindler's List* (1993), graduated from Columbia. So

Columbia College has produced many actors, filmmakers, and directors, including Janusz Kaminski, Declan Quinn, George Tillman, Jr., Bob Teitel, and Theodore Witcher. (*Courtesy of Columbia College.*)

did George Tillman, Jr. and Bob Teitel, the writer/director and producer behind *Soul Food* (1997). Another recent Columbia grad, Theodore Witcher, hit it big with *love jones* (1997). Declan Quinn (actor Aidan's brother, by the way) did the dream-like cinematography for the critically-acclaimed *Leaving Las Vegas* (1996), Peter Teschner edited *Doctor Dolittle* (1998), *Howard Stern's Private Parts* (1997), the HBO film "The Late Shift" (1996), and *The Brady Bunch Movie* (1995), all of which were directed by another former Chicagoan, Betty Thomas. John McNaughton, director of *Henry: Portrait of a Serial Killer* (1986) took classes here too. And these are just some of the better known Columbia students.

"We now are turning out so many high profile alumni that we forget about the artisans and the crafts people," says Ric Coken, assistant chair of the Columbia Film and Video undergraduate division. "We started as a small film school in order to stimulate the creative mind, not technology. But you have to know the technical end if you want to succeed."

"We are really here to find the filmmaker," Coken adds, noting that Columbia students intern on film and television productions throughout the area, including major Hollywood features. "Our students come well-versed in technology and understand what the end product should be," he says.

The Columbia faculty includes many film professionals with significant professional credits in directing, cinematography, editing, producing, sound, and other areas of specialization. International filmmakers often come in for a semester or two, providing cinematic perspectives of different cultures.

Such well-known figures as Spike Lee and Michael Apted have given guest lectures, and successful alumni periodically return to give current students an added incentive. (Interestingly enough, when the film school was in its infancy, Herschell Gordon Lewis taught movie production classes at Columbia.)

Though the Film and Video department has produced a healthy share of working professionals, Columbia graduates from other disciplines have also made their mark in the film and television industry. Most notable are television actors Andy Dick and Isabella Hofmann, as well as Andy Richter, the sidekick on the NBC talk show "Late Night with Conan O'Brien."

For more information about Columbia College, check out their Web page at http://www.colum.edu/.

George Tillman, Jr. & Bob Teitel
The Phenomenon of *Soul Food*

On the weekend of September 28, 1997, the lives of George Tillman, Jr. and Bob Teitel, two Columbia College film school graduates, changed forever. Their film *Soul Food* (1997), which Tillman wrote and directed and Teitel produced, opened at theaters nationwide. Made for $7.5 million, small change by Hollywood standards, *Soul Food* hauled in $11.1 million worth of tickets over that three-day period.

This nationwide take was good enough for second place at the box office. First place went to another new film, *The Peacemaker* (1997) a $50 million budget thriller produced by Steven Spielberg's DreamWorks SKG studio. Starring George Clooney and Nicole Kidman, *The Peacemaker* brought in $12.3 million. One week later, *Soul Food* was the top box office draw in the country and *The Peacemaker* punched in at number two. In a business that's often run by the bottom line, the made-in-Chicago *Soul Food* proved itself a dollar-for-dollar champ. And suddenly Tillman and Teitel were the hottest things in Hollywood.

Tillman, an African-American from Milwaukee, and Teitel, a Jewish kid from Arlington Heights, first met as film students at Columbia College. "I lived in the dormitory at Roosevelt University and so did Bob," says Tillman. "Then we both took the same production class and

Writer/director George Tillman, Jr. (*left*) and producer Bob Teitel (*right*) on location for *Soul Food*. Tillman and Teitel worked together on film projects while students at Columbia College.
(*Photo courtesy of State Street Pictures.*)

that's when we started working together." By the time Tillman and Teitel were seniors, the duo had established a solid working relationship. Teitel handled the business and producing end of the partnership, while Tillman did the writing and directing. Their first film, *Paula*, was Tillman's senior thesis film.

Made for $12,000, which the enterprising duo raised themselves, *Paula* was about a 17-year-old single mother who wants to continue her education beyond high school. Shot in the Uptown area, the film ended up winning six national awards including the Student Academy Award and recognition from the Black Filmmakers Hall of Fame.

With the success of *Paula*, Tillman sat down to write his next screenplay, a feature-length film called *Scenes for the Soul* (1993). Containing a tapestry of stories, the film intermingled characters and situations with different scenes set on the North, South, and West sides of Chicago.

"We used *Paula* as a vehicle to raise money for *Scenes for the Soul*," says Teitel. "We raised $150,000 between 44 different people—everyone from plumbers to stockbrokers. We shot in 1993 and it took us a year for post-production before the film was finally done."

What happened next is the kind of stuff Hollywood legends are made of. With just $400 in their collective pockets and a copy of *Scenes for the Soul* on a video cassette, Tillman and Teitel drove out to Los Angeles in November 1994. "We'd never been to California," says Teitel. "George and I stayed at a friend's house, and we knew one person who knew one person who knew someone at the William Morris Agency. We were fortunate enough to show *Scenes for the Soul* to them and they liked it.

"About a week later we were signed by William Morris and a month later, on December 23, 1994 we sold the film to Savoy Pictures for $1 million."

Savoy went bankrupt in 1995 and the film was never seen. Down, but not out, Tillman and Teitel remained determined. Tillman wrote a new script, a family drama he called *Soul Food*. "I got the ideas from my family in Milwaukee, the Sunday dinners and family dinners that we had," said Tillman. "The get-togethers at my grandmother's, how important and influential she was on the family, how she kept everybody together. I wanted to make a film about that."

"We were supposed to do George's script with Savoy," said Teitel, "but after that fell apart we got it out of Savoy and had a deal to make it for a couple million dollars for a small production company. Since we were tied with William Morris, we were always looking for a soundtrack. Some people suggested we show it to Babyface for just a possible soundtrack."

Kenneth "Babyface" Edmonds is one of the music industry's hottest talents, having won numerous Grammy Awards for both his singing and producing. When he saw Tillman's script, Babyface realized he wanted to do more than the film's soundtrack.

At the time, Babyface and his wife, Tracey E. Edmonds, were starting their own film production company through the auspices of Fox 2000 Pictures (a division of 20th Century Fox). Having just produced the soundtrack album for the movie *Waiting to Exhale* (1995), the Edmonds were looking for the right vehicle to get their company started. Serendipity ensued when the *Soul Food* script crossed their desk. "They felt like this would be a great first project for them to do," says Teitel. "We met in June 1996 and on November 6 we started shooting."

With the Edmonds' connections, it wasn't hard to get Vanessa L. Williams or Vivica Fox signed on to the cast. Next was Chicago-based actor Irma P. Hall. "We were huge fans of Billy Bob Thorton's film, *A Family Thing* (1996), which starred Irma," said Teitel. "Once we saw that movie we knew without a doubt that she was *Soul Food's* Mother Jo."

Still, getting *Soul Food* up and running the way Tillman and Teitel wanted wasn't an easy task. "Originally they didn't want me to direct the film because my first film didn't come out and they didn't know anything about me," says Tillman. "But we stuck to our guns. I knew I could always raise the money independently if I had to. They gave in and then they wanted to shoot the film in Los Angeles. I wanted to shoot the film in Chicago. I didn't know anything about Los Angeles neighborhoods. I feel comfortable in Chicago and I held out again."

"Shooting in Chicago is the only way we would make the film," added Teitel. "They didn't want us to shoot in Chicago and we said we were going to walk and we did. For a couple of days *Soul Food* was off because of that.

"Finally," says Tillman, "they gave in to shoot in Chicago. I wanted to stick to my guns and do what I believe in and it worked out to our advantage. We gave them the final script in August and two months later we had production.

"Everything just happened so fast, I didn't have time to think about it. I was a little intimidated beginning to work with Vanessa L. Williams, Vivica Fox, and Michael Beach. They had the most experience. But they were the coolest people. Vanessa was the coolest person I ever worked with in my entire life. She listened to everything I said and was just great. No one really questioned the things I was doing. They knew it was my story. It was the type of project where everything really clicked together."

"Chicago was completely accommodating," says Teitel. "A lot of people we went to school with worked on the set as the crew. There were a lot of familiar faces. I can honestly say that they actually looked out for us in a way that I don't think they would have looked out for anybody else."

"It wasn't an easy shoot. It was a 36-day shoot, six days a week with an ensemble cast and a little kid who could only shoot nine hours a day and he was in nearly every scene. It probably should have been a 40-some-odd-day shoot but we had to finish by Christmas time. And you know Chicago in November and December! Everybody was sick. George at one time had a 105° temperature and they had to put an IV in his arm."

Returning to Los Angeles, Tillman and Teitel worked hard to put the film together. "Early on," says Tillman, "when I saw the first cut, I was worried about what I had. I just felt like, 'God, I've got a piece of shit here! It's just people talking!'

"Then we had two test screenings and we scored around 95 to 98 out of 100 on the testing, which is as high as Fox ever had. Everyone was just clapping, a big applause, and I felt really good. That made me actually start feeling better, that we had a really good chance to make some money."

Soul Food was a huge success and for good reason. The film is an insightful look at family life, honestly portraying the whole gamut of emotions that bubble to the surface when crises strike. The actors comprise one of the best ensemble casts in American cinema since Philip Kaufman's *The Right Stuff* (1983) Williams, Fox, Long, Hall, Beach, Phifer, and youngster Brandon Hammond work well together—their warmth for one another radiates from the screen. Watching *Soul Food* you really believe these characters are a family.

By January 1998, *Soul Food* brought in $43.4 million at the box office, making it a certifiable hit. The home video release was also a best seller, as was the soundtrack album.

Now a true Hollywood success story and operating on their own terms, Tillman and Teitel have a two-year deal with Fox. The duo, through their production company State Street Pictures, remains committed to producing the same kind of quality films they made as students.

"I think everything that George writes, because he writes what he knows, will always be done in Chicago," says Teitel. "Of course, if we find a script that takes us somewhere else, we'd have to do that, but if we had a choice I'd live there right now and shoot there all the time. I still have a home in Chicago. I get back as often as possible."

➡ THE BLACKSTONE HOTEL
636 S. Michigan Avenue

Built in 1909, the Blackstone Hotel was designed by Benjamin Marshall and named after Timothy Blackstone, a Chicago railroad magnate whose mansion once stood at this site. The hotel is 22 stories tall, with a three-story limestone base.

The Blackstone has particular historical significance in the annals of American politics. In 1920, when the Republican Convention whooped it up in Chicago, top honchos locked themselves in Suite 804-805, lit their cigars, and debated over who would be their party's next presidential nominee. When the team finally emerged, Warren G. Harding was their anointed candidate and "the smoke-filled room" became part of the American vernacular.

There is also some notoriety to the Blackstone. Many years ago, there was a murder in a room which today is permanently closed to guests. Rumor has it this killing was a gangland hit. The victim wasn't so eager to shed his mortal coil and stuck around to haunt the joint. Strange things supposedly happened to anyone who stayed in the room. In fact, New York mob boss Lucky Luciano refused to stay at the Blackstone whenever he was in town because of this specter.

When the film *Hoodlum* (1997), which featured Luciano as a major character, was looking for 1930s period locations, a location scout checked out possibilities at the Blackstone. He asked to take pictures of this room and hotel officials reluctantly allowed him. The scout, however, was warned that his photographs of this room probably wouldn't turn out. When the pictures were finally developed, a strange white blur appeared in every image.

The tourist theater crowd aren't the only out-of-towners who like the Blackstone. Hollywood filmmakers have been using this classic old hotel for quite some time. Andrew Davis, a hometown boy made good, came here for *Above the Law* (1988) and *The Package* (1989). *Only the Lonely* (1991), *Rent a Cop* (1988), *The Babe* (1992), and *My Best Friend's Wedding* (1997) also used the Blackstone, as did the television series "Early Edition."

The hotel's elegant Crystal Ballroom was used for some scenes in the offbeat satire *The Hudsucker Proxy* (1994). The same ballroom was the site of the exuberant dance scene in *love jones* (1997). This charming romantic tale marked the directorial debut of Theodore Witcher, a graduate of Columbia College, which is just down the street.

The Blackstone also stood in for an Atlantic City hotel for Martin Scorsese's *The Color of Money* (1986). It's here where the cute but dumb pool hustler, played by Tom Cruise, checked in while waiting for his chance to play in a major national tournament.

For reservations at the Blackstone Hotel, call 312-427-4300.

➡ CHICAGO HILTON AND TOWERS
720 S. Michigan Avenue

Designed by the firm of Holabird and Roche for hotelier James W. Stevens, this Chicago landmark was once the largest hotel in the world. When it opened its 3,000 guest rooms in 1927, the Stevens Hotel (as it was first named) boasted such amenities as an 18-hole rooftop golf course complete with real grass, a private library with more than 25,000 books, a five-lane bowling alley, an indoor ice rink, a 27-seat barber shop, and a 1,200-seat theater featuring the latest in "talking picture equipment."

In 1942, as part of the war effort, the Stevens was purchased by the United States Army for a mere $5 million, a real bargain considering that construction alone cost $30 million. By 1945, the hotel had changed hands again and took on the name of its new owner, Conrad Hilton. Significant renovations reduced guest rooms to 2,200 and later to 1,543, but the hotel lost none of its glamour. Over the years, the Hilton added a pair of Imperial Suites, a fully-equipped athletic room, an International Ballroom, and five restaurants. In 1985, at a cost of $185 million, the hotel was completely renovated for modern standards and re-christened the Chicago Hilton and Towers.

The Hilton and Towers was featured in the opening scene of *Primal Fear* (1996), where Richard Gere makes his entrance at a Catholic Charities event. It doubled as New York's Plaza in *Home Alone II: Lost in New York* (1992), providing a home away from home for Macaulay Culkin. Julia Roberts shared a claustrophobic moment in Hilton elevators with Cameron Diaz in *My Best Friend's Wedding* (1997). The hotel has also been featured in the syndicated television remake of "The Untouchables" (1993-94) and *The Fugitive*'s sequel *U.S. Marshals* (1998).

Director Andrew Davis first used the Chicago Hilton and Towers in *The Package* (1989). Shot in the midst of a brutally cold Chicago winter, Davis staged an outdoor rally across the street on the edge of Grant Park, where protesters decried a visiting Soviet premier. This scene was shot on one of the coldest days of the year, with a biting wind-chill sweeping off the lake.

The Package also featured the hotel's Grand Ballroom as the site of a presidential dinner. A magnificent 12,640-square-foot space, the Grand Ballroom is trimmed with 22-karat gold leafing, original frescoes, and crystal chandeliers.

Davis revisited the Grand Ballroom in *The Fugitive* (1993). It was here where wrongly convicted Dr. Richard Kimble (Harrison Ford) burst in on shocked conventioneers and untangled Dr. Charles Nichols' (Jeroen Krabbe) twisted trail of corporate corruption and murder. The hotel then transforms into an action-packed labyrinth as Ford, Krabbe, and lawman Samuel Gerard (Tommy Lee Jones) dovetail into a thrilling chase through the Hilton and Towers' promenade roof, elevator shaft, and laundry room.

While there's some deliberate confusion amidst the sheets, steam, and flying metal I-beams of the climactic laundry room sequence, the crates labeled "Palmer House" shouldn't throw sharp-eyed viewers. No, the sequence wasn't shot at different hotels and then edited together. Rather, the elaborate Chicago Hilton and Towers laundry takes up three stories of the hotel, making it one of the largest industrial laundries in the country. Not only does this facility handle the many sheets slept on by Hilton and Towers guests, they also take in wash from the nearby Palmer House Hilton at State and Monroe.

To book a room, make dinner reservations, or inquire about banquet facilities at the Chicago Hilton and Towers, call 312-922-1400 or 1-800-HILTONS.

➡ **GRANT PARK**
Michigan Avenue between Randolph Street and Roosevelt Road

Stretching roughly from Randolph Street on the north to Roosevelt Road on the south and bordered by Michigan Avenue and the lake, Grant Park's scenic beauty is another of those great places that visually declares "Chicago and nowhere else" on screen. With its wide assortment of summer music programs at the Petrillo Bandshell (Columbus Drive and Jackson Boulevard), the annual Taste of Chicago foodfest in July, and acres of park space, Grant Park provides filmmakers with a rich diversity of settings. To the west, Chicago's downtown buildings majestically rise and the panoramic view at sunset can't be beat.

For a historical viewpoint, check out Haskell Wexler's *Medium Cool* (1969). Shot documentary style in the midst of the controversy surrounding the 1968 Democratic Convention, *Medium Cool* accurately portrays the madness of the time as members of the Chicago Police Department brutally confront Vietnam War protesters.

Joe Mantegna, Joe Pantoliano, and Brian Haley tromped through the park in their hapless kidnapping efforts in *Baby's Day Out* (1994), while Demi Moore and Rob Lowe pitched woo and softballs here in *About Last Night...* (1986). The latter film, a romantic comedy based on David Mamet's acerbic play, *Sexual Perversity in Chicago*, was originally scheduled for a summer production. "The play ends with Jim Belushi's character describing girls on the beach," said co-screenwriter Denise DeClue. "By the time we were shooting it was fall and we couldn't do beach. So we decided to do softball in Grant Park. The production company had to put leaves on the trees because all the real leaves had already fallen."

The Petrillo Bandshell, the center of Chicago's annual Fourth of July fireworks show, was the site of an explosion-filled declaration of personal independence by everyone's favorite 12-stepper, Stuart Smalley (Al Franken), in *Stuart Saves His Family* (1994). The bandshell can also be seen in the slight, yuppie coming-of-age picture, *Windy City* (1984).

Studs Terkel on *Medium Cool*

"And there's the moment when Jonathan Hayes, the associate producer, shouts 'Look out Haskell, it's real!' "
—Studs Terkel on *Medium Cool* (1969)

During the filming of *Medium Cool*, director and native Chicagoan Haskell Wexler turned to Studs Terkel for advice on Chicago neighborhoods. "I knew Haskell from when he was going to Francis Parker High School," Terkel recalls. "He'd been away for awhile and he wanted certain things [in the movie]. I showed him different things here and there, certain people that he met. I was sort of his cicerone you might say, I was his guide around town...but Haskell's so good he would have done it without me.." Regardless, Wexler expressed his gratitude by giving Terkel screen credit as "Our Man in Chicago."

Medium Cool is a landmark film, shot in the midst of the turmoil surrounding the 1968 Democratic Convention. The scanty plot follows television cameraman Robert Forster (seen in 1997's *Jackie Brown*) and his soundman Peter Bonerz (who later became familiar to audiences as "Jerry the dentist" on the Chicago-based television sitcom "The Bob Newhart Show") as they examined the societal chaos of the times. In the process, Forster meets Verna Bloom, an immigrant from Appalachia now living in an Uptown apartment with her 13-year-old son.

What gave the film its sense of immediacy was the documentary-style shooting and incorporation of footage from inside the International Amphitheatre where the Democratic Convention was held. Wexler heightened the realism by actually shooting scenes in the middle of the Grant Park riots. Bloom wore a bright yellow dress during filming, which was a stark contrast to the dark colors worn by the Daley cops as they squared off against the Yippies and their followers.

"Nelson Algren said that never has he seen such a scene with the fusion of reality and fantasy together," says Terkel. "The yellow dress... the mother running through [the riots], as an actress, an actress running through a scene...in which an actual scene is occurring at that moment.

"It wasn't a documentary in that sense. This is an actress playing a role in a plot, such that it is, with an actual moment and the cops beating the crap out [of people] and the actress is seen in it running through, which is a remarkable moment, I think. And there's the moment when

Jonathan Hayes, the associate producer, shouts 'Look out Haskell, it's real!' You have a crazy combination of Haskell doing a documentary at the same time he wants a story line. I've never seen anything quite like it before.

"I find it tremendously exciting. Haskell himself...he is unique. He's a marvelous cinematographer, he's a committed man, of course...but that isn't it, either. He's a certain kind of revolutionary, in the good sense—revolutionary in technique. He'd done something no one quite did before."

➡ **BUCKINGHAM FOUNTAIN**
Congress Parkway and Lake Shore Drive

Buckingham Fountain, located on the eastern edge of Grant Park, is one of the city's splendors. Modeled after the Latona Fountain at Versailles, this memorial display of shooting water and colored lights was dedicated on August 26, 1927 by Chicago socialite Kate Buckingham in honor of her late brother Clarence. The basin holds 1.5 million gallons of water, and 133 jets can blast up to 14,000 gallons per minute through the fountain.

Nia Long and Larenz Tate shared a sweet moment at Buckingham Fountain in *love jones* (1996). Shot on a fog-shrouded night, the fountain provides an ethereal backdrop as the two lovers nuzzle in the mist. It's one of the most romantic scenes in any Chicago movie.

For a less idyllic view, consider the popular Fox Television sitcom "Married With Children." The opening credits of this obnoxiously funny, Chicago-based series began with the Buckingham Fountain shooting water high in the air to the sounds of Frank Sinatra's hit "Love and Marriage." The weekly tales of Al and Peg Bundy and their two children, Bud and Kelly, brutally savaged sitcom family stereotypes and was a surprise hit that lasted for ten seasons, from 1987 to 1996. "Married With Children" wasn't just popular with Americans: foreign viewers, particularly German audiences, were enthralled by the show. (In fact, a "Married With Children" ring of Internet sites exists on the World Wide Web, with pages available in English, German, and Swedish.) In 1994, when World Cup soccer came to Chicago, city tourist officials quickly learned to steer TV-mad European visitors to Congress Parkway and Lake Shore Drive, where they could make a pilgrimage to what is known overseas as "Bundy Fountain."

Buckingham Fountain is open from May 1st through October 1st. The water shoots up from 11:00 a.m. to 11:00 p.m., with colored light displays every night from 9:00 to 11:00 p.m.

NATIVE SON (1950 & 1986)

Richard Wright's 1940 landmark novel of a young African-American caught in a trap between social forces and his own deadly mistakes has been filmed twice. The first version, made in 1950, starred Wright himself as his anti-hero Bigger Thomas; the second, released in 1986, featured Victor Love in the role.

Native Son is an emotionally-charged story, fueled by racism, classism, radical politics, and sexuality. Hollywood, circa 1950, clearly wasn't ready for such powerhouse material. Yet European director Pierre Chenal was a great admirer of the book and was determined to capture it on film. Wright himself was enlisted by Chenal to play his fictional creation, though the author was much too old for the part. Though the majority of the production was shot in Argentina, Chenal did some location work in Chicago, the setting of *Native Son.*

The film's opening sequence includes shots of the Wrigley Building, Buckingham Fountain, State Street, and the legendary Riverview amusement park. Chenal contrasts these shiny exteriors with the bleak world of Chicago's South-Side "black belt," where Bigger lives with his family. Ultimately, this first version of *Native Son*, while ambitious, falls well short of its good intentions. Still, it remains an interesting, if flawed, historical curio and worth the price of a video rental.

The second screen version of *Native Son* was made as part of the Public Broadcasting System's "American Playhouse" series. Released theatrically before appearing on PBS, this *Native Son* boasts a strong cast: Matt Dillon as the radical Jan, Elizabeth McGovern as Mary Dalton, Carroll Baker as Mary's Mother, Geraldine Page as the Dalton's maid, Oprah Winfrey as Mrs. Thomas, and newcomer Victor Love as Bigger. In a small role, as one of Bigger's buddies, was Ving Rhames, who would develop into a powerful film actor with his role as mob boss Marcellus Wallace in Quentin Tarantino's *Pulp Fiction* (1994).

While the ensemble works well together, the script unfortunately was much less than the sum of the cast's collective talents. At some points the film lurches unevenly from scene to scene. Choppy transitions also work against the compelling nature of the story.

The 1986 *Native Son* did make good use of Chicago locations to achieve a 1930s period look. Scenes of Bigger's neighborhood were shot around the 6300 blocks of South Martin Luther King Drive and South Greenwood. In contrast, the opulence of the Dalton's lifestyle was captured in the Hyde Park area. Some scenes were also shot in Logan Square, around the 3100 block of West Logan.

The Dalton residence was located at 49th Street and South Drexel. A gothic-style mansion, designed in a similar style to many of the buildings at the neighboring University of Chicago campus, this house is actually the living quarters for a group of Serbo-Croatian Greek Orthodox priests.

➡ **LAKE SHORE DRIVE**

Starting at 5700 North, where Sheridan Road and Hollywood Avenue connect, and heading south to 67th Street, Lake Shore Drive offers a spectacular view of both Lake Michigan and the city's skyline, taking drivers past universities, posh condominiums, museums, beaches, Navy Pier, and much more. During the day, it's an entertaining drive (as long as it's not rush hour), but at night its a spectacular panorama of Chicago's light and color. Needless to say, Lake Shore Drive is a very attractive location for filmmaking.

If you want to see what the Drive has looked like over the years, head to the video store. One of John Wayne's few non-Westerns, *Brannigan* (1975), featured the Duke as a Chicago cop who ends up tailing some bad guys to England. Though the local scenes barely last five minutes, the opening credits feature a ride down the long-gone "S" curve. *Medium Cool* (1969) also gives a glimpse of the "S" curve, as well as other parts of the Drive in its opening credits, as the camera follows a motorcycle courier rushing news film to a television station.

Because of its uninterrupted length, the Drive is ideal for movie chases. The grand finale of *The Blues Brothers* (1980) begins its downtown demolition derby at a stretch of the Drive along McCormick Place. LSD also was the starting point for the high-octane chase sequence in *Risky Business* (1983). Driving his dad's purloined Porsche, containing high-priced call girl (Rebecca DeMornay) and his very nervous friend Miles (Curtis Armstrong), future enterpriser Joel Goodson (Tom Cruise) leads pissed-off pimp Guido (Joe Pantoliano) on a wild ride extending all the way to Highland Park. "I don't believe this," moans Armstrong. "I've got a trig mid-term tomorrow and I'm being chased by Guido, the killer pimp."

Apparently the Drive has an attraction to North Shore movie teens with heisted parental automobiles. The indomitable Ferris Bueller (Matthew Broderick) "borrowed" a red Ferrari from the father of his neurotic friend Cameron (Alan Ruck), then picked up girlfriend Sloan (Mia Sara), and enjoyed an energetic drive up and down the Drive in *Ferris Bueller's Day Off* (1986). Had they been there a few years earlier, the intrepid trio might have seen one of LSD's more unusual movie sites: a gun-toting, bicycling priest in the action-packed *Three the Hard Way* (a.ka. *Three Tough Guys*) (1974), which featuerd a threesome of a different sort: Jim Brown, Fred "The Hammer" Williamson, and Jim Kelly.

Still, the real winners of Hollywood's "how to creatively use Lake Shore Drive" derby inevitably belongs to *When Harry Met Sally* (1989) and *My Best Friend's Wedding* (1997). Native Chicagoans couldn't help but smirk when University of Chicago graduates Billy Crystal and Meg Ryan leave the campus on a road trip for New York City and somehow wind up several hundred blocks out of their way as they cruise south along North Lake Shore Drive. It may have been an unexplained bad turn on the part of the characters, though director Rob Reiner undoubtedly wanted to capture the scenic skyline of North LSD.

My Best Friend's Wedding's cinematic reconstruction of the Drive is even more blatant. In one sequence Julia Roberts is seen entering the northbound lanes of LSD near McCormick Place, then pulls off the Drive in the southbound lane around Delaware Street. Just how Roberts was able to pull off this incredible maneuver is probably best left to a bemused Chicagoan's imagination.

➡ **THE FIELD MUSEUM OF NATURAL HISTORY**
Roosevelt Road and Lake Shore Drive

Founded during the Colombian Exposition in 1893, the Field Museum of Natural History has been a versatile location for filmmakers. *The Package* (1989) utilized the building's Romanesque columns as a stand-in for a government building in Washington, D.C. *Music Box* (1989) and *She's Having a Baby* (1988) also featured scenes at the Field Museum, as did *Continental Divide* (1981). In this preposterous, but amiable romantic comedy, a Mike Royko-like columnist, played by John Belushi, succumbs to his romantic side by confronting his former lover, visiting lecturer and naturalist Blair Brown.

A fine example of Chicago geographical movie magic begins at the

Field Museum in the 1996 feature *Chain Reaction*. Keanu Reeves begins a chase sequence on the second floor of the Field Museum, then dashes through the airline exhibit of the Museum of Science and Industry before ending up back at the Field. How Reeves gets from Roosevelt Road to 57th Street and back again so quickly is one of *Chain Reaction*'s biggest mysteries.

The biggest Field Museum production is the surprise 1996 box-office hit *The Relic*. Based on a novel by Douglas Preston and Lincoln Child, *The Relic* turned the Field Museum into a veritable spookhouse, complete with labyrinth hallways and staircases, slamming doors, icky bugs, and one vicious monster with a taste for human brain matter holed up in the tunnels beneath the museum.

The producers looked at six other cities, before settling on the Field Museum. "[The Field Museum] was exciting because of what it could offer to us as filmmakers," recalled *The Relic*'s producer, Sam Mercer. Not only was Mercer impressed with the Field's look and layout, "There's also such an image walking up to [the museum] by itself, isolated out there. It's kind of laid out for the camera."[1]

The Relic, a good, old-fashioned monster movie, involves a series of mysterious and gruesome murders taking place in the Field Museum's basement. Meanwhile, in the research halls on the upper floors of the museum, Penelope Ann Miller and Tom Sizemore run around liked crazed ferrets, desperately trying to terminate the devouring dervish.

With all the carnage that takes place in *The Relic*, it's amazing to see that the Field Museum survived intact. This was a case of movie set designing at its best. The two-floor interior of Stanley Field Hall was recreated on Paramount studio soundstages, as was much of the third-floor laboratory facilities and other behind-the-scenes spaces. Observant viewers will notice the famed elephants of the Stanley Field Hall have been replaced in *The Relic* with a pair of giraffes. Though there are other subtle differences, the imitation museum is an almost perfect facsimile of the Chicago facility.

Much of *The Relic*'s action takes place in the coal tunnels beneath the museum. Those tunnels are part of the elaborate system beneath the downtown area, originally created to transport coal and haul away ashes from downtown buildings. Forming something of a dark, underground maze, the tunnels became an indelible part of Chicago lore on April 13, 1992. Construction work near the Kinzie Street Bridge ruptured the wall of the tunnel system, causing a massive subterranean flood.

It's these tunnels where the brain-sucking monster makes its Chicago home. Again, much of the tunnel system was recreated on Hollywood soundstages, though some filming was done in underground passages

The actual Tsavo lions that killed and devoured 140 bridge workers in East Africa in 1898—as depicted in the 1996 film *The Ghost and the Darkness*—are on display at Chicago's Field Museum. (*Photo by George Papadakis. Photo courtesy of The Field Museum.*)

beneath City Hall.

The Relic was another case where Hollywood reality created some confusion for Chicagoans. For movie purposes, the Field Museum was temporarily renamed "The Museum of Natural History." Then, as part of the movie set, the Field Museum hung banners announcing its upcoming, totally fictional *Superstition* exhibit. While a non-show can be explained to bewildered patrons over the phone, the phalanx of police cars, fire equipment, and helicopters surrounding the Field Museum for the film's climax was another story. The city handled numerous calls from people concerned about the seeming emergency situation unfolding at Roosevelt Road and Lake Shore Drive!

There is one more movie connection to be found at the Field Museum. In 1924, the museum acquired the skins and skulls of two African lions killed in the late 1890s by Lieutenant Colonel John Henry Patterson. During construction of a railway bridge across the Tsavo River in East Africa, these lions went on a rampage, killing almost 140 workers. The area was evacuated by terrified villagers, and construction was halted until the lions could be tracked down and killed. Patterson's efforts to stop the lions was documented in the 1996 feature *The Ghost and the Darkness*, with Michael Douglas starring as Patterson.

The film ends with a narrator telling viewers: "If you want to see the lions today, you must go to America. They are at the Field Museum in Chicago, Illinois. Even now, if you dare lock eyes with them you will be afraid."

For information, call 312-922-9410 or visit their Web page at http://

www.fmnh.org./.

[1] Dretzka, Gary, "Unnatural History: The Friendly Field Museum is Transformed into the Menacing Setting of a New Monster-From-Hell Movie," *Chicago Tribune Sunday Magazine* (May 19, 1996).

South Loop

➡ **OLD VAN BUREN STREET**
Van Buren Street between State Street and Clark Street

Take a walk down Van Buren Street between State Street and Clark. It's an impressive stretch of downtown, with its clean streets right in the shadow of the Harold Washington Public Library at State and Congress.

It doesn't seem that long ago that downtown along Van Buren was a haven for cheap bars and single room occupancy hotels. Down and outers roamed the streets—guys like Joliet Jake and Elwood Blues. Before Van Buren cleaned up its act, the street's down-and-out look was a favorite among Hollywood filmmakers.

One of the most popular locations on the strip was the Stag Hotel. This cheap, men-only flophouse was the home of Dan Aykroyd and John Belushi in *The Blues Brothers* (1980). With its proximity to the El tracks, the Stag Hotel was ideal for a great comic setup. The production rented a pair of CTA El cars, then played with them like a giant train set. As Aykroyd stared out his window, the El zips back and forth to the point of absurdity. Look carefully next time you watch *The Blues Brothers* and you'll notice those train cars are sans passengers.

When *The Blues Brothers* was done shooting, Belushi took a can of shaving cream and signed his name on the wall of Jake and Elwood's supposed room. No one wanted to touch this unique autograph and ultimately the shaving cream petrified into a rock-hard signature. When the walls of the Stag Hotel came tumbling down in the late 1980s, Belushi's wall-sized autographed ended up as part of the rubble.

The Stag was where Kirk Douglas holed up while searching for his missing son in Brian DePalma's misfired horror film, *The Fury* (1978). John Travolta was also a movie Stag resident. In *Angel Eyes*, a.k.a. *Eyes of an Angel* (1991), a forgettable flick made before his *Pulp Fiction* (1994) career rebirth, Travolta played a single father down on his luck and living at the Stag. His daughter befriends an abused dog, a turn of events which eventually leads Travolta out of Chicago.

The Big Town (1987), a look at illegal gambling in the 1950s and *A Night in the Life of Jimmy Reardon* (1988), William Richert's autobiographical film starring the late River Phoenix, were two other films that captured the decadent beauty of Van Buren's squalor. Both productions were in Chicago during the fall of 1986 and ended up shooting on Van Buren during the same week.

➡ PACIFIC GARDEN MISSION
646 S. State Street

The Pacific Gardens Mission has been around for more than 120 years, helping Chicago's homeless population through pastoral counseling while providing food and shelter. You can often see people lined up outside the Mission building waiting for a hot meal and a comforting word.

In the science fiction-horror comedy *The Borrower* (1989), Organic Theater actor Tom Towles waits outside the Pacific Garden Mission with other homeless men. Though undoubtedly they all have tales to tell, none could rival that of Towles's character. It seems Towles' head was ripped from his body and slammed onto the neck of an alien creature. Now the creature, outfitted with this former Organic Theater actor's noodle, roams the streets until he can find another head worth grabbing.

For information on the Pacific Garden Mission, phone 312-922-1462 or check out their Web site at http://www.pgm.org/.

➡ FILM ROW
800 S. Wabash Avenue to Wabash and 15th Street

Once upon a time, this strip of South Wabash—now part of the Burnham Park neighborhood, was a hotbed of wheeling and dealing for film exhibitors in the lucrative Midwest markets. During its heyday between the 1920s and the 1940s, theater owners would run from building to building, looking for the latest Hollywood features, cartoons, and newsreels. Posters and press materials, movie projectors, candy and popcorn for the concession stand, screening rooms, and even a place to repair damaged films could all be found along this hustler's paradise. The mile-long string of offices was affectionately known by its denizens as "Film Row."

All the major studios, including Paramount, Metro-Goldwyn-Mayer,

Columbia, and Warner Brothers had offices along the strip. Carl Laemmle, who got his start as a movie exhibitor, moved up to distribution by taking an office on the 800 S. Wabash block. Calling his business the Universal Film Distribution Company, Laemmle eventually pulled up stakes and moved out West to make the product himself. His new company, Universal Pictures, eventually rented an office along Film Row, this time to peddle their own films.

With over one million theater seats to fill throughout the Midwest, owners of theaters ranging from downtown movie palaces to small-town houses flocked to Film Row (or "The Avenue," as it was also known). Naturally, parties on both the distribution and exhibition end wanted the best deal they could get for their money. Competition was fierce, so it wasn't unusual to see bargains being struck on the sidewalk. Why let a theater owner venture into someone else's office when you could sell your movies right on the street? In the 1950s, companies like American International Pictures, which specialized in juvenile delinquent and cheap horror films, ruled the roost along Film Row. During this era, David F. Friedman, who later partnered with Herschell Gordon Lewis on many exploitation features, got his cinematic start working for a film distributor on South Wabash.

With the changing face of the neighborhood in the 1960s, however, the cacophony of Film Row was eventually muzzled. As South Wabash degenerated into a crime-infested area, studio representatives scattered to safer parts of the city.

Today, the neighborhood is on a roll, with fashionable stores taking root along the block. The presence of Columbia College, including, ironically, its new film school facility at 1415 S. Wabash, has given old Film Row a new luster.

➡ **THE COMMUNITY FILM WORKSHOP OF CHICAGO**
1130 S. Wabash Avenue, Suite 302, Chicago, IL 60605

Budding filmmakers will find a friendly home at the Community Film Workshop of Chicago (CFWC), a vibrant institution that's been around since 1971. Originally funded in part by the American Film Institute and the Chicago Office of Economic Opportunity, the CFWC provides hands-on film training at bargain prices.

This is a great place to learn all aspects of the film and video arts, from scripting to post-production. Aesthetics and film history classes are also available, as are summer programs for high school students. And if you become a member of the CFWC, you'll have access to low-cost equipment rental, sound transfer, and 16mm editing facilities.

The CFWC is committed to putting cameras into the hands of all Chicagoans, regardless of age, education, or background. Over the years, graduates of the program have gone on to success in commercial and independent filmmaking careers.

For more information about the Community Film Workshop, call 312-427-1245 or contact them by e-mail at CFWChicago@aol.com.

➡ **THE ROOSEVELT HOTEL**
1152 S. Wabash Avenue

Looking for a place to stay but can't afford the ritzy downtown hotels? If you're really strapped for cash, you might consider the Roosevelt Hotel, a cheap, single room occupancy establishment.

Despite its lack of amenities, the Roosevelt has been a popular place for movie characters. Matt Dillon stayed here in *The Big Town* (1987). In *Primal Fear* (1996), a scuffle broke out at the Roosevelt between defense attorneys and a possible eyewitness to murder.

Perhaps the most improbable use of the Roosevelt Hotel was in *Straight Talk* (1992), a dimwitted romantic comedy starring Dolly Parton. Playing a hopelessly cheerful Southerner trying to start her life over in Chicago, Parton books a temporary room at the Roosevelt while on her way to fame and fortune. Though the joint has seen its share of down and outers over the years, hosting Dolly Parton on the skids was probably something of a first for the hotel.

One of the many riders in *Chicago Cab* (1998) was also a Roosevelt Hotel resident.

NORTH

INDEX OF ARTICLES

The City

→ NORTH AVENUE BEACH
1600 N. Lake Shore Drive

One of the most popular lakefront gathering spots in the summertime, this is also a favorite site with film and television producers. *About Last Night...* (1986) and *End of the Line* (1987) both had scenes here, as did episodes of "Chicago Hope," "Crime Story," "ER," and "Amerika," the 1986 television mini-series about a Soviet takeover of the United States. Even the party-happy programming of MTV has brought its cameras to North Avenue Beach.

Lou Gilbert began his journey through Chicago after emerging from North Avenue Beach in *Goldstein* (1965). Brian DePalma also took advantage of this lakefront location in his laughably awful thriller *The Fury* (1978). Look quickly among the extras as teen-aged Amy Irving strolls along the North Avenue Beach bicycle path: James Belushi, then a fledgling member of Second City, can briefly be spotted in the crowd.

→ AMBASSADOR EAST
1301 N. State Parkway

Simply put, the Ambassador East is one of Chicago's premier movie sites. It's a place where, if your timing was right, you were apt to bump into Cary Grant, either on the set of Alfred Hitchcock's escapist thriller *North by Northwest* (1959) or perhaps dining in the hotel's fabled Pump Room.

The hotel opened its doors in October 1926. Originally built as a swanky residential and travelers' hotel, the Ambassador East was nearly out of business some six years later when the Depression deeply cut into owner Ernest Byfield's profits. Fortunately, the end of Prohibition and revamping of the hotel's sister building, the Ambassador West, brought this elegant building back from the brink of disaster. The addition of the Pump Room in 1938 sealed the hotel's status as a place for people to see and be seen.

Taking his cue from the spa in Booth Tarkington's novel *Monsieur Beaucaire*, Byfield hired Chicago architect Sam Marx to design a unique dining spot. The result was the Pump Room, an almost ethereal restaurant with crystal chandeliers, murals, blue sapphire walls, and white leather booths. From its opening day, with wait staff wearing scarlet swallow-tails and feathered head pieces, the place was a hit.

In the 1930s and 1940s, movie stars traveling between New York and Hollywood routinely had a three-hour layover in Chicago. Eager to exploit this high-profile clientele, Byfield arranged for personalized limousine service to shuttle celebrities from Union Station to the Pump Room. As a result, the Pump Room quickly became the Chicago restaurant of choice for many famous names. While the celebrities sat along the eastern portion of the restaurant, captivated movie fans took up the western side for food and the opportunity to watch screen idols eat.

Anybody who was anybody was automatically seated in the Pump Room's legendary Booth Number One. This highly coveted seating was established by Gertrude Lawrence, who was starring in the play *Susan and God* at the time of the Pump Room's opening. For 90 evenings straight, Lawrence held court at Booth Number One following each performance.

Booth Number One has seen a veritable who's who of celebrity grace its seats. John Barrymore, Judy Garland and Liza Minnelli, Humphrey Bogart and Lauren Bacall, Jack Benny, Natalie Wood, Lassie, Joan Crawford, Zsa Zsa Gabor, Cary Grant, Mickey Rooney, Frank Sinatra, and Ronald Reagan are just a few of the many Booth Number One guests. During the filming of *The Sting* (1973), Robert Redford and Paul Newman spent every lunch at Booth Number One, never varying from a menu of ham sandwiches washed down with Pilsner.

After Byfield's death in 1950, the hotel passed through a series of hands until finally bought by the Omni Corporation in 1986. The Pump Room also changed ownership more than once and spent 22 years with Chicago restaurateur Rich Melman's Lettuce Entertain You Enterprises. In 1998, the restaurant was bought and remodeled by a Texas-based corporation.

On the big screen, Room 463 of the Ambassador East was where Cary Grant, having survived an attack by a machine gun-wielding crop duster, catches up with Eva Maria Saint in *North by Northwest* (1959). The hotel played a pivotal role in *My Bodyguard* (1980). This charming, coming-of-age story featured Chris Makepeace as the son of the Ambassador East's live-in manager, comedian Martin Mull. Stealing the show was Ruth Gordon as Mull's eccentric mother, who provided unending trouble for the hotel's staff and guests. The Ambassador East also pinch-hits as a Los Angeles hotel for the traveling Chicago Cubs in *Rookie of the Year* (1983). The Pump Room has been in its share of films as well, including the moment where shy cop John Candy introduces girlfriend Ally Sheedy to his inflexible mother in *Only the Lonely* (1991) and the first date between Dolly Parton and James Woods in *Straight Talk* (1992).

To book Room 463 or any other room at the Omni Ambassador East, call 312-787-7200. Dinner reservations at the Pump Room can be made by calling 312-266-0360.

➡ THE FORMER SITE OF EDWIN G. COOLEY VOCATIONAL HIGH SCHOOL (*COOLEY HIGH*)
1225 N. Sedgwick Street

Though the building has been torn down, this address was once the location of Edwin G. Cooley Vocational High School, the inspiration for the 1975 comedy *Cooley High*. Starring Lawrence-Hilton Jacobs, Glynn Turman, and Garrett Morris, *Cooley High* depicted the lives of inner-city high school kids, circa early 1960s.

The film was based on the life of screenwriter Eric Monte, a former Cooley High student who grew up in the nearby Cabrini-Green housing project. Monte, who moved to California after serving in the military, wrote for the television sitcom "Good Times," which was also based in Cabrini-Green. *Cooley High* served as inspiration for another sitcom, "What's Happening."

➡ CABRINI-GREEN
Division and Halsted Streets

The Cabrini-Green housing complex is a case of good intentions gone horribly wrong. Originally built in 1942, this public housing project was intended to provide cheap apartments for Chicago's poor. It was named after Mother Cabrini, a nun later elevated to sainthood for her work with the underprivileged. In 1962, the Chicago Housing Authority added another set of buildings to the area, the William Green Homes. Consequently, the complex became known as Cabrini-Green.

Over time, the Cabrini-Green housing project has become synonymous with gang crime and drugs. The apartments are poorly maintained by the CHA and elevators are constantly breaking down. Though originally meant to help the city's underprivileged, Cabrini-Green has become a testament to urban despondency.

Yet there are glimmers of hope in this ghetto, existing in pockets beneath Cabrini-Green's ugly facade. The Cabrini Connections Film Festival provides children living in the complex an opportunity to make and publicly exhibit their own videos. This on-going project gives the young filmmakers hands-on experience in writing, directing, photography, and editing as they work with production professionals from around Chicago.

One such film, *The Real Cabrini* by Jimmy Biggs, won first place for documentary at the 1997 Chicago Children's Film Festival.

In February of 1994 independent director Joel Goodman brought a camera crew to shoot rock videos for the Slick Boys. This trio of Chicago cops, Eric Davis, Randy Holcomb, and James Martin use rap music as a way of connecting with kids and offering an alternative to the uglier sides of Cabrini. "When we were out there shooting," says Goodman, "Cabrini-Green residents came up to us, rapping positive lyrics and it was an incredible sight to see. It was 15 below, but everyone came out, eyes wide open to see in their backyard an independent production using some of their own residences. It really gave these young kids hope that there's something more out there than the problems of Cabrini-Green." These videos have taken the positive message of the Slick Boys to nationwide television and have been shown on "Nightline," "Oprah," Black Entertainment Television, and in other venues.

Hollywood has also come to Cabrini-Green. The 1970s CBS television sitcom "Good Times" was set here and featured shots of the housing complex in the opening credits. More recently, the pre-*Hoop Dreams* (1994) basketball drama *Heaven is a Playground* (1991) made extensive use of Cabrini-Green locations.

The cult horror film *Candyman* (1992) was likewise shot inside the housing complex. In this low-rent thriller, an anthropologist studying urban legends makes her way through the elaborate tunnel system of the ominous Cabrini-Green towers. These tunnels were actually carved out by gang members, who bashed their way through the walls of vacant apartments.

➡ CHICAGO FILMMAKERS
1543 W. Division Street, Chicago, IL 60622

Whether you are interested in highly personal, non-commercial movies, want to learn more about the filmmaking process, or need to rent equipment, Chicago Filmmakers has what you're looking for. Founded in 1973 by three students from the School of the Art Institute, the organization has grown into one of the city's most important resources for independent filmmakers.

Filmmakers offers Chicagoans an alternative to the usual commercial fare of your local multi-screen commercial theater complex. Through their Kino-Eye Cinema, Filmmakers provides a local outlet for short experimental films, avant-garde work, and documentaries. They also do co-presentations with other local film entities, including the School of the Art Institute, the Goethe Institute, and Facets Multimedia. One of Chicago Filmmakers' most important contributions to the local movie scene is their sponsorship of

"Reeling: The Chicago Lesbian & Gay International Film Festival." (See Appendix A on p. 323 for more information).

Classes at Filmmakers cover a wide range of cinema production, including sound, editing, screenwriting, producing, and camera work. Selections range from one-night seminars to full ten-week courses. Equipment rental and editing facilities are also available for non-commercial moviemakers. Additionally, Chicago Filmmakers has membership options and volunteer opportunities for everyone from students to professionals to plain old film lovers. Membership privileges include discounts on class tuition and supplies, equipment access, special rates for a wide variety of movie magazines, and, perhaps most important, technical consulting on film projects from the talented Filmmakers staff.

For more information, contact Chicago Filmmakers at 773-384-5533. Their Web site address is www.chicagofilmakers.org, and they can be reached by e-mail at programming@chicagofilmakers.org.

JIM SIKORA

"The stories I'm interested in seem to seep up out of the ground here. In Los Angeles they have to bring the water in, here we have to keep the water at bay. We're in a swamp and it's very rich."

Spend a day with Jim Sikora and you'll get a hyperactive lesson in movie history. His mind is a nimble encyclopedia of film—Sikora knows the directors, the stories, the shot compositions. Visit his apartment and chances are there'll be a movie playing on the VCR and Sikora will want to know what you think. Movies are as important to him as life itself, with a passion for cinema that recalls the famous film appetites of French director Francois Truffaut or American director Martin Scorsese. "My approach to film," Sikora says, "is I genuinely love movies."

Sikora got hooked at an early age, inspired as a child after his father took him to see Stanley Kubrick's *2001: A Space Odyssey* (1968). It set off a creative spark, burning into his brain the notion that anything was possible through the movies. Storytelling, artistic expression, psychology, entertainment—all were vital parts of what movies could be.

That's reflected in Sikora's work. His features, made independently on lower-than-low budgets, include *Walls in the City* (1994), *Rock and Roll Punk* (1998), and the edgy *Bullet on a Wire* (1996). Sikora, like so many filmmakers of his generation, learned how to make low-budget films as a kid playing around with Super 8-millimeter films.

"In grade school," Sikora recalls, "I was doing stuff for years. Someone gave my folks a crappy, used GAF Super 8 camera. I would smuggle it out of their closet and walk around just looking through it, not with film. I had a paper route and saved up money so once in a while I would actually buy film and load it in there and shoot. The light meter battery was fucked up, so my film was all overexposed.

"I read about this technique about taking India ink and painting on film, so I took the overexposed film and started doing stuff like that and projecting it and seeing how it would turn out. I'd get these fragmented mosaics. You could do anything with this format. You could take it, cut it up, put it back together, just geeky, art manipulation."

Following high school, Sikora took a few college courses, then joined the Army and ended up stationed in Germany. He took his love for film with him. Getting a hold of a Super 8 camera, Sikora started hanging out with local skinheads and started shooting. Naturally, this was in defiance of military regulations. The resulting film, *Drool*, recorded a day in the life of these alienated neo-Nazis: running around, hanging out, and shooting dope at a Nuremberg stadium where Adolf Hitler once addressed thousands.

After being discharged, Sikora jumped into film school at Columbia College, got bored, and dropped out. He figured he'd learn more making films on his own without having to pay a lot of tuition. Once more, he picked up the Super 8 camera and started shooting.

"Super 8 was an affordable medium that was 'film' as opposed to video," said Sikora. "If you can manipulate Super 8 you can work in any other medium as far as controlling film. I think most filmmakers now don't go to Super 8, they go right to video. It kind of undermines the term 'filmmaker.' There's no film involved.

"Back in the early 1980s, when I got started, video tape was cheaper, but Super 8 film was still an option to artists and novice filmmakers. It was a cheap option and still affordable. Maybe you had to sacrifice rent money or lunch money or steal film or whatever. But it was film!

"Still, today, digital technology, digital video, nothing beats film. I'm glad I learned how to shoot on film. I really fell in love with shooting film and the idea of film because really, by and large, it hasn't changed in over 100 years."

Sikora gradually developed a reputation as Chicago's "King of the Super 8s." He even went as far as to book the Three Penny Theater on North Lincoln Avenue for a group show of kindred spirits working in this small format. His work was described as edgy and raw, but one thing was for certain: the boy had talent. And while he wasn't going through regular distribution channels, his work was getting screened.

While working as a phone solicitor for the Goodman Theater, Sikora hooked up with performance artist Paula Killian. Killian's dark humor and intense stage presence instantly clicked with Sikora. He proceeded to cast her in *Walls in the City* (1994), a trilogy of stories in which Killian plays the lead female in all three sections. *Walls in the City* featured a virtual who's who of Chicago's cutting-edge art scene from the early 1990s. David Yow of the band Jesus Lizard, artist/actor/writer Tony Fitzpatrick, and the late, great poet Lori Jackson all had roles, as did Bill Cusack, a member of Chicago's premier acting family.

The film looked at life in Chicago's underbelly: dirty bars, cheap apartments, and low-rent liquor stores. Contrasting these almost clichéd images of poverty chic, Sikora shot endless, haunting footage of the city's downtown glamour. The squalor of the streets becomes the walls for gleaming downtown.

With less than an hour's running time, Sikora clearly had matured as a story teller, while losing none of his ragged sensibility.

"One of my ideas about film is the intersection of documentary and narrative fiction," he says. "You picture yourself at an intersection, only take away the traffic signals where you have these wonderful accidents. That's how I consider my work, specifically at that intersection as opposed to a well-regulated intersection. I like working with non-actors, free-improvisation."

That attitude helped considerably with Sikora's next film, *Bullet on a Wire* (1996). Taking a cue from his days at the Goodman, Sikora's first full-length feature, shot in black-and-white, revolved around a telephone solicitor involved in the shadier ends of the business. Jeff Strong plays Raymond, a lumbering, bald-headed loner. Desperate to connect with the outside world, he takes records from the women's clinic his sister (Killian) works. Raymond calls the home of one patient and falsely informs her parents that the young lady is pregnant and HIV positive. From there, *Bullet* spirals out into an intense study of people living on the fringe of society.

Originally budgeted at $30,000, Sikora only managed to raise five grand for the production. Rather than wait until he had the complete nest egg, Sikora simply went ahead and made the film with what he had.

Jim Sikora, local independent filmmaker (*above*).
Jeff Strong in *Bullet on a Wire*, an edgy exploration of people living on
the fringe of society and Jim Sikora's first full-length feature (*below*) .
(*Photos by Jim Alexander Newberry. Courtesy of Jim Sikora.*)

"We had to reduce the shooting schedule," he says. "Ideally, I wanted to shoot over 20 days, but I reduced it to seven. Exponentially, if you multiply the final budget times 20, it comes out to roughly the same. I just had to work that much harder to get things done in seven days as opposed to 20 days. Same thing, only you really have to have your shit together, I guess, and be a slave driver and know what you want.

"It wasn't easy. Logistically, we had a lot of problems, a lot of tough maneuvers. I had to be a real field marshal with the crew and coax the actors. It was harder on the crew. The actors weren't aware of how hard I was on the crew. At one point the crew almost mutinied halfway through the week. But then I won their affection; we finished it and we were sad when it was over. At least most of us were!"

A lesser filmmaker might have thrown in the towel working under these conditions. The minuscule budget also forced Sikora into some expense-cutting creative decisions. Forced to find a set in a hurry for the telephone solicitor headquarters, Sikora ended up filming in the basement of an animal hospital.

"Those cages just worked out wonderfully. I don't think a set designer could have done a better job. You know, the telemarketers were in cages, imprisoned, defined by their job. So what appeared to be a limitation we made work for us. I think that's part of using what you have. To most people it's 'omigod, we can't do that,' but you make those limitations work for you. Limitations allow you to be more creative."

Another of *Bullet's* low-rent sets was a newly built lock-up at 29th and California. Shooting in this pristine, unopened jail is another example of Sikora's chutzpah and unwavering approach to moviemaking. "It just happened that they just built the place and the population wasn't in there," he said. "So we had a window of time of one week, ironically during the time that we were shooting. We had a $100 million set at our disposal. We called and asked and they said 'okay.' "

The completed *Bullet on a Wire* belies its limitations. The film is a muscular piece of work, delving headfirst into a nightmare world. Yet it's not without a few laughs; indeed, Sikora's sense of humor in *Bullet* plays like a cinematic version of dark Franz Kafka jokes.

"I didn't need to spend $100,000, $200,000, $500,000 to do *Bullet*," says Sikora in retrospect. "Although it looks like we spent money on it, we didn't. The reason it looks that way is because we don't suck. We did our homework."

As *Bullet on a Wire* makes its way around the festival circuit, Sikora's reputation is building. The film was the closing selection for the 1997 Chicago Underground Film Festival. It also played the Munich Film

Festival, South by Southwest Film Festival, Slumdance (an alternative to Robert Redford's Sundance festival), the Fort Lauderdale Film Festival, the New York Underground Film Festival, and the Rotterdam International Film Festival. Most recently, *Bullet* played at the prestigious Anthology Film Archives in New York, where it earned Sikora alternating high praise and bad reviews throughout the Manhattan print media.

Though Sikora is now getting some overdue respect in the film world, he remains a steadfast Chicagoan. "Why leave?" he says. "Number one, I was born here. The stories I'm interested in seem to seep up out of the ground here. In Los Angeles they have to bring the water in; here we have to keep the water at bay. We're in a swamp and it's very rich. There's a lot of history here and my roots go very deep. I was born here, I have a lot of identity here.

"I think you have to grow and the only way to grow is to support others you believe in but not to come under this pretension of saying 'this is the community.' It has to happen organically. You cannot force this thing to happen. You cannot force a movement."

For information on ordering Sikora's films on video, contact Provisional Films at 307-742-3418 or fax them at 307-742-3047.

➡ **CELLULOID MOVIE BAR**
1805 W. Division Street

Looking to share a champagne cocktail with the denizens of Casablanca? How about a vodka martini (shaken, not stirred) with 007? Then head to the Celluloid Movie Bar, a popular nightspot that features nightly flicks with your drinks. The movie theater-like seating of Celluloid is a great place to have an adult beverage and enjoy movies projected on a large video screen. Seeing films here is definitely more of an interactive experience than your standard movie house, however. Bar patrons have been known to cheer the good guys, boo the bad guys, and recite dialog in unison with on-screen performers. Films at Celluloid range from cult favorites like *Caddyshack* (1980) and *Dr. Strangelove* (1964) to recent box office attractions.

Another great reason to check out Celluloid is the bi-monthly screenings devoted to Chicago's independent scene. On the first and third Monday of each month, the bar shows films made by local talent. There's no cover charge on these nights, which provide a wonderful opportunity to see what the local filmmaking community is all about.

To find out what the Celluloid Movie Bar is playing, call 312-707-8888.

➡ MILWAUKEE , NORTH, & DAMEN AREA—WICKER PARK

These three streets converge to form one of the city's busiest corners in the thriving Wicker Park neighborhood. Once upon a time, this area was the stomping grounds of writer Nelson Algren; today it's home to an attractive mix of pierced punks, artists, yuppies, and the vestiges of a once-thriving Latino community. Restaurants, galleries, funky little coffee shops, music stores, bars and clubs dot the area, though operations come and go, changing names and management with surprising regularity.

Maybe that on-going change has something to do with this area's uncanny popularity with movie companies. One area-location scout recalled a three-week period in which the short-lived television series "EZ Streets," the pilot show for TV's "Early Edition," another television pilot called "For the People," and the movie *Michael* (1996), starring John Travolta, all shot scenes in this Wicker Park area. *Soul Food* (1997) and *love jones* (1997) are also recent films to use the neighborhood environs as a background for dramatic action.

In *Red Heat* (1988), made before the area was a hip-happening mecca, Soviet cop Arnold Schwarzenegger and wiseguy Chicago detective James Belushi followed some bad guys

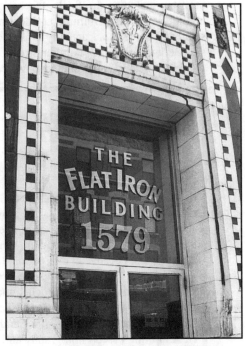

The Flat Iron Building (1579 N. Milwaukee Avenue)—home to art galleries and office space—has been used as a background for several movies, including *Red Heat* and *Blink*. (*Photo by Holly Pluard.*)

through this area holing up in their car just outside the Flat Iron Building,

1579 N. Milwaukee Avenue. The Flat Iron Building, which normally houses art galleries and office space, became an apartment building in *Blink* (1994), home to Madeline Stowe's character.

Perhaps the most ingenious use and non-use of the Milwaukee/North/Damen area was at the end of *Michael*. In this charming fantasy film, John Travolta plays a fallen, chain-smoking, pot-bellied angel. Found living with Jean Stapleton in an Iowa farmhouse, Travolta is brought back to Chicago by William Hurt, Andie MacDowell, and Robert Pastorelli, three reporters for an *Enquirer*-like tabloid. At the film's end, Travolta and Stapleton dance a merry waltz in the well-known streets of this Wicker Park neighborhood.

Or do they?

Watching the finished product, it's hard to argue that *Michael* ends anywhere but in the Milwaukee/North/Damen area. Though about a third of the film, including the finale, takes place in Chicago, the production spent about nine weeks filming at locations throughout Texas. The ending sequence of *Michael* actually was shot in Austin, Texas. The downtown skyline and seemingly familiar streets of Chicago were added to the scene thanks to the miracle of computer-generated backgrounds.

"Basically, *Go Fish* completely, radically changed my life and gave me a career."
—Guinevere Turner, writer/producer/actor, *Go Fish*

Girl meets girl. Girl loses girl. Girl gets girl. On the surface, *Go Fish* is a charming, sweetly sexy date movie. Yet this comic lesbian romance, shot on a less-than-bare-bones budget in the creative environs of Wicker Park, surprised the independent film community, to say nothing of its creators, and became an international hit.

The film began as a creative project between University of Illinois-Chicago alumnus Rose Troche and her significant other, Guinevere Turner. "We were going out," said Turner. "Rose had just graduated [from UIC] and I had graduated from Sarah Lawrence in New York. She had a BFA in Film/Video/Photography and I had my little, useless Bachelor's of Arts degree—not useless, but not practical. We just started talking about how we wanted to make a film together. I said, 'well let me write something and you can shoot it.' At that point it was an idea for a 15-minute film. The more we talked about it and the more we talked to other people, it just sort of grew to the point of becoming an hour long and we said, 'hell, if we're going to make an hour long movie, why not just make a feature?' "

Through a network of friends, Troche and Turner found Ann Rosetti, a local cinematographer, "who was happy to suffer through the whole process with us for free," says Turner. "We shot it on weekends and after work. I would come home to my apartment, which would be full of c-stands and wires and everything, make the phone calls and make sure the food was coming and get in front of the camera." In addition to co-writing and co-producing *Go Fish* with Troche, Turner also played one of the two romantic leads.

"All together we shot for about 45 days, but that was over a two-year period," Turner recalls. "It started out [with us] buying film stock, which is like 60 bucks for 12 minutes of black-and-white film. When we had film, the rest of the [production] was very much thanks to the Chicago university system—Rose was at UIC (since she was still working there so she could borrow equipment), we had someone at Northwestern, we had someone at the Art Institute, someone at Columbia. We would ask everyone if we could use their privileges to borrow equipment, and it would be this crazy, mad 'take the van around these colleges, and gather all the equipment, get it to where ever we're shooting' shoot."

It was a crazy way to [make a movie], but it was free! I think we actually rented equipment only twice. Our basic strategy for raising money was never doing anything but just talking about this movie. Part of our strategy of having benefits as a way of letting people know what's going on. We had never made more than $1,000 at a benefit.

"About three-quarters of the way through shooting we really ran out of money and were about to get evicted. At this point, Troche hooked up with New York producer Christine Vachon and her partner, Tom Kalin, a School of the Art Institute graduate who had directed *Swoon* (1992), a retelling of the Bobby Franks murder case. Vachon passed the word to John Pierson, the moneyed guru of the modern independent film movement. "Pierson eventually gave us the $50,000 we needed to finish, which to us was a million," says Turner.

Once completed, *Go Fish* was entered into the prestigious Sundance Film Festival, the Robert Redford-sponsored annual event held in Park City, Utah. The off-beat story of lesbian romance was an instant audience hit, and Troche and Turner's labor of love was picked up for distribution by Samuel Goldwyn.

"After Sundance, we were like 'what the hell? how did this happen?'" says Turner. Though the strain of making the film broke Troche and Turner's collective wallet, as well as their personal relationship, the duo found themselves in the enviable position of being independent film darlings. What's more, *Go Fish* was becoming an international phenomenon.

"We really thought we were going to make a film that was going to go to gay and lesbian festivals in America if we were lucky, and we ended up all over the world." Turner recalls. "We went out of our minds. We used to laugh all the time, because we'd have a limo coming to pick us up to bring us to the airport to fly us to Spain and we wouldn't even have three dollars to tip the driver. We went to Germany, Spain, England. Rose went to Italy, Ireland, and Australia. We both went to Israel and Japan. These are all countries where the movie was distributed and it was shown in China as well. In England and in Israel *Go Fish* was really well received, Israel in particular. I just never would have thought it in a million years. Israelis just really love American independent films. I think because it was American and the culture gap between Israel and here is so wide and so different, they could love *Go Fish* for being an independent film, which was really refreshing. Walking around in Tel Aviv and seeing my image on a poster everywhere was just like 'wow.'

"It's funny the things that *Go Fish* has been compared to. I was sitting with Rose the other day watching this independent romantic comedy, and as we were watching this, [it occurred to us that] on some level the plot of *Go Fish* is so formulaic and the things that happen in it are traditional romantic comedy elements. And we were like 'did we create an incredible cliché and not even realize it?' I think it makes a big difference that it's just women. That's the whole idea, that it's just like men and women or men and men or whatever. *Go Fish* is about the same crazy rituals we all go through."

Today Turner and Troche both live and work in New York. Troche recently completed her second feature, while Turner has appeared in several films and is writing scripts. Though both are now making films in New York and England, Turner emphasizes that *Go Fish* could only have come out of the Chicago independent movement.

"*Go Fish* is truly a product of Chicago. People see it and say 'did you shoot that in New York or whatever?' We shot in such tiny little spaces you can't even tell where the hell we are, but the fact of the matter is we never could have made the film the way we made it in New York. There's a spirit in Chicago of people when you say, 'oh, we're going to do this and this' everyone's like, 'oh, can I come and help,' whereas in New York everyone here is like 'fuck that, I've got my own shit to do. I've moved to New York to do my thing.' I feel like the film is the product of a certain kind of working class ethic, family oriented— 'let's all do something together' kind of spirit that to me is really a part of what

➡ ST. MARY'S CHURCH
1800 N. Wood Street

There's nothing like the action at a neighborhood church and in *Above the Law* (1988), St. Mary's sees plenty. There's the traditional stuff like the baptism of a new born infant and compassionate activities like hiding political refugees from South America. Of course, in between the wine and wafers, there's also a bombing that sends bloodied churchgoers flying through the pews. Just a typical day in the neighborhood chapel, at least when cop Steven Seagal is a parishioner. And look closely at that baptism scene: Seagal's wife is played by an up-and-coming talent named Sharon Stone.

➡ THE SECOND CITY
1616 N. Wells Street

In the mid-20th century at an abandoned second-floor chop suey place at North and LaSalle, comedy was forever changed. A group of friends, including Paul Sills, Mike Nichols, Elaine May, and Sheldon Patinkin, split from their classes at the University of Chicago, took over the former restaurant, and turned it into a theater called The Playwright's Theater Club. Along with pals David Shepherd, Barbara Harris, Ed Asner, Zohra Lampert, Eugene Troobnick, and Byrne and Joyce Piven, the group threw together production after production.

By 1955, the company had regrouped both name and technique. Under the banner "The Compass Players," this troupe, aided by newcomers Severn Darden, Shelly Berman, Roger Bowen, Jerry Stiller, Anne Meara, and Alan Arkin, hurled themselves into Chicago nightclubs.

The cast of The Second City, 1960 (*left to right*): Eugene Troobnik, Barbara Harris, Alan Arkin, Paul Sand, Bill Mathieu, Mina Kolb, Severn Darden, and Andrew Duncan. (*Photo by Dick Klein. Courtesy of The Second City.*)

The Second City (1616 N. Wells St.), home to improvisation, has produced many famous actors, writers, and directors who have had a major influence on television and film. (*Photo by Dick Klein. Courtesy of The Second City.*)

With their invigorating, free-style theater known as "improvisation," the Compass gang took theater games developed by Sills's mother, Viola Spolin, and staged rollicking comedy reviews. No subject was too sacred, no person was too revered to escape the satirical skewer of the group. Their home base was the Hi-Hat, a bar at 1152 E. 52nd Street, then the Dock at 6472 S. Lake Park, and finally the Off-Beat Room at 6344 N. Broadway. All these venues have since dried up, but what was spawned on those dirty stages has become an international phenomenon.

A second Compass group, including Del Close, Nancy Ponder, Jo Henderson, and Theodore J. Flicker, played St. Louis for awhile. Back in Chicago, Sills hooked up with newcomers Bernie Sahlins and Howard Alk and began the troupe's next phase. Throwing together a cast including Sahlins, Alk, Bowen, Darden, Andrew Duncan, Harris, Troobnick, and Mina Kolb, the gang took over an abandoned Chinese laundry at 1842 N. Wells Street, then tossed in a piano, a rudimentary stage, a few tables, and some chairs. Re-christened "The Second City" (the title of a *New Yorker* magazine piece about Chicago written by legendary journalist A. J. Leibling), the group staged its first show on December 16, 1959.

"I consider it a halcyon period for creative acting," says Avery Schreiber, a member of the troupe during the early 1960s. Indeed, this little storefront theater was quickly attracting national attention. New York-based magazines ranging from *The Nation* to *Time Magazine* sent writers to Chicago to see what the hell was going on, literally and figuratively, in The Second City. Out of these sketch comedy revues grew a mighty cultural force. Next thing you know, Nichols and May are doing Broadway. Shelly Berman's comedy routines are laid down on vinyl and sold in record stores across the country. Alan Arkin's doing movies. Stiller and Meara take the foibles of their marriage to comedy clubs. Theodore J. Flicker's writing Elvis pictures and directing *The President's Analyst* (1967), which quickly becomes a cult classic. Nichols wins an Oscar for directing *The Graduate* (1967)! And things are just beginning.

As the 1960s expanded the American political, social, and cultural consciousness, The Second City grew from a scrappy Chicago-based theater into an American institution. Needing more room than before, during 1967's *Summer of Love*, the troupe moved into a built-to-order home at 1616 N. Wells, the heart of Old Town.

Throughout the late 1960s and into the 1970s, The Second City's reputation for seat-of-your-pants sketch comedy expanded. Companies were opened in Los Angeles, Toronto, and Detroit. Second City played New York and developed a touring company that traveled from podunk town to podunk town like old-time vaudevillians.

Over the years, Second City troupes rose and fell on the strength of their versatile casts. The overall roll call reads like a who's who of American comedy, a veritable checklist of top stage, television, and film talents: Alan Alda, Jane Alexander, Dan Aykroyd, John Belushi, James Belushi, Peter Boyle, Jack Burns, John Candy, Dan Castellaneta, Del Close, Bill Cusack, Melinda Dillon, Paul Dooley, Robin Duke, Chris Farley, Joe Flaherty, Aaron Freeman, Rick Hall, Valerie Harper, Isabella Hoffman, Anthony Holland, Bonnie Hunt, Henry Jaglom, John Kapelos, Tim Kazurinsky, Richard Kind, Robert Klein, Linda Lavin, Eugene Levy, Shelley Long, Andrea Martin, Tim Meadows, Brian Doyle-Murray, Bill Murray, Mike Myers, Mick Napier, Bob Odenkirk, Catherine O'Hara, Gilda Radner, Harold Ramis, Joan Rivers, Paul Sand, Dick Schaal, Avery Schreiber, Jim Sherman, Martin Short, Joyce Sloane, David Steinberg, Betty Thomas, Dave Thomas, Nancy Walls, George Wendt, and Fred Willard. And that's just a sampling.

Now owned and operated by Andrew Alexander, who helped develop the original Toronto troupe, The Second City has evolved into a theatrical institution. Its influence can be felt at many levels, from the numerous improvisational comedy troupes playing Chicago bars on any given night to

Del Close

"I remember there was sort of an omen."

Del Close, one of the early forces behind Second City and a distinguished figure in Chicago's improvisational theater scene, periodically works as a character actor in films. Among his many roles, Close has played a corrupt alderman in *The Untouchables* (1987), a gynecologist in *Goldstein* (1964), and a baseball team owner in Penny Marshall's wartime baseball drama, *A League of Their Own* (1992), where he beheld an extraordinary backstage event:

"We were shooting out at the McCormick Mansion (I later would end up playing Col. McCormick in, of all things, the television version of *The Untouchables*). I was the owner of the team Madonna played for. The owners were very reluctant to rent out the mansion because they heard about movie companies and the kind of damage they can do, but somebody twisted an arm somewhere and they rented the mansion. They shot a lot in and around it. I remember, there was sort of an omen. The day before I got involved in the shoot, somebody got stung by a bee and almost died from going into an anaphylactic shock.

"We were doing this scene in one of the dining rooms in the mansion. In order to get a light grid up above the table, they built a 2 x 4 frame to hold the lights and had something holding up the 2 x 4s. A dozen people were at the table talking with Gary Marshall about how baseball was going to survive with the absence of many players during World War II. What were we going to do? Could we have girl's baseball? I remember one of my lines was 'Girls can't play baseball!' and I would do the 'girl-throwing-the-ball' gesture. Unfortunately this did not wind up in the film!

"My friend Gary Houston, really a fine actor who does a lot of stage work here in town, also had a part in this scene. Gary is rather annoyed with a lot of theatrical superstitions. Now, there's a lot of down time sitting around the table as they move the camera around to get the reaction shots of everybody. We were talking about a lot of theatrical superstitions and how foolish he thought it was for actors to refuse to quote from the Scottish play [Shakespeare's *Macbeth*] backstage. I was saying to him, it's not a superstition, it's science. It can be demonstrated that whenever anybody quotes from the Scottish play or uses the title of the play, something untoward happens. He was going on how this is plain old foolishness. I said, 'just wait, you'll see. It will happen because you called it to happen.'

"Right about that point, the light grid fell onto the table! The light grid with steaming hot lights was supported by the table, otherwise it would have crashed us all to the ground. One guy broke a collar bone. I remember catching Gary's eyes as we were climbing up from under the table. I just had this sort of grin on my face, sort of like saying 'you see? Does this prove my point?' It's clear that the superstition is not just a theatrical convention. It extends to films as well!"

the highs and lows of television's comedy war-horse, "Saturday Night Live." Homer Simpson is voiced by Dan Castellaneta, a former Second City player. Betty Thomas gained national attention on the television ensemble drama "Hill Street Blues," then came into her own as a film director with such features as HBO's "The Late Shift" and *Howard Stern's Private Parts* (1997), the wild and wonderful Howard Stern film biography. Bill Murray became America's favorite wiseguy. Bob Odenkirk revitalized television comedy on HBO. Joan Rivers brought her whacked-out sense of humor to cable's QVC shopping channel, becoming a multi-millionaire in the process of hawking her own designer jewelry. The list of alumni accomplishments is as off-beat and varied as any Second City review.

Today, in addition to the mainstage and Toronto troupes, The Second City offers Second City ETC, which stages original reviews at a theater in Pipers Alley around the corner from the Wells Street main stage. The Second City also has an actor's training program, a children's theater, and a corporate division, which creates made-to-order industrial films and corporate entertainments.

For ticket information, contact The Second City at 312-337-3992. If you're interested in Second City classes call 312-664-3959. The Second City Web site is at http://www.secondcity.com.

THE SECOND CITY AND THE MOVIES

Although its alumni have gone on to be some of the best known names in the television and movie industry, The Second City has a small, but important part in Chicago's film history. During the 1960s, the theater itself turned into a venue for the so-called "underground" film movement. And for one brief, horrifically failed moment, The Second City company itself attempted to bring feature filmmaking back to Chicago.

In 1966, a non-profit organization known as the Aardvark Film Associates regularly held court at Poor Richard's in Old Town. A showcase for films of such avant-garde talents as Stan Brakhage and Kenneth Anger, the Aardvark screenings attracted film devotees from around the area. An important venue for alternative cinema, these screenings eventually moved to The Second City on Monday nights, when the mainstage was dark.

One of the Aardvark regulars was Roger Ebert, who was in his early years as the *Chicago Sun-Times'* movie critic. "You had this so-called 'film generation,' " he recalls. "People were going to the movies in a different spirit. The Aardvark screenings were really exciting. People came with their 8-millimeter or 16-millimeter films in cans and they were screened. You saw abstract films, you saw films in which people were playing with the surface of the film by scratching it or burning it or dying it. You saw found films that were altered in various ways, you saw pseudo-documentaries, and real documentaries and all in an atmosphere of great daring, because some of these films included a little nudity too."

With the success of the Aardvark Cinematheque, Second City made plans to open its own film division. Dubbed "The Second City Film Center," this planned co-op was designed to assist independent filmmakers. It was hoped that camera equipment and editing space would be added, as well as becoming an information resource for such necessities as grants, film festivals and contests, regular screenings, and, of course, a pool of acting talent.

Unfortunately, these ambitious plans faded over the next few years. For awhile, The Second City Film Center was involved in distribution, booking films by avant-garde and experimental filmmakers, as well as classic silent films. Short jazz films from the 1940s, featuring such talents as Louis Jordan, the Nat "King" Cole Trio, Jack Teagarden, Billie Holiday, and Louis Armstrong, were also released through The Second City Film Center. Local filmmakers also took advantage of Second City, most notably Philip Kaufman. *Goldstein* (1963) and *Fearless Frank* (1967) made extensive use of Second City players, including Anthony Holland, Severn Darden, and Del Close. (See Philip Kaufman profile, page 301.)

In late 1967, Second City made its next leap into the movie business when it announced plans to film *The Monitors*. Based on a science fiction novel by Keith Laumer, the plot followed a group of outer space invaders who take over Earth and begin regulating human behavior.

A slew of Second City veterans, including Avery Schreiber, Murphy Dunne, Peter Boyle, Alan Arkin, and Barbara Dana were brought back to Chicago to appear in the film. Rounding out the cast were some well-known 1960s television actors, including Susan Oliver ("Peyton Place"), Larry Storch ("F-Troop"), Guy Stockwell ("Adventures in Paradise," also Dean Stockwell's brother), and Sherry Jackson (Danny Thomas's daughter on "Make Room for Daddy"). Other disparate talents appearing in the film included Keenan Wynn, Ed Begley, Stubby Kaye, and bandleader Xavier Cugat. Even Illinois senator Everett Dirksen was hired to do a cameo appearance. Chicago actors Mike Nussbaum, Byrne Piven, and Sidney Grossfield also had parts, as did a child actor named Adam Arkin. The son of Alan Arkin, Adam made a more notable impression as an adult, playing in the Chicago-based television drama "Chicago Hope."

The Monitors was a joint production of Second City, Chicago-based camera manufacturer Bell & Howell, and Harold Goldman Associates Inc., a California production company. Produced by Bernie Sahlins, *The Monitors* even managed to get something no other Chicago film of the era could possibly claim—a whole-hearted endorsement from Mayor Richard J. Daley.

To this day, Daley's contempt for Hollywood portrayals of his beloved city is legendary. Hizzoner, as Daley was often referred to, couldn't stand to see Chicago or its police department portrayed in a negative light and for many years made it difficult for out-of-town filmmakers to use Windy City locations. Said one Chicago policeman who occasionally dealt with Hollywood crews, "If it's not *Mary Poppins*, the mayor doesn't want it."[1]

Yet on September 19, 1967, when plans for *The Monitors* were announced at a press conference, Mayor Daley was singing a very different tune. "We have a wonderful city to be part of a motion picture project," he declared. "We have anything anyone wants to shoot. We have a wonderful lakefront."[2] Daley promised full cooperation from the various city departments.

Though the Mayor's benevolent cinematic attitude may take many people by surprise today, anything seemed possible on that glorious September morning. Feature filmmaking was coming back to the city, produced by and starring Chicagoans. A new day was dawning in the city's history.

But then production on *The Monitors* began.

Shooting was to begin in late November, but ultimately was delayed until February of 1968. Studio work was done at Chicago's former movie playground, the old Essanay Studios at 1345 W. Argyle Street. "It was good being on that lot," Schreiber recalled. "I felt like we were part of Chicago film history again." In addition to the studio work, location shooting was done at the University of Illinois-Chicago, Meigs Field, the Randolph Street Armory, the Outer Drive East Apartments, the Field Museum, and a quarry southwest of Chicago.

"We did our damnedest," says Schreiber. But ultimately, *The Monitors* was a series of good intentions gone woefully bad. Clumsily directed by Jack Shea (who later worked on a series of television shows ranging from "The Waltons" to "Growing Pains"), the film never developed its satirical potential. Instead, the few people who did see *The Monitors* were subjected to a series of stilted moments that were painfully unfunny. "I was cut out of *Goldstein* (1964)," Schreiber lamented some 30 years later. "I wish I was cut out of *The Monitors*!"

Released in 1969, *The Monitors* took a much-deserved critical bashing. The film quickly disappeared into the footnotes of movie history, and Daley returned to his old stance on filmmakers. It was up to future mayors including, ironically, Richard J. Daley's son, Richard M. Daley, to oversee Chicago's rebirth as a Midwestern Hollywood.

[1] Witt, Linda, "Mayor Daley Meets the Sundance Kid or How the Movie Business Came Back to Chicago," *Chicago Magazine* (January, 1974): 70.

[2] Anderson, Jon, "Multimillion-Dollar Group Formed to Shoot Movies Here,"

➡ **STEPPENWOLF THEATRE**
1650 N. Halsted Street

In the world of Chicago theater, where storefront troupes come and go with Darwinian regularity, the Steppenwolf Theatre Company is legendary. This scrappy ensemble, famous for bringing a pugnacious sensibility to the stage, has nailed something all fledgling Chicago companies dream of: unbridled success that has become world-renowned.

To look over the list of ensemble members is to understand Steppenwolf's importance not only to theater but also on film and television production. People like John Malkovich, Laurie Metcalf, Gary Sinise, John Mahoney, and Joan Allen are household names to movie fans around the world. The film, television, and stage work of Steppenwolf members have earned Oscar nominations, Emmy awards, and Tony

Terry Kinney (*standing*) and Gary Sinise (*sitting*) in a scene from Steppenwolf's production of Michael Weller's *Loose Ends*. (*Photo by Lisa Ebright. Courtesy of Steppenwolf Theatre.*)

awards.

Steppenwolf got its start in north suburban Highland Park. In 1974, Sinise and his old high school pal, Jeff Perry, along with Perry's Illinois State University comrade Terry Kinney, slapped together a theater company. The company name was nabbed from a handy copy of Herman Hesse's novel someone happened to have. Later, after incorporating as Steppenwolf Theatre Company, the trio found it too expensive to switch monikers. For better or worse, they were Steppenwolf.

Within a couple of years, other ISU graduates migrated north and joined the company. Malkovich, Metcalf, and Moira Harris were among this group. They staged their shows at Highland Park's Immaculate Conception Church, 770 Deerfield Road, in a minuscule basement theater. Rent was ten bucks a month, the ideal price for a group of starving actors.

From the start, Steppenwolf was committed to the ideal of ensemble acting. The collective developed a muscular approach to production, emphasizing emotional dynamics in their performances.

Moving to the Jane Addams Hull House Center, 3212 N. Broadway, in the city, Steppenwolf grew in size and reputation. Allen, Mahoney, Glenne Headly, and Rondi Reed were among the new members. The enhanced ensemble tackled such meaty works as Harold Pinter's *The Caretaker*, Samuel Beckett's *Krapp's Last Tape*, and Eugene Ionesco's *Exit the King*. In just six years, the company had evolved into a considerable theatrical force.

The 1980s proved to be even more lucrative. Steppenwolf acquired its own space in 1982, moving into a 211-seat theater at 2851 N. Halsted. Shows that opened in Chicago played in New York at prestigious venues like the Lincoln Center for the Performing Arts and the Circle Repertory Theatre. In 1985, the troupe was given a Tony Award for Regional Theatre Excellence. Three years later, John Steinbeck's estate gave permission for Steppenwolf to adapt *The Grapes of Wrath* for the stage. This ground-breaking production took Chicago by storm, then moved to the LaJolla Playhouse in California and the Royal National Theatre in London, England. Eventually *The Grapes of Wrath* moved to Broadway; it won the Tony awards for Best Play and Best Director for the 1989-1990 season.

When ensemble members hit Hollywood in the early 1980s, their impact resounded at all levels of the industry. Malkovich's film debut, as a blind man in *Places in the Heart* (1984) earned him an Oscar nomination.

Steppenwolf Theatre (1650 N. Halsted St.), producer of many acclaimed actors, playwrights, and directors.(*Photo by Michael Brosilow. Courtesy of Steppenwolf Theatre.*)

The intensity he brought to his roles, whether in an art film like *The Object of Beauty* (1991) or something as blatantly commercial as *Con Air* (1997), was pure Steppenwolf.

Other members quickly followed. Laurie Metcalf won several Emmys for her supporting role on the sitcom "Roseanne." Sinise developed into a screen chameleon, easily switching from regular guy to historical figure to boiling madman. He also directed a remake of John Steinbeck's *Of Mice and Men* (1992), starring as George opposite Malkovich's Lenny. Allen, Perry, Headly, Mahoney, and others became well-known figures to movie and television audiences worldwide.

Despite this global reach, the ensemble remains committed to Chicago and their home theater. Members routinely plan their film schedules to allow for Steppenwolf productions, and periodically hold movie previews in Chicago as fundraisers for the theater. In 1991, Steppenwolf Theatre Company moved to 1650 N. Halsted in a specially-built complex. The building holds a mainstage with a seating of 510, while a studio theater seats between 100 to 300, depending on the show.

For more information, contact Steppenwolf Theatre's switchboard at 312-335-1650 or check out their homepage at http://www.steppenwolf.org.

John Mahoney
A COMMITMENT TO CHICAGO

"When I got the Commitment to Chicago Award from the Chicago Film Critics Association, it was amazing. I couldn't believe they were giving me an award. It was like getting an award for having the sense to order surf and turf instead of hamburger. I mean, who would not want to live here?"

John Mahoney is a guy who truly loves life and the daily miracles it brings. Warm and completely unassuming in a profession that's rife with ego-driven personalities, Mahoney has carved out a unique niche as an actor. He's your next-door neighbor, he's your uncle, he's the guy at the corner bar. Whether you're watching him in hit films like *Moonstruck* (1987), *Say Anything* (1989), *Barton Fink* (1991), and *The American President* (1995), or as part of the crackling ensemble of the sitcom "Frazier," Mahoney's genuine warmth is embodied in his characters. Even in *Betrayed* (1988), where Mahoney plays a father figure to a group of white supremacists, his basic humanity rises above the character's uglier side. "All I ever wanted was to raise my crops and raise my boy," he tells undercover FBI agent Debra Winger. "The bank took my farm and Vietnam took my son." In this subtle, understated performance, it's hard not to feel some sympathy for the man, despite his abhorrent beliefs.

"I think that whatever that Chicago style of acting is that is so successful and done such great things for Joe Mantegna and John Malkovich and Dennis Franz and me, I learned all that here and I've got that to be thankful for," says Mahoney. "Basically, it's just an ordinariness that you just don't get in a lot of other places. It's a willingness to throw things away. It's a willingness to let the words go instead of hoarding them and eking them out. It's a willingness not to make every single semi-colon fraught with meaning. I think that's what a Chicago acting style is. Very down to earth, very throwaway. I learned that here, and that has carried me very, very far. It's carried me to Broadway, it's carried me to a Tony Award, it's carried me to a lot of great movies with some of the greatest directors in the world, so I owe an awful lot to Chicago. I think of myself as a Chicago actor and I think of my style of acting as a Chicago style."

Though his unadorned Midwestern accent smacks of Chicago, Mahoney actually is a British native. "I come from a very, very poor, Irish-Catholic family, eight kids, brought up in post-war England and we didn't have a pot to pee in," says Mahoney. "I fell in love with America when I first came over here. It's like some things you fall in love with right away. It was like 1951 and I was 11 years old. We came over to visit my sister, who was a war bride, and as soon as I saw America, I knew this is what I wanted."

Determined to become a U.S. citizen, Mahoney joined the Army in 1959 as a way of speeding up his citizenship process. In the process, he worked hard to drop his native British accent. After his discharge, Mahoney enrolled in Quincy College (later Quincy University) in Quincy, Illinois. "I had a lot of friends from Chicago as classmates and they'd say 'come on home, spend the weekend,' and I'd say 'oh, okay.' Well, once again, it was like seeing the United States for the first time. I saw Chicago and I just absolutely thought 'this is it! This is where I want to live the rest of my life.' That's never changed, it really hasn't.

"And I don't know why."

Mahoney taught college English earning his Master's degree at Western Illinois University, then made the move to Chicago where he went into publishing. "I was an associate editor on *The Quality Review Bulletin*, which is the journal of the Joint Commission on the Accreditation of Hospitals. Yeah, I had a good job in the Hancock with a nice big private office on the 37th floor." Seemingly, Mahoney had achieved the great American dream. Yet at age 37, despite the outward appearance of corporate success, the 9-to-5 route left him unfulfilled.

"I was making good money, but I was just at a point where I knew I wasn't happy and I had to do something with my life. I had to at least try something else and sort of racked my brains about what I'd ever done in my life that made me happy. Then I went to England to visit my family and I saw this incredible production of Tom Stoppard's play *Jumpers* at the National Theater. I came back to Chicago and I saw this incredible version of Arthur Miller's *A View from the Bridge* at the St. Nicholas Theater. I noticed that they were offering classes and I thought, 'this is it, this is it. I've got to try this before I get one day older.'

"When I was a kid I did a lot of theater in England. I was a member of the Stratford Children's Theater. I was a character actor, even when I was 12. I loved it!"

So, throwing caution to the proverbial wind, Mahoney quit his cushy downtown job and plunged into a life in the theater.

"I started at St. Nicholas Theater and enrolled in an acting class taught by Steven Schachter. Steven was getting ready to direct David Mamet's new play at that time, which was *The Water Engine*. David was there in residence. I got cast out of the class and into David's new play. It was my first professional role. I played a small part and when the play extended, one of the actors had to leave and I was sort of 'promoted' to another part. That part required me to be a member of Actor's Equity [the professional stage actor's union]. The next play I did at St. Nicholas was *Ashes* and that's where I met John Malkovich.

"John had the lead in *Ashes* and we got along very well. When the Steppenwolf Theatre moved from Highland Park to Chicago, each member was asked to bring in one person to double the size of the company. I was the one that John asked, so I sort of owe a lot to John Malkovich."

At the same time, Mahoney got to know another would-be actor, Chicago policeman Dennis Farina. "Dennis and I go back a long way. I was in the first play he ever did. We were doing some television, too. There was a show being produced here called "Chicago Story." I had a recurring role in that. John Malkovich was cast in one episode of that and Dennis Farina happened to be in the same episode. Well, John fell in love with Dennis, he thought he was the greatest guy, so when we were doing *A Prayer for My Daughter* at Steppenwolf, John asked Dennis if he would understudy one of the leads. Dennis said, 'oh, I'd love to.' He was still working as a cop at the time. One thing led to another and Dennis ended up taking over the role. Dennis played a policeman in the production and I played the murderer. He got to beat me up on stage every night, which he loved. He was a cop for a long time and he used to say, 'oh, if I just had enough money to become an actor!'

John Mahoney in the Steppenwolf Theatre Company's American premiere of Simon Gray's *Stage Struck*. (*Photo by Lisa Ebright. Courtesy of Steppenwolf Theatre.*)

Mahoney was on the move himself. He and Farina had supporting roles in a powerful PBS film, *The Killing Floor* (1985). A post-World War I era drama, *The Killing Floor* was set at the Chicago stockyards. The rise of the labor movement and the infamous race riots of 1919 are part of the film's tableau. "That was a wonderful movie," says Mahoney. [Director] Bill Duke was so much fun. He loved what I was doing because I was so mean. I had this sort of streak. I just turned my nose up at everybody and was nasty to black people and white people alike. Duke loved it; he got a big kick out of that. He was great to work with.*

"I did a lot of small parts in made-for-TV movies and then was cast in *Code of Silence* (1985). That was my first feature." *Code of Silence*, directed by native Chicagoan Andrew Davis, featured martial arts expert Chuck Norris as a tough cop chasing down corruption and the mob. Norris's on-screen partner was Mahoney's old pal, Dennis Farina. Mahoney had a wonderfully silly bit part as a robot technology salesman who demonstrated a fully-armed radio operated mini-tank to Chicago's Finest. "I had a great time. I loved working for Andy Davis; he was a real sweetheart. I was very nervous because it was my first feature. He was very good about that, and he was very patient with me. It was a lot of fun."

After *Code of Silence*, the parts got a little more respectable. Mahoney continued working with Steppenwolf, then went to Broadway with a production of the play *House of Blue Leaves*. That earned him a Tony Award for Best Supporting Actor. Within a few years, Mahoney had carved out a nice career as a character actor in films and television. Yet he refused to make a permanent move to Los Angeles, instead maintaining a residence in west suburban Oak Park and commuting to where ever he had to be. And when the occasional Chicago-based movie project came his way, Mahoney jumped at the chance to participate.

"We shot the bank robbery scene for *Betrayed* (1988) downtown. Actually, that was sort of a bonus. I knew we were going to be filming in Canada, and I wasn't too happy about that because I'd already done *Moonstruck* (1987) and *Suspect* (1987) in Canada, and I didn't particularly want to go there to film *Betrayed*. Half-way through shooting they said, 'oh, and by the way, we're going to be in Chicago for a week during the bank robbery,' and it was just like, 'Oh! Wonderful!' The thought of actually being in Chicago and going home at night instead of having to stay in a hotel was just great. I was very happy about that. It was especially wonderful for Ted Levine and me because we lived here. [*Betrayed's* director] Costa-Gravas loved the city. In fact, I think because of that week here he came back to film *Music Box* (1990)."

Twenty years after taking a leap of faith, Mahoney's life gamble has paid off beyond his wildest dreams. Best of all, he has an opportunity most actors dream of. He gets to live in a city he loves and commute to film and television jobs. And when Mahoney's not on a set somewhere, he's back in his adopted hometown, often doing a play as part of the Steppenwolf ensemble. "Chicago has been fabulous for me as an actor. My career got started here. All the theaters are here. I learned my craft here. I learned basically how to act here, and I don't dislike Hollywood and I'm not a snob. A lot of people will say, 'oh, L.A. is a cultural desert,' and all that. I don't believe it for one minute. I've seen great opera out there, I've seen wonderful symphonies, I've seen wonderful theater out there. It's just not for me.

"Chicago has got a personality like no other city. New York has got a great personality, too. Los Angeles has no personality. London's got a great personality. Paris, of course, has a great personality. And so does Chicago. It's almost like a person instead of a city.

"When I got the Commitment to Chicago Award from the Chicago Film Critics Association, it was amazing. I couldn't believe they were giving me an award. It was like getting an award for having the sense to order surf and turf instead of hamburger. I mean, who would not want to live here? And I know I'm not in a minority, because when I'm out in California, working on 'Frazier' or working in movies, people will say, 'where are you from?' and I'll say 'Chicago' and they'll say, 'oh my God, I did such and such a movie there and such and such a show there, I did this there, I did that there. I love it! I'd be out there in a minute if it wasn't for the winters.' They do! People love this city. All the cast of 'Frazier' came in to see *The Man Who Came to Dinner* at Steppenwolf, and they all made sure they came and spent an extra four or five days here because they just love it. I don't know what it is. How do you describe this city?

"It's so tough and yet so tender, and it's so forgiving."

*Duke later came back to Chicago to direct another period drama, *Hoodlum* (1997).

➡ CHARLIE TROTTER'S
816 W. Armitage Avenue

One of the North Side's most fashionable eateries, Charlie Trotter's was the restaurant where Julia Roberts poured her heart out to pal Rupert Everett in *My Best Friend's Wedding*. Look for restaurateur Trotter himself, who did a cameo appearance in the scene.

For reservations at Charlie Trotter's, call 773-248-6228.

➡ FACETS MULTIMEDIA, INC.
1517 W. Fullerton Avenue

"Chicagoans are very lucky to have so many wonderful film opportunities
...it's a good film town..."

—Milos Stehlik, founder and director, Facets Multimedia, Inc.

Originally founded as a screening alternative to bring foreign works to Chicago, Facets Multimedia, Inc. has blossomed into one of the nation's premier film resources. It's the only place in town where you can catch a Rainer Werner Fassbinder retrospective, rent a Herschell Gordon Lewis flick, create your own Eastern European film festival for the VCR, take appreciation classes like "Ideology and the Body in Pasolini's Cinema" or "Film Noir and the Hollywood Blacklist," or even bring the kids to see the best children's films from around the world. Roger Ebert wasn't hyperbolizing when he called Facets "a temple of great cinema...an amazing place."

Facets Multimedia, Inc. is the brainchild of Milos Stehlik, a Czechoslovakian native who came to Chicago in 1962. Eager to create a showcase for Eastern European film in Chicago, Stehlik and a partner started showing films at a rented theater on the corner of Halsted and Armitage. "It was kind of a strange situation," Stehlik remembers. "Even though the films were quite successful at this theater, [the owners] were kind of jealous of it, so we decided to come up with a theater on our own. Our first location was at the Resurrection Lutheran Church in Lakeview."

Forced to find a new location, Facets eventually found a permanent home at 1517 W. Fullerton. The building was originally a department store, then served as headquarters to *Die Hausfrau*, a German-language journal "with a big circulation in Argentina!" Stehlik notes. Facets bought the building and took up residence in May of 1977, using volunteer construction to transform the space into a movie theater.

Over the years, Facets' reputation has grown considerably. Today it houses two theaters, one for film screenings and the other for video projections. As venues for foreign films disappear, Facets thrives as a showcase for international cinema. "The number of sub-titled films being distributed in America is going down," Stehlik notes. "Foreign film in America is not in its best state. There's a lot of challenges for audiences." Fans of independent, low-budget films have also found a haven at Facets.

As part of their commitment to comprehensive film-going for Chicago, Facets brings in guest lecturers who represent many aspects of contemporary filmmaking. Werner Herzog, Claude Charbol, the late Louis Malle, Robert

Altman, Errol Morris, and Dusan Makavejev have all spoken at Facets, giving Midwesterners a unique opportunity to speak with world-renowned directors.

In 1982, the non-profit institution took a huge leap of faith into the slowly-growing market of home video rental.

"That was done gradually and with great fear and trepidation," says Stehlik. "Roger Ebert encouraged us a great deal. He kept saying, 'why don't you do something in video?' Easier said than done! Initially, we took the plunge and bought 140 tapes which were pretty much the standard 'art house' repertory films like Fellini's *8 1/2*. We taped the boxes to the wall with Velcro and whenever someone wanted to rent a tape, the projectionist went to the basement and got it. We basically reinvested all the rentals into buying more tapes."

Today Facets Video carries more than 33,000 tapes. Stehlik firmly maintains the same focused approach to video that he used for Facets' screenings.

"The largest part of our income is selling tapes nationally to individuals, institutions, and other video stores. We have a licensed line [of films] which is a couple of hundred titles that we own the North American rights for. [We got into that] by knowing filmmakers who were here over the years, who did workshops, with whom we had some kind of association. We started saying 'your work should be out and be seen.' "

Facets Video carries a variety of film-related books and, in association with Academy Press, has also published guides for gay/lesbian, African-American, and non-violent/non-sexist children's videos. Be sure to pick up a copy of Facets Video's thick catalog—the rich offerings within blow Blockbuster Video stores' stock out of the proverbial water. It's no wonder that Facets' repeat customers include directors Martin Scorsese and Jonathan Demme.

Video has been an asset to another important part of Facets—its many film appreciation classes. "Oddly enough, what made classes possible was video," Stehlik says. Facets held classes off and on for a few years, but the high cost of film rental often made tuition cost prohibitive. Owning an extensive video library has essentially allowed Facets to bring down class fees. The classes in film history and aesthetics consider an expansive range of topics. Viewing includes works from the silent era, world cinema, American independent films, and Hollywood blockbusters—sometimes all of which are represented in a single thematic course. Unlike many film institutions, Facets recognizes the importance of films for children. If you're looking for an alternative to Disney pictures or endless Barney videos, Facets has what you're looking for. Facets also holds an annual children's film festival every autumn.

Since those first screenings at Halsted and Armitage, Facets Multimedia has become an important resource for local filmmakers and institutions. Their commitment to Chicago's filmmaking community is reflected through on-going relationships, screenings, and video distribution. The work of local documentary stalwarts Kartemquin Films and Tom Palazzolo can both be rented through Facets Video. Additionally, Facets has co-sponsored a number of programs with the Film Center at the Art Institute, Chicago Filmmakers, and the Goethe Institute.

For membership information, film schedules, and workshop information at Facets Multimedia, call 773-281-9075. The video department can be reached at 1-800-331-6197. Facets Multimedia also maintains a presence on the internet at http://www.facets.org.

TOM PALAZZOLO

"If you were to put together Tom Palazzolo's complete works, you would have an interesting underground record of Chicago over the last 30 years."
—Roger Ebert

Combining the urban realism of documentary, with the poetic grit of Nelson Algren's writing, Tom Palazzolo has carved out a unique niche among Chicago-based filmmakers. "I really like Chicago, doing documentaries on Chicago and people in Chicago," he says. "Urban settings are where I'm the most comfortable."

Palazzolo came to Chicago in 1960 for studies at the School of the Art Institute. "I got interested in photo and film and got into underground and experimental film scene." He began making his own experimental documentaries and was a regular at the legendary Aardvark Cinematheque in the late 1960s. In 1968, Palazzolo went to the Mid-East with a group of independent filmmakers as part of a government program to show other cultures how much freedom Americans have. After returning home, he was hired to teach at the City Colleges of Chicago. Over the years, Palazzolo established himself as one of the premier documentary filmmakers working in the city.

"I like the margins of things," he says today. "I don't make shocking films, but I do like the humanity of people sort of on the out-there, the lower end of society. I like marginal people and places like Riverview." Palazzolo's subjects cover a wide spectrum of fringe culture. His wonderful documentary *I Married a Munchkin* is a warm-hearted portrait of a married pair of little people, one of whom played a Munchkin in MGM's classic musical *The Wizard of Oz*. Another of Palazzolo's works looks at the ragtag National Socialist Party of Frank Colin as they plan a march through the heavily Jewish suburb of Skokie. "[These neo-Nazis] were more pathetic and sad than anything else," Palazzolo observed. "I try to make [my films] as personal to me as I can and as personal as I can. I've also done a couple of experimental films which in a way are documentaries. I used some performance artists and did *Calagari's Cure*, a sort of a funny remake of the silent German expressionist film *The Cabinet of Dr. Calagari*. Because I'm in this art environment, I did these weird painted sets. It really was kind of an 'art comedy.' "

Palazzolo's work has been shown at many prestigious venues, including New York's Whitney Museum and the Museum of Modern Art. Locally, Chicago Filmmakers and the Film Center also screen his films, and Facets sells compilation videos of Palazzolo movies. Perhaps the best place to catch his work is on WTTW-Channel 11's popular show *Image Union*, which features Palazzolo's work on a regular basis.

➡ **KARTEMQUIN FILMS**
1901 W. Wellington Avenue

Though they're well known as the folks who made *Hoop Dreams* (1994) a reality, Kartemquin Films is a long-standing Chicago institution. Since its inception in the late 1960s, Kartemquin has been a thriving hub for socially-conscious documentary filmmakers. In 1998, the Chicago Film Critics Association presented Kartemquin partners Gordon Quinn and Jerry Blumenthal with the "Big Shoulders" award, honoring their "ongoing efforts to promote filmmaking [which] best exemplifies the bold, innovative, and independent spirit of Chicago."

"I came to school at the University of Chicago in 1960," recalls Quinn. "I got involved in the Documentary Film Group there and met a guy named Jerry Temaner. At that time there was no film department at the University. Then it was a 'God forbid you should do anything with your hands!' kind of attitude."

Following graduation, Quinn worked in New York, then returned to Chicago after Temaner called with the possibility of doing a film with fellow U of C alum Stan Carter about an old-age home. The result was a documentary called *Home for Life*. The trio formed their own film company, Kartemquin, which took its moniker from a conglomeration of the Carter, Temaner, and Quinn names.

"We formed Kartemquin in 1966 with the original concept to make films about social issues," says Quinn. "What we found very quickly was you had to do more than just show people the problems. You also had to have the political forces and the power to actually change things."

Carter left the following year and Jerry Blumenthal joined Kartemquin. The company offices moved from Hyde Park to the North Side, but Kartemquin's mission remained the same. "Gradually we became politicized and our films became more political," says Quinn. "We made a series of films sponsored by Catholic Adult Education, including *The Inquiring Nuns* (1968) and *Thumbs Down*. There were a few other films, and we took on a more anti-Vietnam war flavor."

The Inquiring Nuns is a particularly moving experience, based on a simple, but profound idea. Shot in 1967, the film follows two nuns through the streets of the city as they ask people "Are you happy?" The responses provide a unique snapshot of Chicago and the mood of the country as tensions were mounting over the Vietnam War and civil unrest.

By the late 1960s/early 1970s, Kartemquin had evolved into a collective of about 12 people. People from the labor movement, teachers, and other socially-concerned individuals all lent a hand to produce films that spoke to, rather than about, issues. Yet in order to survive as a company, Kartemquin also produced industrial and educational films. "We realized if we were going to survive and be independent we needed to have a way of also doing things that paid," said Quinn.

"The collective was a group of people that we gathered around us in

Gordon Quinn and Jerry Blumenthal of Kartemquin Films shooting Leon Golub in his New York City studio for the documentary, *Golub*. (*Photo by Tom Sullens. Courtesy of Kartemquin Films.*)

1972," says Blumenthal. "Basically, the idea of the collective was that you bring together people from a variety of backgrounds, all of whom shared this notion that film, the kind of documentaries that we were interested in, ought not to be produced in a vacuum by people who were just filmmakers. The films ought to be produced in a context where the relationship between the filmmaker and the subject had some real teeth to it. This way the subject that we worked with and the ultimate distribution and use of the film were all tied together from the very beginning."

Through the 1970s and 1980s, Kartemquin produced a series of social portraits, looking at the problems of Chicago's inner city through the eyes of children, in such films as *Winnie Wright, Age 11* (1974) and *Now We Live on Clifton* (1974). In 1981, when the Pullman rail car factory threatened to close, the Kartemquin cameras documented the struggles between labor and management. "In *The Last Pullman Car* (1983) we went back and told a 100-year history," says Blumenthal. "What we did was follow a steelworkers' local that was trying to save its jobs. Pullman was closing and going into another business. In order to understand what was happening to them, we had to go back and include 100 years of labor relations and the industrial history of what happened at Pullman.

"That was a very important thread in our work during the 1970s and early 1980s, a desire to use film as a way of providing some sort of historical, political, and economic analysis to underlie the stories we were telling. But we never stopped telling the stories—the human story was always up front, and that's why we made a film."

Kartemquin's next big project was *Golub* (1988), a study of the artist Leon Golub. "It just so happened that the Leon Golub retrospective was at the Museum of Contemporary Art," Blumenthal recalls. "We sort of knew Leon from way back when he was a Chicago artist. I went down to see the exhibit and I said, 'hey why don't we do a film about this?' Everybody thought that was not such a bad idea because of Leon's political interests and because he's such a powerful artist. His art seemed to us to have the capacity to really move people to think about what was going on around them outside the museum. Leon brought the real world into the museum in a particularly compelling way, a very aggressive way.

"We began the project back in 1985. It took us three-and-a-half years to finish and it was not so much because of funding. We had money from the Focus Infinity Fund and eventually got a series of grants from various funds and arts councils. We got a big grant from the National Endowment for the Arts. But we were sort of letting out into new territory, making a film about art and trying to figure out how to tell that story in a way that would really involve the film audience in the same way that the spectators in the gallery are involved in Leon's paintings. We had to use all kinds of devices to fold it all together—how to use music and archival footage in a way that was very different from our earlier films.

"In those earlier films, when we did historical passages they were very separate from the passages in the present; in other words, the film would sort of stop and we would say 'now we have to look at 100 years of history.' You would do that 10-or-15 minute passage, then come back to the story in he present. But when you've got Golub painting about mercenaries, about death squads, about stuff that's going on around you on television every night, how do you convey that sense of the present, the presence of all this information and all this kind of incredible political, moral turmoil, and brutality? How do you tie that all together and make it seamless? That was a pretty intense experience for us, those three-and-a-half years.

"I think that we succeeded in solving that problem and making a good movie. It was very different from anything we had done prior to that."

For their three-decade-plus relationship with the city, the Chicago Film Critics Association honored Kartemquin with their "Big Shoulders" award, recognizing Quinn and Blumenthal's "ongoing efforts to promote filmmaking [that] best exemplifies the bold, innovative, and independent spirit of Chicago."

"There's a lot of good synergies between different groups and people in Chicago," says Quinn. "There's a certain amount of support for each other. Chicago is a very good climate to remain independent but not having to compete so hard for your survival."

Video cassettes of Kartemquin's documentary work is available for rent/sale at Facets Multimedia.

➡ **THE BIOGRAPH THEATRE**
   2433 N. Lincoln Avenue

➡ **THE THREE PENNY THEATER**
   2424 N. Lincoln Avenue

The best action to play at the Biograph Theater didn't happen on screen. On July 22, 1934, the notorious bank robber John Dillinger stepped out of the Biograph doors into a hail of FBI bullets.

John Dillinger's story has been told often, sometimes right, sometimes wrong, and more often than not, in a mixture of fact, fiction, and fantasy. What follows is a thumbnail sketch of the Dillinger saga.

Dillinger was born in Indianapolis, Indiana, on June 28, 1902. In 1923, Dillinger joined the United States Navy, but soon went AWOL with no intentions of returning. The following year he turned to crime, trying to hold up a store in his hometown of Mooresville, Indiana.

Dillinger was caught and thrown in the slammer. Paroled in 1933, he gathered a few like-minded individuals and started robbing banks. By 1934, the Federal Bureau of Investigation was hot on the Dillinger case. Certainly killing two cops and two FBI agents along the way made the hardened criminal an especially favored target for the Feds who listed him as Public Enemy Number One. Though Dillinger tried to change his looks through plastic surgery, he couldn't evade the law.

On July 22, 1934, Dillinger went to the Biograph with his girlfriend of a few weeks, Polly Hamilton, and Hamilton's landlord, a Romanian immigrant named Anna Sage.

Unbeknownst to Dillinger or Hamilton, Sage was facing deportation for helping run a prostitution ring. When Sage met Hamilton's new beau, a guy named "Jimmy Lawrence," she instantly realized he was the notorious bank robber. Despite plastic surgery, Dillinger was still recognizable.

Hoping to cash in on the substantial reward, as well as block the deportation charges against her, Sage went to a police officer who had been investigating her case. On July 20, 1934, she promised she could deliver Dillinger to the FBI. On the morning of July 22, Sage informed the local FBI office that she, Dillinger, and Hamilton would be going to either the Marbro Theater at 4124 W. Madison or the Biograph that evening. Two teams of agents were dispatched to stake out the theaters.

That night, the threesome went to the Biograph. On the bill was *Manhattan Melodrama*, a gangster drama starring Clark Gable as racketeer Blackie Gallagher (Mickey Rooney also had a small role, playing the young Gallagher). At 10:30 p.m., Dillinger and company exited the theater, where FBI Agent Melvin Purvis, along with other Feds and some Chicago cops, were waiting. Dillinger ran down the alley next to the theater, but was cut down in a shower of bullets.

The next morning, the story was all over the news wires. Sage was singled out as the mysterious "Woman in Red" who had betrayed America's most vicious bank robber.

The story of Dillinger's demise has been told numerous times on screen. Tough guy Lawrence Tierney played the title role in the 1945 film *Dillinger*. *Gang Busters* (1955) and *The FBI Story* (1959) portrayed the FBI's point of view. *Appointment with Death: the Last Days of John Dillinger* was released in 1971. The 1973 *Dillinger* featured Warren Oates as the notorious bank robber, while Robert Conrad essayed the role in *The Lady in Red* (1979). Baby-faced Mark Harmon starred in a made-for-television "Dillinger" in 1991. The most unlikely spin on the story was the 1995 feature *Dillinger and Capone* starring Martin Sheen as John Dillinger and Oscar winner F. Murray Abraham as Al Capone. Apparently some producer got the wise idea of pairing Chicago's two most notorious gangsters together on screen, a partnership that never existed in real life.*

Across the street from the Biograph, at 2424 N. Lincoln, is one of Chicago's most interesting movie theaters, the Three Penny. This theater specializes in second-run art films and great weekend midnight movies. Either way, the low ticket prices provide you with one of the best movie bargains in town.

The Three Penny does have something of an unusual history. It opened in 1912 as a nickelodeon theater. During the 1960s, it was run by John Rossen, a former member of the illustrious Abraham Lincoln Brigade. Rossen, an outspoken leftist, showed films like *The Battle of Algiers* (1966) and *Salt of the Earth* (1953), a long-banned movie that had been made in secret by several talents who were blacklisted in Hollywood during the 1950s. Later, the Three Penny became a pornographic theater, gaining some notoriety when it hosted the Chicago debut of the controversial hard-core sex film, *Deep Throat* (1972).

In the early 1980s, the theater took on new ownership and took on the art house status it enjoys today.

To see what's playing at the Biograph, call 773- 348-4123. If you want the Three Penny's schedule, call 773-935-5744.

* Dillinger just doesn't live on at the movies. For another perspective on the Dillinger legacy, check out Ursula Bielski's *Chicago Haunts: Ghostly Lore of the Windy City* (Lake Claremont Press, 1997).

➡ LINCOLN PARK ZOO
2200 N. Cannon Drive

The Lincoln Park Zoo, one of the city's most popular attractions, was founded in 1868 with the gift of two white swans courtesy of the folks running New York City's Central Park. Today the zoo has more than 1,000 animals and provides visitors with one of the best walks the city has to offer.

The movies have also had a good time at Lincoln Park Zoo. If you head to the great ape house, you can pretend to see where Joe Mantegna, Joe Pantoliano, and Brian Haley squared off with a gorilla in *Baby's Day Out* (1994). (Their encounter actually was filmed on a soundstage.) Chuck Norris took a stroll through the zoo in *Code of Silence* (1985); so did David Schwimmer in *Kissing a Fool* (1998).

Head to the Lincoln Park Lagoon and you'll find the site where high school bully Matt Dillon shoved around Adam Baldwin before receiving his comeuppance from Chris Makepeace in *My Bodyguard* (1980). The performances in this film were wonderfully natural, marked by the easy stylings of then-unknown Chicago actors Baldwin and Joan Cusack.

The Lincoln Park Zoo Web site is at http://www.lpzoo.com/. The zoo is open 365 days a year from 9 a.m. to 5 p.m., and admission is free. For more information, call 312-742-2000.

➡ **JOHN BARLEYCORN'S FROM *PRIMAL FEAR***
658 W. Belden Avenue

"Se Habla Beethoven." That's the motto of this great Lincoln Park tavern where hotshot attorney Richard Gere tipped a few when not working on the case of a lifetime in *Primal Fear* (1996).

➡ **ROBERT DENIRO'S APARTMENT IN**
***MAD DOG AND GLORY* (1993)**
635 W. Belden Avenue

Mild-mannered police photographer Wayne "Mad Dog" Dobie (Robert DeNiro) leads a pretty quiet life on this pretty quiet stretch of Belden until he inadvertently saves the life of mob boss/fledgling stand-up comic Frank Milo (Bill Murray) in 1993's off-beat comedy *Mad Dog and Glory*. The second half of the title comes in the form of Uma Thurman, a sort of feminine "gratuity" Murray passes on to the reluctant DeNiro for a week.

Pay close attention to the climactic fight scene outside this apartment and you'll notice a few subtle differences. Extras don't quite look the same from shot to shot and DeNiro manages to get his hair cut, then grow it back in between shots. You can credit this mysterious movie magic to that unique Hollywood convention, the test screening. This practice, designed to make all films everything to all potential viewers, is a standard for major movie studios. Unreleased films are trotted out before select audiences, responses are tallied, and alterations are made based on these reactions.

The original ending to *Mad Dog and Glory* had Murray's character beating the living daylights out of DeNiro's character. Defeated, DeNiro goes back into his apartment and sits on his couch. Thurman, who disappeared during the fight, comes walking in the door and sits down next to DeNiro—their fledgling love appears to have hope.

That's not what you see in the final cut, of course.

"Nobody liked that ending in the test screenings," recalls *Mad Dog and Glory* producer Steve Jones. "Audiences hated the fact that the Raging Bull got his ass kicked by Bill Murray. We kept saying 'it's not the Raging Bull!'

But it didn't matter.

"So we added a second half to the fight. The DeNiro character gets in a whole bunch of licks. We shot it literally a year later. DeNiro's hair had been cut down for *This Boy's Life* (1994), Bill had gotten bigger, and we couldn't get back some of the guys who were in Murray's gang. If you look really closely at all of the extras, after DeNiro throws that punch, they're all different extras. Look at the people across the street, see what they're wearing, they're all completely different. DeNiro throws a punch one year and it lands the next."

John McNaughton & Steve Jones

One used to be a day laborer, a carnival worker, and a bartender before becoming a small-time video director. The other came from the advertising industry, where he animated spots for big name clients like Captain Crunch and McDonalds. Together they form a brilliant team, creating films that push creative and artistic boundaries. In the dog-eat-dog world of independent movie-making, John McNaughton and Steve Jones have emerged as two of Chicago's most original talents.

Their story begins in 1985 with an Oak Forest-based video company. Maljack Productions Incorporated (MPI) was on a roll. Formed by Waleed and Malik Ali, the sons of a Lebanese immigrant, MPI got into the video-releasing business in the early 1980s, just as the great home video boom was about to take off. Acquiring the rights to such films as *Beckett*, *8 1/2*, the Beatles' movies *A Hard Day's Night*, and *Help!* and television shows like "Dark Shadows" and "The Honeymooners," the Ali brothers quickly racked up some significant profit. Their net worth increased with "The Superbowl Shuffle," a music video made by the Chicago Bears en route to their 1985 national championship.

MPI also released non-fiction videos. A deal with the ABC network resulted in a 14-tape set, *The Greatest News Stories of All Time*. In 1987, when Oliver North became an unlikely American hero for his Iran-Contra testimony to Congress, MPI released a video of North's hearing within five days, under the title *Oliver North: Memo to History*.

Having gotten a handle on video distribution, the brothers decided to take a leap into the production end of the business. John McNaughton, a freelance video director who worked with MPI, suggested a film based on the crimes of Henry Lee Lucas, a notorious serial killer McNaughton had seen profiled on television. The Alis liked the idea; after all, serial killer horror films like *Friday the 13th* (1980) and *Nightmare on Elm Street* (1984) had been immensely successful. McNaughton hooked up with Steve Jones, who'd designed the MPI logo as a freelance job. The duo was provided with $100,000, McNaughton wrote a script with the Organic Theatre's Richard Fire, and a trio of unknown actors was hired.

Playing Henry was Michael Rooker, an intense, handsome Chicago actor. Tom Towles was Henry's dimwitted friend Otis, and Tracy Arnold played Otis' sister Becky. McNaughton used a documentary style to explore the ugly world of these three characters. No moral judgment is made on Henry's actions. If anything, the audience looks over his shoulder. The result is terrifying. *Henry* wasn't the cartoonish violence of the *Friday the 13th* movies. We see the aftermath of Henry's work in stark reality.

"The people we made it for thought it was too arty, and the people who were artists thought it was too gory," says Jones. "We ended up in this no man's land."

Part of the film's terrible beauty came from Rooker's chilling performance. Henry could be anybody. He was the guy with a broken down car you tried to help. He was the jerk you tried to sell a hot TV. You take his order at a restaurant and smiled when he flirted with you. He was the man at the door who'd come to fumigate your house. No matter what your relationship was, he'd kill you.

In an age where serial killers are glorified on film, television, and in countless cheap paperbacks, *Henry* pulled no punches. The Alis didn't know what to make of McNaughton and Jones's work. They'd been expecting a standard shock-thriller. Teens head out for fun. Slowly the group gets picked off by an unseen murderer. Audience jumps at prerequisite scene of victim scared by cat...then killer strikes. Last member of the group manages to escape...but so does psychopathic fiend. Watch the whole formula again in numerous sequels.

Henry, on the other hand, was stark, brutal, and got under your skin. It was also an undeniable work of art. It played at the 1986 Chicago Film Festival to critical acclaim. Audiences recoiled in horror and praised the film's artistic merits.

Shocked by the realistic nature of *Henry*, the MPAA ratings board slapped the film with an "X." That meant no distributor would touch *Henry*. Essentially, the film had been blackballed before it had a chance. Enter a miracle via the Music Box Theatre. (See the Music Box entry on page 216 for another take on *Henry*.)

"We ended up in this no man's land," says Jones, "but then Erroll Morris, who made *The Thin Blue Line* (1988), guest-directed the 1989 Telluride Film Festival. He chose *Henry* as one of his three movies that the audience sort of had to see. When Morris stood up and said 'this is a great work,' everybody looked at *Henry* in a different light and it sort of took off from there."

Three years after it was completed, *Henry* had become a cult hit. Suddenly other theaters around the country wanted to show the film. New York critics put *Henry* in their annual Best Films of the Year lists. Time magazine decried *Henry's* MPAA "X," boldly stating "...this movie rates an X as in excellent."

McNaughton and Jones' next collaboration was a science fiction horror comedy, *The Borrower*. (1991) "That's another sad story," says Jones. "We made *The Borrower* for a company called Atlantic Entertainment, who made their money doing a picture called *Teen Wolf* (1985) with Michael J. Fox. But they went out of business while we were making *The Borrower*. So after we raised the $2 million to make *The Borrower*, they took $400,000 of it just to stay open. So by the time we got our film done, there was no company. Then all of their creditors came and there was a bankruptcy. We couldn't even get the picture away to show it to anybody! It was an asset in the bankruptcy.

"Finally, Cannon Films bought it. I don't know what they did, but they determined not to try to release it theatrically. When we finally heard that Cannon had it and was sending it straight to video, we begged them, 'please, can we release it theatrically?'

"We got the Music Box and a couple of other places to show *The Borrower*. We screened it at the Seattle Film Festival but then Cannon immediately had the video released, so we never had a chance to open wide like we wanted to."

Still, McNaughton and Jones persevered. Martin Scorsese, it turned out, was enthralled by *Henry*. He gave the Chicago outsiders a chance at the mainstream with *Mad Dog and Glory* (1993). "Scorsese called John and said, 'I've got this idea for a screenplay. Maybe you want to do it,' says Jones. "*Mad Dog and Glory* was a great screenplay. John and I said 'Yeah, we'll do it.' Then Scorsese asked 'What do you think if I offer it to my friend Bob?' 'Bob?' 'Yeah, Bob DeNiro.' We said, 'Well yeah if you want to, go ahead.' Like we're going to tell Marty 'No!'

"Up until that point, *Mad Dog and Glory* was supposed to be an $8 or $9 million movie. We were thinking of casting guys like Joe Mantegna. Once DeNiro got involved, it changed considerably. The budget doubled. DeNiro was the guy who suggested casting Bill Murray. You know, the more money you bring into a picture, the more people you have telling you how to spend it. It became much more of a studio picture once DeNiro got involved, but on the other hand we got to work with him!

"We started *Mad Dog and Glory* in New York. We did preproduction work, but then Scorsese had to deliver a picture to Universal after Steven Frears backed out of doing *Cape Fear* (1991) with DeNiro. Marty took over that picture and they put us on hold. The producer came over to our office and said, 'You know that movie you were going to do? Well, you're not going to do it now. You'll do it next year.' We said, 'yeah, sure.' The head of production at Universal said, 'No, no, I'm telling you, you'll make this movie next year.' As things turned out, they told us the truth.

"But we were out of business at this point. Since we had nothing to do, John and I decided to call back one of the guys who'd called us up. One of them was Eric Bogosian, who had sent John a fan letter about *Henry*. We were talking to him and he said, 'you know, I'm trying to do a movie of my live show, but I don't want to talk to you guys about that.' We said, 'Talk to us, we just lost our job!'

"We ended up filming his live show in Boston with Ernest Dickerson, who was Spike Lee's cinematographer at the time. We did a big version of what he was doing on stage in New York City. John and I left what Bogosian was doing completely alone. We said, 'you do what you do, and we'll make the set a little bigger.'

"So we did our interpretation of what Bogosian did for a company called Avenue Pictures. They even advertised the release for about 200 theaters. It got released in 20 and then Avenue Pictures went out of business! Once again, we had a picture that didn't get seen very much, but we got some good reviews and had some good times. Strangely enough, the people who bought it to release on video were MPI.

"Because of union labor charges, Universal decided to move *Mad Dog and Glory* to Chicago, which was fine for us. We got to stay home! We changed everything in the script to Chicago locations. John and I got to pick locations, like the water sculpture down on the river, so we had a little more fun.

"While we were editing *Mad Dog*, I picked up a *Chicago Tribune* magazine article about Jeff and Jill Erickson. They were this couple who robbed banks and then Jill had killed herself when they got caught. I said, 'look at this, this is a great story.' I called the woman who wrote the article but she wouldn't return my calls.

"We went back to New York to finish *Mad Dog* and I saw a headline in the *New York Times*: "Jeff Erickson Killed in a Shoot Out." I started calling the writer again, but she wouldn't return my calls and I couldn't figure out why. It turned out somebody else had already optioned her material.

"A year later somebody sends us a screenplay. It was really good. We didn't have another picture and John was doing television. Finally, people at William Morris said, 'If you are willing to work with Luke Perry, we can probably raise enough money to make this movie.' John and I looked at Luke's rodeo movie, *8 Seconds* (1994), and agreed that he'd be fine. Luke's an innocuous, suburban guy.

"Then they said, 'By the way, you can have this newcomer, Ashley Judd.' John and I said 'Okay, lets go!' Once again, we got to work here. We shot in the O'Hare area, in just about every suburb around the airport. Hanover Park, Hoffman Estates, River Grove...these were all the places that Erickson actually went. We were in the actual bank that he held up. When we captured him in the movie it was the same parking lot that they really captured him in. That was kind of interesting.

"We used Triton College in River Grove for the rehab scenes and Triton's Cernan Space Center for the planetarium. We had so little money, that whenever we shot someplace, we'd have two more scenes that we could shoot real close by.

"*Normal Life* was made for theatrical release—or so we thought! But meanwhile, the money people said 'Oh well, you know, we don't want to bother putting it out in theaters. We'll just sell it to HBO. John yelled and screamed a lot and got them to release it in New York and Chicago.

"Once again, we just seemed to have this string of pictures that would never get released and then we'd get these great reviews. *Henry; The Borrower*; *Sex, Drugs and Rock 'n' Roll;* and *Normal Life* all got incredible reviews!"

Still, McNaughton and Jones have persevered. Their most recent film, *Wild Things* (1998), was released nationwide—in theaters! But the duo have yet to "go Hollywood." Both continue to live and work in Chicago.

"As long as we can keep on working, there's no need to go out to Los Angeles," say Jones. If you're in a bar in L.A., 95 percent of the people would be talking about movies. The other five percent would be talking about the music industry. "I prefer to live in a place that's a little more real. There's no such thing as working class L.A. The fact that Chicago is not a film industry town makes people here want to really work extra hard, really be craftsmen at what they do."

➡ **FRANCIS J. DEWES HOUSE**
503 W. Wrightwood Avenue

A stately former mansion (and once home to the Swedish Engineers Society of Chicago), this wonderful Lincoln Park building is notable for the male and female statues beneath the wrought iron balcony. The period look of the Dewes House served *The Babe* (1992) and *Hoodlum* (1997) well. It has also shown up in such contrasting pictures as Patrick Swayze's cop-action flick *Next of Kin* (1989) and the off-beat Julia Roberts comedy *My Best Friend's Wedding* (1997). Television's "The Untouchables" (1993-1994) and "Early Edition" (1996-the present) have likewise filmed scenes here.

➡ **"O'NEILS" FROM *ONLY THE LONELY (1991)***
3369 N. Clark Street

In *Only the Lonely* (1991), this hangout at the corner of Roscoe and Clark became "O'Neils," the neighborhood Irish pub. Maureen O'Hara, mom of shy cop John Candy, lifted her drink in salute to Candy's girlfriend Ally Sheedy here. In another drinking scene, one with a bit more edge to it, Candy and his uniformed colleagues brought in a deceased pal for one last round.

For Brian DePalma's big screen version of *The Untouchables* (1987), the whole block was redressed as 1920s storefronts.

➡ **BREW & VIEW AT THE VIC THEATER**
3145 N. Sheffield Avenue

Looking for a combo of a late night movie and cheap eats? Then check out Brew & View, one of the city's most entertaining spots for both movie and people watching. The Brew & View is actually an off-shoot of the Vic Theater. When not hosting rock concerts or comedy shows, the Vic turns into a movie theater, albeit one that serves beer and pizza. What's more, this is one venue where talking during the show isn't a faux pas. Patrons tend to be on the rowdy side (midnight movies and beer...go figure), which makes this an ideal place to watch action flicks or robust comedies.

For a schedule of upcoming Brew & View movies, call 312-618-8439.

➡ **WOMEN IN THE DIRECTOR'S CHAIR**
   3435 N. Sheffield Avenue, #202, Chicago, IL 60657

Women in the Director's Chair (WIDC) is devoted to making film an accessible medium for women. One powerful statement to their effectiveness: The Women's Caucus of the Director's Guild of America published a report showing that over a 35-year period less than 20 out of more than 7,330 major motion pictures were directed by women; yet within its first four years of existence, WIDC had shown the work of more than 200 female directors.

WIDC was formed in 1980 as a showcase festival for female film and video artists. Today the alliance has grown into a thriving community resource, including a video archive of more than 200 tapes. The collection includes several works geared towards health, youth, and racial issues, all of which are available for screening by non-profit organizations.

Another aspect of WIDC is the annual film festival held every March during Women's History Month. They also have a traveling festival available nationwide to universities, libraries, and museums. Ongoing programs include work-in-progress screenings, Spanish language screenings, an African-American history celebration, lesbian pride screenings, and year-round programming for incarcerated women.

One of WIDC's most important outreach programs is "Girl Talk," an educational program run at the Juvenile Temporary Detention Center in Chicago. Through screenings, discussions, and creative production classes, WIDC members provide young women an opportunity to express themselves and learn more about the issues they face.

For more information on Women in the Director's Chair, call 773-281-4988.

➡ **3400-3459 SOUTHPORT AVENUE**
   (BETWEEN ROSCOE & CORNELIA)

Today Southport Avenue is a trendy stretch of coffee bars, nightclubs, shops, and a combination laundromat/drinking establishment. But for a few days in 1991, this stretch of Southport was transformed into 1916 Boston for the baseball biography, *The Babe* (1992), starring John Goodman as Babe Ruth.

But how do you get businesses to close up shop, induce the CTA to re-route buses and trains, and transform video stores into early 20th-century establishments? *The Babe* production company had to complete 65 different contracts with the many businesses and private residences on Southport to cover loss of clientele, parking problems, and other factors of daily living in this busy neighborhood.

Once this was completed, facades were built in front of businesses to establish a period look. Nearly 20 truckloads of mud and hay covered the street between Roscoe and Cornelia, while transportation was reduced to a few vintage automobiles and some horse-drawn wagons.

The on-screen result was terrific. For a few moments, Southport did become that busy 1916 Boston neighborhood where Ruth swaggered down the street.

➡ **THE MUSIC BOX THEATRE**
3733 N. Southport Avenue

"Our mission is to supply what our customers want to see," says Chris Carlo, who co-owns the Music Box Theatre with partner Bob Chaney. That philosophy of film exhibition may seem like a quaint anachronism, particularly in an era driven by multiscreen movie complexes. Carlo and Chaney's commitment to their patrons, however, has resulted in a loyal following since they reopened the Music Box in 1983. Today, this beautiful mini movie palace is one of the best places in the country to enjoy a filmgoing experience.

The Music Box Theatre opened in 1929 as a neighborhood alternative to the more palatial downtown movie houses. It was intended as a "second-run" theater, meaning that once a film had completed its run in the bigger Loop theaters it would be recycled to local movie houses. It was considered relatively small in comparison to downtown houses, with the capacity for 800 patrons. Though the Music Box was built with the new sound technology in mind, it was equipped with room for an orchestra as well as a pipe organ should the talkies go bust. The ceiling, which remains a notable feature to this day, was painted dark blue and outfitted with twinkling lights and moving clouds.

Debuting on August 22, 1929 with *Mother's Boy*, a forgettable studio comedy starring crooner Morton Downey, Sr., the Music Box quickly settled into its role as a second-run theater. One major exception to this rule was the opening of Charlie Chaplin's anti-fascist comedy *The Great Dictator* (1940). The politically-charged nature of this film was unsettling to big-ticket theater owners, particularly as the United States was still officially neutral about entry into World War II. Consequently, *The Great Dictator's* Chicago opening was limited to the Music Box and its South Side sister theater, the Romova, which was located at 35th Street and Halsted Street. Chaplin and his co-star, comedian Jackie Oakie, attended the film's Chicago openings with the director making a personal appearance at the Romova while Oakie met with fans at the Music Box.*

The Music Box continued to thrive through the 1960s, but gradually attendance dwindled. By the mid-1970s, the theater was barely attracting enough patrons to justify its existence. On November 24, 1977, the theater manager closed shop for the night and went to sleep on the lobby couch. The manager, nicknamed "Whitey" by people in the theater's Lakeview neighborhood, never woke up. He had held the same position since the Music Box's grand opening.

Over the next few years, various attempts were made to re-open the Music Box. For a time it showed Spanish-language features and later, Arabic films. Like so many failing theaters, the Music Box even did time as a showcase for pornography. All that changed when Carlo and Chaney bought the theater in the spring of 1983, intending to turn it into a revival house.

"The Music Box just knocked us out," says Carlo, "we thought it was going to be great. We made the landlord a ridiculous offer and he took it. He actually admitted that he thought that we would fail but we would fix up the building so he could run Colombian floor shows in here. He was a Colombian doctor."

The Music Box reopened as a full-fledged movie showcase in August 1983, almost 54 years to the day after its grand debut. Two locally-themed movies, *Wabash Avenue* (1943) and *In Old Chicago* (1937), made up the theater's first double feature. Initially, the Music Box showed a new double feature every three days. Eventually they switched over to a daily schedule change. The changing face of movie distribution, however, was about to change the nature of the Music Box.

By the mid-1980s, the home video market had made a powerful impact on revival movie theaters. Film companies stopped making new prints of old films, and circulating prints were often unviewable. The availability of repertory favorites on video was another major issue. The habits of moviegoers clearly were changing, and the few revival theaters left in Chicago gradually began to close their doors.

Rather than throw in the proverbial towel, Carlo and Chaney decided to change with the times. They made a slow transition from revival house to repertory movie theater. "We starting to pick up one-week runs of documentaries and independents that couldn't get run anywhere else," Carlo says. "We started making money for distributors of little films, and the distributors of medium films came to us. Basically, they wanted us to provide box-office return on films that wouldn't normally get booked in larger theaters."

In 1986, the Music Box hired a film booker to find out what was available on the independent circuit. Being independent rather than part of a chain, many film distributors wanted to deal with Carlo and Chaney because they did everything themselves, from advertising to creating the popular Music Box schedule calendars that are widely distributed throughout Chicago. These calendars have been an important part of the theater's marketing since it reopened in 1983. Today, the Music Box annually prints more than 270,000 calendars.

The success of the theater as an art house is, in Chaney's words, "plain dollars and cents. You present films at the Music Box for a fraction of the cost to open at a chain." Ultimately, this led to the theater's next major development, the addition of a second screening facility in 1991. An adjacent storefront was remodeled into a 104-seat mini-house with a decor that complemented that of the main theater.

"We'd play a film for a week or two on the main screen," says Carlo "and as the audience got smaller we could still do almost 300 people a day with three shows.

The opening of the second theater also allowed Carlo and Chaney to return to a limited revival format. On weekends, the Music Box plays older fare and documentaries, using the smaller theater for its early-afternoon matinees.

Today, the Music Box is equipped to run everything from 1920s silent features to current trends in foreign films, documentaries, and American independent movies. They have projectors that can run older films at silent film speed, thus avoiding the "herky-jerky" look silents have when run on modern movie projects. The Music Box also has 16-millimeter projectors, which are used largely for documentaries and independent features that are only available in this smaller format.

In addition to showing movies, the classic look of the Music Box has made it a popular film location for Hollywood. Local boy made very good, John Hughes, has repeatedly turned to the Music Box for his features. "John Hughes has been very good to us," says Carlo. Hughes' first feature with Music Box scenes was *Only the Lonely* (1991), directed by Chris Columbus. Though ultimately the Music Box scenes were cut from the film's final release, Hughes did have the theater's candy counter overhauled for the film. For *Curly Sue* (1991), a kid comedy starring James Belushi and Kelly Lynch, Hughes rebuilt the candy counter again and this time used the theater as inspiration. "We were playing a 3-D porno film as our midnight show," says Carlo. "That's where the 3-D glasses came from in *Curly Sue*. We had 3-D glasses in the theater and Hughes thought it would be really funny to see them on screen. That's what led to the popcorn-stealing scene in *Curly Sue*. All that was written right on the set."

A traditional musical event at the Music Box appears in the film

Solstice (1993). Every December, the theater holds a Christmas sing-along in conjunction with the perennial Jimmy Stewart-Frank Capra favorite *It's a Wonderful Life* (1946). This annual event ultimately inspired local director Jerry Vasilatos, a Columbia College film school graduate who lost his right leg in a freak subway accident. The film revolves around a young man who rediscovers the real spirit of the holidays after going to the Music Box sing-along.

Though the theater has undergone massive change since it first opened its doors in 1929, there is still a theater mainstay. According to Carlo and Chaney, the spirit of Whitey, the long-time theater manager, still lives in the Music Box. "We call him 'manager emeritus' because he acts that way," says Chaney who offers up an example of how Whitey has favorably intervened on their behalf.

"We take care of a lot of the maintenance here ourselves," says Chaney. "I think it was before the film festival one year....all of the lights on the emergency circuit, which are the aisle lights, and the wall sockets in the auditorium on the left side were all out. The fuse blew up.

"I did an invocation to Whitey. I just verbally started talking to this man and said 'you've got to help me find this problem. I can't have a whole row of lights out for the opening of the film festival. Now you know where the problem is.' Whitey or something told me to go down and turn on a certain switch. I would not have done that. There wasn't anyone else around but me. Chris had gone. I just decided to verbalize, I said 'it certainly couldn't hurt.' I didn't want to spend two days crawling around checking every circuit. I fixed the whole thing in a matter of about 30 minutes, put in a new porcelain circuit in the socket, eliminated the switch, and saved myself a whole lot of time.

For more information, call the Music Box Theatre at 773-871-6604 or visit their Web site at http://www.musicboxtheatre.com.

*Oakie played "Benizo Napaloni, Dictator of Bacteria," an obvious caricature of Italy's Benito Mussolini, while Chaplin lampooned Adolph Hitler as "Adenoid Hynkel, Dictator of Ptomania." During production, Oakie took great pleasure in trying to out-maneuver Chaplin for laughs, a competition that clearly shows up in the final cut. During the filming of one scene, an exasperated Chaplin finally dropped the comedy gauntlet. With cameras rolling, Chaplin broke character, smiled wickedly at his co-star, and told him, "If you really want to steal a scene from me, you son-of-a-bitch, just look straight into the camera. That'll do it every time."

Sources:
Robinson, David. *Chaplin: His Life and Art.* New York: McGraw-Hill, 1985, 502.
Music Box Web page at http://www.musicboxtheatre.com.

Ron Dean

"I was protecting the coat."

It's one thing to be a former Chicagoan who comes back to town to make movies. But what's it like for Chicago actors who don't make the big jump to Los Angeles?

Ron Dean is a local actor who worked with such theater companies as Second City, Steppenwolf, the Goodman, Organic, Wisdom Bridge, Northlight, and Victory Gardens. "Chicago is great for theater," he says. "For someone who wants to be in film in Chicago, it's kind of like wanting to live in Iowa and be a whaler."

You may not know Dean by name, but you probably know his face. He's Emilio Estevez's father in *The Breakfast Club* (1985). He's the guy in The Ginger Man sitting next to Paul Newman in *The Color of Money* (1986). In *Code of Silence* (1985) and *Above the Law* (1988), he plays a cop pal of Chuck Norris and Steven Seagal respectively. In *The Fugitive* (1993), he's one of the detectives who interrogates Harrison Ford after Ford's wife, Sela Ward, is brutally murdered.

Dean also had a good part in *The Package* (1989), playing a shadowy figure within a larger conspiracy plot. It gave him a chance to work on screen opposite an old friend of his from the Organic Theater, Dennis Franz.

"Dennis is fun to work with," says Dean. "He's always looking for bits. There's never a scene that goes by that he doesn't do a little something.

"In *The Package*, part of my wardrobe was a beautiful leather jacket. I was wearing it through every scene. I don't think there was one scene where I didn't have it on. I loved that jacket. 'After the movie is over,' I told the wardrobe people, 'I'll buy this jacket.' They said 'yeah, after we're done you can have it.'

"The last scene I was in was my big death scene. I was supposed to get shot and fall down. Well, I didn't want to fall down on this beautiful jacket. In the scene, I come out of the bathroom when I'm supposed to be guarding someone. I come out of the bathroom and Franz catches me and I pull a gun on him. Well, I don't want to get shot and fall on my coat. So the first time we did the scene, I went into the bathroom and took off my

You may not know local actor Ron Dean by name, but you probably know his face. Dean has had roles in numerous Chicago-shot films, including *The Breakfast Club, The Color of Money, Code of Silence, Above the Law, The Fugitive,* and *The Package.* (*Courtesy of Ron Dean.*)

coat. I come out and [director Andrew Davis] says, 'wait a minute, why are you carrying your coat?' I said, 'well, he [my character] just took a shit...he wouldn't be wearing a coat.' Andy says, 'well, that makes sense.'

"So then when I fall after I get shot, I drop the coat off to the side, gently. Then Franz comes over and checks my pulse. We shot this sequence several times, and all of a sudden it dawns on Dennis that I was protecting my coat. So now he's coming in the next take and he's trying to step on my coat. I was supposed to be dead and I'm trying to kick my coat away!"

Dean remains a steadfast resident of the city, long after many of his colleagues headed west for fame and fortune in Hollywood. "As much as I enjoy doing movies, I'm a dyed-in-the-wool Chicagoan," he says. "I was a Chicagoan long before I was an actor, and I'll be a Chicagoan after they stop hiring me as an actor. I just don't want to live anyplace else."

➡ METRO
3730 N. Clark Street

Looking for the Next Big Thing in pop music? Then check out Metro, the Midwest's premier showcase for cutting-edge bands. The Smashing Pumpkins, Ministry, and Liz Phair all learned their chops on the Metro stage before moving on to national fame and glory.

When Hollywood needs a nightclub scene, Metro's darkened ambiance nicely fills the bill. Joan Jett (ex-member of the Runaways and leader of the Blackhearts) and her movie brother Michael J. Fox played here in *Light of Day*'s (1987) look at the day-to-day world of struggling rock bands. Supposedly set in Cleveland, a good chunk of the film was acutally shot in Chi-town.

In *Blink*, Madeline Stowe played a member of The Drovers, a real-life Chicago band that brings a Celtic lilt to their music. Metro is where cop Aidan Quinn first notices Stowe as she plays Irish fiddle.

For more information, call Metro at 773-549-4140 or visit their Web site at http://www.metrochicago.com/.

➡ JESSICA LANGE'S APARTMENT BUILDING IN *MEN DON'T LEAVE*
510 W. Belmont Avenue

It looks like Chicago, but it was supposed to be Baltimore in *Men Don't Leave* (1990), a sweet romantic drama starring Jessica Lange. This building on the corner of Belmont Avenue and Sheridan Road was were Lange lived with her son, a local actor by the name of Chris O'Donnell.

➡ BELMONT HARBOR
Belmont Avenue at Lake Michigan

Fans of the dark suburban nightmare, *Risky Business* (1983), will instantly recognize this popular lakeside attraction. Belmont Harbor is where Joel Goodson (Tom Cruise) exchanged words with his girlfriend-for-a-night, Lana (Rebecca DeMornay), then clung to the hood of his father's Porsche as the car slowly rolled into Lake Michigan.

On a lower comedic note, Dan Aykroyd's Jerry Lewis-like feature, *Dr. Detroit* (1983), did some shooting at Belmont Harbor.

➡ GLORIA SWANSON BIRTHPLACE
341 W. Grace Street

"I feel sure that unborn babies pick their parents," Gloria Swanson wrote in her 1980 autobiography, *Swanson on Swanson*. "I waited for the right moment between a young man named Joe Swanson and his wife Addie, before I willed my way from infinity to the second floor of 341 W. Grace Street in Chicago. I decided to be a girl."[1] Will your way to this Lakeview location if you want to walk the streets where Swanson spent her first few years before entering the picture business at Essanay Studios on Argyle Street.

[1] Swanson, Gloria, *Swanson on Swanson* (New York: Random House, 1980), 12.

GLORIA SWANSON

Chicago-born Gloria Swanson spent her early teen years as an extra at Essanay Studios before moving to Hollywood where she would eventually rise to film stardom. (*From the collection of Arnie Bernstein.*)

➡ BREWSTER BUILDING
2800 N. Pine Grove Avenue (at Diversey Parkway)

This is one of the North Side's most beautiful condominium apartment buildings. Built in 1893, the Brewster Building was designed by R.H. Turnock. Its stately elegance is marked by polished red marble moldings on the windows and doorways and the beautiful grillwork of the cage elevator and stairway banisters. Overall, this is a visually stunning edifice—perfect for all kinds of films.

The Brewster has seen it all, from action films like *Running Scared* (1986), to the comic romance of *She's Having a Baby* (1988), to the over-the-top horror of *Child's Play* (1988). *Hoodlum* (1997) effectively used the building's vintage look to help recreate Chicago as 1920s New

York City.

The Brewster briefly housed one of cinema's greatest names. Legend has it that when Charlie Chaplin worked at Essanay Studios during the early months of 1915, he stayed at the Brewster Building's luxurious penthouse suite.

➡ CHICAGO CEMETERIES IN THE MOVIES
- Graceland Cemetery, 4001 N. Clark Street
- Jewish Graceland Cemetery, 3869 N. Clark Street
- Rosehill Cemetery, 5800 N. Ravenswood Avenue
- Bohemian National Cemetery, 5300 N. Pulaski Road
- Oak Woods Cemetery, 1035 E. 67th Street
- Burr Oak Cemetery, 471 E. 31st Street

Cemeteries make great film locations. Shooting in a necropolis, with its ornate art work and the inherent drama of the grave, amidst mausoleums and memorials, offers a wealth of possibilities for moviemakers.

On the North Side, Graceland Cemetery, 4001 N. Clark Street, was the location for the fireman's funeral in *Backdraft* (1991). Don't look in Graceland for the Volunteer Firefighter's Monument where the funeral was held; that memorial is actually part of Rosehill Cemetery, north and west of Graceland. A replica of this memorial was created specifically for the film and temporarily installed at Graceland.

Another movie funeral shot in Graceland was for the low-rent horror flick, *Damien: Omen II* (1978). That burial ceremony took place just north of the Potter and Bertha Palmer grave site, one of Graceland's landmark monuments. *The Naked Face* (1984)—a Roger Moore thriller, *The Negotiator* (1998), and the television series "Early Edition" have also made use of Graceland.

Just south of Graceland, on the other side of Irving Park Road, is a smaller cemetery known as Jewish Graceland at 3819 N. Clark Street. Made up of four separate cemeteries, Jewish Graceland ironically served as the site of a Catholic burial in *Running Scared* (1986). Fake snow had to be strategically placed around the cemetery plots to cover Hebrew lettering and the six-pointed Stars of David carved into many of the graveyard's tombstones. *Flatliners* (1990), a surreal examination of life after death, also did some shooting at Jewish Graceland.

Movie-wise, Rosehill Cemetery, 5800 N. Ravenswood, is where *Next of Kin* (1989) staged its shoot 'em up finale. Another film to send bullets flying through the normally quiet graveyard was *U.S. Marshals*. Standing in for the Queens borough of New York, Rosehill actually combined with Bohemian

National Cemetery, 5300 N. Pulaski, to form the extensive grounds where Tommy Lee Jones, Wesley Snipes, and a mini-militia of good guys and bad guys exchanged gunfire.

On the South Side, Oak Woods Cemetery was the place where Mama Jo was buried in *Soul Food*. Located at 1035 E. 67th Street, Oak Woods is one of the city's oldest graveyards. For history buffs, Oak Woods is an outstanding place to take a stroll. The graves here range from physicist Enrico Fermi to athletes Jesse Owens and Cap Anson. Among the more infamous residents is Big Jim Colosimo. A major crime boss in the 1910s, his assassination in 1920 ultimately led to the rise of Al Capone. Oak Woods is also the final resting place of two Chicago mayors: William Hale Thompson and Harold Washington, the city's first African-American mayor. Washington died in the fall of 1987. Ironically, Bernard Epton, who ran as the Republican candidate against Washington in 1983, died a few weeks later and is buried not far from his former rival.

Finally, there is Burr Oak at 471 E. 31st Street. It's here, at this South Side burial ground, where the funeral scene of *Cooley High* took place.

For more information on Chicago cemeteries, check out Matt Hucke's wonderful *Graveyards of Chicago* Web site at http://www.graveyards.com.

➡ **WGN TELEVISION STUDIOS**
2501 W. Bradley Place

Since it first hit the airwaves in 1948, WGN-Channel 9 television has been a bedrock of Chicago broadcasting. Owned by the Tribune Corporation (WGN stands for the *Chicago Tribune's* motto "World's Greatest Newspaper"), Channel 9 has been known for its pioneering efforts in television programming. In the 1970s, Phil Donahue came here from Ohio to launch his nationally-syndicated talk show. Of course, a few generations of Chicago children grew up with various incarnations of the beloved Bozo the Clown, an anchor of WGN's broadcasting empire. Tickets for a Bozo taping remain as highly coveted as a Bulls courtside playoff seat.

Part of WGN's success was the savvy move to get involved with the cable television industry. Today, no matter what city you travel to in the United States, you're bound to find a WGN broadcast.

Movie-wise, WGN was the launching pad for William Friedkin. Starting out as a lowly mailroom assistant, Friedkin worked his way up through the ranks at the station and eventually headed to Los Angeles. In 1971, Friedkin won the Best Director Oscar for *The French Connection*, one of the all-time great cop movies.

WGN also served as a movie set for Oliver Stone's surreal satire,

Natural Born Killers (1994). Robert Downey, Jr., playing a sleazy Australian tabloid reporter, shot his television control room scenes at the Channel 9 studios.

For more information on WGN, its history, and schedule, check out the station Web site at http://www.wgntv.com.

➡ **LANE TECHNICAL HIGH SCHOOL**
2501 W. Addison Street

In *Wildcats* (1986), a football comedy starring Goldie Hawn, Lane Technical High School did double duty. In the film's thin story, Hawn loses her teaching job at "Prescott High," a suburban institution, then, improbably enough, becomes head football coach at the inner-city "Central High." Both schools were played by Lane Tech. Incidentally, look carefully at Hawn's players. Two of her athletes are Wesley Snipes and Woody Harrelson, who moved from supporting parts to star status, teaming up in *White Men Can't Jump* (1992) and *Money Train* (1995).

The Lane Tech homepage is at http://www.lanehs.com/.

THE POOL HALLS OF
The Color of Money

 In 1986, Martin Scorsese, Paul Newman, and Tom Cruise came to town to film *The Color of Money*, a sequel of sorts to the classic 1961 film, *The Hustler*. Newman won an Oscar for recreating the role of "Fast Eddie" Felson, a retired pool shark now taking young hustler Cruise under his wing. The premise had the duo traveling the Midwest, with Cruise gaining experience in various pool rooms before moving on to bigger stakes in Atlantic City. On screen, we see a road trip. In reality, you can recreate *The Color of Money* journey with only one foray outside Chicago city limits.

Start at Fitzgerald's, the popular Berwyn nightspot at 6615 Roosevelt Road. That's where Newman first spies Cruise and sees potential in this talented, hopelessly cocky pool player. (Fitzgerald's also showed up as "The Tear Drop Lounge" in the 1987 comedy *Adventures in Babysitting*.) Chicago's Finest Billiards at 6414 S. Cottage Grove represented the South Side. Up North, *The Color of Money* shot scenes in The Ginger Man at 3740 N. Clark, Chris' Billiards at 4637 N. Milwaukee, and Family Billiards at 8100 N. Ashland.

Significant action took place at St. Paul's Billiards at 1415 W. Fullerton when Cruise got the snot beat out of him by some nasty thugs. A beating of a different sort took place at the North Center Bowling Alley at 4017 N. Lincoln. It's here where Newman, the old-school shark, is out-hustled by a young hustler, played by Forrest Whitaker.

➡ **THE GREEN MILL**
4802 N. Broadway (at Lawrence Avenue)

The history of the Green Mill is packed with stories that rival Hollywood's fictional creations. This popular jazz club opened in 1907 under the name Pop Morse's Roadhouse. The establishment changed hands three years later and was given a new name: The Green Mill Gardens. With Essanay Studios just a few blocks north on Argyle Street, the Green Mill became a popular place for actors to congregate. Western star and studio co-owner Bronco Billy Anderson was known to ride his horse to the Mill after a day's shooting, tie the steed to a hitching post, and head inside for a few drinks. Wallace Beery was another Green Mill regular from the Essanay lot; legend has it that Charlie Chaplin stepped in a time or two during his brief Chicago stay as well.

Aside from the Essanay gang, vaudeville performers passing through town would stop by the Green Mill in between their shows at the nearby Uptown and Riviera Theaters. Al Jolson, Eddie Cantor, and Sophie Tucker were among the many stars who frequented the Green Mill during this era.

The 1920s ushered in the brave new world of Prohibition. Though alcohol was now banned from coast to coast, the new teetotal culture had little effect on Green Mill business when Al Capone's henchman "Machine Gun" Jack McGurn bought a partial ownership of the club. Capone and company held court in a booth along a wall, affording them a good view of the entertainment on stage as well as the entrance.

Under McGurn's rule, the Green Mill played a role in what is now a show business legend. During the 1920s, entertainer Joe E. Lewis was a club

The Green Mill (4802 N. Broadway), a popular jazz club which opened in 1907, has been blown up on-screen in *Thief*, and seen in *Soul Food*, *Prelude to a Kiss*, and others. (*Photo by Holly Pluard.*)

favorite. McGurn offered the rising singer-comedian a $650-per-week deal for exclusive engagements. Lewis boldly declined the offer, telling McGurn that he had a more lucrative proposal from the New Rendezvous Cafe, located at Clark Street and Diversey Parkway. McGurn, not one to take "no" for an answer, warned Lewis, "You'll never live to open."

Unperturbed, Lewis left the Green Mill. On November 2, 1927, he began his engagement at the New Rendezvous, where his comedy review was capped by a series of McGurn jokes.

Eight days after opening, Lewis was attacked in his room at the Commonwealth Hotel, 2747 N. Pine Grove Avenue. Three McGurn thugs, brandishing guns and a hunting knife, proceeded to cut Lewis's throat from ear to ear. After severing his vocal cords, the trio mutilated Lewis's face and split the scene.

Though bleeding profusely, Lewis managed to open the door of his room and crawled into the hallway. He was found by hotel personnel, rushed to a local hospital, and spent seven hours in surgery. The message was clear. If Lewis wasn't working for McGurn, then he wasn't going to entertain anybody.

Amazingly, Lewis survived this brutal assault. Though he required extensive speech therapy, Lewis returned to the nightclub circuit, playing the New Rendezvous for a while. Then, at the behest of Scarface himself, Lewis returned to the Green Mill. Eventually the comic went to Los Angeles, where he had some limited success in the picture business. In 1957, Hollywood turned this violent tale into *The Joker is Wild*, starring Frank

Sinatra. Over the years, Lewis remained a Chicago favorite, playing numerous engagements at the Chez Paree nightclub.

With the end of Prohibition and the Capone era in Chicago, the Green Mill once more became a legal operation. From the 1930s to the 1960s, it was a popular nightclub, boasting of big name jazz acts on its small stage. In the 1970s, the club slipped in stature, relegated to "dive" status, and inhabited by assorted barflies and down-and-outers. Then, in 1986, the Green Mill was bought by Dave Jemilo, who sunk money and hard work into restoring the club to its former grandeur.

Jemilo's efforts paid off. Today the Green Mill is one of the hottest night spots in town. Jazz acts here range from Von Freeman and Ed Petersen to the swinging retro sounds of the Mighty Blue Kings. Sunday nights are devoted to rowdy, slightly pretentious "poetry slams" where contestants throw egos out the window, get on stage, and read poetry (sometimes written on the spot) to the cheers and jeers of the audience.

For filmmakers, the club's interior, modeled after the famous Uptown House of Harlem, offers a unique setting. It's a nightclub, it's a seedy bar, it's a place to take a date. That's the beauty of this great place—at least from a Hollywood perspective.

Thief (1981), an intense study of a professional burglar and the first film for director and former Chicagoan Michael Mann, utilized the Green Mill for several scenes. The bar served as a sort of headquarters for the main character, played by James Caan. The Green Mill was also setting for a pivotal moment between Caan and crime boss Robert Prosky.

Thief's legacy lives on at the Green Mill to this day. The end of *Thief* has a determined Caan destroying any place associated with his past, including his home and car dealership. Caan also firebombs the Green Mill, destroying the front of the building in a massive explosion. In order to blow up the club without actually leveling it, a facade was built to cover the Green Mill's real door and picture window. The flashing "Green Mill Lounge" was detonated in a wild mix of fire, electricity, and popping light bulbs. The obliterated sign was quickly replaced with an exact replica, which remains a club fixture to this day.

On a less violent note, the Green Mill was a place of leisure for characters in the romantic comedies *Prelude to a Kiss* (1992) and *Kissing a Fool* (1998). Kathleen Turner, in the title role of private eye *V.I. Warshawski* (1991), hung out here, as did the mob family of *Next of Kin* (1989), a far-fetched thriller featuring Patrick Swayze as a Chicago cop.

In the painfully unfunny comedy *Folks!* (1992), Tom Selleck's absent-minded father, Don Ameche, ended up wandering into the Green Mill, the setting for an all-black South Side bar, for a little socializing. The Green Mill also played an all-African-American South Side bar in *A Family Thing*

(1996). In an oddly touching scene, a drunken Robert Duvall, having recently learned he was born to an African-American mother, interrupts a private party at the lounge. Awkwardly, Duvall, a white Southerner dressed in simple, dirty clothing, tries to ingratiate himself with a group of friends, explaining that he, too, is a member of their race.

Soul Food (1997) used the Green Mill as the debut club for the band Milestone, a group formed by Michael Beach's character. The band featured the film's executive producer, Kenneth "Babyface" Edmonds, on guitar and vocals.

To find out who's playing at the Green Mill, call 773-878-5552.

Source: Bergreen, Laurence. *Capone: The Man and the Era.* New York: Touchstone, 1996, 251-54.

➡ THE UPTOWN THEATER
Broadway at Lawrence Avenue

The Uptown Theatre, built in 1925 and located on Broadway a half block north of Lawrence, was featured in *Home Alone II: Lost in New York.* (*Photo by Holly Pluard.*)

Located half a block north of the Green Mill, the Uptown Theater was once the North Side's golden movie palace. Built at a cost of $4 million by Balaban & Katz, the Uptown opened in August of 1925.

Eight stories tall, the Uptown combined modern technology with a regal Spanish Renaissance decor. Hanging from the ceiling of the five-story lobby was a magnificent chandelier. The theater itself contained 5,000 seats (still not enough for the estimated opening night crowd of 12,000!), a custom-made Wurlitzer organ (at the time, the world's most expensive), and a full-sized orchestra pit. Best of all, this movie palace had an elaborate air conditioning system—no small accomplishment for the 1920s.

The Uptown offered patrons the latest in Hollywood features, as well as big name vaudeville acts. A night at the Uptown meant glamour, prestige, and a good time for countless Chicagoans.

Then came the Depression. With declining revenues, theater maintenance was cut back and the Uptown underwent a slow, painful decay. Second- and third-run movies replaced the lavish premieres, and by the late 1970s, the Uptown was mainly a venue for rock-and-roll shows. Ultimately, the theater closed its doors in 1981.

If you want a glimpse of what exists behind the plywood covering the Uptown Theater doors, check out *Home Alone II: Lost in New York* (1992). The grand lobby of the theater was remade into a Manhattan toy store for this John Hughes/Chris Columbus slapstick comedy.

➡ PEOPLE'S CHURCH
941 W. Lawrence Avenue

The People's Church was built in 1926 for the congregation of progressive Chicago clergyman Dr. Preston Bradley. Today the building is used by theater companies and for public meetings. In the 1930s-period gangster drama *Hoodlum*, the People's Church was transformed into New York's Harlem Faith Church.

➡ LOYOLA UNIVERSITY OF CHICAGO
6525 N. Sheridan Road

The camera sweeps across Lake Michigan, zeroing in on a solitary figure walking along a rocky beach, framed by campus buildings. Against the brilliance of a rising sun staring him in the face, an isolated young man (Kiefer Sutherland) dramatically declares "Today is a good day to die."

So begins *Flatliners* (1990), a surreal story of medical students who attempt to cheat death. This histrionic opening took place at Loyola's North Shore Campus; other scenes were shot in Hyde Park and the Museum of Science and Industry. Trivia buffs will note that *Flatliners* is the movie where Sutherland and co-star Julia Roberts became romantically involved before their very public, pre-wedding breakup.

The Suburbs

➡ **EVANSTON TOWNSHIP HIGH SCHOOL**
1600 Dodge Avenue, Evanston, Illinois

In *Rookie of the Year* (1993), Evanston Township High School was transformed into a junior high where pint-sized pitching sensation Thomas Ian Nicholas was a student. Actors Joan Cusack and Jeremy Piven are two real-life alumni of this north suburban institution.

➡ **NORTHWESTERN UNIVERSITY**
North Sheridan Road in Evanston, Illinois

➡ **NORTHWESTERN MEMORIAL HOSPITAL**
Superior Street and Fairbanks Court in Chicago

Founded on June 14, 1851, Northwestern University is one of America's premier schools, with a sprawling campus along the Lake Michigan shoreline in north suburban Evanston. A second campus, in downtown Chicago, comprises Northwestern's law and medical schools.

The Northwestern School of Speech includes divisions in Communication Studies, Radio/Television/Film, Theater, and Performance Studies. The film program is housed in the Barbara and Garry Marshall Studio Wing of Louis Hall, on the north end of the campus. Yes, that's the same Garry Marshall who hit it big in Hollywood as a television writer and film director. A 1955 alum of Northwestern's Medill School of Journalism, he was the driving force behind the television sitcoms "The Odd Couple," "Happy Days," and "Mork and Mindy." Marshall later switched to movies and directed a string of comedy films including *The Flamingo Kid* (1984), *Pretty Woman* (1990), and *Nothing in Common* (1986), which was partially shot at Marshall's alma mater.

Northwestern provides a full range of film production and history classes, sometimes working in tandem with other departments in the School of Speech. Guest lecturers have included Robert Altman, playwright Alan Ayckbourn, Richard Benjamin (class of 1960), Ellen Burstyn, William Daniels (class of 1950), producer Robert Greenhut, Gene Hackman, playwright Tony Kushner, Cloris Leachman (class of 1948), John

Malkovich, *My Best Friend's Wedding* co-star Dermot Mulroney (class of 1985), Robert Redford, David Schwimmer (class of 1988), and Gary Sinise.

In addition to Marshall, Benjamin, Daniels, Leachman, Mulroney, and Schwimmer, Northwestern has produced a considerable array of film and television talent. Laura Innes (of "ER" fame, class of 1979), comic actor Richard Kind (class of 1978), "Seinfeld's" Julia Louis-Dreyfus (class of 1982) and her husband, writer/producer Brad Hall (class of 1980), screenwriter Dana Olson (class of 1980), and Kimberly Williams (class of 1993) all trod the boards at Northwestern.

Northwestern also provides the north suburbs with a real treasure: the A&O Film Series in the Norris Center on the Evanston campus. With a programming smorgasbord of classic Hollywood fare, foreign films, recent hits, and great schlock flicks, the A&O series provides one of the best (and cheapest) places in the area to catch a good movie.

When it comes to Hollywood productions, Northwestern's ivy-covered buildings and beautiful lakefront locations provide filmmakers with a wealth of opportunities. *Nothing in Common* (1986) featured both the Evanston campus and the downtown Northwestern University Hospital. The film story revolved around Tom Hanks, a self-centered yuppie who must come to terms with his dying father, played by Jackie Gleason. Hanks' movie girlfriend Bess Armstrong held the on-screen job of an acting teacher at Northwestern, with her classes meeting in Annie May Swift Hall. Meanwhile, Gleason was hospitalized at the downtown medical center.

Baseball player cum scholar Tom Berenger hung out at Northwestern's Deering Library in *Major League* (1989). While on campus he might have caught a lecture at the Technological Institute where Dan Aykroyd ruled the classrooms in the painfully unfunny comedy *Dr. Detroit* (1983). When not being seduced by older women in glass elevators, the prep school boys of *Class* (1983) lived in Northwestern dormitories.

Other films shot at Northwestern's downtown campus include *The Babe, Richie Rich,* and *With Honors*—which made some good use of the campus backdrop.

Two other Northwestern-based films are worth noting. In 1942 some students from the School of Speech took a camera to north suburban Winnetka and filmed Henrik Ibsen's classic play, *Peer Gynt*. Making his film debut in the title role was none other than Charlton Heston. Seven years later, many of the same gang scouted out Romanesque buildings in Evanston and Chicago, then used these locations (including the downtown post office and the Elks Club at Diversey Parkway and Sheridan Road) to shoot a lakeshore version of William Shakespeare's *Julius Caesar*. Heston had the role of Marc Antony and David Bradley, who directed both films, played Brutus.

After *Julius Caesar*, Heston and Bradley both ended up in Hollywood. With his solid looks and considerable talent, Heston quickly rose through the ranks to become one of America's premier screen actors. Bradley's adventures in Tinseltown were less fortunate. His first studio effort as a director was *Talk About a Stranger* (1952), which starred former Chicagoan and future First Lady Nancy Davis (later, of course, Mrs. Ronald Reagan). Clashes between Bradley and studio chieftains, however, led to the quick demise of his career. Bradley's last film, *Madmen of Mandoras* was released in 1963. This film was recut in 1968, with new footage edited in and released under the title *They Saved Hitler's Brain*. A seemingly permanent denizen of the Hall of Worst Films Ever Made, *They Saved Hitler's Brain* loosely revolves around some mad scientists who keep the former Furhrer's animated noggin in a jar.

Happily, Bradley reinvented himself, taking his love for silent movies and becoming one of the country's leading film archivists. He was personally responsible for rescuing thousands of silent films from the cinema dustheap. Upon Bradley's death in 1997, this invaluable collection was willed to Indiana University.

For more information about Northwestern University, check out their Web site at http://www.nwu.edu/. The School of Speech also maintains one of the Internet's best movie sites, The Chicago Moving Image Scene, at http://www.rtvf.nwu.edu/chicago/.

➡ **SITE OF OLD NILES EAST HIGH SCHOOL**
Lincoln Avenue at Skokie Boulevard, Skokie, Illinois

When Niles East High School closed its doors in 1980, the north suburbs lost an educational institution but gained a movie facility. Part of Skokie School District 219, East's demise was instigated by declining enrollment. Yet the building itself, which was razed a few years ago, was a moviemaker's dream. Complete with hallways, classrooms, a gym, lockers, and other scholastic accouterments, Niles East found new life as a movie set.

In the early to mid-1980s, John Hughes almost single-handedly carved out the north suburbs as a hotbed of adolescent movie locations. With *Sixteen Candles* (1984), *The Breakfast Club* (1985), and *Ferris Bueller's Day Off* (1986), Hughes put together an off-beat trilogy of films which were solidly rooted in the Skokie-Wilmette-Winnetka-Glencoe-Highland Park region.

Yet someone beat Hughes to the punch, with a film that crystallized the culture of north suburbia: Paul Brickman and *Risky Business* (1983), a star-making vehincle for young actor Tom Cruise. He played Joel Goodson, a high school senior worried about his future and curious about matters sexual. Niles East served as both Cruise's school and home. Scenes inside and outside the school are obvious. The exterior sequences for the house cum brothel were filmed at a private residence in the north suburbs. The interior of the home, however, including the famous living room where Cruise danced in his underwear to the music of Bob Seger, were sets built inside the school's old gymnasium.

Not to be outdone, Hughes brought his first group of high schoolers, led by Molly Ringwald and Anthony Michael Hall, to Niles East, where he filmed some scenes of *Sixteen Candles*.

➡ WALKER BROTHERS ORIGINAL PANCAKE HOUSE
153 Greenbay Road, Wilmette, Illinois

In *Ordinary People* (1980), Robert Redford's Oscar-winning adaptation of Judith Guest's novel, Timothy Hutton and Dinah Manoff met at this Wilmette restaurant to trade life stories over coffee. They should have stayed for the apple pancakes. Walker Brothers is practically an institution in Wilmette, serving up a delectable array of breakfast creations. The apple pancake is a meal unto itself; eat one and you'll be hooked for life.

➡ WINNETKA CONGREGATIONAL CHURCH
725 Pine, Winnetka, Illinois

Remember how Kevin Bacon felt over his nuptials to Elizabeth McGovern in *She's Having a Baby* (1988)? The happy couple had their ceremony in this quiet Winnetka church.

➡ THE *HOME ALONE* TOUR

Home Alone (1990) was a phenomenon. Written and produced by John Hughes and directed by Chris Columbus, the film's thin plot revolved around a youngster (Macaulay Culkin) accidentally left home during the Christmas season while his family flew off for a Paris vacation. Two bungling burglars, played by Joe Pesci and Daniel Stern, attempt to rob Culkin's seemingly empty home, only to be thwarted by the youngster's Rube-Goldberg booby traps.

Home Alone was shot in early 1990, making extensive use of several north suburban locations. Using a car and a good map, fans of the film can tour *Home Alone's* public sites. (What you won't find in the list below is the house where Culkin squared off with Pesci and Stern, since this is a private residence.)

First head up to Winnetka and the Hubbard Woods Pharmacy at 940 Greenbay Road. The exterior of this business was used as the drugstore where Culkin stocked up on supplies. His actual purchases were made a bit further from here, inside Kenilworth's Blann Pharmacy at 400 Greenbay Road. Unfortunately, neither drug store is still in business.

Culkin's second foray for reserves was made at the Grand Food Center grocery store at 606 Greenbay Road, also in Winnetka. Playing the puzzled grocery clerk in this scene is Tracy J. Connor, a wonderful Chicago-trained comic actor who made her film debut in *Home Alone.*

Nearby, at the corner of Greenbay Road and Gage Street, is Hubbard Woods Park. Here's where Culkin ran pell-mell from his mysterious next-door-neighbor Marley (Roberts Blossom).

Towards the end of the film, Culkin heads into Trinity United Methodist Church at 1024 Lake Street in Wilmette. Once he steps inside, however, the young hero takes a huge location jump. Though the exterior of the church is in Wilmette, interiors were shot at Grace Episcopal Church at 924 Lake Street in Oak Park. It's here where Culkin again meets Blossum and we learn the true story of this strange man.

Culkin wasn't around when Grace Episcopal was the setting for another Chicago-area movie. In 1978, two years before Culkin was born, the nuptials for Robert Altman's *A Wedding* were held at this house of worship.

➡ NEW TRIER WEST HIGH SCHOOL
7 Happ Road, Northfield, Illinois

When New Trier West closed down in 1984, John Hughes' movie machine moved in. The former high school's three gymnasiums were converted into movie sets where Hughes filmed parts of *Sixteen Candles* (1984), *Uncle Buck* (1991), and *Curly Sue* (1991). *Uncle Buck* also used the New Trier West exterior as the school where title character John Candy dropped off his niece and nephews. New Trier West reopened in 1998 as an all-freshman school.

Interestingly, New Trier West's sister school, New Trier (formerly New Trier East) in Winnetka, has been a spawning ground for several film personalities. Ann Margret, Rock Hudson, Charlton Heston, Adam Baldwin, and *About Last Night...* (1986) director Edward Zwick are all alumni of this North Shore institution, which is often described as one of the finest public high schools in the country.

➡ **THE *WIZARD OF GORE* MAGICIAN'S THEATER**
Edgewood Middle School
929 Edgewood Road, Highland Park, Illinois

Yes, it looks like an innocent middle school, but behind these ominous doors lies the theater where Herschell Gordon Lewis's *Wizard of Gore* (1970) plied his gruesome trade. "My kids were in school at Edgewood," Lewis recalls. "I made a deal to rent the school auditorium. It was perfect for us, a little theater. Production was at a time when school was out, so we had use of the place. So that's where we shot the magician stuff."

Herschell Gordon Lewis

"The Godfather of Gore"

He graduated from Senn High School, then earned his bachelor's and master's degrees in journalism from Northwestern. After obtaining a doctorate in psychology he taught English at Mississippi State University. He has worked in television and advertising and has authored numerous books on direct marketing. He's a connoisseur of the fine arts, penning volumes on such varied topics as plate collecting and Norman Rockwell. So what is Herschell Gordon Lewis's best-known contribution to film history?

Gore.

Known among horror fans as "The Godfather of Gore," in the 1960s and early 1970s Lewis personally annihilated every taboo Hollywood filmmakers had set for themselves. *Blood Feast* (1963) featured a maniacal caterer with a taste for human innards. *2000 Maniacs* (1964) was a carnival of torture as Confederate ghosts wreaked vengeance on hapless northerners. Other titles, like *A Taste of Blood* (1967), *The Wizard of Gore* (1970), and Lewis's swan song, *The Gore-Gore Girls* (1972), continued to break new ground in on-screen carnage, if not artistic merit.

Just how does a genteel college professor make the switch to low-budget gore movie monarch? Having grown bored with teaching, Lewis turned to broadcasting and eventually became a producer for WKY-TV in Oklahoma City.

Eventually he returned to Chicago and joined an advertising agency founded by a friend from Lewis's Northwestern days. When the agency failed, Lewis bought an interest in a small industrial studio at 218 S. Wabash. His partner was one Marty Schmidhofer, though the company was called Lewis & Martin Films. This name was less a matter of homage and more towards practicality. There wasn't enough room for Lewis & Schmidhofer Films on their building!

The affable, innocuous Herschell Gordon Lewis, director, producer, "king" of low-budget gore films of the 60s and 70s. (*Photo by Arnie Bernstein.*)

Lewis Martin Films managed to stay afloat through work on business and government films and television commercials. "One day somebody said to me 'how do you make any money in your business,' because I was complaining about the nature of the film business in Chicago. I said the only way to make money in the film business is to shoot features. He said, 'then why don't you shoot features.' I said, 'well, nobody shoots features in Chicago.' He said, 'why not?' It occurred to me, this is where the whole thing started with Charlie Chaplin at the old Essanay Studios.

So I said, 'what the hell.' "

That "what the hell" resulted in Lewis's first feature production company, Mid-Continental Films, a consortium of friends "who thought the movie business had some glamour to it," Lewis jokes. "The company was to shoot two movies. The first one was called *The Prime Time* (1960) and it was a mistake from beginning to end in every conceivable way."

Filmed at the Fred Niles Studio (today occupied by Harpo

Productions) and in areas just outside the city, *The Prime Time* is notable mostly as the film debut of Karen Black. * Also known as *Hell Kitten*, the film was a grade-Z "teens in trouble" flick, a popular commodity at the time. Despite production problems which largely involved union salaries, *The Prime Time* was completed and ready for audiences.

"We made a deal with a company called Modern Film Distributors at 1325 S. Wabash. The place was run by Irwin Joseph, who was an old time, hard-bitten film distributor—my kind of guy!

"Irwin had a young fellow named Dave Friedman, who was his assistant. Dave and I became quite friendly. We made a deal to distribute *The Prime Time* with a picture someone had made a few years earlier called *Carnival Story* (1954). At that time you had to put a double feature together or else the theaters, in their consummate wisdom, would say 'well, yours was the second feature, you get $50 flat and they'd say to the other guy, 'well, yours was the second feature, you get $50 flat.' If you controlled both sides of a double feature, they couldn't say that. We opened the picture in Madison, Wisconsin and began to run ads in *Variety*, but nothing much happened."

Down, but not out, Lewis decided to direct the next feature himself. *The Living Venus* (1960) detailed the fictional rise and fall of a Hugh Hefner-like magazine editor. Cheesy, but fun, the movie featured a very young Harvey Korman as *Pagan Magazine's* head photographer.

Again, Modern Film Distributors was to deliver the goods to audiences. "We were mid-way through the course and no film rentals were coming in," says Lewis. "We were playing dates, no film rentals. We were buying prints, no film rentals. When we became somewhat

A scene from Herschell Gordon Lewis's *Living Venus*, a fictionalized story of a Hugh Hefner-type magazine editor. (*Courtesy of Herschell Gordon Lewis.*)

Scenes from Herschell Gordon Lewis's *Living Venus* (*above* and *below*).
(*Courtesy of Herschell Gordon Lewis.*)

demanding about the film retals, Modern Film Distributors folded, went belly up, kaput! I had sold Lewis and Martin for my share of the investment in Mid-Continent Films. And so, like an O. Henry story, I was left with no studio and no friends. The whole thing was a low point, one of many in my life.

"So I moved in full-time with another industrial film studio. They didn't have any space for me, so my office was the screening room. I would sit in front of the screen and when they wanted to look at something, I would have to duck down. But I was also directing stuff for them just to keep bread on the table. This went on for six months or so.

"One day Dave Friedman walked in and said, 'I've got a deal for you. Al Sack (a film distributor in Dallas) will pay us $9,000 if we can make a one-reel movie in color with cute girls in it.' We were planning this thing and in came a fellow named Jack Curtain, who worked for a film lab in New York, and asked about what we were working on. I said, 'we're shooting this thing for Al Sack.' Curtain said, 'I'll make you a deal. You shoot 70 minutes (the running time for full-length feature in those days). If you'll shoot 70 minutes, no lab bills will be made until 30 days after the answer print is made.'

"That's the story behind *The Adventures of Lucky Pierre* (1961). We found this knock-down comedian named Billy Falbo, who was perfect for the role. We shot it in a couple of days at Dave's drive-in theater in Joliet. It was late October and it was cold. The girls had blue nipples—good heavens! The final film ran 6,300 feet, exactly 70 minutes. We only bought 8,000 feet of raw stock so we cut the slates off and that's all there was. In fact, we didn't have enough to make a trailer! Tom Dowd, who owned the Capri Theater, agreed to play *Lucky Pierre* and we made one print. It ran nine weeks and in that one play date we made more money than the picture cost us to make. "I said, 'well, how long has this been going on?' "

Lucky Pierre was part of a genre known as "nudie cuties." A precursor to today's multi-million dollar pornography industry, nudie cuties are fairly innocent by modern standards.

"Based on *Lucky Pierre* and our quick earnings, Dave and I went to Florida and shot a nudist camp film called *Daughter of the Sun* (1962). I had a little Volkswagen bus just crammed with equipment and we'd shoot anything for anybody. The key to shooting movies was: it's getting cold in Chicago so we better go to Florida and shoot something!"

Lewis and Friedman made several more nudie cuties, but were rapidly burning out on the genre. "Our feeling was we better break new ground. The question was, what kind of movie could we make within the budget range we had that theaters would play and major companies wouldn't make. It was a short list. Now there's no list!

"But in the early '60s, nobody was shooting pictures with a lot of blood in them. We decided to take a chance on a gore movie; so a gore movie it was!"

The result was *Blood Feast* (1963). Shot on a minuscule $24,000 budget, the story revolves around "Fuad Ramses" (Mal Arnold), a caterer who specializes in the delectable "Egyptian feast." The main dish of this spread is, of course, human flesh, served up in steaming, dripping chunks. Ramses goes on a killing spree to obtain fresh tidbits, only to be stopped in the end by a diligent police detective. To be kind, the ensemble is unaccomplished but the film never pretends to be anything more than what it is—good, clean gory fun.

The film still holds fond memories for Lewis. "I've seen a lot of folklore on *Blood Feast*, on how it came to be, because it was the first of its type, and yes, it's a footnote to motion picture history, but that's underselling it," he says emphatically. "*Blood Feast* broke open a door that had not only been shut, but had been sealed, and filled in with lead, and we smashed right through it. The only way to do gore was with a low-budget picture where the entire movie industry wouldn't be on your neck, saying 'what are you trying to do?'

"We shot all of *Blood Feast* in Miami Beach in five or six days. When we were cutting the thing back in Chicago on my old editing table, people couldn't bear to watch it, not because the acting was so terrible, but because of the gore scenes. I said, 'oh my God, what have we done here? No one's going to watch this movie!'

"So we decided to open it in Peoria. We had a partner in that movie named Stan Kohlberg who owned the Starlight Drive-In outside Chicago and another theater in Peoria. We figured, if we die in Peoria, who would know? We not only didn't die in Peoria, we crocked 'em. Of course, we pulled out many stops. We had these vomit bags and printed on them was 'you may need this when you see *Blood Feast*.' We had an ambulance with a mars light running and we put together a 'wowser-bowser' of an ad campaign. Word got out about the movie. I said to Dave, 'my gosh, I can't believe this. What would happen if we made a good one? What would happen if we did this right?' "

Following the unexpected success of *Blood Feast*, Lewis cranked out gore movies like cinematic sausages. Forsaking expenses other filmmakers face, such as a production crew, Lewis often served as producer, director, cameraman, editor, and composer. In winter he would head to Florida for the hospitable filming weather. Spring and summer brought production back to Chicago, where extensive use was made of area locations. For the most part, Lewis's movies were popular in theaters and drive-ins throughout the south and western United States and rarely played in Chicago or other northern cities.

In the late 1960s, Lewis branched out with biker flicks and sexploitation movies, and showed some versatility by making two children's pictures. Often working in multiple capacities on each film, Lewis adopted a variety of pseudonyms, including Lewis H. Gordon, Mark Hansen, George Parades, Armand Pays, Sheldon Seymour, and Sheldon S. Seymour.

Though the film work kept him busy throughout the decade, Lewis opened a successful ad agency in the Wrigley Building. He also returned to education on a part-time basis, teaching graduate courses in marketing at Roosevelt University for 20 years and training film students for five years at Columbia College.

Not just satisfied with making movies, for a time Lewis was also an exhibitor. He owned the Adelphi, the 400, and the Devon movie theaters in the Rogers Park neighborhood, and for a brief, shining few months in 1968, Lewis ran The Blood Shed on North Wells Street.

"Old Town had sprung to life as a sort of bohemian haven," Lewis recalls. "A friend who owned a building there said 'why don't we put in a theater?' I said, 'first of all, the zoning will kill us. And the inspections will kill us and we need projectors.' 'But you have projectors,' he said. The projectors I had were taken off a Navy destroyer from World War II, where they would screen movies for the crew.

We paid off the City of Chicago so they wouldn't kill us with the inspections and we called our theater "The Blood Shed." We'd screen things like the original *Dracula* (1931) with Bela Lugosi, and in the middle we'd break the movie and two people would run in front of the screen. We'd turn the lights up, then one guy would slit the throat of the other and drag him out.

"We started off very strong. Then the newspapers, spurred by what, I don't know, refused to take our ads because of the word 'blood,' which struck me as a rather strange kind of censorship. We changed the name to Cinema Bizarre, but that didn't help us at all because part of the image left. People thought it wasn't the same thing anymore and business fell off.

"Then there was the 1968 political convention in Chicago. One night here came this mob, boiling up Wells Street, smashing up windows, kicking at things, throwing stones, putting paint on windows. We were largely spared, maybe just a crack in the door. But that was the end. From that point on we did no business. And a couple of days later we found some kid with his hand stuck in the Coke machine, kicking and screaming because we caught him. I said, 'that's enough.' It had ceased to be a profit center of any sort, so we simply closed the place down without notice and went our way."

Lewis's last hurrah in Chicago was the 1972 feature, *The Gore-Gore Girls* (also known as *Blood Orgy*). Notable as the first film ever to be rated "X" for violent content, *The Gore-Gore Girls* was shot in Old Town and other North Side locations. It also featured comic Henny Youngman playing, oddly enough, a wisecracking nightclub entertainer. But by now, Lewis had relocated to Florida and was altogether sick of the movie business.

In the mid-1970s, he switched careers—again, with no regrets. Turning his talents to direct marketing, Lewis become one of the industry's leading experts.

Despite his retirement from filmmaking, the legions of Lewis cultists has grown around the world. All of this came as a surprise to Lewis, who let go of his copyrights. "I got into another business and I pledged my movies as collateral. I thought it was funny that the partners accepted them. When the business went under, I said 'take the movies, they're old' and much to my astonishment somebody else bought them. And I didn't say, 'you fool,' but I couldn't understand why someone would want these films. Well, of course now I understand why, because *Blood Feast* has sold over 150,000 videos."

Lewis did maintain copyright on his scores for *Blood Feast* and *2000 Maniacs*, which were released as soundtrack albums on Rhino Records. "Now, twice a year I get cigar money," Lewis laughs.

And what about a comeback in the picture business? Says Lewis, "Every now and then I get a phone call or a piece of mail or an e-mail or a fax or something saying let's make another movie or how about *Blood Feast II*?" I have scripts for two movies: one is *Blood Feast II* and the other is *Herschell Gordon Lewis' Grim Fairy Tales*. I like what I'm doing today but, of course, the fire horse has to answer the bell. If a deal comes up, yeah, I'm there, though I don't expect it.

"But my bag is packed just in case."

* Nude footage of Black romping around a quarry was later destroyed at the insistence of Black's agent.

➡️ **LAKE FOREST ACADEMY**
1500 W. Kennedy Road, Lake Forest, Illinois

Is Lake Forest Academy a private prep school or flexible movie location? Actually, it's both. Located on 140 acres of wooded property, Lake Forest Academy has played a considerable role both in education and recent Chicago film history.

Founded in 1857, Lake Forest Academy provides a college preparatory education within a unique setting. Though always located in north suburban Lake Forest, a 35-minute drive north of Chicago, the Academy has been headquartered at the former estate of meat-packing magnate J. Ogden Armour since 1948.

Hollywood is no stranger to the unique splendor of this gorgeous campus. Unfortunately, its first foray onto the Academy grounds was less than exemplary. *Damien: Omen II* (1978), the second movie adventure of Satan's spawn, turned Lake Forest Academy into a military school. The evil title youngster was enrolled here, using it as a headquarters to commit his crimes against humanity.

Two years later, Robert Redford, Timothy Hutton, Mary Tyler Moore, and Donald Sutherland entered the grounds for *Ordinary People* (1980). The production made extensive use of the wooded campus and school buildings. So did *The Babe* (1993), a retelling of the Babe Ruth legends, when the campus was turned into a baseball spring training facility. For another example of Lake Forest Academy as a movie playground, see *The Package* entry below.

For more information about Lake Forest Academy, call 847-234-3210 or visit their Web site at http://www.lfa.lfc.edu/index_g.html.

 The Package (1989)

A ndrew Davis' 1989 film *The Package* was among the last of a dying genre breed: the Cold War thriller. Incorporating historical events with the worst nightmares a conspiracy theorist could conjure up, the film explores a shadow alliance of Soviet and American officials who want to sabotage an impending nuclear peace treaty.

The Package stars Gene Hackman as Johnny Gallagher, an Army sergeant who inadvertently stumbles onto an assassination plot of the Soviet premier during an impending visit to Chicago. The action opens in what was then East Berlin, switches to Washington, D.C. and winds up in the Windy City. Yet, with the exception of some establishing footage shot in East Germany, the entire film was made in the Chicago area.

"In preparing *The Package*, we visited East Germany, including Berlin," says Davis. "Once you've seen the real location, it's easy to compare and analyze what similarities exist in Chicago. Many Germans immigrated here at the turn of the century and created architecture exactly like they had at home."

The film opens with a peace conference between Soviet and American military officials. The meeting takes place in a chalet outside the Black Forest—or so it would appear. Head north to Lake Forest Academy in suburban Lake Forest and you'll find yourself transported to East Germany, at least as far as *The Package* is concerned.

Another major scene involves a shooting within the Black Forest witnessed by Hackman and his troops. The scene was filmed just outside the city, in a forest preserve on Archer Avenue in south suburban Palos Hills. Add German police cars, American troops, and a few explosions amidst the snow-covered trees, and there's nothing within the sequence to suggest this is anywhere but Germany.

The film's title comes from Gene Hackman's initial mission: to bring insubordinate soldier Tommy Lee Jones—"a package"—from Germany to Washington, D.C. Hackman picks up Jones along a bridge between East and West Berlin. Look closely at the scene though and you may spot some familiar-looking buildings in the background.

Hackman actually picks up Jones at the Cermak Road bridge at Canal Street. By far, this is one of the most creative movie redecorating jobs Hollywood ever pulled off in Chicago. The bridge was outfitted with barbed wire, guard booths and ominous warning signs with German lettering. Filmed in the dark of night, the sequence has all the look and feel of a Cold War-era border. When dawn broke, some early morning commuters were reportedly a bit perplexed over the apparent invasion taking place on Cermak Road.

"We were able to find old hospitals and residential areas, specifically in the Pullman neighborhood, which had the flavor of Berlin," says Davis. With a little set dressing, the Pullman area was turned into the streets of Berlin, where an American soldier is rousted from his bed by the conspirators and hurled into a complicated web of deceit.

Switching locales to Washington, D.C., Davis again was able to shoot in and around Chicago. O'Hare Airport became Washington National Airport. The stately exterior of the Field Museum stood in for a government building where Pam Grier (who also appeared in Davis's *Above the Law* in 1988) is gunned down. The highways outside the city doubled for roads leading out of Arlington, Virginia.

WEST

INDEX OF ARTICLES

The City

➡ JANE ADDAMS HULL HOUSE MUSEUM
The University of Illinois at Chicago
800 S. Halsted Street

"...In the days before the inspection of films and the present regulations for the five-cent theaters, we established at Hull-House a moving picture show."

—Jane Addams, *Twenty Years at Hull-House*, 1910.

Social pioneer Jane Addams understood the power of art to germinate ideas. Consequently, painting, music, and theater became a powerful factor in the vitality of Addams's Hull House. With the development of motion picture technology, Addams decided to make part of Hull House a nickelodeon for neighborhood children. Though she had to combat objection to the new medium by many of her peers, Addams insisted on holding regular screenings. When her experiment ended, Addams worked closely with local officials to improve the quality of neighborhood motion picture theaters.

The Jane Addams Hull House Museum is open weekdays from 10 a.m. to 4 p.m. and Sundays from noon to 5 p.m. Admission is free. For more information, including booking group tours, call 312-413-5353 or visit hte Hull House homepage at http://www.uic.edu/jaddams/hull/hull_house. html.

➡ COOK COUNTY HOSPITAL
1835 W. Harrison Street

Cook County Hospital, the largest and busiest medical facility in the city, consists of 13 common buildings and has more than 500 physicians on staff. As a public hospital, it is a true lifeline for many Chicagoans unable to afford medical insurance.

The hospital played a pivotal role in *The Fugitive* (1993). It's here where Harrison Ford, a brilliant surgeon on the run, begins his search for the mysterious one-armed man who killed his wife. Disguised as a janitor, Ford uses the prosthetics lab to research possible suspects, but ultimately gives himself away when coming to the aid of a misdiagnosed youngster.

Cook County Hospital was also used for scenes in *Red Heat* (1988) and

Hero (1992). Independent filmmaker Jim Sikora shot part of *Walls in the City* (1994) outside the hospital, opening the movie's second tale with local artist/actor Tony Fitzpatrick lighting up a cheap stogie to celebrate his release from the medical facility.

When it comes to show business, Cook County Hospital is best known as inspiration for NBC television's popular show "ER." This Emmy-winning dramatic series revolves around the people who work in the "Cook County General Hospital" trauma unit, though no actual production takes place within the real hospital. The "ER" team does get to Chicago from time to time to shoot exterior scenes around town.

For more information about the real Cook County Hospital ER, check out the Trauma Unit's Web site at http://www.rush.edu/Departments/Trauma.

➡ MID-CITY NATIONAL BANK
800 W. Madison Street

The White Supremacists of *Betrayed* (1988) attempted to further their twisted underground movement by staging a holdup at this near-Loop bank.

➡ FULTON STREET MARKET
600 - 800 W. Fulton Street

Head to Fulton Street for a wide variety of fruits, vegetables, bullets, bodies dropping, and cars crashing. Typical day at Chicago's center for restaurant produce? Not really, but then again most produce workers don't look like steely-eyed undercover cop Nico Toscani (Steven Seagal) and his drop-dead gorgeous, tough-as-nails partner Delores Jackson (the irrepressible Pam Grier) in *Above the Law* (1988). The first of the film's many action sequences is set here.

➡ HARPO STUDIOS
1058 W. Washington Boulevard

At first glance, this building doesn't seem that different from anything else in this Near West Side neighborhood. But don't let first impressions fool you. Behind the facade is a billion-dollar empire that can be summed up in one word: Oprah.

When Oprah Winfrey came to Chicago in 1984, her initial role was to serve as host of WLS-TV's morning talk show, "A.M. Chicago." Within a few years, Winfrey had mastered the talk show form and recreated it in her own image. The program was renamed "The Oprah Winfrey Show," and dived headfirst into oddball Americana, with topics ranging from celebrity interviews to dysfunctional families to frank discussions of that old ratings stand-by, sex.

Legend has it that Quincy Jones saw a broadcast of "The Oprah Winfrey Show" while staying at a Chicago hotel. This led to Winfrey's being cast in Steven Spielberg's *The Color Purple* (1985), an Oscar nomination for Best Supporting Actress, and, ultimately, unbridled success. Shortly after finishing work on *The Color Purple*, Winfrey took her show national. Acquiring the 1058 W. Washington building, she started her own production company, dubbed Harpo. The title was no tribute to Harpo Marx, but rather a backwards spelling of Winfrey's first name.

The Harpo Studios building has some significant history. It's original purpose was as the Second Regimental Armory. The Armory served as temporary morgue for victims of the 1915 Eastland disaster, and spirits of these drowned souls are rumored to haunt the building to this day (see Ursula Bielski's *Chicago Haunts: Ghostly Lore of the Windy City* for more details).

The Armory's vast spaces made it ideal for film production, and eventually the building was transformed into the Fred Niles Studios. For years these soundstages were a center for commercial and industrial filmmaking though occasionally feature filmmakers made use of the facility. Herschell Gordon Lewis came to Niles Studios for his first nudie cutie, *The Prime Time* (1960). Arthur Penn and Warren Beatty also utilized the Niles facilities for some of the surreal street scenes of *Mickey One* (1965).

Harpo Studios (1058 W. Washington), home to *The Oprah Winfrey Show*, is a state-of-the-art television and film production center. (*Photo by Holly Pluard.*)

Today Harpo Studios is a state-of-the-art showcase for film and television production. *Code of Silence* (1985), *Men Don't Leave* (1990), and *Only the Lonely* (1991) are a small sampling of Chicago-shot Hollywood productions which made use of the Harpo soundstages. Winfrey-produced television films like "The Women of Brewster Place" and "There Are No Children Here" have also been based out of Harpo. But the heart and soul of this building is the mega-empire of Oprah Winfrey.

For tickets to "The Oprah Winfrey Show," call 312-591-9222.

➡ **THE CHICAGO ACADEMY OF THE ARTS**
1010 W. Chicago Avenue

New York has the High School for the Performing Arts, which inspired the 1980 movie and subsequent television series *Fame*. In the Windy City, we have the Chicago Academy of the Arts. This private high school is for students who aspire to careers in visual and performing arts, offering studies in music, theater/musical theater, dance, visual art, and communication arts. Offering fully-accredited, college preparatory classes in the morning, afternoons are devoted to the study of a student's chosen discipline. The Academy lists Oprah Winfrey, David Mamet, Bob and Delores Hope, Elizabeth Taylor, Ben Vereen, Carol Channing, and Irv and Essee Kupcinet among its many benefactors.

Famous alumni of the Academy include Lara Flynn Boyle, best known for her work on the cult television series "Twin Peaks," as well as such Chicago-based movies *Wayne's World* (1992), *Baby's Day Out* (1994), and "Since You've Been Gone" (1998); and Adam Rifkin, whose work ranges from directing and writing the little-seen black comedy, *The Dark Backward* (1991), performing under the name "Rif Coogan" in such forgettable junk as *Bikini Squad* (1993), and scriptwriting for the big-budget Dreamworks comedy, *Mouse Hunt* (1997).

For more information on the Chicago Academy for the Arts, call 312-421-0202 or visit their Web page at http://www.mcs.net/~academy.

HOOP DREAMS (1994)

"*Hoop Dreams* showed me how supportive this city is of independent filmmakers. Everywhere we went people were at least willing to listen to our cries of help."
—Fred Marx, editor/co-producer *Hoop Dreams*

"(This) is one of the great movie-going experiences of my lifetime."
—Roger Ebert

"It's a beautifully made documentary about two kids in the inner city trying to realize their dream of playing professional basketball."
—Number Six of David Letterman's "Top Ten Signs the Movie You're Watching Will Not Win an Academy Award," as featured at the 1995 Academy Awards Ceremony

In the early 1980s, when Steve James was a graduate student in the film program at Southern Illinois University in Carbondale, he spent what little leisure time he had playing basketball at the school's recreation center. While on the court, seeds for making a film about basketball germinated in James's head. "For whatever reason it was in my mind," says James. "One day at the rec center there, it turned out for some odd reason I was the only white guy in the gym. It just struck me that the whole feel of the place was very different. It was one of those kind of things where it seemed very different and it just dawned on me it would be interesting to do a film on what basketball means to the black ballplayers and the whole nuance of the game in the street.

"The film was really going to be more about the street game, the pickup game like we played in the gym. That was sort of the dawning of the idea."

A few years later, with M.F.A. in hand, James moved to Chicago. "Chicago seemed like a good, literally and otherwise, place to go. But at the same time I also knew that basketball was a religion in Chicago, and I thought this would be a good place to pursue this basketball project.

"So I came up to Chicago and like a lot of people, I had an M.F.A. in film production. I quickly found out that this wasn't terribly meaningful. Even though I had this fancy degree, I was working as a production assistant for commercial production companies. That was fairly humiliating. I met some nice people who became very helpful to me, but it was very tough to stock the drink cooler and sweep the floor a lot."

Still, James nurtured his idea of a documentary on street basketball. He got in touch with Fred Marx, a fellow M.F.A. graduate from SIU. After graduating, Marx had spent a few years in China, lived in New York for a while, and eventually came to Chicago. "Steve was my best buddy in grad school," recalls Marx. "I remember Steve and I had discussions about the basketball project during grad school. In our correspondence back and forth when I was in China, he suggested forming a partnership around making films and that sounded good to me.

"In April 1986, in my mother's backyard in Champaign, we had our first official *Hoop Dreams* meeting. We sort of carved out how we would make it. It was a full 15 months before we actually shot anything. We spent a year doing research and fundraising."

Once this preparatory work was completed, James and Marx went to Kartemquin Films in hopes of getting some support. "These two very tall guys walked in with this idea for a film about street basketball," recalls Gordon Quinn. "They had a small grant from the Illinois Arts Council, which let me know they at least knew the basics of fundraising and were serious."

"We gave Gordon the proposal," says James, "and he was intrigued with it. At that point the film was going to be a half-hour long documentary. It was going to be done in six months, and focus on a single court on the streets of the city.

"We spent a good part of 1986 trying to raise money without a lot of success, despite Kartemquin's name and reputation. The fact that I, being the director, didn't have any track record to speak of and Fred not having any track record to speak of, we were unable to raise any money. And the subject! People just didn't use sports as a very serious subject of inquiry for a documentary.

"I finally got a $2,000 Illinois Arts Council grant and we used that to start. That's when we hooked up with Peter Gilbert."

Gilbert, one of Chicago's most respected cinematographers, had a longtime association with Kartemquin and documentary filmmaking. "They were looking for someone to shoot a 30-minute short film on street basketball," says Gilbert. "I've always been a huge hoops head. I said, 'Let's use my equipment. If we're going to do it, let's do it professionally.' Steve and Fred had been writing grants for a long time. One of the things we all talked about was that unless you're really established, the only way you can get money for projects is to go out and shoot something so you have a demo, something that you can bring to people along with a proposal.

"So we went out and literally in the first two or three days of filming we met Arthur Agee. Then we went out to St. Joseph's High School in Westchester and met William Gates. It became pretty immediate that we were going to follow them through four years. Here's this inner-city kid out at a white suburban high school and this coach is saying to him, 'if you stay here and play basketball for me, you'll go to college. I'll get you into college, I promise you.' That was the hook. We had to follow these kids for four years."

Steve James adds, "We went to the Agee and Gates families and it was fine with them. I don't think they had a sense of what *Hoop Dreams* was going to be. Neither did we. If either of us had, we probably would have said 'no.' The film just kind of evolved, because at first without money we didn't film that often and then it just snowballed and as it got more and more interesting, we became more obsessed and then eventually we got some funding."

Still, that funding wasn't enough to live on. "For the first three years, we had only $2000, so we all worked," said Gilbert. "We did whatever we could to work. When I started *Hoop Dreams*, I was still working with Barbara Kopple on the documentary *American Dream* (1990). We all did different things, anything we could do to make a living."

"I was pretty much living hand to mouth," says Marx. "I would take jobs that would support me for a while, then stop working for a while in order to work on the film and be broke, then go back to having to take jobs again. That's pretty much how it went for me."

"I was production-managing on commercials," says James. "Eventually Kartemquin employed me to make smaller, educational documentaries, which really saved me. We would juggle all that, so shoot days for *Hoop Dreams* were always 'grab what you can.'

"People would pitch in. If we needed a camera, they would get us a camera, they would lend us a camera; if we needed lights, they would lend us lights. When we needed editing to finish the film, we went to IPA and Scott Jacobs gave us this incredible deal because he just wanted to help us get *Hoop Dreams* made. He believed in the film and that it was good for Chicago.

"That was the kind of pitching in [that was done] on behalf of a project that had no money, a documentary that wasn't going to make anybody who helped us become famous. We certainly didn't believe it was going to make us famous. We thought it was going to be on PBS at 10 o'clock on some Tuesday night and no one would even see it."

"We shot an average of one day a week over the four years," said

Marx. "The way that broke down, sometimes we shot pretty often, seemingly every day, and sometimes we didn't shoot for months." Notes Gilbert, "We probably shot a total 250 days over the entire course of the four years. Heavy the first year, very little the second year, then it got heavy again junior/senior year."

"Shoot days were always grab what we could," says James. "I would stay in touch with the families consistently, either by phone or stop by because Arthur's family didn't have a phone. I developed, I think, close relationships with the families. That didn't just happen out of the shooting, it happened with calling them up at night. There were times when Sheila Agee [Arthur's mother] would say things like 'Who would want to see this story? Why would anybody want to see this? This is such a terrible story, you know, with Bo [Arthur's father] gone and on drugs. I've never been off welfare all my life.' I used to tell her, 'Sheila, I really think you're going to speak to people in a way they haven't heard it before.'

"It took a while for them to trust us. With Arthur, the trust didn't come, really, until he was kicked out of St. Joe's and we didn't go away. I remember going to one of his games when he first played for Marshall High School's sophomore team. He said, 'After I got kicked out of St. Joe's, I didn't think you guys would be interested in me.' He was thinking that we were only interested in him because he was going to the NBA. I think he got that sense that we weren't going anywhere despite what had happened to him and he began to open up more.

"With William, he was always more open, but his family, his mom in particular, didn't open up until his junior year when he blew out his knee. She saw that we really truly were concerned for him and were trying to do whatever we could to help...not just film, but help. She didn't want to be filmed until then. We hardly filmed her until junior year because she didn't trust us. She'd tolerate us because William wanted to do this, but she didn't trust us."

"I'd say by junior year, we knew what an amazing story it was," says Gilbert. "It got Shakespearean. It got to be more incredible all the time and you got more and more involved with these kids' lives. Not only is there a lot of story that we couldn't put into the film, but it was an amazing experience to get to know those people and get to know the families. It's the kind of thing that documentary allows you that no other kind of filmmaking can and it's a big rush.

"We eventually started to get good material and things started happening," says James. "Eventually we got funded, though we never got a lot of funding. *Hoop Dreams* was made for a shoestring through the end.

"During the editing I tended to steer away [from interaction between Arthur and William and the filmmakers], in part because I didn't want people to see us as self-aggrandizing, 'Oh, look at this great relationship they have with these guys.' With us being white and them being black subjects, it would be easy for people to get very cynical about that and think that we were putting stuff like that in just so you would think that we were good guys.

"I went into making this film thinking that, hey, I was a liberal and still am, and had very liberal notions about racial justice and racism in America and all that, but I still viewed black people as symbols more than human beings—as symbols of poverty or symbols of hope, or symbols of this or symbols of that. Getting to know the families the way I did was eye-opening. I was crying while we filmed Sheila getting her nursing degree.

"*Hoop Dreams* got accepted at the Sundance Film Festival and that, in and of itself, we were obviously pleased about. Sundance only accepts 16 documentary films into competition and there's generally 200 to 300 entries. We were generally thrilled that happened.

"During the first two nights of the festival Siskel and Ebert did their television review of the film. At that point in time, the only place you could see the film was at Sundance. It wasn't in distribution. All the Sundance screenings were sold out. Siskel and Ebert did this nationwide plug for the film for the express purpose of us getting distribution, which is a pretty unusual thing. They really championed the film."

"We were able to see *Hoop Dreams* before it played Sundance film festival and our show was its kind of public unveiling," says Ebert. "Both Gene and I felt that it was so important that we reviewed the film before it even had a distributor. Our review appeared on the weekend that Sundance opened and we said 'we hope people go to see this film.'

"By the time Peter, Fred, and I got to the festival," says James, "*Hoop Dreams* seemed basically to be the buzz of the entire festival, documentary or fiction, which was pretty heavy and pretty fun, obviously.

"We won the audience award at the end of the festival, which was the best award we could have won. At that point, for a three-hour documentary looking for theatrical distribution, winning the audience award was a real boost towards the effort."

After eight years of hard work for no money, James, Marx, and Gilbert were suddenly overnight sensations. *Hoop Dreams* was picked up for distribution by Fine Line Feature. Warner Brothers studios became interested in buying the story rights to the property as a fiction film, with

Spike Lee as executive producer. James was flown out for a meeting with Lee and came back the same day. Because of NCAA rules, neither Agee nor Gates could receive any kind of direct compensation for their participation in *Hoop Dreams*.

Then came the Oscars and the next chapter in the *Hoop Dreams* saga. "There was a lot of talk leading up to the Oscar nominations that we should be a shoo-in to win Best Documentary," said James. "There was even a lot of talk that we would be the first documentary to break through and be nominated for Best Picture. There was a lot of press about this.

"Of course, the day the nomination decisions came down, we rendezvoused at Kartemquin. The publicists for Fine Line had arranged for media people to be there and capture the moment, because they were hoping for this Best Picture nomination or at the very least, a Best Documentary nomination.

"So it ended up being a big dud because neither happened. We got nominated for Best Editing, which was very satisfying for me as a co-editor.*

"It [not being nominated] was just a momentary disappointment. The award nominations were at 7 o'clock in the morning. I got home and my phone rang about 9 o'clock and it was Ebert, who says to me, 'This is an outrage! Aren't you just outraged about this?' and I said, 'Well, I don't know. I kind of take the long view.'

"The next best thing to us getting a Best Picture nomination was what happened, which was to get nothing because it created this big firestorm of controversy. It became the lead of a lot of articles, it became the headline: '*Hoop Dreams* Slighted!' instead of '*Forrest Gump* Gets Ten Nominations!' If we had gotten the nomination, it would have been buried in the stories because that was expected.

"So Fine Line ran with that. They were hoping for a Best Picture nomination but this was the next best thing. They beat that horse as best they could, drumming up as much controversy as they could about this outrage and wringing their hands over it and all that. *Hoop Dreams* opened wide around the country that following week. We actually went from being in about 50 theaters at most to being in more than 250."

In the wake of their post-*Hoop Dreams* success, James and Gilbert formed their own production company, Longshot Films, through a deal with Disney studios, while Marx became an independent director. In 1997 James and Gilbert made *Prefontaine*, a feature film for Disney's Hollywood Pictures division, about the late Olympic runner Steve Prefontaine. The two also maintain close ties with Kartemquin. In 1998, Gilbert and Kartemquin's Gordon Quinn went to Vietnam to film a documentary for network television. "Vietnam: Long Time Coming," follows a group of American veterans returning to Vietnam for a cross-country bicycle race.

Though they received many offers to resettle in Hollywood, all three of the *Hoop Dreams* trio remain committed to Chicago. "If you spent any time in L.A.," says James, "the weather's great and all, but the thing is, it's such a movie mad world and a crazy world. It feels so disconnected from everyday life. I always breathe a sigh of relief after a trip out there, to come home and just live in a neighborhood where everyone on the block doesn't work in the movie business."

* *Hoop Dreams* was co-edited by James, Marx, and Bill Haugse.

Frederick Marx
INDEPENDENT DIRECTOR AND PRODUCER/EDITOR OF *HOOP DREAMS* ON WHY HE CONTINUES TO WORK IN CHICAGO

Chicago is a logical place for me to be. I can see myself in a kind of broad tradition of the Nelson Algrens, the Studs Terkels, people who try to do socially meaningful work. So I think it's a city that's an appropriate place for a socially conscious filmmaker to be. I'm interested in thoughtful, humanistic, no nonsense work. I'm interested in art, but art that means something and is accessible. So Chicago is perfectly situated both geographically and sort of philosophically/ intellectually between two coasts, if you want to make Los Angeles all business, all entertainment, and New York sort of all art, as it were. I think being in the middle is sort of good for me."

Frederick Marx, director/editor/ producer of *Hoop Dreams*. (*Courtesy of Frederick Marx.*)

"I realize that in the wake of the success of *Hoop Dreams*, I could have gone to L.A. and I could have spent two to three years taking meetings, talking to people, going on endless rounds of shmoozing, and maybe, maybe I would have gotten the opportunity to direct *Porky's 7* or something....something I wouldn't necessarily believe in at all. So I thought, 'do I really want to be spending the next two to three years of my life to maybe have this chance?' And the answer to me was 'no.' The bottom line for me becomes: I'd rather fail at making fulfilling movies than succeed at making unfulfilling ones."

In addition to *Hoop Dreams*, Frederick Marx's films include *Higher Goals, Out of Silence, Dreams from China, Hiding Out for Heaven,* and *Dream Documentary.* He can be reached through his Web site at http://www.fmarxfilm.com/.

Peter Gilbert

AMERICAN DREAM, THE OSCARS, AND FAMILY

Peter Gilbert is well-known as one-third of the *Hoop Dreams* team. He has considerable experience as a cinematographer, having shot documentaries for such luminaries as Michael Apted (*35 Up*) and Barbara Kopple (*American Dream*). His work has won him respect around the world, yet he remains close to Chicago and all the possibilities it offers. "There's a really good group of filmmaking people here," he says. "It may be smaller than Los Angeles, but people here are very supportive of each other. Chicago is a very easy city to struggle in."

"I get to go and work with really brilliant filmmakers during the day. I've been very lucky. But I also am lucky because I have a normal life here where people just go 'fuck you! So you make movies, who cares?' It's a great thing.

"Probably one of the most bittersweet nights of my life was when *American Dream* won the Academy Award for Best Documentary in 1991," says Gilbert, who served as the film's director of photography. His joy at seeing Kopple's victory was well-deserved. The two of them had worked many long hours, often for no money, on this moving documentary chronicling the struggle between corporate giant Hormel and a strike by union workers. As the film unfolds, we witness a community cracking under the pressure of this battle. The toll of the strike isn't just financial—emotions are thrust into the crucible of this seemingly unending dispute.

The day before the Oscar ceremony, Gilbert's mother suffered a massive stroke. "Barbara mentioned my name on TV in her acceptance speech," Gilbert recalls. "My mom had just had her stroke. She was in a coma. It's like, here's the one thing I would want my mother to see. We used to joke about it. They lived through this with me, getting calls at 3:30 in the morning, Barbara asking, 'Where's Peter? Can you find him?' All of this!...and my dad, not totally understanding this and why do you not get paid...all that stuff.

"And here's this thing. For me it was this unbelievably, bizarre, bittersweet moment because Barbara was generous enough to talk about me but I couldn't really enjoy it. Honestly, at that moment, none of us thought my mother was going to live. I went to the hospital that night and told her.

"I didn't get one call from an agent: I didn't even have an agent nor did they come after me. But I got 300 phone calls from my name being mentioned on the Oscars . . . not from entertainment people. My dry cleaner called me! The important thing, even though my mom was sick, I was able to go and tell her. To me, that was a big deal."

Cinematographer Peter Gilbert (*left*) and director Steve James (*right*) of *Hoop Dreams*.
(*Photo by Gita Saedi. Courtesy of Long Shot Films.*)

Gilbert's mother spent seven weeks in a coma before regaining consciousness. Her recovery was nothing short of miraculous. And just a few years later, she saw her son achieve national recognition for his work on *Hoop Dreams*.

➡ **MIDWAY AIRPORT**
5500 - 6300 S. Cicero Avenue

The city's first major airport, Midway, was originally known as Chicago Municipal Airport. It opened in 1927 and quickly developed a reputation as the world's busiest airport, a position that now belongs to O'Hare International Airport on the Northwest Side. In 1949, when 3.2

million passengers passed through its gates, Chicago Municipal Airport was renamed in honor of the World War II Battle of Midway.

Midway has been used in just a handful of films. In *Henry: Portrait of a Serial Killer* (1986), dimwitted Otis (Tom Towles) picks up his sister Becky (Tracy Arnold) here.

Midway played a more pivotal role in Alfred Hitchcock's cross-country thriller, *North by Northwest* (1959). Having just been arrested for creating an art gallery disturbance, Roger Thornhill (the rakish Cary Grant) is brought to Midway by two Chicago cops. Shocked that he's being taken to the airport rather than jail, Grant demands some answers. He's quickly handed over to master agent Leo G. Carroll ("F.B.I....C.I.A....O.N.I...We're all in the same alphabet soup," he tells Grant), and the already twisted plot takes another sharp turn.

Look closely during this scene and you'll notice two men in the background. Extras? Hardly. During the shoot, Bill Blaney, an airport worker at the time, and one of his colleagues sneaked onto the runway to sneak a peek at Cary Grant. Upon seeing the two men on the runway, Blaney recalled, Hitchcock was outraged. The master of suspense berated the duo for ruining his shot and ordered them to leave. Nevertheless, Blaney and his pal remained in the final cut, giving *North by Northwest* a slightly more realistic look, albeit through a volunteer effort!

➡ *THE UNTOUCHABLES* **APARTMENTS**
22nd Place and Hoyne Avenue
Racine Avenue and Harrison Street

Looking for a good cop, circa the Prohibition era? In *The Untouchables* (1987) Kevin Costner (a.k.a. Elliott Ness) lived at 22nd Place and Hoyne Avenue. His mentor, played by Sean Connery, lived a little further north at the corner of Racine Avenue and Harrison Street.

➡ **WALT DISNEY BIRTHPLACE**
1249 N. Tripp Avenue

In this house on December 5, 1901, Flora Disney, wife of Elias Disney, gave birth to her fourth son. The child was named Walter Elias Disney.

The Disney family later moved to Kansas City, where young Walt developed an interest in drawing. Returning to Chicago in 1917, the Disneys took up residence at 1523 Ogden Avenue on the Near West Side. Walt persisted in his dream of becoming an illustrator. After graduating from

McKinley High School, he studied at the Chicago Academy for the Arts. His teachers at the Academy included professionals from the *Chicago Herald-Examiner* and the *Chicago Tribune*. Walt was introduced to the developing art of cartooning, a medium he instantly fell in love with.

The rest, as they say, is history.

Source: Mosley, Leonard. *Disney's World*. New York: Stein and Day, 1985.

▭▭▭▭▭ Balaban and Katz Theaters

The movie business would not be the same in America had it not been for two entrepreneurs from Chicago. As photoplays evolved into a lucrative form of popular entertainment, Barney Balaban and Sam Katz operated a string of theaters throughout the city and suburbs that set the standard for motion picture exhibition.

Balaban, the son of Russian-Jewish immigrants, grew up on the Near West Side, near the thriving Maxwell Street Market. In 1908 Balaban pooled financial resources with his brother Abe and purchased the Kedzie Theater at Kedzie Avenue and Roosevelt Road. The venture proved successful. Within a year the brothers added a second theater.

By 1915, Balaban had acquired a new partner, Sam Katz. The duo hatched a plan to build a theater of their own, the Central Park Theater. Located at 3535 W. Roosevelt Road, the building today houses the People's Church of God-Christ, a rather ironic evolution in the grand scheme of things. In the minds of the Balaban brothers and Sam Katz, the Central Park was a sanctuary for Chicago moviegoers.

Designed by Cornelius and George Rapp, the Central Park featured 400 velour-covered seats, beautiful chandeliers, and hand-painted wall murals. The beautiful interior had an added benefit, ice-cooled air that offered Chicagoans relief from the often grueling summer humidity. In addition to showing the latest movies from Hollywood, this picture palace also featured live entertainment.

Gradually the Balaban and Katz empire expanded beyond its West Side roots. Their holdings included theaters on the North and South Sides and in the suburbs. Some of their better-known playhouses included the downtown Apollo at Randolph near Clark Street, which today is the site of the outdoor art facility, Gallery 37; Belmont at 1635

W. Belmont (today a condominium complex); Bel-Park at 3231 N. Cicero (now a bingo parlor); Biltmore at 2046 W. Division (now demolished); Century at 2828 N. Clark Street (today the popular Century Mall); Congress at 2135 N. Milwaukee Avenue (today it's a multi-use concert hall); Coronet on Chicago Avenue in Evanston (now occasionally used for theatrical productions); Gateway at 5216 W. Lawrence Avenue (now the Polish community's Copernicus cultural center); Granada at 6427 N. Sheridan Road (tragically demolished despite a valiant effort to save this beautiful theater); Howard at 1621 W. Howard (an abandoned shell of a building today); Lakeside at 4730 N. Sheridan Road (now the Columbia College Dance Center); McVickers at 25 W. Madison (demolished); Marbro at 4124 W. Madison (demolished); Maryland at 855 E. 63rd Street (demolished); Norshore at 1749 W. Howard (demolished); Nortown at 6230 N. Western (one of the last palaces of Balaban and Katz's to survive, it was chopped up into a multi-screen cinema in the late 1970s and is now abandoned); Paradise at 231 N. Pulaski Road (this theater inspired an album by the Chicago-bred rock band Styx—both the group and the theater have since been leveled); the original Regal at 4719 S. Parkway (demolished); Riviera at 4746 N. Broadway (now a popular site for rock concerts); Roosevelt at 110 N. State Street (demolished); State-Lake at 190 N. State Street (now the home of WLS/ABC television and radio studios); Tivoli at 6325 S. Cottage Grove (demolished); and Tivoli at 5021 Highland in Downers Grove (still operating). Two other Balaban and Katz showcases were the Chicago and Uptown Theaters (see separate entries).

Balaban and Katz theaters emphasized classy presentation. The theaters were mini-palaces, often with grand auditoriums that could seat anywhere from 500 to 2,000 customers. Lobby chandeliers, of course, were a prerequisite. Ushers wore spiffy red uniforms, complemented by spotless white gloves.

Ultimately, Barney Balaban and his smart business acumen attracted the attention of Hollywood. In 1936 Paramount Studios came calling. Balaban sold Paramount two-thirds of his theater chain and eventually became president of the studio.

This ultimately led to legal troubles for the Balaban and Katz chain. In 1948, with the case of U.S. versus Paramount, the Supreme Court ruled that film studios unfairly had a stranglehold on film distribution. In essence, by supplying top-notch entertainment only to the Paramount-owned Balaban and Katz theaters, Hollywood executives

Balaban and Katz's Paradise Theater: the rock group Styx was inspired to record a tribute album to this now-leveled movie palace which once stood at Crawford (now Pulaski) near Washington. 1929-30. (*Chicago Historical Society photo CRC-4007-7-9.*)

had conspired with theater owners to control the movie distribution market. Paramount and other major studios had to release control of their theater chains, a move that ultimately led in part to the downfall of the classic Hollywood system.

Balaban, in the meantime, retained his position as Paramount's president until his retirement in 1967. He was subsequently named honorary chairman of the board, a title Balaban held until his death in 1971. (His nephew, Bob Balaban, continues working in the family business as an actor and director.) The Balaban and Katz theater chain was renamed ABC-Great States in the late 1960s and was sold to Plitt Theaters in 1974. Ultimately, the chain was bought by Canadian-based Cineplex Odeon.

And therein lies another irony in the Balaban and Katz legacy. In their heyday of the 1920s and early 1930s, a Balaban and Katz theater meant a night of elegant moviegoing. From the moment you arrived at one of their many movie palaces, you knew you were in for something special. The grand architecture, the curtains parting from the screen as the film began, and the snappily-dressed theater personnel all pointed to one thing: moviegoing was something special and all patrons deserved royal treatment. Compare that ideal to what is offered today by the legal inheritors of the Balaban and Katz tradition. The next time you're at an anonymous movie complex with its small screens, thin walls, and shopping mall atmosphere, close your eyes and imagine attending a show at the old Central Park Theater.

It must have been a slice of movie-going heaven.

Sources:
Mast, Gerald. *A Short History of the Movies*, Third Edition. Indianapolis: Bobbs-Merrill, 1981, 260-1.

Sawyers, June Skinner. *Chicago Portraits*. Chicago: Loyola University Press, 1991, 20-2.

WWW: *Explore Chicago Movie Theater* (http://www.suba.com/~scottn/ explore/sites/theaters)

➡ **METRO GOLDWYN MEMORIES**
5425 W. Addison Street

Looking for a video copy of *Call Northside 777*? Need a life-sized Charlie Chaplin for your living room decor? Then head to Metro Goldwyn Memories, Chicago's premier shop for old-time movie memorabilia. Opened by local radio nostalgia guru Chuck Schaden and his partner Dave Denwood in 1976, the store has expanded from its original Irving Park Road location to this larger West Addison Street facility. Metro Goldwyn Memories specializes in old movies on video and classic radio programs on audio.

Metro Goldwyn Memories is open from 10:00 a.m. to 6:00 p.m. Mondays through Saturdays and noon to 5:00 p.m. on Sundays. For more information, call 1-800-538-6675.

➡ **R.S. OWENS & COMPANY**
5535 N. Lynch Avenue

Tucked away in a little pocket of the Northwest Side is one of the most important manufacturing plants in the world, at least as far as the denizens of Hollywood's dream factory are concerned. Movie talents work hard to win a coveted Academy Award statuette, which are produced here at R.S. Owens & Company, a Windy City trophy company which has an exclusive contract to produce Oscars only for the purposes of the Academy of Motion Picture Arts and Sciences.

If you aren't in the movie business, maybe you have a chance to nab one of the other trophies produced by R.S. Owens. They also make the mementos handed out to winners of MTV Video Awards, Emmys, and the advertising industry's Clio awards.

➡ O'HARE INTERNATIONAL AIRPORT

Located on the far Northwest Side and surrounded by suburbs, O'Hare International Airport is considered the world's busiest airline terminal. On a typical day more than 165,000 passengers come and go through O'Hare's gates.

The airport was originally a military airfield and manufacturing facility known as Orchard Place. A remnant of this history can be found on baggage tickets: the ORD luggage tags attached to O'Hare-bound luggage is a contraction of the former name. In 1949, Orchard Place was renamed after Navy Lieutenant Edward "Butch" O'Hare, a World War II Medal of Honor winner lost in action over the Pacific on November 23, 1943. In 1955, O'Hare began operations as a commercial airport.

Filmmakers love O'Hare, though it's taken awhile for the airport to warm up to cameras. Early films to use O'Hare as a backdrop include Philip Kaufman's *Goldstein* (1964) and an off-beat political satire, *The Steagle* (1971).

It took another 12 years for the next major production to land at O'Hare. In *Risky Business* (1983), O'Hare was the airport where Tom Cruise's parents left town for vacation, then waited endlessly upon their return for a ride home. A few scenes for the Billy Crystal-Gregory Hines cop buddy flick *Running Scared* (1986) also took place here, as did the "planes" portion of *Planes, Trains and Automobiles* (1987). *The Package* (1989) used O'Hare as a substitute for a Washington, D.C. airline terminal. Gene Hackman took a nasty hit to the head in an O'Hare bathroom, enabling his "package," Tommy Lee Jones, to disappear.

With *Home Alone* (1990), O'Hare came into its own as a popular movie location. The John Hughes-written and produced/Chris Columbus-directed kiddie comedy made significant use of the American Airlines terminal. American had allied itself with the production in exchange for on-screen promotion. This slapstick comedy, while not the most creative film ever made, was an enormous hit, going on to become the biggest grossing comedy in movie history.

In *Home Alone* O'Hare not only played the Chicago airport; it also stood in for the Paris airline terminal. Ultimately, that's been a running theme in the *Home Alone* trilogy. *Home Alone II: Lost In New York* (1992) had O'Hare playing New York's Kennedy Airport, while *Home Alone III* (1997) pretended Chicago's airline hub was the San Francisco airport.

My Best Friend's Wedding (1997) is another example of the airport switcheroo. In an early scene, Rupert Everett drives Julia Roberts to LaGuardia Airport, located in the Queens borough of New York City. Sharp-eyed Chicagoans will note that the duo drive under the Mannheim Road overpass—quite a detour from the East Coast.

Next thing you know, Roberts is landing at the United Airlines terminal at O'Hare. There she shares an accidental kiss with her old pal Dermot Mulroney, a prelude to the romantic chaos Roberts is about to unleash.

O'Hare has also shown up in such varied films as *Rookie of the Year* (1993), *Music Box* (1990), *Sleepless in Seattle* (1993), *The Jackal* (1997), *U.S. Marshals* (1998), and television's "Early Edition."

The Suburbs

➡ **MAINE NORTH HIGH SCHOOL**
9511 W. Harrison Street, Des Plaines, Illinois

Once a high school, now the Central Management Services for the State of Illinois, the former Maine North had a brief stint as one of John Hughes's mid-1980s movie high schools. Though the title came from a nickname New Trier students in Winnetka gave their Saturday detention group, *The Breakfast Club* (1985) was shot at Maine North.

The Breakfast Club revolves around five archetypal high schoolers: The Athlete (Emilio Estevez), The Princess (Molly Ringwald), The Brain (Anthony Michael Hall), The Criminal (Judd Nelson), and The Basket Case (Ally Sheedy). Assigned Saturday morning detention for various crimes, the quintet proceed to push each other's buttons, whine about life, and come to the mutual conclusion that adults in general and parents in particular are at the root of all adolescent evils.

The film was shot outside of Maine North, where the kids were dropped off in the morning and picked up at the end of the day. Most of the action takes place in the school library, which actually was a set built in the old Maine North gymnasium.

Perhaps the unrelenting teen angst of *The Breakfast Club* was a little too much for Hughes. The next year he returned to Maine North with something considerably lighter, *Ferris Bueller's Day Off* (1986). The exterior of the school building and classroom interiors were the prelude to Ferris (Matthew Broderick) and company's mad trip to downtown Chicago.

➡ **THE CHURCH FROM *A WEDDING* (1978)**
Grace Episcopal Church
924 Lake Street, Oak Park, Illinois

A bride, a groom, two wildly disparate families, and a minister barely able to get through a ceremony. You're at *A Wedding* (1978), Robert Altman's over-the-top satire of marriage ceremonies and receptions. The whole shebang gets started in this beautiful Oak Park house of worship. Macaulay Culkin also made a stop here during *Home Alone* (1990).

Behind the Scenes on Robert Altman's *A Wedding*

"I thought it was like going to summer camp."
—Steven B. Poster, ASC

In the summer of 1978, filmmaker Robert Altman brought a crew of 60 technicians and an all-star cast, including Mia Farrow, Lauren Hutton, Paul Dooley, Howard Duff, Dina Merrill, Nina Van Pallandt, Carol Burnett, Geraldine Chaplin, Pam Dawber (in a pre-"Mork & Mindy" role), Pat McCormick, Desi Arnaz, Jr., a newcomer named Dennis Franz, and the First Lady of American Movies, Lillian Gish, to Lake Bluff for a comic extravaganza. Titled *A Wedding* (1978), the film revolved around two unlikely families coming together to celebrate a marriage. The majority of the shoot took place on the estate of Aleka Armour, widow of meatpacking magnate Lester Armour.

This elegant Sheridan Road home, complete with a guest wing and servants' quarters, was ideal for Altman's plans. It occupied 64 acres of a wooded area along Lake Michigan, giving the large cast plenty of physical room to romp through *A Wedding's* multitude of storylines. In return for using the mansion, Altman agreed to make a considerable donation to Mrs. Armour's favorite charity, the Rehabilitation Institute of Chicago. Altman also promised to hold a fundraising premiere of the film on behalf of the Institute.

So Mrs. Armour moved out and a cast of crazies moved in. Steven Poster, who has photographed such films as *The Boy Who Could Fly* (1986), *The Cemetery Club* (1993), *Rocket Man* (1997), and the made-in-Chicago features *Next of Kin* (1989) and *Opportunity Knocks* (1990), was then a young film technician.* "I thought it was like going to summer camp," Poster says, recalling the making of *A Wedding*. "Here we had this huge estate. You had to get into a van and be driven up this long kind of camp road. Every actor in the movie was there every day for that entire summer. Altman worked that way. He wanted to have everyone there.

"There was a real party atmosphere on the set. People hung out together. Everyone went to dailies at night. It seemed more like people on vacation than 120 people making a movie.

"The children working in the movie would love to have Carol Burnett do her Tarzan yell. Everyday, somewhere on the Armour estate you would hear way off in the background this wonderful person doing her Tarzan yell.

"One day I was sitting in the front of the main house. There was a big circular driveway and this huge limousine drove up. Maureen O'Sullivan, Mia Farrow's mother, got out of the car. At that moment, somewhere on the estate, Carol was doing her Tarzan yell because the kids got her to do it again. For a second, I saw Maureen O'Sullivan's eyes glass over. Of course, she had played Jane opposite Johnny Weissmuller's Tarzan. I think she thought she was back in the Tarzan movies! It was hysterical. Carol found out about it later and was extremely embarrassed. It was one of those golden moments."

O'Sullivan wasn't the only member of Hollywood's glamour age to visit the set of *A Wedding*. Grace Kelly, a.k.a. Princess Grace of Monaco, was another visitor. And of course, cast and crew had the rare privilege of working with one of Hollywood's legendary actors, Lillian Gish. Gish was the star of the silent cinema's first American epic, *The Birth of a Nation* (1915), directed by film pioneer D.W. Griffith. Her performance in the chilling picture *Night of the Hunter* (1955) is a classic example of great screen acting.

"Working with Lillian Gish was like working with a fairy princess," Poster said. Gish played a family matriarch who dies early in the film and subsequently spends the whole film in her deathbed. "She was in the bedroom the whole movie," Poster recalls. "While preparing a camera set in the shooting room, she would rest in another room and tell stories of the old days to crew members."

Finally, the summer came to an end, the filmmakers packed up, and Mrs. Armour moved back in. The Armour estate was ultimately sold and broken up into a series of smaller lots.

* Poster is also an advocate for his profession and currently serves as Vice President and the Chairman of Publications for the American Society of Cinematographers and as National Second Vice President of I.A.T.S.E. Local 600 Cinematographers Guild.

DENNIS FRANZ
From Maywood to Hollywood

He got started as an actor to impress a girl. It's that simple.

As a high school student living with his family in west suburban Maywood, Dennis Franz was involved with baseball, football, and swimming. When his girlfriend auditioned for Arthur Miller's *The Crucible*, a stock play for any high school thespian, Franz decided to take a shot at acting himself. "I sat there and thought, 'I can do this,' " Franz recalls. He ended up getting a part, though his girlfriend was passed over. The romance ended, but a career was born.

After high school, Franz attended Wright Junior College, then transferred to Southern Illinois University in Carbondale. He graduated with a bachelor's degree in speech and theater, then returned home to find a draft notice waiting for him. Having little choice in the matter, Franz ended up serving with a reconnaissance unit in Vietnam for 11 hellish months.

When his tour of duty ended, Franz decided to make a go of it in the theater. It was the early 1970s, a time when Chicago theater was on the verge of a great new movement. "It was a wonderful place to learn your basics and gave you a sense of appreciation for the work of others that I've never forgotten," says Franz. After working with a few different troupes, Franz ended up with the Organic Theater Company. There he became close friends with another up-and-coming actor, Joe Mantegna.

Franz, Mantegna, and the Organic members helped usher in a renaissance era for Chicago theater. With director Stuart Gordon, they created shows that still are fondly remembered some 20-plus years later. *The Wonderful Ice Cream Suit, Cops, Switch Bitch, The Sirens of Titan,* and *Bleacher Bums* provided theatergoers with a fresh approach to performance. "People in Chicago made the effort to see a small theater company," says Franz, "and we appreciated it. The spirit was contagious."

At the same time, Franz was breaking into the movies. His first role was as a thug who provided front money for a group of musicians in *My Main Man from Stony Island,* the directorial debut of Andrew Davis. He and Mantegna also appeared in a small, independent film, *Towing,* which satirized the ruthless tactics of the notorious Lincoln Towing Company.

In 1978, Franz was asked to audition for the role of a Chicago cop in Brian DePalma's horror film, *The Fury.* "I had gone to audition," he remembers, "and I went in for the preliminary with [casting director] Lynn Stalmaster. I thought it went fairly well and was waiting for a callback. Finally, I got tired of waiting and went to a John Wayne double feature at a movie theater in Berwyn.

(*Courtesy of Cynthia Snyder Public Relations.*)

"I called my answering machine and there was a message from Meshach Taylor, another member of the Organic company. I thought he was just horsing around but he said, 'the people from *The Fury* have been looking for you all day!'

"I thought to myself, 'Man, did I blow this one!' But it turned out that Brian DePalma was hanging around town for an extra day. I went down to where the auditions were being held and ran into the room. Some guy with a beard was there, I didn't know who it was. As things worked out, I got the part and later found out the guy with the beard was actually DePalma!" Though Franz's part in *The Fury* was minor, it ended up working out quite well for him. He later had significant roles in DePalma's *Dressed to Kill* (1980), *Blowout* (1981), and *Body Double* (1984)

After another small part, this time in Robert Altman's *A Wedding* (1978), Franz decided to head west and try his luck in Hollywood. He picked up minor roles in TV shows like "The A-Team" and "Matlock," then got a role in a new series "Chicago Story," which was shot in the Windy City "I thought, 'well, this is a pretty great way to come back home,' says Franz. "I got a per diem to live in an apartment I normally couldn't afford!"

"Chicago Story" led to Franz's big breakthrough: a guest shot on TV's "Hill Street Blues." He played Sal Benedetto, a venal member of the police force who turned out to be a hit with viewers. Series creator Steven Bochco offered Franz a role on the television baseball drama "Bay City Blues," but when the show was canceled, Franz was written into "Hill Street Blues." His new character, Norman Buntz, was another bad cop and proved to be just as popular as Benedetto was with the series' fans.

Franz vaulted between films and television, including another role with Andrew Davis in the 1989 film *The Package*. With his gruff exterior and hard-edged Chicago accent, Franz was perfectly cast as Gene Hackman's cop buddy. By now he had become something of a quintessential movie and television cop, reflecting a tough blue collar sensibility.

In 1993, Franz reunited with Bochco for what is thus far his finest hour: playing Detective Andy Sipowicz on the ABC television drama "NYPD Blue." Sipowicz is a recovering alcoholic, withdrawn from those he loves and struggling with prostate cancer. Shading his performance with the many natural complications of being human, Franz brings out all the nuances of Sipowicz's good, bad, and ugly personality.

The part has brought Franz much-deserved respect as a serious actor. He has won several Emmy Awards for Lead Actor in a Drama Series, the Golden Globe award, and honors from Viewers for Quality Television. When his colleagues in the Screen Actor's Guild instituted awards of their own, Franz's "NYPD Blue" work earned him the very first SAG honor for

Best Performance in a Drama and Best Ensemble Acting in a Drama.

"Never in my wildest dreams did I ever think I'd get this far," Franz says reflectively. "I used to watch award shows when I was a kid and I thought, 'I don't know where these people come from but it's sure not from Maywood, Illinois.' That still ran through my mind when I won the Emmy. It's like it's not happening to me. I've gone a lot further than I ever could have hoped to achieve.

➡ **AMERICAN MOVIE PALACE MUSEUM/**
THEATRE H ISTORICAL SOCIETY
York Theatre Building, 2nd floor,
152 N. York Road, Elmhurst, Illinois

If you long for the days when going to a movie theater meant stepping through the doors of something spectacular, then head to the western suburbs of Chicago. Nestled on the second floor of the York Theatre in Elmhurst, you'll find the remnants of a by-gone era. Though the location seems unlikely, the American Movie Palace Museum is a genuine treat. The museum highlights a grand period of moviegoing, from the 1920s through the 1940s. Here you'll find old posters, blueprints, photographs, programs, and other memorabilia from long-gone movie palaces. They even have the conductor's stand, saved from the orchestra pit of the razed Granada Theater, on display. The collection covers a vast sweep of global filmgoing, with information on more than 7,000 theaters, both American and foreign.

As part of the Theatre Historical Society of America, the museum offers considerable research facilities for students, historians, and movie buffs. Staff members will also comb through the archives for an hourly fee.

Admission to the museum is free of charge (although donations are accepted) Tuesday through Friday from 10:00 a.m. to 4:00 p.m. No appointments are necessary. Weekend and evening open houses are also occasionally scheduled.

For more information, including research rates, call the Theatre Historical Society of America at 630-782-1800 or visit their Web site at http://www2.hawaii.edu/~angell/thsa/.

➡ **AURORA, ILLINOIS**

Ah, beautiful Aurora, Illinois. One of Chicago's western suburbs, it ranks as the area's best place to relax among fragrant palm trees or beautiful

Rocky Mountains while nibbling on pastries from Stan Mikita's Donut Shop.

Okay, okay, so there aren't any palms or peaks in Aurora. But in *Wayne's World* (1992) and *Wayne's World II* (1993), just about anything is possible. So what if California streets substituted for Aurora? It's the spirit of Aurora that really counts! But be prepared for tart disappointment: though both films paid homage to the former Black Hawk hockey star, you won't find any donut shops topped by a mechanical Stan Mikita amidst Aurora's swaying palm trees.

The Most Excellent *Wayne's World* Tour

In *Wayne's World* (1992), cable access TV star Wayne (Mike Myers), his sidekick Garth (Dana Carvey), and their pals drive around Chicago, looking for aimless laughs. Their oddball tour takes the group past some of the area's most unusual outdoor sculptures.

Want to take this tour yourself? Start on the South Side, home of Capitol Cigar Stores Incorporated, 6258 S. Pulaski Road. This is where the boys gazed in amazement at the ultimate in cigar store Indians. Perched on the roof of this neighborhood tobacco shop is a giant Native American, outfitted in loincloth, headband and feather, and with his arm held aloft.

Though it only took Wayne, Garth, and company a few moments, your drive to the next stop, the North Side's Superdawg Drive-In at 6363 N. Milwaukee will take a little longer. It's worth the time. Superdawg is home to the most delightfully gaudy advertising sculpture in the city. High atop this fast food joint is a pair of anthropomorphic hot dogs, one male, one female. The male, flexing his muscles for all the world to see, is decked out in a Tarzan-like leopard skin while his female companion gazes on adoringly.

After taking in the delights that Superdawg has to offer, head west towards suburban Berwyn. At the Cermak Plaza, 7043 Cermak Road, is "Pinto Pelt," perhaps the ultimate in bizarre outdoor sculpture. It's hard to miss this piece, with its eight cars impaled onto a giant spike. Created by artist Dustin Shuler, the Pinto Pelt is to Berwyn what the Daley Center Picasso is to Chicago. Rumor has it the Berwyn police department breaks in new recruits by sending them out to the Cermak Plaza, with instructions to investigate an eight-car pileup.

➡ WOODSTOCK, ILLINOIS

A cynical weatherman. A dreamy television producer. A town caught up in its annual festivities. That's *Groundhog Day* (1993), an ethereal romantic comedy starring Bill Murray and Andie MacDowell as star-crossed colleagues who stumble towards romance. The story, set against the backdrop of the annual Punxsutawney, Pennsylvania Groundhog Day Festival, takes place over a 24-hour period, one that repeats itself over the course of 30-plus days. Only Murray is aware that time refuses to march on, an experience that by turns acerbic and sweet gradually teach lessons of love.

In recreating Punxsutawney, director Harold Ramis needed a location that visually represented small-town America, while providing a conducive atmosphere for shooting a major motion picture. Unsuccessful in his initial search of Illinois, Ramis was on verge of sending location scouts to Pennsylvania. A drive through Woodstock changed everything

Located about an hour northwest of downtown Chicago, the town was founded in 1837 as "Centerville," and changed its name to Woodstock four years later. In its 160 years of existence, Woodstock has grown into a picturesque community and serves as the seat of McHenry County.

Before *Groundhog Day* was ever conceived, Woodstock was home to several movie-related people. Chester Gould, creator of comic strip cop Dick Tracy, got his start here. The square-jawed detective inspired a series of low-budget films in the 1940s and a big-budget rendition by Warren Beatty in 1990. Today the Chester Gould/Dick Tracy Museum resides in Woodstock and every June the Chamber of Commerce stages the "Dick Tracy Days" festival. Orson Welles, the boy-genius behind *Citizen Kane* (1941), also spent his early creative years in Woodstock. Sent to an all-male boarding school located just outside of town, Welles earned his initial acting and directing credits in Woodstock by staging shows at the Woodstock Opera House.

So, chock-full of history and blessed with a unique, small-town look, Ramis settled on Woodstock as Punxsutawney's stand-in. The town square offered him a filmmakers dream: a series of wonderful locations all within walking distance from each other. What's more, Ramis found himself emerged in a friendly community that was glad to cooperate with the often crazed atmosphere of moviemaking.

"Shooting in small town like that, in one place, you get to be a citizen of the town," Ramis recalls. "You go from never having seen the place to being the leading citizen of the town. Everyone welcomes the movie people. You kind of become part of the community. And as much as they love you, people on the movie will fall in love with the place itself."

Groundhog Day was shot largely in Woodstock's historic town square which is anchored by the beautiful Woodstock Opera House (121 Van Buren Street). In the movie, the Opera House played the Pennsylvania Hotel, where Bill Murray leaps from the tower, only to live and see another February 2 roll around. Ironically, the Opera House is rumored to be haunted by a similar jumper. (See Ursula Bielsksi's *Chicago Haunts: Ghostly Lore of the Windy City*.)

Across the street from the Opera House, at Van Buren Street and Johnson, is Square Park. The southwest corner of the park stood in for Punxsutawney's famed "Gobbler's Knob," where Phil the Groundhog makes his annual entrance. Incidentally, that is Bill Murray's brother, gravel-voiced writer/comedian Brian Doyle Murray playing the Mayor of Punxsutawney during the Groundhog Day festivities. A few yards east, near the corner of Van Buren and Benton, is the site where Murray and MacDowell had several snowball fights on their rocky road to love.

Along Johnson Street, between Van Buren and Cass, is Tavern on the Square, the bar where Murray, MacDowell, and Chris Elliott, the camera-man, enjoyed a few adult beverages. At 101 Cass Street, you'll find one of the movie's recurring jokes and landmarks—the icy puddle that Murray first stepped into but gradually learned to avoid over the course of his endless day. Further east at 109 East Church is the bowling alley that served as "Wayne's Lanes." A few blocks further is Woodstock's Moose Lodge, Chapter 1329. Located at 306

See a free filming of *Groundhog Day* in the lovely Woodstock Opera House during Woodstock's annual "Groundhog Days" festival.
(*Photo by Don Peasley.*)

Clay Street, this is where Groundhog Day's big dance scene took place.

Heading along Jefferson Street, go to the northwest corner of Jefferson and Calhoun Street. Drive carefully—this is the spot where Murray and the groundhog took a suicidal plunge after a high speed chase. Apparently Murray and his rodent co-star had their differences off-screen. Over the course of shooting, Murray was bitten at least twice by the feisty groundhog.

The Cherry Street Inn, the bed and breakfast where Murray supposedly stayed, is actually a private residence in Woodstock. Only the exteriors of this stately house were used; interiors were shot at a home in Cary, Illinois.

"The shooting of Groundhog Day sort of froze Woodstock in a certain way," says Ramis. "The movie got connected with the identity of the town." Indeed, the film became something of an event for Woodstock. With the belief that any time is a good time for celebrating, Woodstock now holds the annual "Groundhog Days" festival, a five-day jubilee honoring the town and its movie. Events include a "Taste of Groundhog Days," featuring cuisine of area restaurants, an ice-sculpting exhibition, a special February 2nd breakfast, a free screening of the film at Woodstock's Opera House, and a walking tour of Woodstock's *Groundhog Day* locations. In the past, this jaunt has been led by Ramis himself, who dedicated a plaque at 101 Cass Street to mark the spot of Bill Murray's puddle nemesis.

For more information about Woodstock's Groundhog Days, call 815-338-2436 or 815-338-0542.

The Restoration of Orson Welles' *Othello*
THE MOOR MEETS DIGITAL TECHNOLOGY IN WESTMONT

1937. Orson Welles, an alum of suburban Woodstock's Todd School for Boys, forms the Mercury Theater along with fellow actor John Houseman. The next year, he scares the pants off America with his radio adaptation of H.G. Wells science fiction tale "The War of the Worlds." Welles continues with his Mercury company, doing radio and theater. He gains a considerable reputation for his staging of William Shakespeare's plays, including *Voodoo Macbeth* with an all African-American cast and a modern-dress version of *Julius Caesar*.

1941. By now Hollywood has discovered Welles. After a few false starts, he's given the opportunity to direct, co-write, and star in his first feature length film. Only 27, Welles comes up with *Citizen Kane*, which wins an Oscar for Best Original Screenplay. Today this landmark film is universally acclaimed as the best movie ever made.

But in 1941, *Citizen Kane* is a box office flop. RKO Studios takes a $150,000 bath on the project. It will take years before adoring movie fans and critics vault *Kane* to its rightful place in movie history.

1948. By now, Welles is almost persona non grata in Hollywood. Still a respected actor, his directorial work has suffered from studio powers-that-be more interested in bottom line figures than masterpieces. Having proven to be a commercial liability, Welles scrambles out of Southern California and heads to Europe.

1949. Still fascinated by the dramatic qualities of Shakespeare, Welles sets out to film *The Tragedy of Othello: The Moor of Venice*. One of Shakespeare's best works, *Othello* has everything a director could possibly want: political intrigue, moments of unforgiving violence, and a sexually-charged interracial relationship. Filming this play becomes Welles' obsession.

Broke, but not broken, Welles sets out to make his dream a reality. Over the course of the next four years, he shoots *Othello* on location in Europe and North Africa. Never mind that he has less than a shoestring budget. Never mind that his original Iago and first two Desdemonas end up quitting. Welles perseveres. He takes parts in other directors' films to raise needed cash, including a highly acclaimed performance as Harry Lime in Carol Reed's *The Third Man* (1949). He cons camera operators out of leftover film at the end of a day's work, then uses this stock to shoot *Othello*.

Though troubled by technical considerations, Welles maintains a strong artistic vision. For the vital sequence in which the character of Cassio is murdered, costumes are unavailable. Forced into a creative corner, Welles resets the scene in a Turkish bath and garbs his actors in towels. This last-minute improvisation pays off in an eerie and unforgettable moment.

Welles puts together his final cut in 1952 and enters *Othello* in the Cannes International Film Festival. Audiences are bowled over by the results. Despite the technical difficulties, including a slightly out-of-synch soundtrack, *Othello* is a hit. Welles is honored with the Golden Palm, Cannes' highest award.

Though European audiences loved *Othello*, it takes three more years for the film to hit American theaters. When *Othello* finally opens in the United States, it is barely noticed. Critics hate Welles' film, and box office returns amount to a paltry $40,000. *Othello* quickly sinks from the theaters without a trace.

Thus was the rocky start of Welles' *Othello*. A brief attempt was made to revive the film in 1960 with little success. Some interest in the film lingered over the years and in 1978, a documentary on the making of *Othello* was broadcast on German television. Occasionally, a 16-

millimeter print would show up in college classrooms, but for all intents and purposes, Orson Welles' *Othello* was considered another noble Welles failure. And after Welles' death in 1985, it appeared *Othello* would never see movie or video screens again.

Then Michael Dawson entered the picture.

Dawson is a 1978 graduate of Southern Illinois University's film program and owner of Intermission Productions, a company in suburban Westmont which specializes in television commercials, music videos, movie trailers (coming attractions), and documentaries. For several years Dawson had been working on a biographical documentary on Orson Welles, called—appropriately enough—*Citizen Welles*. "It's been an epic effort," says Dawson, "and it's been put on the back burner a couple of times." In the process of putting together the documentary, Dawson became friends with Welles' daughter Beatrice.

"In terms of her assisting me with the documentary, she contacted me and said some company was trying to re-release *Othello* in Italy," said Dawson. "She was very upset about it because it was one of the few things she had inherited through her mother's estate and she wanted that stopped. At the time I thought, 'If you're going to stop something like that from being re-released, the best thing to do is to find the master elements. Once you're in possession of the master elements, you have at least some physical control over the film.'

"Beatrice said the theory is that *Othello's* master elements were burned up and lost in Paris in the mid-1950s. I took the lead and said, 'Let me see if I can find it.'

"We did some research and made some phone calls and subsequently found the master elements for *Othello* in a New Jersey warehouse. Through documents Beatrice provided through her mother's estate and her attorney, she was able to get those elements released and sent to Intermission Productions. It basically remained underneath my dining room table for some time, then we deposited *Othello* in a bank vault. We found a bank in Westmont that had a large enough safety deposit box where we could put the boxes of film in.

Opening a can of original nitrate negative of Welles' *Othello* at WRS Laboratories in Pittsburgh, PA. (*Courtesy of Intermission Productions, Ltd.*)

"The original camera negative was about 85 percent nitrate film, which is very fragile. About 5 percent of the film was blown-up from 16-millimeter to 35-millimeter, and the rest of it was safety film. At the time, I was thinking in terms of my documentary. The plan was, if I could get the original master elements, I'll have pristine shots to work with which are certainly much better to put in the documentary.

"But as I began looking at *Othello*, I began to realize that part of the legacy of Welles is that he went off and became 'independent' years before it came in vogue. He essentially would continue to make these masterpieces, he would just do so under increasingly difficult circumstances. The thing that suffered was not Welles' 'canvas,' so to speak, or his visual aesthetics, but post-production, primarily post-production sound."

Indeed, Welles realized during production that sound would inevitably be a problem—no small quandary when it came to recording Shakespeare's rich language! He deliberately shot some sequences without sound, with plans to dub actors' voices in during post-production. Consequently, the lips of *Othello's* characters were often hidden as a way of covering this technological difficulty.

"Welles had a situation where often he would do things on the cheap or he would run out of money," says Dawson. "Or he would be provided with a particular facility where they would do post-production work in an unsupervised situation and sometimes technicians would make mistakes. Those mistakes would end up as part of the final product and the mythology would begin...the mythology being that Orson Welles was going downhill. A large school of critics considered certain technical flaws of Welles' to be aesthetic flaws.

"But what we began to realize was that new technology existed, specifically in terms of digital sound. We could fix some of the problems that Welles had faced. Now with *Othello*, one of the things that was problematic was that the original music score was distorted on the soundtrack. You could not only not hear a lot of the musical nuances, you really couldn't get the real flavoring of it."

Dawson brought in Michael Pendowski, a composer and arranger, to recreate the film score of Francesco Lavagnino and Alberto Barberis. Pendowski went over the film, carefully transcribing every note. Once the score was committed to paper, members of the Chicago Symphony Orchestra and the Lyric Opera of Chicago were hired to record a fresh version of *Othello's* haunting background music.

Using digital technology, Dawson's crew was able to fix *Othello's* poorly synched dialog through slight stretching or compressing of specific shots. Other technical problems, such as muddied sound effects, were also cleaned up. Once the sound was fixed, *Othello* was remixed in stereo.

The final product eventually was transferred from the delicate nitrate film to D-1, a component digital video. "It's the highest form of digital video presently available," says Dawson. "Unfortunately, the public has never seen that version. It's too bad, because the visual quality of D-1 was able to go leaps and bounds above what we were able to do at the film level.

"The film was released and to wide critical acclaim. There were huge write-ups in everything from the magazine *American Cinematographer* to the *New York Times*.

"Restoring *Othello* helped correlate the theme of my documentary in that it kind of created a revisionism. Now that some of the technical flaws had been eliminated, people were able to appreciate the film. They're not being distracted by poor lip-synchronization or an over-modulated music score. Without those distractions present, audiences were able to absorb *Othello*." Indeed, the highly-respected *New York Times* film critic Vincent Canby wrote that this restored *Othello* was on par visually with *Citizen Kane*.

After this amazing effort, the film premiered at the Film Center at the School of the Art Institute in a benefit performance. *Othello* ultimately was released to great acclaim at theaters around the world. In the end, *Othello* was an artistic triumph larger than Welles himself could have possibly imagined.

Reach Intermission Productions at 630-654-0200. Check out the *Citizen Welles* Web site at http://citizenwelles.com, for more information on *Othello* and Dawson's *Citizen Welles*.

Michael Dawson, owner of Intermission Productions and the producer responsible for employing digital technology to fix poor sound quality in the restoration of Orson Welles' *Othello*. (*Photo courtesy of Intermission Productions Ltd.*)

SOUTH

INDEX OF ARTICLES

The City

➡ MAXWELL STREET DISTRICT POLICE STATION
943 W. Maxwell Street

Opened in 1888, in part as a response to the Haymarket Riots, the former Maxwell Street District police station is listed on the National Register of Historic Places. Legend has it Al Capone once spent a night in the station lockup. After more than 100 years of service, the building was closed in 1997 and is now owned by the University of Illinois-Chicago.

Movie fans will probably recognize the Maxwell Street District as the police station Edward Norton is brought to for questioning in *Primal Fear* (1996). (Interiors were filmed at a now-closed police precinct at 39th and California.) However, the Maxwell Street precinct is better known as the station house shown in the opening credits of the 1980s police drama "Hill Street Blues." This landmark television series revolved around the cops of an unnamed city and included Chicago actors Betty Thomas and Dennis Franz among its cast.

➡ U.S. SOCCER FEDERATION BUILDING
1811 S. Prairie Avenue

Okay, you say your movie is about a Catholic bishop who runs the Archdiocese of Chicago, only it turns out that he's also a crazed sex maniac and gets murdered by a sweet-faced young man who appeared in the clergyman's homemade pornographic videos and you want to film it where?

With a hook like that, it was obvious from the word go that the makers of *Primal Fear* (1996) weren't going to be doing a whole lot of creative work in

The U.S. Soccer House (1801-1811 S. Prairie Avenue) served as the location for the opening murder scene in *Primal Fear* (1996) and also appeared in *Chain Reaction* (1996). (*Courtesy of the U.S. Soccer Federation.*)

cooperation with the officials of our local Catholic church. Consequently, a substitute rectory had to be created for the murder scene. To accomplish that, *Primal Fear* came to the U.S. Soccer Federation Building on Prairie Avenue.

This gorgeous mansion is one of many to be found along the Prairie Avenue district. Owned by the Chicago Architecture Foundation, the house now serves as offices of the U.S. Soccer Federation. To turn the home into a cathedral and rectory required a bit of movie magic. Across the street from the property was a warehouse. A false front was built to link the two structures together. This created "Saint Michael's Cathedral" where the bishop is murdered.

The U.S. Soccer Federation Building was also used in the Andrew Davis thriller *Chain Reaction* (1996).

➡ **ALL-AMERICAN NEWS**
2901 S. Prairie Avenue

Before television beamed daily news into our living rooms, audiences hungry for pictures of major events soaked in the weekly newsreel. Such series as *March of Time* and *Fox Movietone News* kept film audiences informed and entertained. The only thing it seemed to be missing was the weather report.

Yet, like so many Hollywood productions of the 1940s, newsreels all but ignored African-American viewers. To serve this important audience, three Chicagoans—Joseph Plunkell, E.M. Gluckman, and J.R. King—formed the All-American News. Intending to bring an improved kind of news and entertainment to African-American filmgoers. The All-American News released its first newsreels in October 1942. Aiming to help with the country's war effort, All-American News released some films under the title *March of Freedom*. "[These newsreels] will record each week the activities of Negro men and women in the service of their country throughout the world," the company stated.

Other newsreels from All-American News examined how the Urban League looked at America's labor struggles, introduced audiences to President Franklin Delano Roosevelt's personal valet, and provided information about the famed Tuskegee Institute. Sports and entertainment figures were also highlighted. The newsreels also included advertisements for Chesterfield tobacco products.

In 1946, All-American News shut down its newsreel production and switched to entertainment films. They made several short pictures with Lollypop Jones, a popular comic in the African-American community.

Another All-American production, *Killer Diller* (1948), was a musical revue featuring the Nat "King" Cole Trio, comedian Jackie "Moms" Mabley, and *Gone with the Wind's* (1939) Butterfly McQueen. Poor production values and eventual financial hardship overtook the All-American News mission. By the time the 1950s rolled around, All-American News was out of business.

Source: Sampson, Henry T. *Blacks in Black and White: A Source Book on Black Films*, 2nd Edition, Metuchen, N.J. & London: Scarecrow Press, Inc., 1995.

 # A Raisin in the Sun (1961)

In 1959, the debut of a young, Chicago-born playwright was honored with the New York Drama Critics Circle Award. Lorraine Hansberry's *A Raisin in the Sun* was the heartfelt story of a South Side family trying to break the cycle of poverty amidst a society pervaded by racism. Written seven years before Dr. Martin Luther King Jr.'s march through Marquette Park, Hansberry's words urged Broadway audiences to examine the myriad difficulties faced by poor African-Americans in Chicago and elsewhere.

Two years later, the film version of *A Raisin in the Sun* (1961) was released to wide critical acclaim. It was honored at the Cannes Film Festival with a special Gary Cooper Award for its eloquent expression of "human values." Certainly, *A Raisin in the Sun* was a revolutionary film far ahead of its time. Featuring a dynamic cast, including original Broadway stars Sidney Poitier and Claudia MacNeil, the film takes on such profound issues as racism, intra-racial differences, and abortion. Few, if any, Hollywood productions of the era could lay claim to such complexity.

Although *A Raisin in the Sun* is a fine screen rendition of the stage play, the film was only part of Hansberry's original movie script which included several Chicago-based scenes portraying the daily life of her characters. "Born to the romance of the [Carl] Sandburg image of the great city's landscape, I was excited by the opportunity to deal with it visually and sent the formerly housebound characters hither and yon into the city," she wrote. [1]

Hansberry's additional scenes "opened up" the stage play, giving her characters context beyond the claustrophobic atmosphere of their small apartment. Director Daniel Petrie, who got started in Chicago as director of the television program "Studs Place," shot scenes in a variety of area locations including the Calumet (now Bishop Ford) Expressway, the South Chicago steel mills, the Loop, and the Victory Monument at 35th and Martin Luther King Drive.

Hansberry's fresh material, however, resulted in a film that ran more than three hours. These scenes, which amplified Hansberry's themes on America's racial divide, were consequently edited from the final version. Hollywood was not ready for such straightforward cultural statements in 1961. What remained of the Chicago footage were some exterior shots on the South Side, a shot of Poitier waiting on Michigan Avenue for his employer, and the scene in which the Younger family visits the house MacNeil has bought with her late husband's insurance money.

One of Hansberry's cut scenes involved a conversation between Sidney Poitier's character, Walter Lee Younger, and Herman, a white liquor store proprietor.[2]

Herman was played by Studs Terkel, acting under his given name Louis. "Lorraine Hansberry wrote in a part for me," Terkel recalls. "You see me listed in the credits on screen as Louis Terkel. They forgot to cut it out."[3]

A Raisin in the Sun remains an American classic nearly four decades after its initial release. In 1994, Hansberry's complete screenplay, painstakingly edited by her former husband Robert Nemiroff and with commentaries by Margaret B. Wilkerson and Spike Lee, was published.

[1] Hansberry, Lorraine, "A Raisin in the Sun: The Unfilmed Original Screenplay," (Signet: New York, 1994), xxviiii.

[2] Author's interview with Studs Terkel.

[3] *Ibid.*

➡ **POMIERSKI & SON FUNERAL HOME**
1039 W. 32nd

In *Hoodlum* (1997), the climactic final scene of Laurence Fishburne attending services for his associate Chi McBride took place at this South Side funeral parlor.

➡ **COMISKEY PARK**
300 W. 35th Street

Home of baseball's Chicago White Sox, the mall-like Comiskey Park on 35th Street is the second incarnation of Comiskey Park. The original, first known as White Sox Park, opened on July 1, 1910. Designed by Zachary Taylor Davis, with input from team owner Charles Comiskey and pitcher Ed Walsh, Comiskey Park stood for 80 seasons.

Old Comiskey, got into the movie business late in its life. Scenes from *Red Heat* (1988) and the climactic scenes of the obscure *One Cup of Coffee* (1991) were shot here. Sadly, the stadium's look and age-old beauty were never really captured on film until the very end with the Chris Columbus romantic comedy, *Only the Lonely* (1991).

The film revolved around a shy Chicago cop (John Candy in a nice change of pace from his usual comic stylings) and his attempts to woo a mortician's assistant (Ally Sheedy). Candy's character has some pull with the groundskeepers at Comiskey, which enables him to treat Sheedy to a sweet post-game, on-field picnic. While the pair dine, they are treated to a special fireworks show, Comiskey Park trademark that was instituted by former owner Bill Veeck. Though it's an unlikely "only in the movies" moment, the scene had a special kind of charm. It's also a tad bittersweet, particularly to fans of the old ballpark.

Shooting took place on a warm October Friday, just a few days before demolition was to begin on old Comiskey. "It was a special night," recalls Jacolyn J. Baker, a location manager on the film. "Everybody knew that this was going to be the last time anybody would be in Comiskey Park since they were going to start demolition on Monday. Everybody brought their families out. It was an unusually balmy night, about 70 degrees—a perfect Indian summer night. In between takes, people were playing catch on the field. You felt that this history was about to be taken [away]. It was really special. We all knew it was going to be the end."

The new Comiskey Park opened the following spring on April 18, 1991. The park was bigger, shinier, and had better sight-lines, but lacked the warmth of old Comiskey. Still, it looked pretty good in *My Best Friend's Wedding* (1997), the off-beat Julia Roberts comedy where Cameron Diaz played the daughter of White Sox owner Philip Bosco.

➡ **THE *BACKDRAFT* TOUR**

In 1990, film production came to a halt in New York City when technician and crew members went on strike. Consequently, director Ron Howard, then in the preliminary stages of *Backdraft* (1991), decided to relocate his epic story of big city firefighters to Chicago. The Big Apple's loss was definitely the Windy City's gain.

The production team ended up staying most of the year, providing considerable employment for local talent both in front of and behind the camera. In addition to the main story involving Robert DeNiro, Billy Baldwin, Kurt Russell, Scott Glenn, Donald Sutherland, Rebecca DeMornay, and other name actors, *Backdraft's* second unit shooting costs ranged between $15-$20 million. Filming things like fire trucks rushing to a scene, helicopter shots of fires, and other sequences that connect the main action, the *Backdraft* second-unit operated like a small-budget movie within the larger production.

Numerous city firehouses were utilized during the film. The Chinatown station at 4195 S. Archer served as the main headquarters for the firefighters. Robert DeNiro, playing an arson investigator, shot his office scenes at a shuttered firehouse at 39th and Albany. Other fire stations utilized were at 1401 S. Michigan, 212 W. Cermak, and 4317 S. Paulina, along with the Chicago Fire Department garage at 3100 S. Sacramento.

Kurt Russell played a grizzled firefighting veteran separated from his wife, Rebecca DeMornay, and estranged from his rookie fireman brother, Billy Baldwin. Having nowhere else to turn, Russell lived in a boathouse located at the Marinus Marine, 1990 S. Lumber, near 18th and Canal Street.

Of course, *Backdraft* wasn't all work and/or personal angst. For a good time, the firefighters relaxed at O'Sullivan's Tavern, 495 N. Milwaukee. The 24-hour White Palace Grill at 1159 S. Canal was also used for on-screen R&R.

Backdraft culminates in an apocalyptic inferno, which was staged at the former Cuneo Press Building, 455 W. Cermak, at the river. Long since abandoned, the empty warehouse was carefully rigged by special effects experts so that the seemingly out-of-control blaze was always safe for the production team. The result was a magnificent destruction, perfectly maintained by a team of movie experts.

That's not to say *Backdraft* didn't have any errors. Veteran firefighters undoubtedly got many kicks out of all the mistakes made by their silver screen counterparts. You never saw Kurt Russell run into a building wearing breathing apparatus, a necessary element in modern firefighting. The final sequence contains another major faux pas. The heat factor alone would have been blistering to the skin, yet Scott Glenn runs around the blaze sans his protective gear.

The biggest fire error in *Backdraft* was a matter of simple physics. Next time you see the film, watch how flames lick their way along ceilings. In reality, a building burns from the floor and moves up, not from the topside down. For movie purposes, these burning ceilings were shot in specially-constructed rooms, which were set on fire, then filmed upside down. While unrealistic to be sure, the overall effect gave *Backdraft's* fires a sinister look and feel.

JANE ALDERMAN
JANE ALDERMAN CASTING

(*Courtesy of Jane Alderman.*)

"We have a great work ethic in Chicago. You've got actors who are willing to work, they're good, they're not seen all the time. They're great faces, they're real people."

You may not recognize Jane Alderman's name but chances are you've seen her listed in the credits for many films and television shows. She's an important player in Chicago filmmaking, having worked on such productions as *Four Friends* (1981), *Bad Boys* (1983), *The Color of Money* (1986) *Lucas* (1986), *Child's Play* (1988), *Poltergeist III* (1988), *Music Box* (1989), *Backdraft* (1991), *The Babe* (1992), *Candyman* (1992), *Natural Born Killers* (1994), *A Family Thing* (1996), *love jones* (1997), and the television series "Early Edition" (1996-present).

Her company, Jane Alderman Casting, helps place local actors in supporting roles for the many feature films that come through town. "We are hired by the production company or the producer to find the actors for the project," she says. "To do it is truly, I believe, an art. You can't just say 'I know Bobby, Bobby's a nice guy, he's 30, he can be a cop.' You can't just do that. There has to be a whole look to a picture. If I brought someone in for the part of a cop, the director could say, 'That's really nice but that's not the way we're going. I want all of our cops to look like they're on "Baywatch." He looks like he could be from Manhattan or any other city.'

"My casting takes me places and into cultures I would never venture into normally. Prisons, baseball players, Vietnamese refugee centers. You have to get into so many diverse cultures to learn what's a reality. For instance, if you go into a coffee shop on the South Side, you can't just say we're filling up waiters and patrons in a coffee shop on the South Side. You're going to have to go around and see who sits around in coffee shops and then that's the reality. You match that look and what the director likes. Martin Scorsese's tastes are completely different than Garry Marshall's.

"If the lead is Robert DeNiro and this person has a scene with him, then he's got to be one of the finest actors. Even if the actor says something like 'oh I'm sorry sir, your bus left' and he's opposite DeNiro, there has to be a presence with that actor. Otherwise he'll evaporate into nothingness because DeNiro's so powerful. To have a very strong actor, even if it's for just one line, up against somebody that brilliant, is smart.

"I loved working on *Backdraft* (1991). That took me into the fire culture, both arsonists and firemen and learning their code. That really was so exciting. I found a lot of real firemen who could act—and there are firemen actors just like there's cop actors.

"What was very exciting, and I've had this happen before, is where you get actors who don't know about the kind of people they're playing. Getting them together and finally watching everyone learn from each other was great. I had a quite a few real firemen in long, big roles. They took the actors under their wings and taught them everything about fighting fires. At the same time the actors, like Billy Baldwin and Kurt Russell, were giving the firemen acting tips."

"For *The Color of Money* (1986) I had to find pool players, real ones that could possibly act. There were some real ones that Scorsese wanted in the movie as themselves. I found myself on this network of pool and pool halls in the city. Word got out really fast within that pool underground. My phone rang off the hook a lot. I'd get champs, former champs, some of the most fascinating characters I have ever met. I'd go out just about every night into various pool halls in the city. My favorite was the one they actually shot it in, The Ginger Man. You would go and talk to the owner or manager and they'd say 'see Puffy. Puffy has been doing this for awhile and was in Atlantic City and won the championship.'

"In several pool halls I would arrange for these guys to shoot pool and do their tricks. Scorsese could talk to them, then take them off into a corner and have them read.

"What I had to be careful was that every pool hall was absolutely smoke-filled and Scorsese was totally allergic to smoke. I was actually worried about it. Somehow we aired the place out; no one was allowed to smoke and I asked that everyone who came in to be interviewed not smoke in their cars. It worked out all right."

➡ **THE MARX BROTHERS' HOMES**
- **4649 S. Calumet Avenue**
- **4512 W. Grand Boulevard**

In 1910, Chicago was a choice location for entertainers to call home. Situated in the middle of the country, the city provided a central base of operations for touring performers as they traveled from town to town and theater to theater. Three of vaudeville's major circuits, Orpheum, Pantages, and Sullivan and Considine, had important booking agencies in town. So, when Minnie Marx decided to move her family of comedians to Chicago from New York, it was a sound business decision.

The Marx family act, touring at that time as "The Four Nightingales," first took up residence at 4649 S. Calumet Avenue. Quickly outgrowing the place, they moved to a three story brownstone at 4512 W. Grand Boulevard, the first home that the family owned. The Marxes stayed there for the next 12 years. Today that location is the site of a soft drink distributor.

Minnie's boys would later change their names, throw their prepared material out the window, and ultimately revolutionize the art of comedy. Ad-libbing a new show night after night, the Marx Brothers honed their characters on vaudeville stages across the country. Legend has it Leonard, Adolph, Julius, and Milton were given the names Chico (originally Chicko), Harpo, Groucho, and Gummo in a poker game aboard a train just outside of Galesburg, Illinois. The baby of the family, Herbert, took on the moniker Zeppo a few years later.

The Marxes later bought some land outside of Chicago in LaGrange and made a miserable attempt to become farmers. "The first morning on the farm," Groucho later wrote, "we got up at five. The following morning, we dawdled in bed until six. By the end of the week we were getting up at noon, which was just enough time for us to get dressed to catch the 1:07 to Wrigley Field..."

Sources:
Arce, Hector. *Groucho*. New York: Perigee Books, 1980.
Marx, Groucho. *The Groucho Phile*. New York: Bobbs-Merrill, 1976.

➡ **PALACE LOAN COMPANY**
216 E. 47th Street

Looking for a bargain? So were Joliet Jake and Elwood Blues in the 1980 romp *The Blues Brothers*. The Palace Loan Company, complete with a wonderful outdoor mural painted on the building's outdoor wall, was where the singing siblings and their bandmates came to buy instruments from shopkeeper Ray Charles.

➡ GERRI'S PALM TAVERN
446 E. 47th Street

In *Mercury Rising* (1998), Bruce Willis hung out and hid out in the South Side neighborhood bar (never mind that the movie indicated Willis lived on the North Side!). Director Harold Becker loved the atmosphere of the place and even hired the owner to play the movie bartender. The short-lived television series "EZ Streets" (1996) also shot some scenes here. In its glory days of the 1940s, the Palm Tavern was a jazz hot spot. Headliners like Ella Fitzgerald and Louis Armstrong were regulars on the bandstand.

➡ *SOMEWHERE IN TIME* LOCATIONS

Somewhere in Time is one of those movies that somehow takes on a life of its own. A romantic tale, this period film revolves around Richard Collier (Christopher Reeve), a modern Chicago playwright who becomes fascinated with the portrait of a long-dead stage actress, Elise McKenna (Jane Seymour). Thanks to a mysterious time warp, Reeve is able to travel back through the years to meet his beloved.

The film earned fair to dismal reviews when it was released in 1980, but has developed a cult following that rivals *The Rocky Horror Picture Show* (1975). Today, fans gather at the annual SIT convention, held at the Grand Hotel on Mackinac Island, Michigan, where the majority of the film was shot. However, there are a few Chicago locations where SIT devotees can make a pilgrimage.

Christopher Reeve's Richard Collier lived in a comfortable loft apartment, located at 1855 N. Halsted Street. If that's not enough for you, head south to the Blackstone Library at 4904 S. Lake Shore Drive, where Reeve did some research on Elise McKenna. Incidentally, keep your eyes open for quick appearances by two Second City actors, Tim Kazurinsky and George Wendt. Both had minor roles in *Somewhere in Time* before moving on to bigger things.

If you want to hook up with other *Somewhere in Time* fans, try INSITE: International Network of *Somewhere In Time* Enthusiasts, c/o Bill Shepard, P.O. Box 1556, Covina, California, 91722. The Web address for INSITE is http://w3.one.net/~voyager/sitin.html. You should also check out the

Somewhere In Time homepage at http://somewhereintime.pair.com.

➡ **THE MUSEUM OF SCIENCE AND INDUSTRY**
57th Street and Lake Shore Drive

Nestled off Lake Shore Drive in the Hyde Park neighborhood, the Museum of Science and Industry was originally built in 1893 for the Columbian Exposition. Dubbed "The Palace of Fine Arts," the building was loosely modeled on a variety of Greek temples on the Acropolis at Athens. It later housed a collection which ultimately was turned over to the Field Museum in 1920.

The building remained empty for the next several years. A $5 million donation from philanthropist Julius Rosenwald revitalized the former Palace of Fine Arts for the 1933 Century of Progress Exposition. Now dedicated to highlighting technical achievements, the building was renamed "The Museum of Science and Industry." It's been a staple for school field trips and a genuine Chicago treasure ever since.

For movie lovers, the Museum of Science and Industry has a lot to offer. Hollywood pictures shot here include *Damien: Omen II* (1978) and *Endless Love* (1981). *Flatliners* (1990) staged its surreal Halloween festival here, making effective use out of the looming Greek columns on the museum's exterior. Take a trip inside to the airplane exhibit and you'll see where Keanu Reeves leaped around on a model 747 fuselage during the chase sequence of *Chain Reaction* (1996). If you want to recreate other moments in Reeves's flight, you'll have to go to the Field Museum. Through the magic of movie editing, two of the city's most popular attractions were fused together, much to the amusement of audiences in multiplexes around town. (Also see the Field Museum entry, p. 160.)

The museum is also home to a couple of movie-related permanent exhibits. Colleen Moore's Fairy Castle is sheer delight. Moore was a silent screen star who personified the jazz babies of the flapper era. One of Hollywood's highest paid talents during the 1920s, she retired from the picture business a few years after talkies arrived. Moore invested her earnings in the stock market and ultimately made a fortune. One of her hobbies was the construction of this Fairy Castle, which houses more than 1,000 miniaturized items.

The Fairy Castle is nine square feet and actually is made up of 200 separate parts. The majority of the structure is made out of aluminum. It also has its own electrical system and running water.

The museum's second attraction is the World War II vintage U-505 German submarine. This U-boat, one of only three in the world, was captured by American forces during a battle off the coast of Africa. Brought to Chicago in 1954, it remains one of the Museum's most popular attractions. It's cinematic significance? When German director Wolfgang Petersen was researching his World War II epic *Das Boot* (1982), a gripping tale of life aboard a German submarine, extensive research was done at the U-505 in order to maintain on-screen accuracy.

Additionally, the Museum of Science and Industry is home to one of the two Imax Theaters in the city. True to the mission of this institution, the films screened here use imagination and a sense of wonder to look at the world's gains in science and industry. (See the Navy Pier entry for more information about Imax technology.)

The Museum of Science and Industry is open every day of the year except Christmas Day. Hours: 9:30 a.m. - 4:00 p.m. weekdays; 9:30 a.m. - 5:30 p.m. Saturday and Sunday. For admission prices to exhibits call 773-684-1414 or check out the Museum's interactive Web page at http://www.msichicago.org.

ANDREW DAVIS
Born and Bred on Chicago's South Side

If Woody Allen is Manhattan's cinema laureate, then Andrew Davis is Chicago's action equivalent. Born and bred on Chicago's South Side, Davis has made the majority of his films here, including *My Main Man from Stony Island* (1978), *Code of Silence* (1985), *Above the Law* (1988), *The Package* (1989), *The Fugitive* (1993), and *Chain Reaction* (1996). Although he now lives and works in southern California, even the name of his production company, Chicago Pacific Entertainment, reflects his Windy City background.

"In the infamous summer of 1968," says Davis, "I graduated from the University of Illinois and began one of the most exhilarating experiences of my young career, having the fortune to work with Haskell Wexler on *Medium Cool* (1969). The streets were alive with a new culture, a new political awareness that was taking over the country."

Medium Cool is one of the quintessential made-in-Chicago movies. Shot at the height of the political tension sweeping the country in 1968, the film blends fact and fiction through documentary style shooting. Some of the film's most compelling moments capture the brutality of the riots that swept Grant Park during the Chicago Democratic Convention.

Within a few years, Davis graduated from 2nd unit to cinematographer, photographing a series of B horror and crime pictures. While the films may have been forgettable, Davis used the opportunity to hone his craft and prepare for his next career move. "Trying to direct without understanding the camera, to me, is like someone conducting a symphony without reading music," he says. In 1977, he came home to Chicago, script in hand, ready to make his mark as a director.

The result was *My Main Man from Stony Island* (a.k.a. *Stony Island*), a loosely autobiographical story about some kids putting together a rock band. Davis shot in his old Stony Island neighborhood (where his family was one of the last white families to move out of the area), in the Kenwood neighborhood, and along the El, a favorite Davis location in this and subsequent films. The cast included Organic Theater members Dennis Franz and Meshach Taylor in their film debuts. Other soon-to-be famous *Stony Island* names included Rae Dawn Chong and Susanna Hoffs.

Following *Stony Island*, Davis returned to the B picture circuit, working as a cinematographer on the critically acclaimed teen film *Over the Edge* (1979). His next directorial effort was *The Final Terror* (1981), another low-grade horror film, which featured another cast of future stars: Joe Pantoliano (who would later appear in Davis's 1993 film *The Fugitive*), Rachel Ward, and Chicagoans Daryl Hannah and Adrian Zmed. Davis was also cinematographer for the exploitation classic, *Angel* (1984). ("High school student by day...Hollywood hooker by night!" blared the film's sensational ad campaign.)

The next year brought Davis back to Chicago, this time to direct martial arts champion Chuck Norris in the action film *Code of Silence* (1985). This is a film clearly made by someone who knows Chicago streets and neighborhoods. Using sites like the Chicago Cultural Center and the Wrigleyville area, Davis carved out a unique territory within the city to stage his action sequences. Alleyways become endless mazes and crowded downtown streets crackle with danger. A death-defying leap off the roof of a moving El train into the Chicago River takes on the feel of a thrill-packed ballet. "*Code of Silence* uses Chicago locations as well as any film I've ever seen," says Roger Ebert.

Davis's next feature, *Above the Law* (1988) marked the debut of another martial arts maestro, Steven Seagal. As per genre expectations, the plot was packed with twists, gunfire, and fight sequences. Yet within the formulaic constraints, Davis again showcased the city neighborhoods, shooting extensively on the South Side. Once more, the El played a crucial role in the action as one bad guy falls to his death from the Executive House onto the train tracks. Though we never see a body hit the rails, a quick electrical flash says it all.

Having mastered the action sequence, Davis took on a more ambitious challenge with his next Chicago picture, *The Package* (1989). A complex political thriller, *The Package* turned Chicago into Cold War-era East Germany and Washington D.C. (And just how did Chicago metamorphose into these locations? Turn to page 245 to find out.)

"Andy's great because he's really an actor's director," says Chicago-based actor Ron Dean. "A lot of times he'll set up a situation and we'll improvise our way through it. He's a lot of fun to work with."

Dean played key secondary roles in several Davis pictures, including *Above the Law, The Package,* and *The Fugitive.* This latter film is probably Davis' most popular Chicago-based work. A clever re-working of the 1960s television show, *The Fugitive* starred Harrison Ford as a doctor falsely accused of brutally murdering his wife (Sela Ward). As Ford eludes U.S. Marshal Tommy Lee Jones (in an Oscar-winning supporting role), Davis takes us on a complex tour of his home town. "Andy knows Chicago very well," says veteran location scout Bob Hudgins. "When you scout with him it's very frustrating because he knows the city better than location people!"

With *The Fugitive*, Davis takes audiences to well-known sites, such as the Hilton Towers, the El, City Hall, Cook County Hospital, and the downtown St. Patrick's Day Parade. Yet he makes these locations fresh, injecting tension in every sequence.

Interestingly, many of the locations of *The Fugitive* were the same places Davis utilized in *The Package*. The Pullman area, the Loop, the downtown El, and the Hilton Towers all played significant roles in these two thrillers. "If you watch *The Fugitive* and *The Package* back to back," notes Michael Malone, a location manager who worked on both films,

Director Andrew Davis, in the D. P. Carlson's *Chicago Filmmakers on the Chicago River* project, aboard a fireboat—representing the blue-collar sensibility of many of his films. (*Photo by Jessica Feith. Courtesy of D.P. Carlson.*)

"you'll see they have a similar rhythm. A lot of the major points in each movie happens at about the same time (movie-wise) and in or near the same location."

In the wake of *The Fugitive's* success, Davis brought *Chain Reaction* (1996) to Chicago as well. A sort of scientific thriller, *Chain Reaction* combines the labyrinth plot of *The Package* with the tight-wire tension of *The Fugitive*. The film was shot at several locations, including the University of Chicago and Hyde Park neighborhood, the Lake Calumet Water Reclamation Plant, the Field Museum and Museum of Science and Industry (combined into one institution through the magic of Hollywood), and the Michigan Avenue bridge. This latter location was at the heart of *Chain Reaction's* biggest set piece, a chase up the raised bridge.

The Package, The Fugitive, and *Chain Reaction* (1996) have another important aspect in common—they were all shot in winter. Though filmmakers love Chicago, for the most part they've avoided location work during the months of December through March. Yet Davis has brought his big budget features to his hometown during its most notorious season. Why?

"Chicago is definitely not Hollywood," he explains. "Every character [in my films] has to endure something just to get out of his or her door. So there is a struggle to every scene. It takes you someplace that nobody would dare go."

Considering the double whammies of snow and bitter-cold wind chill factors, this metaphoric sense of struggle that winter brings to the city certainly enhances this sensibility. But in addition to artistic concerns, Davis also has a practical reason for leaving sunny Los Angeles for the icy environs of his hometown.

"I use winter in Chicago to my advantage because it is so cold there is no one to get in the way of the shooting crew," he says.

➡ THE UNIVERSITY OF CHICAGO
Hyde Park

In 1891, William Rainey Harper founded the University of Chicago in Chicago's South Side Hyde Park neighborhood. In its century of service, the university has become one of America's most prestigious institutions. Nobel Prizes abound throughout the faculty roster, particularly in the field of economics.

Filmwise, U of C has a great deal of significance. In 1932, a group of students founded the Documentary Film Group, commonly referred to as

Doc Films. Devoted to the exhibition and discussion of cinematic arts, Doc Films is the oldest continuously running student film society in the United States.

Which of the following sounds like a more fulfilling cinematic experience to you: drooling as Bruce Willis detonates some dastardly rapscallions or engaging in a thoughtful deliberation over genre and authorship in postclassical cinema? If the latter is what you crave, check out the University of Chicago Film Studies Center. Located in Cobb Hall at 5811 S. Ellis Avenue, the Film Studies Center (FSC) concentrates in three specific areas: film education and research in Cinema and Media Studies courses, archive and collections in the Gerald Mast Film Archive (named after the University's highly-renowned late film historian), and film and media-related events and activities.

The University of Chicago Cinema and Media studies offers undergraduate, graduate, and doctoral degrees in film studies. Classes concentrate on cinematic theory and history. For those who want to make movies as well as study them, the program offers referrals to other area institutions where students can learn production skills.

The University's Film Archive contains more than 3,700 film, video, and laserdisc titles, ranging from Hollywood features to non-commercial avant garde work.

Of course the University of Chicago has also shown up on screen from time to time. In *When Harry Met Sally* (1989) Billy Crystal and Meg Ryan begin their decades-long friendship at the main quadrangle near University and 58th Avenues. It's never explained though how the couple gets sidetracked on their road trip to New York City and end up on the North Side of Chicago—heading south on Lake Shore Drive.

Looking for a little life after your death? Parts of *Flatliners* (1990), a neo-gothic, postmortem drama, were filmed around the University and in the Hyde Park neighborhood.

Andrew Davis has brought his last three locally-shot productions to the University of Chicago. Before taking it on the lam in *The Fugitive* (1993), Dr. Richard Kimble (Harrison Ford) was based at "Chicago Memorial Hospital." Don't look for their number in the phone book: Chicago Memorial was actually the re-dressed University of Chicago Hospital at 5812 S. Ellis Avenue.

One of the University of Chicago's most historical events ultimately served as a backdrop for Davis' 1989 film *The Package*. On December 2, 1942, in a converted squash court beneath Stagg Field, Italian physicist Enrico Fermi led a group of scientists in the world's first controlled nuclear reaction. Splitting the atom ultimately led to development of nuclear weapons, which brought an end to World War II but a beginning to the Cold

War.

After Stagg Field was torn down, the University installed the Henry Moore sculpture "Nuclear Energy" at the site of this flashpoint. In *The Package*, much of the plot revolves around a U.S.-Soviet pact on nuclear weapons. Davis filmed the symbolic signing of this fictional arrangement in front of the Moore sculpture, heightening the dramatic qualities within the moment.

Chain Reaction (1996) was the third Davis film to shoot around this illustrious institution. Keanu Reeves played a University of Chicago researcher (typecasting, this was not!), who assists in an experiment to harness energy from water molecules. When rogue elements within the project blow up a good chunk of the South Side, Reeves finds himself inadvertently tangled in a web of deceit. Most of the Hyde Park scenes took place at the Museum of Science and Industry, though Reeves' movie girlfriend, Rachel Wiecz, lived in an apartment building at 4801 S. Ellis Avenue.

For more information on the University of Chicago, check out their Web site at http://www.uchicago.edu/. Doc Films is also on the Web at http://bsd.uchicago.edu/doc/. The Film Studies Center maintains an excellent movie-related Web site at http://www-college.uchicago.edu/FSC/Research. html.

Philip Kaufman

"In general, back then, film seemed very fresh and Chicago seemed very fresh. It seemed like you could start a new type of filmmaking."

One of America's most intelligent and literate filmmakers, Philip Kaufman has directed such compelling films as *The White Dawn* (1973), *Invasion of the Body Snatchers* (1977), and an adaptation of Czech writer Milan Kundera's novel, *The Unbearable Lightness of Being* (1988). His screen version of *The Right Stuff* (1983), Tom Wolfe's chronicle of the Mercury astronauts, is an American masterpiece, skillfully combining social satire, history, and the human story behind the space program. Kaufman also provided the original story for *Raiders of the Lost Ark* (1981) and wrote the screenplay for

Clint Eastwood's *The Outlaw Josey Wales* (1976).

In 1990, working with his wife Rose, Kaufman adapted Anais Nin's memoirs into the lyrical *Henry and June*, a biography of writers Henry Miller, Nin, and Miller's wife June. It was a fitting subject for the director. After meeting at the University of Chicago in 1962, Nin encouraged Kaufman to become a filmmaker.

Kaufman grew up on Chicago's North Side and attended college at the University of Chicago. He then enrolled in Harvard Law School, but ended up returning to U of C to work on a Master's in history.

After living in San Francisco, and then Europe, Kaufman returned to Chicago. Exhilarated by the new styles of filmmaking that were sweeping France, Czechoslovakia, and other European countries, Kaufman took Nin's advice and in 1963 began work on his first motion picture.

Teaming up with co-writer/producer/director Benjamin Manaster, Kaufman reworked a Hassidic tale of Martin Buber into a $50,000 satire, *Goldstein* (1963). "It was sort of a fable of a young couple whose relationship is falling apart," says Kaufman. "The young guy encounters a prophet—Elijah, really—who comes out of Lake Michigan and is supposed to be this kind of bum and unrecognizable guy who we leave a seat for at the table. He's played by Lou Gilbert who I'd seen in one of Harold Pinter's plays, *The Homecoming*. Gilbert had been blacklisted [in the 1950s]. He was a good friend of Studs Terkel and Nelson Algren's. Algren also tells a wonderful story in *Goldstein*. There were also a lot of Second City people in the film—Del Close, Severn Darden, Anthony Holland.

"Our offices were on the North Side, around Rush Street. I'd been living in Europe for a couple of years and seen the New Wave [films] and there really wasn't much being done in America. So for us, it was the idea of starting a New Wave of filmmaking based on local talent in Chicago.

"*Mickey One* (1965), Arthur Penn's movie, was shooting when we finished editing *Goldstein*. *Mickey One* was still shooting because I remember Francois Truffaut was in town. He was visiting Alexandra Stewart, who he was involved with at the time. She was in *Mickey One*. He came to the first screening of *Goldstein*. During one scene he jumped to his feet and started applauding, which was great! He didn't speak English, he just loved the visuals. [In the scene] Severn Darden and Anthony Holland were itinerant abortionists. This was before abortions were legal and they were flown in for the occasion to perform

[one].

"We'd gone out to the airport to shoot. These itinerant abortionists are flying into Chicago and this plane, suddenly as we were photographing it, smoke started coming out of the back end. It sort of pulled out of the landing pattern and went right over the camera and in the film we suddenly put in the sound of screeching brakes and cut to the long corridor of United Airlines where you heard the crash-tinkle of an airplane crashing and Muzak began. Severn Darden and Anthony Holland, seemingly the only two survivors, come walking down the long corridors as if nothing's happened and the first line is 'they said they'd serve dinner, but they only served snacks!' And Truffaut jumped to his feet. He thought that was great."

Goldstein was entered in the 1964 Cannes Film Festival, where French director Jean Renoir hailed it as "the best American film I have seen in 20 years." The film was awarded the Prix de la Nouvelle Critique, the festival's prize for new filmmakers. This honor was shared with another rising filmmaker, Bernardo Bertolucci, and his work *Before the Revolution* (1964).

"*Goldstein* showed for a while. It showed in New York and Los Angeles and had a very good run in Paris and then it disappeared! And that's how things happen."

Kaufman's next film was *Fearless Frank* (1967), originally titled *Frank's Great Adventure*, which featured an unknown actor named Jon Voight in his movie debut. "I'd seen him off-Broadway in New York in a play *A View From the Bridge*. Dustin Hoffman was the stage manager of that play and Robert Duvall was in it.

"*Fearless Frank* was a comic book—a sort of pop art kind of thing. It was narrated by Ken Nordine. Frank was sort of an amalgam of all the superhero types of characters. He's a young country boy who leaves his country home, comes to the big city, and is shot and killed before the credits begin. The credits turn into this kind of comic book which was drawn by a Chicago artist named Ellen Lanyon.

"It was sort of a parable of the Vietnam time, of how the idea of doing good by fighting evil was not necessarily to be taken at face value as we'd grown up believing as the comics had told us. David Steinberg was in there. Ben Carruthers who was in *Goldstein* as well. I'd seen him in John Cassavetes's *Shadows* (1960), and David Fisher who was another actor in that. Again, a lot of Second City people [were cast]. The cameraman on *Fearless Frank* was Bill Butler who went to Hollywood and shot *Jaws* (1975) and a number of big films."

Following *Fearless Frank*, Kaufman headed west and ultimately was signed by a major studio. Moving into the world of bigger budgeted films, Kaufman rose through the ranks to become one of Hollywood's pre-eminent directors. Still, he looks fondly back on his early days in Chicago.

"In general, back then, film seemed very fresh and Chicago seemed very fresh," Kaufman says. "It seemed like you could start a new type of filmmaking. There was a beginnings of a New York kind of cinema. John Cassavetes and Shirley Clarke were just beginning to make an alternative cinema in New York. But there really wasn't that kind of thing in Chicago and it was tough. It was hard to get recognition, hard to break through with some of the New York critics. There was a certain kind of competitiveness as to which way the independent movement should go."

➡ **THE *MONKEY HUSTLE* BLOCK PARTY**
6300-6400 S. Ellis Avenue

On a summer day in 1976, this stretch of South Ellis turned into one big movie set. Block parties are nothing new, but throw in some cameras, a script, and a few hundred well-fed neighborhood extras and you have a movie scene. That's essentially what happened here for a scene in *Monkey Hustle* (1977), a goofy caper comedy starring Yaphet Kotto and Rudy Ray Moore.

By the way, look closely in that crowd of extras and you'll see future film writer-director-actor Robert Townsend. Before going on to such features as *Hollywood Shuffle* (1987), *The Five Heartbeats* (1991), and *Meteor Man* (1993) and the television sitcom "Father Hood," Townsend made his movie debut playing a street band member in the *Monkey Hustle* block party.

➡ **SOUTH SHORE CULTURAL CENTER**
7000 S. South Shore Drive

The South Shore Cultural Center is a bastion for theater, special events, and a wonderful summer jazz festival. The grounds of this former country club also make for a great movie location. *A League of Their Own* shot a few scenes here, as did *The Blues Brothers*. Television's "Early Edition" and the syndicated version of "The Untouchables" have also brought camera crews to the South Shore Cultural Center.

IRMA HALL

SCREEN CHAMELEON

When I was a kid growing up, one of the things that pushed you to do your best all the time was the fact that you were representing your family, your church, your school, your neighborhood, your race, your country—you had this big bag! I still do that. Whenever I'm doing a project, I'm very conscious that I'm representing not only my family and friends, but also Chicago actors."

Irma Hall is a screen chameleon. Whether she's playing the family matriarch in *Soul Food* (1997) or the mysterious voodoo practitioner in *Midnight in the Garden of Good and Evil* (also 1997), the Chicago-based actor completely disappears into her roles. Watching any of her films back to back, you'll find it hard to believe that she's the same person, so complete is her character transformation. Off screen, Hall is a vivacious and deeply spiritual person, who brings a lifetime of experience to her work.

"I was in Dallas, Texas teaching school and working for a newspaper, the *Dallas Express*. I was the publicity person for my school, so when I heard the oldest black newspaper in Dallas was in trouble because they were short-staffed, I went and volunteered. I figured that would kill two birds with one stone. I'd be doing something to help and I would make sure our school news got in the paper.

"I became the cultural page editor, and they also needed someone to cover school sports and eventually sports. I ended up doing sports, period! I knew this lady named Peggy Taylor who was an agent. She told me that Raymond St. Jacques was coming to Dallas to look at it as a possible location for his film *Book of Numbers* (1973) and that I should interview him. Someone sent him a copy of all the articles I had written. He liked them and asked if I would work as interim publicist for the first five weeks until his regular publicist could come to Dallas. I said great, because I was going to get a chance to learn to do something else.

"I also write poetry and was involved in a group called Advancing Artists and Writers. We had just gotten a grant for workshops for young people in the summer. St. Jacques heard I was reading some poetry and asked me to read for a part in the film. I got the part because they thought I read well and I said, 'Well, I teach school. I hope I read well!'

"Originally it was just a day's work but when he saw me in the dailies, St. Jacques said he was going to expand the role and that I had a lot of natural talent. I was what they called 'an instinctive actor' and I should develop it. As God would have it, there was a young man named Reginald Montgomery who was the first black clown with Ringling Brothers. He was in Dallas as a guest director for the Dallas Theater Center. I had met him through some of my ex-students. Montgomery asked me if I would work with him to found a community theater and that I would be the executive director. I found myself plunged headlong into community theater for the next five years.

"That's how I learned the craft. I figured if God gave me the talent then I'm obligated to develop it. But I really felt it was something I was supposed to use in my teaching. I was interested in showing students how they could use theater in school. I did that for the next 12 years until 1984 when my arthritis got so bad and my parents got so sick that I had to retire.

"When I retired I had to take my entire funds in the teacher retirement to pay up all my bills. So I had no money! I said, 'Well God, get me to 62 now with this!' And so He did! I wanted to get to 62—I said at least I'll have a regular social security check coming in. Up until then I was working mainly on stage and doing what they call 'day player bits.'

"I came back to Chicago to take care of my parents in 1987 and have been here ever since. After my father died, it's like he went and started working for me because right away between him dying and being interred I got a role in the television movie "The Kid Who Loved Christmas" (1990). Then I got a day's work on Oprah Winfrey's television series "The Women of Brewster Place" (1990).

While doing these small television roles, Hall was becoming an established presence on the local theater scene. "My home theater here is Chicago Theater Company, a tiny black equity house on 500 E. 67th." Hall ended up winning a Jeff Award, then was cast by Steppenwolf in the play *Stepping Out*. The company won a Jeff Award for Best Ensemble and Hall's place in Chicago theater was established. Ultimately she was in productions by the Court Theater, the Illinois Theater Center, and Northlight Repertory. Hall also worked at the Old Globe and the San Diego Repertory in San Diego, the Cleveland Playhouse at the Great Lakes Festival, and in touring productions that played Winston-Salem, North Carolina; Cincinnati, Ohio; and Rochester, New York.

"Mainly I thought I'd be doing stage work and then every once in a while I'd get a day part in a film. I was in Rochester when I heard about the movie *A Family Thing* (1996). I came back and auditioned for it. I had written a note and put it on my altar table asking God if it was His will to be in the movie.

When I got the part of 'Maotis,' I thought this is the answer to my prayer."

"A few days later, I was extremely tired and took a nap. I didn't hear the phone ring and when I woke up there were two messages on phone. The first one was telling me that my uncle had died and the next one was telling me that I needed to come and audition for the part of Aunt T, a role that all of us who read for it thought was going to someone in Los Angeles. I guess I have these relatives who die and then go and help me! So I went and did the audition. I said 'All right, if I get it fine, then I still have a part, I'm

(Courtesy of Harrise Davidson.)

still going to be in it.' I had to go to Memphis and read and they all liked it. On my birthday, June 3rd, I found out I had the part.

"It's just been lucky for me and that role seemed to be the door opener. It was very surprising to me and I was taken aback. At first I didn't understand what they meant when they said I stole all the scenes. I wasn't trying to upstage anybody. I'm so used to ensemble work and this was such a beautiful ensemble piece and I was thinking, 'oh gosh!' I was worried about that. I said, 'oh well, I didn't intend to do that.' But I remember Robert Duvall used to say all the time on the set 'They're going to say that we were good but that Aunt T stole the show!' I thought they were trying to make me feel good.

"Then I finally began to understand what they meant. It's just that the character stands out. Aunt T, the character herself, was written that way. I had no idea that they were still looking for that character at the time filming was about to begin because I just assumed that some big actress in New York or Los Angeles had that role...we all did.

"After *A Family Thing* I felt so good. Now I could really say 'I'm an actor,' because I was working right along with Robert Duvall and James Earl Jones."

"I happen to be one of those people when I'm working on a project, whether it happens to be stage, screen,or whatever that takes up my total concentration. So it's like I have one foot in the character and one foot in reality. I like to rehearse. I just enjoy the whole process. I hear things [about what happens behind the scenes] and I say, 'when did that go on?' The project is the paramount thing in my mind. I told my daughter, I may look pitiful or something but I've never had a bad experience. Everybody's always sweet and nice to me wherever I go."

Hall's next major project was the sleeper hit, *Soul Food* (1997). "That was indeed a labor of love. I was in L.A. working on a project when George Tillman, Jr. and Bob Teitel came to see me and brought the script to see if I would be interested in doing it."

In Hall's eyes, this project seemed to be fated for her. "When I opened the script, I knew it was something I was supposed to do because the character's name was 'Mother Jo' and my mother's name was Josephine. So I said, 'my mother sent this, I have to do it.' When I read the script I found more reason to think that, because my paternal grandmother was a diabetic and amputee. She had three daughters and her death was similar [to the Mama Jo character]. I said, 'oh my, this is too close.' My mother had a brother who lived with her sister and he had typhoid fever or something when he was a child. It had affected his speech some kind of way, so he rarely talked and he stayed to himself. He always stayed in his room. I knew about him and I said, 'oh wow, he's even in [the script]." It was like whoa—my whole family is in here! So I knew I had to do it.

"I had never met any of those young people before except Michael Beach and I didn't know he was going to be in it. We all bonded so quickly. Brandon, as soon as I saw him, I said, 'that's my grandbaby.' We're still like that. When I see him on other things, like *Men in Black* (1997), I say, 'oh, that's my grandbaby.' It's funny, both of us, our roots are in Louisiana—we just found that out recently.

"I had seen Vanessa L. Williams, Nia Long, and Vivica Fox in various things. I never thought I'd see them in person. They were just so great! It was so much fun. We really got to be like a family. Behind the scenes, they were friends. Brandon and Vivica used to go places together. She was like his big sister or mother. It was very relaxed. No tension, other than us wanting to do a good job.

"The hardest thing for me was lying flat on my back all day. That's hard on you! Everything goes to sleep and you start cramping all over. You're not in bed where you can turn from side to side, you just have to lie there. They would be rehearsing something when I was supposed to be in a coma, especially during the argument and I would be so tickled and I would want to laugh but I couldn't."

Hall ended up winning a NAACP Image Award for her work in *Soul Food*. Now a nationally-recognized character actor, she remains a steadfast Chicagoan.

"I like the atmosphere here. Its conducive to creativity. I tell young people, if you really want to learn your craft, this is a place where if you get two or three people of like mind together and you don't see a theater of your liking, then you start your own! There's a lot of creative energy here. I like the honesty of Chicagoans, I like the work ethic of the Midwest.

"I want to see how much can you grow as a character actor. Living here in Chicago, I still have the opportunity to do stage work. I still have the opportunity to do films. I just don't see a reason from moving away

➡ IMMACULATE CONCEPTION CHURCH
2944 E. 88th Street

This quiet church, nestled on the east side of the city near Commercial Avenue saw a lot of action in *Appointment with Danger* (1951). The story revolved around postal inspector Al Goddard (Alan Ladd) relentlessly pursuing the truth behind a colleague's death. A parish nun, Sister Augustine (Phyllis Calvert), is the only eyewitness to the crime. Ladd goes undercover as a rogue postal worker and infiltrates a gang led improbably by Jack Webb and Harry Morgan. Seeing the two hard-nosed cops from television's "Dragnet" as *Appointment with Danger's* bad guys provides modern audiences with a lot of campy laughs.

The towering spire of Pilgrim Baptist Church. This neighborhood landmark attracted the beam of light which set off *The Blues Brothers'* John Belushi spiritual transformation. (*Photo by Holly Pluard.*)

➡ **PILGRIM BAPTIST CHURCH FROM *THE BLUES BROTHERS***
3235 E. 91st Street

On a mission from God? Joliet Jake Blues (John Belushi) was when he stopped at Pilgrim Baptist Church in the 1980 hit *The Blues Brothers* for a little inspiration and gospel singing by Preacher James Brown. Joliet Jake couldn't have picked a better place for his conversion.

The building was designed as a house of worship by Adler and Sullivan and opened its doors in 1890—not as a church, but as a synagogue. As the neighborhood's original Jewish population moved north to Hyde Park, the West Side, and Rogers Park, the building was eventually converted to a Baptist church. By the mid-1910s, Pilgrim Baptist was a thriving house of worship for African-Americans.

Under the direction of Pilgrim Baptist's organist, former jazz and blues pianist Thomas A. Dorsey, a new type of music—gospel—took root here during the exuberant Sunday services. Over the years, such legendary names as Mahalia Jackson, Sallie Martin, Roberta Martin, Clara Ward, James Cleveland, the Edwin Hawkins Singers, Albertina Walker's Caravans, and the Barrett Sisters emerged from the congregation to become nationally known for their soul-stirring gospel singing.

The towering spire of Pilgrim Baptist is a neighborhood landmark and was absolutely perfect for attracting the beam of light that set off Belushi's spiritual transformation. Another kind of light, the blue neon signs over the church doors, were a gift from the production company, who outfitted Pilgrim Baptist with the eye-catching displays in return for using the building.

For more information about church services at Pilgrim Baptist, call 773-374-8748.

Darryl Roberts

*"When I first started, I had an original vision
of hoping to build the film industry in Chicago."*

D arryl Roberts' quiet, introspective demeanor belies his persistence. A communications major at Kennedy-King College, Roberts found his first professional jobs in radio, first in North Carolina and then in his hometown on Chicago's legendary WGCI. He then switched to promotion, throwing enormous bashes under the title "Partyin' in Chicago." The festivities often drew as many as 10,000 people, thanks in part to Roberts' talent for booking appearances by Michael Jordan and Willie Gault. Such an entrepreneurial spirit inevitably had to be attracted by the movie business.

"I don't know how it happened, but it was 1986," said Roberts. "I was riding down the streets of Los Angeles and I decided I wanted to make a movie.

"I hadn't gone to film school or anything so I went and bought $500 worth of different books on how to direct and read them a couple times each. I told friends I was thinking about making a movie. I asked how much did it cost and they said, 'I think like $5 or $6 million.' At that time I said 'I can't do that.'

"After three months, I said 'let's see if I can do it cheaper and raise $500,000.' I just assumed that if I wanted to make a movie, people would give me money. That didn't happen! I decided to just make a movie with what I had, which turned out to be $31,000. I wrote a script called *The Perfect Model* (1990), which was kind of a Cinderella story."

With his small budget, Roberts couldn't afford the necessary permits required by the city to shoot around Chicago, but people thought it was a student film, so they gave him some slack. Shooting took place largely on the South Side and was completed in a rapid two weeks.

Once he had the film in the can, Roberts worked on getting his film distributed. In November of 1987, he managed to get *The Perfect Model* screened at the Village Theater on North Clark Street. Five months later *The Perfect Model* opened at eight area theaters. Roberts later got the film distributed nationwide in a video release, under the title *Sweet Perfection*.

With the initial success of *The Perfect Model*, Roberts wrote the script for *How U Like Me Now?* (1993), a multi-layered study of life among a group of friends and lovers on Chicago's South Side. "I sent the script to studios and people loved it. And since I made a first film, I had a track record."

Still, Roberts wanted to do the film his way and not under the guidance of movie studio bosses. He raised $300,000 and hired a tech crew that had done several independent films. When it came to casting, Roberts decided to offer a plum role to Darnell Williams, an Emmy Award-winning actor from the daytime television drama, "All My Children." Roberts flew to Los Angeles and didn't come back until Williams agreed to do the film.

Roberts' female lead was Salli Richardson. "Because it was independent, we definitely were stealing shots and working late," said Richardson. "It was the first time I got to be a lead in something so it was a lot of work for me."

Again making creative use of numerous South Side locations, Roberts' *How U Like Me Now?* explored numerous issues within Chicago's African-American community. Class issues, inter-racial relationships, and attitudes between men and women were all explored through the several plot lines that Roberts wove together. And look carefully in a scene shot outside the Village Theater—you'll see a poster for *The Perfect Model* hanging in the window!

Though Spike Lee had opened the door to modern-day African-American filmmakers with the overwhelming success of *She's Gotta Have It* (1986), Roberts found nothing but resistance by movie executives to his finished work. "I knew that I had something, but whatever it was, the studios couldn't see it," Roberts recalls. Though the film was popular with test audiences, no one wanted to distribute *How U Like Me Now?*

So, in the tradition of Oscar Micheaux, Roberts decided to release the film himself. His former employer, WGCI, helped Roberts promote the film and on Labor Day weekend of 1992 *How U Like Me Now?* opened in two Chicago theaters.

The film grossed $13,000 per screen that opening weekend. On a nationwide basis, it was the third largest per screen average for any movie over that three-day period. As a result of this unprecedented success, Roberts final got a distribution deal. *How U Like Me Now?* quickly opened in 15 major cities around the country and was later picked up for video release by Universal-MCA.

"When I first started, I had an original vision of hoping to build the film industry in Chicago," Roberts says today. "I'm also aware that I'm about three or four years behind by being here, as opposed to Los Angeles or New York. But there's a lot of Chicago that no one has ever seen before. Little by little, I want to capture it."

The Suburbs

➡ **THE FORMER DIXIE MALL**
Harvey, IL

Once a thriving shopping center for the south suburbs, Dixie Mall fell on hard times in the late 1970s and eventually went out of business. Then, in 1980, out-of-town interests plunked down $100 grand for the shuttered mall.

The owners quickly installed a vast array of stores, stocked to the gills with new merchandise. A grand re-opening? Hardly. It seems Dixie Mall was acquired by *The Blues Brothers* production team. And their plans had nothing to do with a conventional afternoon of browsing.

In an unforgettable moment of movie mayhem, Joliet Jake and Elwood Blues (John Belushi and Dan Aykroyd) drive their Bluesmobile into Dixie Mall, cops in tow, and proceed to smash everything in sight. Shoppers scatter, merchandise flies through the air like popcorn, cops plow into store windows, no one gets hurt (this is a comedy, after all!), and Jake and Elwood keep on trucking.

Today the mall is an empty shell, with shrubbery bursting through cracks in the barren parking lot.

➡ **STATEVILLE CORRECTIONAL CENTER/**
JOLIET CORRECTIONAL CENTER
Joliet, Illinois

South of Chicago in Will County, is Joliet, Illinois. A unique city in and of itself, it is also home for two Illinois Department of Corrections prisons: the Stateville Correctional Center and the Joliet Correctional Center.

The two penitentiaries are sometimes collectively referred to as "Joliet," and hence leads to some confusion if you're not familiar with the different sites. The original Joliet Correctional Center opened in 1860 as a prison for Confederate soldiers. Following the Civil War, the site was converted to part of the Illinois prison system. Stateville was opened in 1925 and over the years became the main facility for prisoners in Joliet. Today the original prison serves as the Reception & Classification Center for processing all newly-arrived inmates convicted in northern Illinois counties.

Prison films have been popular since the birth of the movies. Shooting a big-budget movie inside a prison, however, poses a unique set of obstacles to any film crew. For one thing, access is restricted within the prison walls. Every item brought onto the set must be catalogued and accounted for at the day's end. The sort of fraternization and horseplay inherent to movie sets must be strictly curtailed.

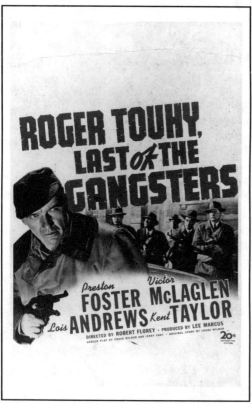

Movie poster for *Roger Touhy: Last of the Gangsters.* (*From the collection of Arnie Bernstein.*)

With that said, it's still not impossible to bring camera crews inside a prison, and Stateville has been cooperative with Hollywood over the years. Director Robert Florey brought Preston Foster, Harry Morgan (then using the name Henry Morgan), and Anthony Quinn to Stateville for the 1944 crime flick *Roger Touhy, Gangster*, a primarily fictional account of the notorious Chicago crime figure.

In *Call Northside 777* (1948), James Stewart comes to Stateville to research the truth of prisoner Richard Conte's story. Filming took place in Cellhouse F, which is designed in the "panopticon," or circular fashion. Filmed in stark black-and-white, this rounded cellblock and an imposing central guard tower made an eerie backdrop as Stewart walked along the balcony to meet Conte.

The cinematic possibilities of Stateville were stretched to the limit by Oliver Stone's over-the-top satire, *Natural Born Killers* (1994). This wasn't just a straight shoot like *Roger Touhy* or *Call Northside 777*. Stone's vision was a hyperkinetic, surreal nightmare, culminating in a frenzied prison riot. Shooting under the strict controls of prison regulations was a daunting challenge, to say the least. Yet Stone pulled it off, creating a compelling sequence that sucks viewers right into the heart of the action.

The entire production team was extremely cautious, because if anything went wrong, no movies would ever be allowed to shoot in Stateville ever again. Interestingly, real convicts were given an opportunity to be film extras for the riot scenes. To be eligible, the prisoners were carefully screened for the least troublesome candidates.

Ultimately, the prison riot went off without a problem. Mingling convicts and stunt men with real guards and their movie counterparts, Stone's hallucination was pulled off without a hitch.

Of course no discussion of movies and the Illinois Department of Corrections would be complete without mentioning *The Blues Brothers* (1980). In the film's opening, Elwood Blues (Dan Aykroyd) picks up his newly-paroled brother Jake Blues (John Belushi), a.k.a. "Joliet Jake," in front of the Joliet Correctional Center gates. What goes around comes around: by the film's end, both Aykroyd and Belushi, along with their reunited Blues Brothers Band, are back in the slammer, providing an invigorating version of "Jailhouse Rock" for an inmate audience.

You can find out more about the Illinois Department of Corrections by visiting their Web site at http://www.idoc.state.il.us/.

Call Northside 777

Despite the holidays' approach, by the first week of December 1932, Chicago seemed to have gone crazy. Though the gangster heyday of Al Capone and his ilk seemed like a bad memory, the city saw six murders in those early winter days. The bloody spree came to a head on December 9, when police officer William Lundy was gunned down while trying to prevent the holdup of a delicatessen at 4312 S. Ashland Avenue.

The pressure was on to solve this brutal murder. With the Century of Progress World's Fair less than six months away, Chicago's Mayor Anton

Cermak wanted the killing solved and solved quickly. (Ironically, in 1933, Cermak himself would be the victim of an assassin's bullet meant for President-elect Franklin Roosevelt.)

Vera Walush, who owned the deli where Lundy was murdered, fingered two local men as the killers. Joseph Majczek and Theodore Marcinkiewicz were brought to trial in 1933 and quickly found guilty. They were sentenced to 99 years each and sent to Stateville Prison in Joliet.

Flash forward 11 years.

On October 10, 1944, city editor Karin Walsh of the *Chicago Daily Times* (a forerunner of the *Chicago Sun-Times*) found an advertisement buried in the classifieds: "$5,000 reward for killers of Officer Lundy on December 9, 1932. Call GRO-1758, 12 to 7 p.m." Walsh assigned reporter James McGuire, a former private investigator, to check out the story. What he found was an amazing tale of perseverance.

Majczek's mother Tillie, a Polish immigrant from the Back of the Yards neighborhood, firmly believed in her son's innocence. To this end, she spent the next 11 years on the night shift, scrubbing floors at Commonwealth Edison's downtown offices. While she and her husband lived on his salary earned at the stockyards, Tillie Majczek saved every penny of her salary to raise the $5,000 reward.

As a human interest story, Tillie Majczek had potential to sell a few papers. McGuire passed his notes onto reporter Jack McPhaul. Wringing Tillie Majczek's account for maximum emotional effect, McPhaul punctuated his story with a quotation from Rudyard Kipling's poem "Mother o' Mine."

Readers hung onto every word as McGuire and McPhaul pumped out story after story. Eventually the twisted truth came out. Vera Walush wasn't just running a delicatessen—her place of business was fronting for an illegal speakeasy. Walush claimed she had hid in a closet during the robbery. But threatened with arrest for brewing black market hooch, Walush suddenly changed her story.

Initially, Walush hadn't been able to identify either Majczek or Marcinkiewicz as the murder suspects. In fact, Walush was twice given the opportunity to pick Majczek out of a police line-up.

At the time, Majczek was on probation for a small-time robbery that netted him all of two dollars. Word got out that Vera Walush was about to finger a neighborhood kid named Ted. Fearing he was the target, Marcinkiewicz hid out the home of his old friends, the Majczeks. When the police came to the door, Joe Majczek told them to come in. "I have nothing to hide," he declared at the time.

The two were arrested and put on trial for Lundy's murder. Their defense attorney was an ex-mob lawyer whose clientele had included gangster Hymie Weiss. When Weiss was assassinated by the Capone gang in 1926, the attorney was hit as well. Though he survived, the remainder of his life was plagued by searing pain. Desperate for relief, he turned to drink. By the time of the Lundy case, the attorney was a raging alcoholic. His drunken courtroom demeanor was pointed out by Majczek, the court bailiff, and even presiding Judge Charles P. Molthrop.

It didn't help. Majczek and Marcinkiewicz were sent to jail and an appeal, written by the defense attorney in the midst of an alcoholic haze, was quickly dismissed. Unbeknownst to the two convicted men, however, new information had been provided to Judge Molthrop.

An anonymous detective informed the judge about some of the shifty tactics used to obtain the guilty verdict. Among other things, Majczek had been held for more than a day before Walush decided to change her story. Hearing this, Molthrop was enraged. He vowed to bring Walush in for perjury charges and rehear the case even if he had to pay for it himself. The State's Attorney's office, fearing backlash from an already outraged public, as well as the police force, took Molthrop aside. The judge was "advised" to drop the case unless he wanted to see his career come to a premature end.

As the story unfolded, Illinois Gov. Dwight H. Green became interested. Majczek was granted a full and unconditional pardon. He was released from prison on August 14, 1945. Eventually it was determined that Marcinkiewicz also had been denied the constitutional right to a fair trial, though his release came five years later.

In Los Angeles, the heart-wrenching story of Tillie Majczek had not gone unnoticed. Darryl F. Zanuck, the legendary producer at 20th Century-Fox was enamored with the story. He sent word to McGuire and McPhaul that their reporting "...is going to be further celebrated by way of the motion picture screen." Two years later, in the fall of 1947, a crew of 70, including director Henry Hathaway and star James Stewart, came to Chicago.

In classic Hollywood tradition, the original story was streamlined, characters were combined, and certain plot elements were left out. Titled *Call Northside 777*, the two reporters were changed to a single character, played by Stewart. McGuire, who did the majority of the street work for the story, was hired as a technical advisor for a fee of $2,500. This payment also included compensation for McGuire's rights to the story. McGuire recreated his investigation, personally taking Stewart on a tour of Chicago's mean streets. Director Henry Hathaway filmed the story in a stark, documentary-like style, bringing his cameras to many of the actual locations where the story unfolded.

Filming took place over ten weeks and made extensive use of South Side neighborhoods. Stewart did much of his investigation at the New City police station, 3501 S. Lowe Avenue, the department's ninth precinct where McGuire uncovered arrest records. Actor Richard Conte, who played Majczek's screen counterpart Frank Wiecek, was interrogated at the Criminal Courts building. Saloons throughout the Back of the Yards neighborhood became darkened pits where Stewart asked questions, eventually leading him to "Wanda Skutnik" (Betty Garde), the Vera Walush character.

One of the film's most gripping scenes was actually shot at Walush's apartment at 725 S. Honore Street. Other scenes were shot along Michigan Avenue, at downtown police headquarters, and along the Chicago River.

Call Northside 777 wasn't just limited to Chicago locations. Hathaway was given permission to shoot inside Stateville Penitentiary, where Stewart looks up Conte for his side of the story. Additional material was filmed in Springfield, including scenes at the old State Capitol building.

The result was a stark, often riveting drama. Stewart's performance was low-key, allowing his character to slowly realize that the truth wasn't always cut and dried. Hathaway's direction was enhanced by Joseph MacDonald's moody cinematography, capturing Chicago at a unique point in its history. Watching the film today, it's amazing how barren downtown looks without the many skyscrapers that have since been built. The climactic resolution, in which a photograph must be sent by wire from Chicago to Springfield, is another of the film's many highlights.

Considering today's technologies of fax machines and e-mail, we have become accustomed to instantaneous information. Hathaway builds genuine suspense as Stewart awaits the precious photograph which may clear Conte—while modern audiences are amazed at the crude machinery every moment in the scene hangs on. Another powerful moment is when Conte submits to a lie detector test to prove his innocence. Administering the test is Leonarde Keeler, who in real-life developed polygraph instrumentation for police investigations. In his only screen role, Keeler handles himself admirably against the professional actors.

And what about the other real-life players? Majczek remarried his wife whom he had divorced after his arrest. Sadly, the rest of his life was troubled by misfortune. After becoming an insurance broker and moving to Oak Lawn, Majczek was involved in a terrible car wreck in 1979 that resulted in massive head trauma. He spent his remaining years in a nursing home and died in 1983.

After his release from prison, Marcinkiewicz changed his name to Marcin and relocated to California. In 1982, he suffered from debilitating eye problems. Fearing blindness, Marcin committed suicide rather than be admitted to a nursing home.

McGuire died in the 1950s. McPhaul, whose reporting also inspired the film *I Am A Fugitive from a Chain Gang* (1932), starring Paul Muni, never got a dime from Hollywood for either film. He continued writing for the *Times* and its successor, the *Chicago Sun-Times,* and retired in the early 1970s. In 1983, McPhaul succumbed to cancer.

Tillie Majczek died in 1964. Officer Lundy's murder was never solved.

Sources:

Greene, Bob, "It Wasn't 777: New Twist to Old Number," *Chicago Sun-Times* (November 12, 1975).

Houston, Gary, "A Real-Life Chicago Murder Mystery: Few Stories Compare with 'Northside 777'," *Chicago Tribune* (January 9, 1995).

Sawyers, June, "The True Story that Led to 'Call Northside 777'," *Chicago Tribune Sunday Magazine* (March 19, 1989).

AFTERWORD

In 1896, armed with a camera, some actors, and a dream to expand the art of motion pictures, Colonel Selig created his first narrative film, *The Tramp and the Dog.*

More than a century later, the modern independent film movement operates in the spirit of Selig's early efforts. With the success of people like Steve James, Peter Gilbert, Frederick Marx, Jim Sikora, John McNaughton, Steve Jones, Rose Troche, Guinevere Turner, Darryl Roberts, and so many others, it's clear Chicago has the resources and talent befitting any moviemaking capital. They may not be as polished as multi-million-dollar Hollywood productions, but Chicago's independents are a determined bunch.

And their numbers are growing. In recent years, the number of local independent productions applying for location permits from the Chicago Film Office has been steady and growing. "That's impressive," says Richard Moskal, "but then you also have to factor in filmmakers who are just going out and shooting without getting any street permits."

Whether above board or guerrilla style, it's clear the Chicago film community is thriving. Joel Goodman and Michael S. Ojeda are two rising members of this fresh new wave. The duo have been friends since kindergarten, growing up in Chicago's north suburbs. "We shot little 8-millimeter films together when we were ten years old," says Goodman.

Today they are on the brink of something bigger. Goodman, who has directed music videos, and Ojeda, an NBC cameraman who has also shot several independent features, are putting together a film of their own. Under the working title, *Alana's Rain*, Ojeda's script is the hard-edged story of a young woman who has fled from the war in Bosnia and now struggles to make it in America. Ojeda will be directing and Goodman will be producing.

Before the cameras even started rolling, Goodman and Ojeda have seen some interest from Hollywood. Yet they are determined to make the film their way and in their hometown.

"The Chicago film community is very hard-working and tight-knit," says Ojeda. "It's easy to shoot here. The city and the neighborhoods are very cooperative. If they see you're a young, independent company, they welcome it."

Adds Goodman, "The magic of Chicago is when a film is made here, the people who live in this town are excited about it."

APPENDIX A:

CHICAGO FILM FESTIVALS

Chicago cinemaphiles live in one of the great film cities. Not only do we have a wealth of resources for learning about and discussing the movies, but Chicago is blessed with an abundance of film festivals. There's something for just about every taste, including experimental, ethnic, and other special interests. There's a festival for children and a festival devoted to cinematic portraits of senior citizens. Though the harsh winter months of December and January are lean, the rest of the year is rich with diverse movie offerings.

The film festivals are listed in chronological order. Dates are approximate, so it's best to contact the sponsoring organization(s) for more information. Phone numbers, street addresses, and Web sites not provided below are available elsewhere in this book.

➡ **THE MARGARET MEAD TRAVELING
FILM AND VIDEO FESTIVAL
Late February/Early March**

This festival, coordinated through the American Museum of Natural History in New York, is held annually at the Field Museum. In the spirit of Margaret Mead, its anthropologist namesake, the festival offers an eclectic series of films about global issues. Contact the Field Museum in January to learn more about what programs will be offered.

➡ **HONG KONG FILM FESTIVAL
March/April**

With Hollywood's discovery of directors like John Woo and Ringo Lam, as well as the clown prince of action films, Jackie Chan, Hong Kong filmmakers are the latest rage with movie junkies. The Film Center of the School of the Art Institute preceded this trend by a full decade. Launched in 1988, the Hong Kong Film Festival extols the virtues of this growing international film capital. Held on weekends throughout March and April, the festival screenings are held at the Film Center. Guest speakers have been known to show up in the past. Contact the Film Center for more information.

➡ WOMEN IN THE DIRECTOR'S CHAIR INTERNATIONAL FILM AND VIDEO FESTIVAL
March

An outgrowth of the Women in the Director's Chair organization, this festival highlights the work of women film and video makers from around the world. In addition to the considerable screen offerings, the festival has panel discussions on artistic and theoretical concerns for women directors, as well as networking opportunities. Contact Women in the Director's Chair for more information.

➡ ASIAN-AMERICAN SHOWCASE
March

Chicago has two Asian-American film festivals to highlight the wide variety of talent within this community. This festival, which is co-run by the Film Center and the Asian-American Media Group Fortune4, offers features and documentaries by Asian-American directors. Panel discussions and guest speakers are also an important part of the festival. For a schedule, contact the Film Center.

➡ AFRICAN-AMERICAN FILM FESTIVAL
March

Held in conjunction with Columbia College Film and Video Department, the African-American Film Festival is devoted to screening the work of emerging artists. Documentaries and features addressing issues in the African-American community, are at the forefront of the festival's mission. Guest speakers and panel discussions are also part of the diverse programming. For more information, contact Columbia College.

➡ CHICAGO ASIAN-AMERICAN FILM FESTIVAL
April/May

The second of Chicago's Asian-American festivals is actually the older of the two. Sponsored by the Asian and Asian-American Studies Program at Loyola University in cooperation with the Asian-American Institute, this broad-ranged festival is not just limited to films. Theater, music, literature, and other forms of artistic expression are also an important part of the month-long activities. Films, both features and documentaries, emphasize the multifaceted range of Asian-American experiences. For more information, contact the Loyola Center for Inter-Disciplinary Programs at

773-508-2935.

→ CHICAGO LATINO FILM FESTIVAL
April

Co-sponsored by Columbia College and Chicago Latino Cinema, the Chicago Latino Film Festival explores the many aspects of Spanish-language moviemaking. Films from Spain, Mexico, Central and South America, Cuba, and the United States are all part of the programming. Symposiums on various issues are held, and guest speakers are an important aspect to the festival proceedings. For more information, call 312-431-1330 or check out the homepage at http://www.chicagolatinocinema.org.

→ SILVER IMAGES FILM FESTIVAL
May

This is the city's most accessible festival, with programs held throughout the city and suburbs. Silver Images, founded by the Chicago-based production company Terra Nova Films, presents films centering around the issues facing senior citizens. You can catch the Silver Image Festival at a number of venues, including Northwestern University, Roosevelt University, the Copernicus Senior Center, and several commercial theaters. For more information, contact Terra Nova at 773-881-6940.

→ CHICAGO ALT.FILM FEST
June

This festival devoted to the works of American independent filmmakers is the latest festival to grace Chicago screens. Founded by local filmmaker Dennis Neal Vaughn, the Chicago Alt.Film Fest concentrates on narrative feature films and short subjects. The overall festival emphasis is on independent Midwestern filmmakers, though directors from other parts of the country are also included. Documentary and experimental works are shown by invitation only. For more information, call Vaughn at 773-525-4559 or check out the festival's Web site at http://members.aol.com/ChiAltFilm.

→ BLACK HARVEST FILM FESTIVAL
August

Another Film Center presentation, the Black Harvest Film Festival, concentrates on the work of African-American and African filmmakers. Emphasis is on independent directors. For more information, contact the Film Center.

➡ **CHICAGO UNDERGROUND FILM FESTIVAL**
August

Looking for something off the beaten path? How about way off the beaten path? Then head to the Chicago Underground Film Festival (CUFF), a delicious array of the modern cinematic cutting edge. All formats, from Super 8-millimeter to video and 35-millimeter films are accepted. Narrative, documentary, and experimental works are shown throughout the five-day festival.

CUFF also presents the Jack Smith Lifetime Achievement Award, named after the 1960s revolutionary experimental filmmaker who succumbed to AIDS. John Waters, director of the cult favorite *Pink Flamingos* (1972), is a past winner of this prestigious honor. For more information on CUFF call 773-866-8660 or check out their Web site at http://www.cuff.org.

➡ **WINDY CITY INTERNATIONAL DOCUMENTARY FESTIVAL**
September

September brings this festival devoted to documentary films from around the world, with screenings at Columbia College, the Film Center, and the Chicago Cultural Center. For more information, call 312-344-7773.

➡ **FESTIVAL OF FILMS FROM IRAN**
October/November

Another international showcase presented by the Film Center, this festival considers the work of Iranian movie directors. If the concept sounds far-fetched to American audiences, consider the working conditions these filmmakers face. With overwhelming government (and sometimes religious) censorship, Iranian directors have produced some wonderfully lyrical work against incredible odds. For more information, contact the Film Center.

➡ **CHICAGO INTERNATIONAL FILM FESTIVAL**
October

The first and biggest of all local film festivals, the Chicago International Film Festival (CIFF) is nothing if not audacious. Founded in 1965, long before film festivals were de rigeur for American audiences, the CIFF whips up an off-beat recipe of international films, independent directors, big name movie stars, and a dash of kitsch.

CIFF founder and artistic director Michael Kutza created the festival with the intent of creating a cultural splash and celebrating the diversity of cinema. Over the years, he's attracted big names to Chicago, including Francois Truffaut, Orson Welles, Harold Lloyd, Bette Davis, Michael Douglas, Roger Corman, Spike Lee, Jodie Foster, and Rainer Werner Fassbinder. In 1968, three years into the CIFF venture, a young director named Martin Scorsese made a powerful impact with his first feature *Who's That Knocking at My Door?*

Though the CIFF has weathered some behind-the-scenes controversy, it still manages to put on a good show year after year. The retrospective "mini-festivals" within the main CIFF give audiences an opportunity to see the body of work for a particular director, producer, or genre topic. In recent years, the CIFF has been adept at booking films which are later released to significant critical and box office respect.

One aspect of the CIFF can't be overlooked: the hyper-sexed festival posters of photographer Victor Skrebneski. Year after year, buffed, beautiful bodies of male and female models, garbed only in a torn CIFF tee-shirt, are featured in the festival posters. "Those pictures helped put us on the map," admits Kutza. "They started as a way to make money. Old-time film festivals like Cannes and Venice featured naked people jumping in fountains. You can't do that in Chicago in October, so that's where we came up with the idea. Ultimately, they either upset you or you like them."

The CIFF also runs two festivals for professional organizations: TV Fest, the International Television Festival for world-wide broadcast productions, and INTERCOM, the International Communications Film and Video Competition for artists in the communications fields.

For more information regarding the Chicago International Film Festival, contact Cinema/Chicago at 32 W. Randolph Street, Suite 600, Chicago, IL 60601, phone 312-425-9400, or check out their Web site at http://www.chicago.ddbn.com/filmfest/.

➡ CHICAGO INTERNATIONAL CHILDREN'S FILM FESTIVAL
October

Thanks to Facets Multimedia, children's films in Chicago don't begin and end with whatever big screen Disney adventure happens to be in release. The Chicago International Children's Film Festival, which started in 1983, is devoted to bringing quality films to younger audiences.

Bringing in films and filmmakers from around the world, the Children's

Festival specializes in short films and animation beyond cartoons. Examples of claymation, hand drawings, sandpainting, and other experimental forms of pixilated movement are all part of festival programming. The audience is encouraged to be an active participant in the creative process. Professional filmmakers are brought in to lead workshops for children, giving youngsters hands-on experience in the rudiments of moviemaking. For more information, contact Facets Multimedia.

➡ **REELING: THE LESBIAN AND GAY INTERNATIONAL FILM FESTIVAL**
November

The annual Gay and Lesbian International Film Festival, which has been around since 1981, is the brainchild of Chicago Filmmaker's Brenda Webb. "The idea behind it was to reach a new audience with experimental films," she says. "It kind of started, in my mind, in reading an article in *Millennium Film Journal* that basically posed the question 'is there such a thing as a gay sensibility in film?' Several filmmakers were cited in the piece, including Kenneth Anger and Barbara Hammer. It occurred to me, wouldn't it be interesting to put these filmmakers in this context as gay or lesbian filmmakers and present that to a community as an opportunity to really reach a new audience. That was sort of the initial impulse for the festival, to show experimental, independent gay and lesbian films by gay and lesbian film and video makers to a new audience.

The festival lasts for two weeks, running films at the Music Box Theatre and one other commercial venue. Though Reeling sticks close to its experimental roots, it also shows work by independent film and video directors, documentaries, and special programs of older gay and lesbian-themed movies. For more information, contact Chicago Filmmakers.

➡ **POLISH FILM FESTIVAL**
November

Sponsored by Chicago's Society for Polish Art, screenings are held at the Gateway Theater, 5216 W. Lawrence Avenue, and Facets Multimedia. For more information, call 773-486-9612.

APPENDIX B:

FILMS SHOT IN CHICAGO AND THE SURROUNDING AREA

The 500+ films below were shot either all or in part in Chicago and/or the suburbs. This list is by no means complete. Many of the silent titles of Selig Polyscope, Essanay, and others have been lost to history. Other films of more recent times can be difficult to catalog due to the sometimes slippery nature of independent film distribution.

Note that this list does not include series television programs, such as "Crime Story," "Lady Blue," "Early Edition," and others.

About Last Night... (1986)
Above the Law (1988)
Adam's Rib (1923)
Adventures in Babysitting (1987)
Adventures of Kathlyn, The (1914)
Adventures of Lucky Pierre (1961)
Alias Billy Sargent (1912)
All the Love in the World (1991)
Allah Tantou (1989)
American Revolution 2 (1969)
And the Children Play (1918)
And This is Free (1964)
Appointment With Danger (1951)
Are Working Girls Safe? (1918)
Ashes of Hope (1914)
An Awful Skate or The Hobo on
　　Rollers (1907)
Babe Ruth Story, The (1948)
Babe, The (1992)
Baby's Day Out (1994)
Backdraft (1991)
Bad Boys (1982)
Barnacle Bill (1918)
Baseball Fan, The (1908)
Baseball Review of 1917, The
　　(1 917)

Battle of Love, The (1914)
Battle of Too Soon, The (1915)
Betrayed (1988)
Big One, The (1997)
Big Score, The (1983)
Big Shots (1987)
Big Town, The (1987)
Bill Bumper's Bargain (1911)
Billy the Janitor (1918)
Birth of a Race, The (1918)
Bix (1991)
Black and White (1915)
Black Sheep, A (1915)
Black Sherlock Holmes, A (1918)
Blank Page, The (1998)
Blink (1994)
Blood Equity (1998)
Blood Will Tell (1914)
Blues Brothers 2000 (1998)
Blues Brothers, The (1980)
Borrower, The (1991)
Brannigan (1975)
Breakfast Club, The (1985)
Breed of Men (1919)
Bride Stripped Bare, The (1967)
Broadway Damage (1997)

Broken Pledge, The (1915)
Brother's Loyalty, A (1913)
Brotherhood of Man (1912)
Bullet on a Wire (1996)
Bullitt (1968)
Bully, The (1918)
Business Rivalry (1903)
Busted Romance, A (1918)
Busy Body, The (1967)
Butch Camp (1997)
C-H-I-C-K-E-N Spells Chicken (1910)
Call Northside 777 (1948)
Campaign (1968)
Candyman (1992)
Captain Ron (1992)
Chain Reaction (1996)
Chains (1912)
Challenge of Chance, The (1919)
Chamber, The (1996)
Chicago After Midnight (1928)
Chicago Cab (1998)
Chicago Calling (1951)
Chicago Deadline (1949)
Chicago Fire Run (1903)
Chicago Firecats on Parade (1903)
Chicago Maternity Center Story, The (1976)
Chicago Police Parade (1901)
Chicago Politics: A Theatre of Power (1985-87)
Chicago Street, A (1898)
Chicago Syndicate (1955)
Child's Play (1988)
Child's Play II (1991)
Christmas Vacation (a.k.a. National Lampoon's Christmas Vacation) (1989)
Citizen Saint (1947)
City of Purple Dreams, The (1918)
City That Never Sleeps (1953)
Class (1983)

Club Paradise (1986)
Code of Silence (1985)
Cold Justice (a.k.a. Father Jim) (1989)
College, The (1964)
Color of Money, The (1986)
Comeback of Barnacle Bill (1918)
Coming of Columbus, The (1911)
Confession, The (1908)
Continental Divide (1981)
Cooley High (1975)
Corner Madison and State Streets, Chicago (1897)
Count of Monte Cristo, The (1908)
Countess, The (1914)
Country Western Hoedown (1967)
Cousin Jim (1916)
Cracked Ice (1917)
Crimson Wing, The (1915)
Crises, The (1918)
Curly Sue (1991)
Damien: Omen II (1978)
Dancing Nig, The (1907)
Deep End of the Ocean, The (1998)
Democracy or a Fight for Right (1918)
Demon Possessed (1993)
Dennis the Menace (1993)
Devil at Your Heels, The (1981)
Dewey Parade (1901)
Discovery (1913)
Do the Dead Talk? (1920)
Do You Wanna Dance? (1997)
Doctor Detroit (1983)
Dollmaker, The (1984)
Dreamer (1979)
Dreamy Dud: A Visit to Uncle Dudley's Farm (1915)
Dreamy Dud: At the Old Swimmin' Hole (1915)
Dreamy Dud: Has a Laugh on the Boss (1916)

Dreamy Dud: He Goes Bear Hunting (1915)

Dreamy Dud: He Sees Charlie Chaplin (1915)

Dreamy Dud: In King Koo Koo's Kingdom (1915)

Dreamy Dud: In Lost in the Jungle (1915)

Dreamy Dud: In Love (1915)

Dreamy Dud: In the African War Zone (1916)

Dreamy Dud: In the Swim (1915)

Dreamy Dud: Joyriding with Princess Zlim (1916)

Dreamy Dud: Lost at Sea (1916)

Dreamy Dud: Resolves Not to Smoke (1915)

Dreamy Dud: Up in the Air (1915)

Dud Visits the Zoo

Dumb Girl of Portici, The (1916)

Dutch (1991)

Eight Men Out (1988)

Elder Brother, The (1914)

End of the Line (1987)

End of the Road, The (1915)

Endless Love (1981)

Every Inch a King (1914)

Excessive Force (1992)

Exile, The (1931)

Eye That Never Sleeps (1912)

Eyes of an Angel (1991)

Fable of Hazel's Two Husbands and What Became of Them (1915)

Fable of the Bush League Lover Who Failed to Qualify, The (1914)

Fairylogue (1910)

Faith of Millions (1927)

Fall of Montezuma, The (1912)

Family Thing, A (1996)

Farmer's Daughter, The (1913)

Fate's Funny Frolic (1911)

Fatty Drives the Bus (1998)

Fearless Frank (a.k.a Frank's Great Adventure) (1967)

Fence, The (1994)

Ferris Bueller's Day Off (1986)

Fingerprints (1914)

Finney (1969)

Fixing the Faker (1918)

Flatliners (1990)

Folks! (1992)

For the Honor of the 8th Ill. U.S.A. (1914)

Four Friends (1981)

Frozen Warning, The (1917)

Fugitive, The (1993)

Funkytown (1998)

Fury, The (1978)

Gaily, Gaily (1969)

Gans-McGovern Fight (1901)

Gentle Julia (1923)

Ghosts (1917)

Ghosts (1917)

Girl in Blue, The (1903)

Girls Just Want to Have Fun (1985)

Gladiator (1992)

Go Fish (1994)

Golden Glove Story, The (1950)

Goldstein (1964)

Golf Champion "Chick" Evans Links with Sweedie (1914)

Golub (1988)

Good Catch, A (1912)

Good Luck in Old Clothes (1918)

Gordian Knot, The (1911)

Gore Gore Girls, The (1972)

Gotch-Hackenschmidt Wrestling Match (1908)

Gotch-Zbyszko World's Championship Wrestling Match (1910)

Grace Quigley (a.k.a. Ultimate Solution of Grace Quigley, The)

Magic Melody, The (1909)
Magic Wand, The (1912)
Mahogany (1975)
Mail Order Bride, The (1912)
Major League (1989)
Major League II (1994)
Mama Medea (1998)
Manhunter (1986)
Marquette Park I (1976)
Marquette Park II (1978)
Masked Wrestler, The (1914)
Maxwell Street Blues (1981)
Medium Cool (1969)
Meet the Parents (1992)
Melody of Love, The (1912)
Men Don't Leave (1990)
Menmaniacs - The Legacy of
  Leather (1995)
Mercury Rising (1998)
Mercy, the Mummy Mumbled
  (1918)
Michael (1996)
Mickey One (1965)
Midnight Run (1988)
Milk Fed Hero, A (1918)
Mo' Money (1992)
Modulations (1998)
Money Talks in Darktown (1915)
Monitors, The (1969)
Monkey Hustle (1977)
Monster a-Go Go (1965)
Moon's Ray, The (1914)
Movie Marionettes (1918)
Murder of Fred Hampton, The
  (1971)
Music Box (1990)
My Best Friend's Wedding (1997)
My Bodyguard (1980)
My Life (1993)
Naked Ape (1972)
Naked Face, The (1984)
Nashville Rebel (1966)

Native Son (1951)
Native Son (1987)
Natural Born Killers (1994)
Natural Born Shooter, A (1915)
Navy Way, The (1944)
Nebata the Greek Singer (1912)
Negotiator, The (1998)
Neptune's Daughter (1912)
New Manager, The (1911)
Next of Kin (1989)
Night Hawks, The (1914)
Night in the Life of Jimmy Reardon,
  A (a.k.a. Jimmy Reardon) (1988)
No Mercy (1986)
North by Northwest (1959)
Nothing in Common (1986)
Now We Live on Clifton (1974)
On the Right Track (1982)
One Wonderful Night (1914)
Only the Lonely (1991)
Opportunity Knocks (1990)
Original Gangstas (1996)
Other Girl, The (1914)
Other Man, The (1914)
Out of the Depths (1912)
Package, The (1989)
Painters, The (1918)
Parents (1968)
Passing Shadow, The (1912)
Pastime (a.k.a. One Cup of Coffee)
  (1989)
Payback (1998)
Peer Gynt (1941)
Penitent, The (1912)ß
Pennies from Heaven (1981)
Penny Philanthropist, The (1917)
People vs. Paul Crump, The (1962)
Perfect Model, The (a.k.a. Sweet
  Perfection) (1990)
Personal Foul (1987)
Piece of the Action, A (1977)
Pioneer Days (1918)

Sweedie's Hopeless Love (1915)
Sweedie's Suicide (1915)
Sweet Adeline (1926)
Switching Channels (1988)
T.R. Baskin (1971)
Taylor Chain I (1980)
Taylor Chain II (1984)
Ten Nights in a Barroom (1909)
That Royle Girl (1925)
They Call Me Bruce (1982)
Thief (1981)
Things Are Tough All Over (1982)
Things Change (1988)
Thirteenth Man, The (1913)
Three Days (1997)
Three Girls Lost (1931)
Three Pals (1916)
Three the Hard Way (1973)
Through the Storm (1914)
Toll of the Marshes, The (1913)
Tomboy and the Champ (1961)
Tony the Fidler (1913)
Touch and Go (1986)
Tough Guys (1973)
Towing (1978)
Trail of the Hunter (1970)
Tramp and the Dog, The (1896)
Tramp and the Dog, The (1906)
Tramp Dog, The (1904)
Trick Bag (1975)
Trinkets of Tragedy (1914)
Trip Around the Union Loop (1903)
Truant Soul, The (1916)
Twilight (1912)
Two Knights in Vaudeville (1916)
U.S. Marshals (1998)
Uncle Buck (1989)
Uncle Sam Awake (1916)
Under Royal Patronage (1914)
Union Station (1950)
Untouchables, The (1987)
Uptown Saturday Night (1973)

V. I. Warshawski (1991)
Vacation (a.k.a. National Lampoon's Vacation) (1983)
Venus Adonis (1966)
Vernon Howard Bailey's Sketch Book of Chicago (1916)
Vice Versa (1988)
View of State Street (1903)
Virtue of Rags, The (1912)
Voice from the Fireplace, A (1910)
Voice of Conscience, The (1912)
Walls in the City (1994)
Watch It (1993)
Wayne's World (1992)
Wayne's World 2 (1993)
Wedding, A (1978)
Weird Science (1985)
What the Fuck Are These Red Squares (1970)
When Harry Met Sally (1989)
When Soul Meets Soul (1913)
When You Hit, Hit Hard (1918)
When You're Scared, Run (1918)
Where Mary? (1919)
While You Were Sleeping (1995)
Whirl of Life, The (1911)
White Roses (1912)
Wildcats (1986)
Wilderness Calling (1969)
Windy City (1984)
Winnie Wright, Age 11 (1974)
Winning an Heiress (1911)
With Honors (1994)
Within Our Gates (1920)
Wizard of Gore, The (1970)
Wizard of Oz, The (1910)
World's Championship Series (1910)
Wrong All Around (1917)
Young Runaways, The (1968)
Your Astronauts (1969)

APPENDIX C:

CHICAGOANS IN THE MOVIE BUSINESS

hicago has been a starting point for a wide variety of film talent. Whether it was someone who was born here, like Robin Williams, or someone who studied at one of the local universities, like Warren Beatty, Chicago and the surrounding suburbs have been the stomping grounds of actors, producers, directors, screenwriters, and other film professionals.

This is by no means an exhaustive list. Consider it a sampling of the movie multitudes who have at one point or other in their respective lives, called the Chicago area "home."

John Agar, actor
Joan Allen, actor
Morey Amsterdam, actor/comedian
Gillian Anderson, actor
Kevin Anderson, actor
Ann-Margret, actor/singer
Alan Arkin, actor
Lewis Arquette, actor
Patricia Arquette, actor
Rosanna Arquette, actor
Ed Asner, actor
Edith Atwater, actor
Darnell Autry, actor/football player
John G. Avildsen, director
Bob Balaban, actor/director
Burt Balaban, director/producer
Adam Baldwin, actor
Jennifer Beals, actor
Warren Beatty, actor/director/
    producer/screenwriter
Rex Bell, actor
Ralph Bellamy, actor
James Belushi, actor
John Belushi, actor/comedian
Richard Benjamin, actor/director

Tom Berenger, actor
Edgar Bergen, ventriloquist/actor
Shelly Berman, actor/comedian
Karen Black, actor
Tempestt Bledsoe, actor
Robert Bloch, screenwriter
Budd Boetticher, director
Beulah Bondi, actor
Tom Bosley, actor
Roger Bowen, actor
Lara Flynn Boyle, actor
Peter Boyle, actor
Marlon Brando, actor
André Braugher, actor
Paul Brickman, director/screenwriter
Edgar Rice Burroughs, screenwriter
Dick Butkus, actor/football player
John Caponera, actor
Allan Carr, producer
Dan Castellaneta, actor
Raymond Chandler, screenwriter
Anna Chlumsky, actor
Del Close, actor
Gary Cole, actor
Nat "King" Cole, singer

Gary Coleman, actor
Robert Conrad, actor
Cindy Crawford, model/actor
Michael Crichton, screenwriter/
    producer/director
Ann Cusack, actor
Bill Cusack, actor
Joan Cusack, actor
John Cusack, actor/screenwriter
Severn Darden, actor
Andrew Davis, director/producer
Clifton Davis, actor
Mark DeCarlo, actor/comedian
Bruce Dern, actor
Andy Dick, actor
Walt Disney, animator/producer
Kevin Dunn, actor
Nora Dunn, actor
Murphy Dunne, musician/actor
Christine Ebersole, producer
Roger Ebert, critic/screenwriter
Dennis Farina, actor
Chris Farley, actor/comedian
Ted Field, producer
Harrison Ford, actor
Bob Fosse, actor/director/
    screenwriter/choreographer
Bryan Foy, producer/director
Dennis Franz, actor
William Friedkin, director/
    screenwriter/producer
Frank Galati, screenwriter
Jenny Garth, actor
Mitzi Gaynor, actor
Jami Gertz, actor
Marla Gibbs, actor
George Gobel, actor/comedian
James Goldman, screenwriter
William Goldman, screenwriter
Benny Goodman, actor/musician
Stuart Gordon, director
Mary Gross, actor/comedian

Michael Gross, actor
Brad Hall, actor/screenwriter/
    producer
Irma P. Hall, actor
Daryl Hannah, actor
Page Hannah, actor
Jessica Harper, actor
Valerie Harper, actor
Barbara Harris, actor
Robin Harris, actor/comedian
Glenne Headly, actor
Anne Heche, actor
Marilu Henner, actor
Charlton Heston, actor
Isabella Hoffman, actor
Celeste Holm, actor
John Hughes, director/screenwriter/
    producer
Bonnie Hunt, actor
Peter Hyams, director
Quincy Jones, composer/musician
Michael Jordan, actor/basketball
    player
Janusz Kaminsky, cinematographer/
    director
John Kapelos, actor
Philip Kaufman, director/
    screenwriter/producer
Tim Kazurinsky, screenwriter/actor/
    producer
Richard Kiley, actor
Richard Kind, actor
Terry Kinney, actor
Robert Klein, actor/comedian
Harvey Korman, actor
Gene Krupa, musician
Rod La Rocque, actor
Frankie Laine, singer
John Landis, director/producer/
    screenwriter
Sherry Lansing, producer
Ring Lardner Jr., screenwriter

Cloris Leachman, actor
Jennifer Lien, actor
Shelley Long, actor
Julia Louis-Dreyfus, actor
William H. Macy, actor
Amy Madigan, actor
Michael Madsen, actor
Virginia Madsen, actor
Jock Mahoney, actor
John Mahoney, actor
Karl Malden, actor
John Malkovich, actor
Dorothy Malone, actor
David Mamet, screenwriter/director
Michael Mann, director/
  screenwriter/producer
Joe Mantegna, actor
Kenneth Mars, actor
Garry Marshall, director/
  screenwriter/producer
Richard Marx, musician
Mary Elizabeth Mastrantonio, actor
Marlee Matlin, actor
Elaine May, director/screenwriter/
  producer/actor
Curtis Mayfield, musician
Paul Mazursky, director/
  screenwriter/producer
Chi McBride, actor
Mercedes McCambridge, actor
Jenny McCarthy, actor
Frances McDormand, actor
Elizabeth McGovern, actor
John McNaughton, director/
  screenwriter/producer
Tim Meadows, actor
Laurie Metcalf, actor
Vincente Minnelli, director
Clayton Moore, actor
Colleen Moore, actor
Polly Moran, actor
Mr. T, actor

Martin Mull, actor/comedian
Dermot Mulroney, actor
Bill Murray, actor/comedian
Brian Doyle-Murray, actor/
  comedian
Mike Myers, actor/comedian
Patricia Neal, actor
Bob Newhart, actor/comedian
Mike Nichols, director/producer
Kim Novak, actor
Mike Nussbaum, actor
Donald O'Connor, actor
Kevin O'Connor, actor
Chris O'Donnell, actor
Anita O'Day, singer
Ken Olin, actor/director
Dana Olsen, screenwriter
Jerry Orbach, actor
Mandy Patinkin, actor/singer
Elizabeth Perkins, actor
Jeff Perry, actor
William Petersen, actor
Byrne Piven, actor
Jeremy Piven, actor
Steven B. Poster, cinematographer
Aidan Quinn, actor
Declan Quinn, cinematographer
Harold Ramis, director/actor/
  screenwriter/producer
Virginia Rappe, actor
Daphne Maxwell Reid, actor
Tim Reid, actor/director
Sally Richardson, actor
Adam Rifkin, screenwriter/director
Joan Rivers, actor/director
Jason Robards Sr., actor
Tony Roberts, actor
Dennis Rodman, actor/basketball
  player
Robert Ryan, actor
Waldo Salt, screenwriter
Tommy Sands, actor

Ben Savage, actor
Fred Savage, actor
Avery Schreiber, actor/comedian
David Schwimmer, actor/director
Seka, actor
William N. Selig, producer/movie
  pioneer
Garry Shandling, actor/comedian
Stan Shaw, actor
Arthur Sheekman, screenwriter
Sidney Sheldon, screenwriter/
  director/producer
Don Siegel, director
Casey Siemaszko, actor
Nina Siemaszko, actor
Gary Sinise, actor
Gene Siskel, critic
Carrie Snodgress, actor
David Steinberg, actor/director/
  comedian
Spankie, actor/comedian
Fisher Stevens, actor
Preston Sturges, director/
  screenwriter
Gloria Swanson, actor
Blanche Sweet, actor
Larenz Tate, actor
Norman Taurog, director/actor
Josh Taylor, actor
Lili Taylor, actor
Meshach Taylor, actor
Robert Teitel, producer
Steve Tesich, screenwriter
Betty Thomas, actor/director
George Tillman, Jr. director/
  screenwriter
Mel Torme, singer/actor
Robert Townsend, director/
  screenwriter/actor
Daniel J. Travanti, actor
Melvin Van Peebles, director/
  screenwriter/actor

Vince Vaughn, actor
Ken Wahl, actor
Irving Wallace, screenwriter
Hal B. Wallis, producer
Sam Wanamaker, actor
Marsha Warfield, actor
Johnny Weissmuller, actor
Raquel Welch, actor
Orson Welles, director/screenwriter/
  actor/producer
George Wendt, actor
Haskell Wexler, cinematographer/
  director
Ted Wichter, director/screenwriter
Kimberly Williams, actor
Robin Williams, actor/comedian
Oprah Winfrey, actor/producer
Billy Zane, actor
Lisa Zane, actor
Robert Zemeckis, director/
  screenwriter/producer
Adrian Zmed, actor
Louis Zorich, actor
Ed Zwick, director

SELECTIVE BIBLIOGRAPHY

Addams, Jane. *Twenty Years at Hull House*. New York: New American Library, 1981.

Arce, Hector. *Groucho*. New York: Perigee, 1980.

Bach, Ira J. *Chicago on Foot: Walking Tours of Chicago's Architecture*. Chicago: J. Philip O'Hara, Inc., 1973.

Bergreen, Laurence. *Capone: The Man and the Era*. New York: Touchtone, 1996.

Bielski, Ursula. *Chicago Haunts: Ghostly Lore of the Windy City*. Chicago: Lake Claremont Press, 1997.

Cawelti, John G., editor. *Focus on Bonnie and Clyde*. Englewood Cliffs, New Jersey: Prentice-Hall, Inc., 1973.

Chaplin, Charles. *My Autobiography*. New York: Pocket Book, 1966.

Cripps, Thomas. *Slow Fade to Black: The Negro in American Film, 1900-1942*. London: Oxford University Press, 1977.

Dardis, Tom. *Harold Lloyd: The Man on the Clock*. New York: Penguin Books, 1984.

Friedman, David F, with De Nevi, Don. *A Youth in Babylon: Confessions of a Trash-Film King*. Buffalo, New York: Prometheus Books, 1990.

Gabler, Neal. *An Empire of Their Own: How the Jews Invented Hollywood*. New York: Anchor Books, 1989.

Gelmis, Joseph. *The Film Director as Superstar*. New York: Doubleday & Company, Inc. , 1970.

Geduld, Harry M. *Focus on D.W. Griffith*. Englewood Cliffs, New Jersey: Prentice-Hall, Inc., 1971.

Hansberry, Lorraine. *A Raisin in the Sun: The Unfilmed Original Screenplay*. New York: Signet, 1994.

Hayner, Done and McNamee, Tom. *Chicago Sun-Times Metro Chicago Almanac*. Chicago: Bonus Books, Inc., 1991.

Heise, Kenan and Frazel, Mark. *Hands on Chicago: Getting Hold of the City*. Chicago: Bonus Books, Inc., 1987.

Katz, Ephraim. *The Film Encyclopedia*. New York: Harper-Perennial, 1994.

Lahue, Kalton C., editor. *Motion Picture Pioneer: The Selig Polyscope Company*. Cranbury, New Jersey: A.S. Barnes and Company, 1973.

Leab, Daniel J. *From Sambo to Superspade: The Black Experience in Motion Pictures*. Boston: Houghton Mifflin Company, 1975.

Leaming, Barbara. *Orson Welles, a Biography*. New York: The Viking Press, 1985.

Lehman, Ernest. *North by Northwest*. New York: The Viking Press, 1972.

Lowe, David. *Lost Chicago*. New York: American Legacy Press, 1985.

Marx, Groucho. *The Groucho Phile: An Illustrated Life*. New York, Bobbs-Merrill, 1976.

Monaco, James. *American Film Now: The People, The Power, The Money, the Movies*. New York: Plume, 1979.

Morton, Jim, editor. *RE/Search No. 10: Incredibly Strange Films, A Guide to Deviant Films*. San Francisco: RE/Search Publications, 1986.

Mosley, Leonard. *Disney's World*. New York: Stein and Day, 1985.

Pierson, John. *Spike, Mike, Slackers & Dykes: A Guided Tour Across a Decade of American Independent Cinema*. New York: Miramax Books, 1995.

Ramsaye, Terry. *A Million and One Nights: A History of the Motion Picture Through 1925.* New York: Touchstone, 1986.

Robinson, David. *Chaplin: His Life and Art.* New York: McGraw-Hill, 1985.

Sampson, Henry T. *Blacks in Black and White: A Source Book on Black Films.* Metuchen, New Jersey: Scarecrow Press, Inc., 1995.

Sawyers, June Skinner. *Chicago Portraits: Biographies of 250 Famous Chicagoans.* Chicago: Loyola University Press, 1991.

————— and Sue Telingator. *The Chicago Arts Guide.* Chicago: Chicago Review Press, 1993.

Schickel, Richard. *D.W. Griffith: An American Life.* New York: Simon and Schuster, 1984.

Sheetz, George H. *The Chicago Flm Industry: Beginnings to 1918.* Unpublished Senior Thesis. University of Illinois at Champaign-Urbana, Department of English, Spring 1974.

Siegel, Arthur, editor. *Chicago's Famous Buildings: The City's Architectural Landmarks and Other Notable Buildings.* Chicago: University of Chicago Press, 1967.

Swanson, Gloria. *Swanson on Swanson.* New York: Random House, 1980.

Sweet, Jeffery. *Something Wonderful Right Away.* New York: Discus, 1978.

Wolfe, Gerard R. *Chicago In and Around the Loop: Walking Tours of Architecture and History.* New York: McGraw-Hill, 1996.

Woodhouse, Sharon. *Know More, Spend Less: A Native's Guide to Chicago.* 2nd edition. Chicago: Lake Claremont Press, 1996.

INDEX

A

E

F

H

n

O

U

V

ABOUT THE AUTHOR

Arnie Bernstein holds a B.A. in Film Studies/Theater from Southern Illinois University and an M.A. in Creative Writing from Columbia College-Chicago. He has contributed to numerous film anthologies, historical encyclopedias, and CD-ROMs. Warner Brothers Television selected Arnie to participate in their Midwest Comedy Writers Workshop. Additionally, his fiction was honored with a grant from the Puffin Foundation. A Chicago native and member of the National Writers Union, Arnie has taught writing, literature, and theater at several area colleges.

Holly Pluard has done extensive photographic work throughout the Chicago area. Her pictures have been selected for juried exhibits at local galleries. She recently was chosen to be a part of the College Program at Walt Disney World.

Bruce Clorfene, editor, has been an advertising account executive, attorney, writer and producer of radio humor, managing editor of a suburban weekly newspaper, and manager of a mystery bookstore. He is currently a screenwriter, freelance writer, writer and producer of newsletters, and freelance editor. He lives in Evanston, Illinois.

PUBLISHER'S CREDITS

Cover design by Timothy Kocher.

Interior design by Sharon Woodhouse.

Photographs by Holly Pluard, and as marked.

Editing by Bruce Clorfene.

Proofreading by Sharon Woodhouse, Susan McNulty, Brandon Zamora, Kimberly Watkins, and Kenneth Woodhouse.

Typesetting by Sharon Woodhouse and Susan McNulty.

Photo Captions by Susan McNulty and Sharon Woodhouse.

Photo Layout by Sharon Woodhouse and Sandie Woodhouse.

Indexing by Brandon Zamora, Susan McNulty, Kimberly Watkins, and Sharon Woodhouse.

The cover of *Hollywood on Lake Michigan* was set in Machine, various Bodega fonts, and Times New Roman. The interior was set with headers in Black OldStyle, Medium, and Medium OldStyle from the BodegaSerif family and the body in Times New Roman.

NOTICE

OTHER TITLES FROM LAKE CLAREMONT PRESS

Chicago Haunts: Ghostlore of the Windy City (Revised Edition)
by Ursula Bielski
From ruthless gangsters to restless mail order kings, from the Fort Dearborn Massacre to the St. Valentine's Day Massacre, the phantom remains of the passionate people and volatile events of Chicago history have made the Second City second to none in the annals of American ghostlore. Bielski captures over 160 years of this haunted history with her unique blend of lively storytelling, in-depth historical research, exclusive interviews, and insights from parapsychology. Called "a masterpiece of the genre," "a must-read," and "an absolutely first-rate-book" by reviewers, *Chicago Haunts* continues to earn the praise of critics and readers alike.
0-9642426-7-2, softcover, 29 photos, $15

Know More, Spend Less: A Native's Guide To Chicago, 3rd Edition
by Sharon Woodhouse,
with expanded South Side coverage by Mary McNulty
Venture into the nooks and crannies of everyday Chicago with this unique, comprehensive budget guide. Over 400 pages of free, inexpensive, and unusual things to do in the Windy City make this the perfect resource for tourists, business travelers, visiting suburbanites, and resident Chicagoans.
0-9642426-0-5, softcover, photos, maps, $12.95

> ## Insiders' Guides to Suburban Chicago
> for locals, visitors, and new residents!

A Native's Guide To Chicago's South Suburbs
by Christina Bultinck and Christy Johnston-Czarnecki
0-9642426-1-3, softcover, photos, maps, $12.95 (Available Feb. 1998)

A Native's Guide To Chicago's Northern Suburbs
by Jason Fargo
0-9642426-8-0, softcover, photos, maps, $12.95 (Available Feb. 1998)

A Native's Guide To Chicago's Western Suburbs and **A Native's Guide to Chicago's Northwest Suburbs** will be also be released in 1999 to complete the series.

ORDER FORM

Please send me autographed copies of the following Lake Claremont Press titles:

A Native's Guide to Chicago, 3rd Ed. _____ @ $12.95 = _____

A Native's Guide To Chicago's South Suburbs _____ @ $12.95 = _____

A Native's Guide To Chicago's Northern Suburbs _____ @ $12.95 = _____

Chicago Haunts: Ghostlore of the Windy City, Revised Ed. _____ @ $15.00 = _____

Hollywood on Lake Michigan: 100 Years of Chicago & The Movies _____ @ $15.00 = _____

Subtotal: _____

Discounts when you order multiple copies!

2 books—10% off total
3-4 books —20% off total
5-9 books—25% off total
10+ books—40% off total

Less Discount: _____

New Subtotal: _____

8.75% tax for Illinois Residents: _____

Shipping Fees

$2 for the first book and $.50 for each additional book or a maximum of $5.

Shipping: _____

TOTAL: _____

Name_____

Address_____

City_____STATE_____ZIP_____

Enclose check, money order, or credit card number.

Visa/Mastercard#_____ Exp. _____

Signature_____

Lake Claremont Press
P.O. Box 25291
Chicago, IL 60625
773/784-7517
LakeClarPr@aol.com

Order by mail, phone, or e-mail.
All of our books have a no-hassles, 100% money back guarantee.